# CULTURE AND POLITICS

# Culture and Politics

## A Comparative Approach

### Second Edition

JAN-ERIK LANE
*University of Geneva, Switzerland*
and
SVANTE ERSSON
*University of Umeå, Sweden*

ASHGATE

Published by
Ashgate Publishing Limited
Gower House, Croft Road
Aldershot, Hants
GU11 3HR
England

Ashgate Publishing Company
Suite 420
101 Cherry Street
Burlington, VT 05401–4405
USA

Ashgate website: http://www.ashgate.com

**British Library Cataloguing in Publication Data**
Lane, Jan-Erik
   Culture and politics : a comparative approach
   1. Politics and culture – Cross-cultural studies
   I. Title   II. Ersson, Svante
   306.2

**Library of Congress Control Number:** 2001099645

ISBN 0 7546 4578 9

Typeset in Times Roman by N$^2$productions.
Printed and bound in Great Britain by MPG Books Ltd, Bodmin, Cornwall.

# Contents

List of Figures                                              *xi*
List of Tables                                               *xiii*
List of Abbreviations                                        *xvii*
Preface                                                      *xix*
Acknowledgements                                             *xxi*

**Introduction: Does Culture Matter?**                       1
   The Cultural Approach                       2
   Culture                                     3
   Outcomes of Culture                         5
   Globalization                               6
   The Framework of Analysis                   7
   The Structure of the Book                   9
   Conclusion                                  11

**PART I    CULTURE AND OUTCOMES**

**Introduction**                                             15

**1  'Culture' and the Concepts of Culture**                 17
   Introduction                                17
   The Early Meanings of Culture               18
   Connotations of Culture                     21
   The Ambiguity of Culture                    24
   New Cultural Theory                         27
      The Backward Society      27
      The Dual Society          27
      The Triadic Society       28
      The Culture Quartet       28
   Political Culture                           31
   Gertz and Cultural Anthropology: A 'Cul de Sac'?   33
   Conclusion                                  35

**2  What Culture Matters For: Outcomes**                    39
   Introduction                                39
   Culture as an Explanatory Factor            40
   Macro-level Outcomes                        42

Political Development                                                    42
Affluence and Poverty                                                   44
Social Development: Equality                                            46
Gender Equality                                                         47
Corruption                                                              48
Dependent Variables and Control Variables                              48
Regional-level Outcomes: Why Does Different Party Support
Vary in Different Regions?                                              51
The USA                                                                 51
Russia                                                                  52
Spain                                                                   53
Switzerland                                                             54
Belgium                                                                 55
India                                                                   56
Summary                                                                 57
Micro-level Data: Individual Values                                     57
The Survey Approach to Values                                          58
Micro-level Outcomes                                                    60
Conclusion                                                              66
Appendix: Countries Included in our Analysis Based on
Different Waves of WVS                                                  68

## PART II  ETHNICITY

**Introduction**                                                        73

**3  Ethnic Groups and Nations**                                        75
Introduction                                                            75
Ethnic Groups                                                           76
Two Types of Ethnic Groups                                              78
Ethnogenesis                                                            79
Ethnic Cores and Nation-building                                        80
Nation and Ethnic Group                                                 82
Nationality and Nationalism                                             83
Herder                                                                  87
Renan                                                                   88
Beyond Nationalism                                                      89
Races                                                                   91
Race: Socially Constructed with Immense Political
Consequences                                                            94
Ethnicity and Society                                                   95
Conclusion                                                              98

**4  Outcomes of Ethnicity**                                            101
Introduction                                                            101

Grand-scale Ethnicity Worldwide                                       102
   Spoken Languages                                                    103
   Language Families                                                    106
   Outcomes of Language Families                                        109
Ethnic Cleavages and Ethnic Structure: Outcomes                      114
   Ethnic Cleavages                                                    115
   Ethnic Structure: Regions and Party Support                         117
Ethnicity and Everyday Life                                          129
   National Pride                                                      130
   Life Satisfaction                                                   131
   Left–Right Orientation                                              132
   Interest in Politics                                                132
   Voluntary Organizations and Political Activity: Joining
   Boycotts                                                            132
   Summary                                                             132
Conclusion                                                           133

**PART III   CIVILIZATIONS**

**Introduction**                                                     137

**5   Civilizations and the Major Types of Religion**                139
Introduction                                                         139
The World Religions                                                  140
Civilizations                                                        141
The Weber Approach                                                   146
Three World Religions: Alternative Classifications                   147
   Hinduism and Buddhism                                              149
   Judaism and Christianity                                            151
   Islam                                                              152
Weber's Theory of Religion                                           155
Mapping the Major World Religions                                    159
Conclusion                                                           164

**6   Religion and its Outcomes**                                    167
Introduction                                                         167
Macro Outcomes: Weber Again                                          167
   Economic Outcomes: Affluence and Economic Growth                    169
   Quality of Life, Gender and Income Equality                         172
   Democracy and Corruption                                            173
   Does Religion Matter?                                               175
   Summary                                                             179
Religious Fragmentation and Outcomes: Macro Level                    179
Religious Structure and Party Support                                182
   The USA: Religion Matters                                           183

Spain: Anti-clericalism 183
Switzerland: Strong Religious Effects 184
Belgium: Strong Cultural Politics 186
India: Ethnicity More Than Religion 187
Summary 188
The Role of Religion for People 189
Summary 191
Conclusion 192

**PART IV LEGACIES**

**Introduction** 197

**7 Historical Legacies and the Colonial Heritage** 199
Introduction 199
The Longitudinal Perspective 200
The Iberian Legacy: The Negative Outcomes of a Spanish
Culture 200
The British Heritage 202
Dividing the World According to Colonial Experience 203
The Impact of Different Colonial Regimes 205
Close and Distant Consequences 209
Do Colonial Cultures Matter? 212
Conclusion 214
Appendix: Colonial Legacies in the Third World 217

**8 Family Structure and Democracy** 219
Introduction 219
The Different Family Cultures 220
Behaviour and Values 223
Classifying Family Cultures 224
The Effects of Family Cultures 227
Conclusion 230

**PART V UNIVERSAL VALUES**

**Introduction** 235

**9 Universal Values: Three Main Theories** 237
Introduction 237
Value Orientations: Behaviour or Attitudes 237
Values as Behaviour: Civic Community 239
Values as Attitudes: Trust 241
Trust in Italy 242
Postmaterialism Theory 244

What are Postmaterialist Values? 245
The Existence of a Postmaterialist Dimension 246
Relevance of Postmaterialist Values 249
Trust Theory 250
New Cultural Theory (NCT) 252
The Consequences of Values: Macro or Micro? 252
Conclusion 254

**10 Value Orientations: How Real Are They?** 257
Introduction 257
The Problem with Values and Value Research 257
Value Inquiry 258
The Relevance of Value Orientations 260
Central Value Orientations 263
Macro: The Spread of Universal Values 265
   Summary 270
The Micro and Macro Relationships Between Values 270
Do Values Matter? 273
Values Matter for What? 275
   Specific Value Impacts 276
   Diffuse Value Impacts 276
The Transfer Mechanism: Election Channel and Policy-making 277
The Macro-level Consequences of Values 278
   Summary 284
The Micro-level Consequences of Values 285
   Summary 286
Conclusion 286

**11 Gender (Sex) as a Major Cultural Cleavage** 289
Introduction 289
Value Orientations Towards Sex as a Cultural Cleavage 290
Gender 293
   Gender: The Macro View 293
   Gender Orientations: The Micro View 297
Homosexuality and Lesbianism 300
   The Micro View 300
   The Macro View 302
Conclusion 302

**12 Conclusion: The Impact of Culture on Outcomes** 305
Introduction 305
The Findings 306
   The Macro Level 307
   The Regional Level 308
   The Micro Level 308

Comparing the Impact of Cultural Factors                          309
   Ethnicity                                                      310
   Religion                                                       310
   Historical Legacies                                            310
   Values                                                         311
How Much Does Culture Matter?                                     312
Muticulturalism – Its Relevance Today                             313
   The Critique of Multiculturalism                               313
   A Multicultural Regime – The Liberal Restrictions upon
   Communities                                                    316
Relevance of Multiculturalism                                     316
Kymlicka: The Institutions of the Multicultural Society           317
Barry: Moral Universalism Destroying Multiculturalism             320

**APPENDICES**
**Appendix A: Macro Data Set: Variable List**                     327
**Appendix B: Regional Data Set: Variable List**                  335
**Appendix C: Micro Data Set: Variable List**                     341

*References*                                                      *345*
*Index*                                                          *359*

# List of Figures

I.1     Framework for the book: culture, outcomes and contexts        9
1.1     Four types of culture                                        29
1.2     The typology of New Culture Theory (NCT)                     29
1.3     Political cultures                                           32
3.1     The two types of nationalism                                 85
3.2     Nationalist movements                                        86
5.1     Basic Weber orientations in all religions                   157
8.1     Basic family institutions according to Todd (1983)          221
8.2     Basic family typology according to Todd (1984)              222
10.1    Value change: micro versus macro                            261
10.2    Individualism (NEWIND) and affluence (LnPPP97) (r=.69;
        N=65)                                                       284
11.1    Opinions on gender equality (GEQ) (percentages)             291
11.2    Opinion on justifiablity of homosexuality (percentages)     292
11.3    Gender development and gender empowerment (r=.725;
        N=102)                                                      293
11.4    Gender equality and gender empowerment (r=.856; N=47)       294
11.5    GDP and GEM (r=.725; N=103)                                 295
11.6    GDP and gender equality (r=.651; N=57)                      296
11.7    Protestantism and gender equality (GEQ) (r=.597; N=57)      297
11.8    Islam and gender empowerment (GEM) (r=-.591; N=103)         298
11.9    Gender equality orientations (GEQ) and attitudes to
        homosexuals (r=.78; N=56)                                   301
11.10   Human development and attitudes to homosexuality (r=.74;
        N=76)                                                       302

# List of Tables

| | | |
|---|---|---|
| I.1 | Groups and cultural identity | 4 |
| I.2 | The key variables at different analytical levels | 9 |
| 2.1 | Absolute distance from the equator (DISEQU) and time since introduction of modernized leadership (MODLEAD) in years by country regions: means | 50 |
| 2.2 | Political interest: macro-regional means (POLINTR) | 63 |
| 2.3 | Political activity: membership of voluntary organizations (VOLORG) – macro-regional percentages – and joining boycotts (JOINBOY) – macro-regional means | 64 |
| 2.4 | Left–right self-placements (LEFTRIG): macro regional means | 65 |
| 2.5 | Life satisfaction (LIFESAT): macro-regional means | 67 |
| 4.1 | Estimates of the number of users of the top ten languages (000s) | 104 |
| 4.2 | Distribution of the world population according to linguistic groups (LINGGRP) | 104 |
| 4.3 | Estimates of English language usage: first (L1) and second (L2) language in the 1990s: by country ranked according to relative size | 105 |
| 4.4 | Distribution of the world population according to language families (LANGFAM) | 106 |
| 4.5 | Distribution of the world population according to linguistic groups (LINGR) | 107 |
| 4.6 | Distribution of the world population according to location (GEO) | 108 |
| 4.7 | Impact of language group on political and socioeconomic variables: bivariate analysis | 110 |
| 4.8 | Impact of language groups on political and socioeconomic variables: bivariate analysis | 112 |
| 4.9 | Overall impact of language groups on political and socioeconomic outcomes: regression analysis | 113 |
| 4.10 | Clusters of ethnic heterogeneous and homogeneous countries (ELF1) | 116 |
| 4.11 | Impact of language on political and socioeconomic variables: correlation analysis | 118 |
| 4.12 | Ethnic fragmentation in the USA in the 1990s: ranking of states | 120 |

4.13   Ethnicity and party strength at state level in the USA:
       regression analysis                                                    121
4.14   Ethnic structure in Russia: ranking of regions in terms of
       homogeneity/heterogeneity (ELFINDEX)                                   122
4.15   Impact of ethnicity on party strength at regional level in
       Russia: regression analysis                                           123
4.16   Impact of ethnicity on party strength at the provincial level in
       Spain: regression analyses                                            124
4.17   Ethnicity and party support in Belgium: regression analysis           127
4.18   Ethnicity and party support in India: regression analysis             129
4.19   National pride by regions of the world as aggregated
       percentages                                                           130
4.20   Ethnicity and life satisfaction: regression analysis                  131
4.21   Ethnicity and interest in politics: regression analysis               133
4.22   Number of significant regression coefficients estimated from
       the impact of ethnicity by country and dependent variables            134
5.1    Major civilizations: population distribution in the twentieth
       century as percentages of total population                            145
5.2    World religions: number of countries                                  160
5.3    Worldwide adherence to the major religions as a percentage
       of the total population: 1900–98                                      161
5.4    Worldwide adherence to the major religions by continental
       area as a percentage of the total population: 1900 and 1994           163
6.1    Affluence and religion: GDP per capita 1990 and PPP per
       capita 1997 in US$                                                    170
6.2    Affluence and religion: economic growth 1960–73, 1973–85,
       1985–94 and 1990–98 – average annual growth by major
       religion                                                              171
6.3    Religion and social development: the HDI, GDI, GEM and
       Gini indicators                                                       172
6.4    Religion and political outcomes: democracy index 1997 and
       corruption 1998                                                       174
6.5    Religion and outcomes: correlations                                   175
6.6    Religion and outcomes: regression analysis                            178
6.7    Religious fragmentation 1900–95                                       180
6.8    Impact of religious fragmentation: regression analysis                182
6.9    Religion and party support at regional level in USA:
       regression analysis                                                   184
6.10   Religion and party support at regional level in Spain:
       regression analysis                                                   185
6.11   Religion and party support at regional level in Switzerland:
       regression analysis                                                   186
6.12   Religion and party support at regional level in Belgium:
       regression analysis                                                   187

6.13   Religion and party support at regional level in India:
       regression analysis                                              189
6.14   Attendance at religious services at least once a week by
       regions of the world                                            190
6.15   Religion and membership in voluntary organizations              191
6.16   Religion and joining boycotts                                   192
6.17   Number of significant regression coefficients estimated from
       the impact of religion by country and dependent variable        193
7.1    The colonial legacy: population distribution in percentages
       around 1950 and 1999                                            205
7.2    Colonial legacies and outcomes: comparing means (total
       sample N=150 at most)                                           207
7.3    Colonial influence: comparing means (Third World sample
       N=103 at most)                                                  208
7.4    Four colonial legacies in the Third World: comparing means      211
7.5    The impact of the colonial legacy on developmental
       outcomes – number of years since independence
       (DECOLYR) and number of years of colonial rule
       (COLRULE): regression analysis                                  213
7.6    The impact of the colonial legacy – British, French and
       Spanish legacies: regression analysis                           215
8.1    Family systems worldwide: the Todd 1983 typology with
       empirical examples                                              225
8.2    Family systems worldwide: the Todd 1984 typology with
       empirical examples                                              226
8.3    Family systems worldwide: the Todd 1983 and 1984 systems        228
8.4    Family systems and civilizations: Pearson's correlation
       coefficients                                                    229
8.5    Family structures and democracy: regression analysis            230
9.1    Civic community and interpersonal trust in Italian regions
       around 1990                                                     243
9.2    Factor loadings on the postmaterialist items: 12-item
       instrument                                                      247
9.3    The meaning of postmaterialism: factor loading items by
       world regions                                                   248
9.4    Impact on party choice in Western Europe of the 1990s:
       bivariate relationships                                         250
10.1   Individualism (INDIV): means                                    266
10.2   Achievement orientation (ACHIEVE): percentages scoring
       high achievement                                                267
10.3   Postmaterialism (POSTMAT): percentages being
       postmaterialist                                                 268
10.4   Trust (TRUST): percentages expressing interpersonal trust       269
10.5   Micro level correlation between values (total sample)            271
10.6   Macro correlations between the indices on universal values       272

10.7   Postmaterialism and developmental outcomes: correlations          279
10.8   The impact of postmaterialism (POSTMAT): regression
       analysis                                                          281
10.9   The impact of interpersonal trust (TRUST): regression
       analysis                                                          283
10.10  Number of significant regression coefficients estimated for
       the impact of macro values by dependent variables                285
10.11  Number of significant regression coefficients estimated for
       the impact of micro values by country and by dependent
       variables                                                         287
11.1   Gender equality and cultural factors: Pearson's correlation       296
11.2   Gender orientation and gender, age, education and income:
       eta correlations                                                  299
11.3   Regression: gender value orientations (GEQ) and value
       orientations, gender, age, education and income (WVS 4th
       wave 1999–2002)                                                   299
11.4   Attitudes to homosexuals and gender, age, education and
       income: eta correlations                                         300
11.5   Regression: attitudes to homosexuals and value orientations,
       gender, age, education and income (WVS 4th wave
       1999–2002)                                                       300
11.6   Attitudes to homosexuals and cultural factors: Pearson's
       correlation                                                       301
12.1   The macro level: impact of culture on political and
       socioeconomic outcome variables – number of significant
       regression coefficients                                          307
12.2   The regional level: impact of culture on party support –
       number of significant coefficients estimated                     308
12.3   The micro level: impact of the independent variables on the
       dependent variables – number of significant coefficients
       when control of other cultural variables has been introduced      309

# List of Abbreviations

| | |
|---|---|
| BJP | Bharatiya Janata Party (India) |
| CP | Communist Party |
| CSPP | Centre for the Study of Public Policy |
| CVP | christian democratic party (Switzerland) |
| CVP | Christian People's Party (Belgium) |
| EC | European Commission |
| EU | European Union |
| FDF | Flemish Democratic Front |
| FDP | liberal party (Switzerland) |
| GDI | Gender Development Index |
| GDP | gross national product |
| GEM | Gender Empowerment Measure |
| GRP | gross regional product |
| GSP | gross state product (USA) |
| HDI | Human Development Index |
| IFOP | Institut Français de l'Opinion Publique |
| INC | Indian Congress Party |
| INCI | Indian National Congress (Indira) |
| INCU | Indian National Congress Party (Urs) |
| JNP | Janata Party (India) |
| NCT | New Cultural Theory |
| NUPI | Norwegian Institute for International Affairs |
| PPP | purchasing power parities |
| PSC | Christian Social Party (Belgium) |
| PSCC | Christian-Social Party (Belgium) |
| PSOE | Partido Socialista Obrero Español |
| RW | Walloon Party |
| SPS | social democratic party (Switzerland) |
| SWP | people's party (Switzerland) |
| UNDP | United Nations Development Programme |
| VB | Flemish Block |
| VU | Volksunie (Belgium) |
| WAPOR | World Association of Public Opinion Research |
| WVS | World Values Survey |

# Preface

This book grew out of our shared ambition to come to grips with two problems, that have caused much debate within political science. They concern both methodology and reality. First, we want to identify a proper place for the analysis of culture in general and values in particular within political science. That is, we need to answer the question 'Is there a coherent cultural approach (CA)?'. Second, we need to explain how the process of globalization impacts on society. In other words, we need to answer the question: 'What is the political relevance of ethnicity, religion, legacies and values in the post-modern society?'.

In our examination of these questions we focus on how compact the groups that carry cultures – so-called communities – tend to be. The basic question that recurs in the various inquiries into many aspects of culture is: does culture matter? Although this focus on *cultural effects* is the *fil d'Ariadne* of our book, we take some time and make much effort to provide a broad overview of the variety of cultures as they exist today.

The perspective in the various chapters is comparative, looking at the impact of different kinds of culture on outcomes. Thus, the consequences of cultures and cultural variation for macro social, economic and political events as well as for individual behaviour at the micro level are investigated focusing on the principal models stemming from a CA framework.

During work on this book the following incident occurred, which meant that one piece of the original manuscript had to be deleted. One of the authors (J-E. Lane) wrote a comment on the book *Switzerland and the Crisis of Dormant Assets and Nazigold* (2000) by Philipe Braillard when this book appeared for the first time in French. The comment was accepted as a review in the *Swiss Political Science Review* on 24 February after the revisions required on 9 and 12 February by the editor-in-chief had been met. However, on 24 March, the editor-in-chief informed that the review would not be published. After a protest from Professor Lane, the journal changed its decision and offered space for Braillard to comment on the review when it was published. When Braillard refused to do so, Professor Lane decided to withdraw the review.

Jan-Erik Lane and Svante Ersson
Geneva and Umeå
December 2001

# Acknowledgements

Svante Ersson's work has been sponsored by a grant from the Bank of Sweden Tercentenary Foundation. We have used data from *The World Values Surveys and European Values Surveys, 1981–1984, 1990–1993, and 1995–1997* by Ronald Inglehart *et al*. (ICPSR 2790), the *Polity II: Political Structures and Regime Change* by Ted Robert Gurr *et al*. (ICPSR 9263), the *Eurobarometer 43.1 bis: Regional Development, Consumer and Environmental Issues* by K. Reif and E. Marlier (SSD0510), and these data sets have kindly been made available to us via the Swedish Social Science Data Service (SSD) in Göteborg. We have further made use of a number of data sets that were available from the Internet, including: the American Religion Data Archive (ARDA), the Central Intelligence Agency (CIA), the Spanish Congreso de los Diputados, the Centre for Studies in Public Policy (CSPP), the World Bank, the Ethnologue: Languages of the World, the Freedom House, the International Monetary Fund (IMF), the Norwegian Institute for International Affairs (NUPI), the Penn World Tables, the Transparency International, the US Bureau of Census, and the United Nations Development Programme (UNDP). We are solely responsible for the interpretations of these data.

We are grateful to Sylvia Dumons in the Political Science Department at the University of Geneva for her extensive assistance and incredible endurance when transforming earlier drafts to final chapters. Thanks are also due to Steven Aufrecht at the University of Alaska in Anchorage, who gave a final most valuable input helping us to correct and improve numerous passages.

# Introduction

# Does Culture Matter?

Several strands of literature point to the importance of culture and communities in politics. In political theory we find a rapidly growing literature dealing with minorities, citizenship and rights, while in political philosophy we find the new ideas about personal identity in the multicultural society. In political sociology, ethnicity, nationalism and religion have again become popular themes for research, but here one should mention in particular the even stronger emphasis on the relevance of values inquiry. Finally, within mainstream political science, competing approaches to the dominant rational choice framework have been proposed, especially for the purpose of analysing the values of communities – cultures – as well as the state responses to 'communal politics': cultural analysis or cultural approaches.

Evolving with great speed during the last 20 years, the research into cultures, groups and rights has resulted in several well-known theories including, *inter alia*, multiculturalism (Kymlicka, 1995), postmaterialism (Inglehart, 1997), nationalism in the postmodern society (Smith, 1998), the politics of recognition (Taylor, 1992), the rise of egalitarianism (Wildavsky, 1991), the trust society (Putnam, 1993; Fukuyama, 1995a), the clash of civilizations (Huntington, 1996) and colonialism as culture (Said, 1994), as well as the conceptions of citizenship (van Gunsteren, 1998). Although these theories contain different ideas and hypotheses about cultures, communities and rights, they all share the ambition to come to grips with the new communal politics.

The purpose of our book is to make a synthesis of these new ideas about politics in the period of globalization, and to examine them through one lens – namely that of *cultural effects*. We make a comparative inquiry into the theme of whether culture matters and, if so, how culture matters in politics. At the core of this volume is the question: is culture theory merely another fad and fashion in the social sciences? How one answers this question depends, we believe, on how one answers the key problem that constitutes the *fil d'Ariadne* – that is, the 'Does culture matter?' theme. Only if culture is important for political decisions (outputs) and results (outcomes) can there be a profound and sustained research interest into the beliefs and values of communities. Our approach is one of several ways of examining the theories and hypotheses put forward in cultural analysis. It differs from the interpretative approach that is typically employed in CA (Geertz, 2000) in that we believe that a fruitful way to organize insights derived from cultural analysis is to focus on outcomes, especially since the traditional anthropological and ethnographic tools of inquiry place more emphasis on local knowledge than on true generalizations (Willis, 2000; Geertz, 2001).

Thus, we argue that one needs to make empirical inquiries into how culture matters and which culture matters the most. In relation to various forms of culture such as ethnicity, religion, legacies and values as they occur in today's postmodern world, especially in the world's wealthier countries, one needs to research the occurrence of *cultural effects*. For instance, while ethnicity is certainly becoming more relevant in politics, nationalism seems to be faltering (Smith, 1998). Is it true that some religions are expanding while others are declining in size and relevance, and that religious fundamentalism is on the advance not only in Islam and Hinduism but also in Protestantism and Judaism (Anton, 2001)? Certain historical legacies are still strongly relevant in politics such as, for instance, orientalism – that is, the view of the West on Arabs and Arab culture (Said, 1995). Finally, not all values have equal importance in political life. We will be examining this cultural variety more closely and probing its political implications for decisions and outcomes as it is outlined in cultural analysis. We suggest that, for our perspective, culture may be seen as comprising ethnicity, religion, historical legacy and universal values, and we will inquire into what roles these cultural items play in terms of outcomes in society and politics.

## The Cultural Approach

If the predominant approach in the social and economic sciences – rational choice – is biased towards understanding human behaviour on the basis of maximising self-interest (Ordeshook, 1992; Stevens, 1993; Shepsle and Boncheck, 1997; Hinich and Munger, 1997), then other aspects of human interaction would need a different framework of analysis – namely a cultural approach. When behaviour is oriented in terms of altruism or values, then cultural approaches yield better explanations than the rational choice approach (Etzioni, 1988; Thompson *et al.*, 1990, 1999; Ellis and Thompson, 1997). In turn, altruistic behaviour may be oriented in terms of ethnic, religious or universal values, as well as traditions.

During the 1990s culture theory became very topical in political science, reflecting a surge of interest in the politics of ethnicity, religion and civilizations – all of which relate to how people search for identity by adhering to the values of social groups. This increased interest in cultural approaches to politics can be seen as a way of counterbalancing the rational choice approach which focuses on the maximization of interests, while neglecting the cultural setting of preference formation (Wildavsky, 1987).

When interpreting events and trends as they have unfolded worldwide since the 1970s, one often encounters arguments to the effect that an ethnic or religious revolution has slowly but consistently been taking place. Community politics is at least as relevant as associational politics. Ethnic and religious identities appear to have increased their relevance considerably, in some cases strikingly – especially when the political consequences of ethnic or religious communities are examined. The doctrine that argues that communities are very important in society is now labelled 'communitarianism' and nowadays has many adherents (Mulhall and Swift, 1996).

Yet, contrary to this argument about the growing importance of communities, it has been claimed that globalization increases the relevance of an entirely different kind of identity – namely, the identification with universal values. Here, we will look at several of the issues involved in postmodern cultural identity by taking an empirical approach, inquiring if and how values matter for decisions and real outcomes in politics and society. In particular, we will inquire into whether values matter *extrinsically* – that is, whether a variation in values or value orientations brings about different social, economic and political outcomes.

The main question thus becomes: do countries with different cultures also display significant political differences in terms of, for example, democracy and policy-making or election results? The analysis of culture is organized into four parts: ethnic cultures, religious cultures, legacies and universal cultures. The consequences of culture will be researched in relation to differences between countries around the globe in a set of outcomes at a macro level, but we will also deal with the impact of culture on the regions within a country and at the micro level – that is on individuals.

## Culture

This book is an inquiry into the main theories about culture from the perspective of cultural effects – for example, the relevance of cultural variation for the understanding of why countries differ in terms of political decisions and outcomes, as well as social and economic outcomes. The analysis concentrates on information about the 1980s and 1990s, as we wish to contrast the argument that cultural differences matter with the counterargument that the world is becoming more homogeneous due to the globalization process.

Culture is the identity of one kind of social group – in other words, the communities. Communities, we suggest, have two basic aspects. First, one may single out the nature of the ties among the members of a social group – that is, whether or not the group is compact. A high level of compactness implies that the group is characterized by strongly shared cultural identity and that it is capable of engaging in collective action. Groups with individuals who seldom interact or have few common ties are characterized by a low level of compactness.

Second, one may pinpoint the nature of the cultural identity itself. It may be oriented towards communal values or it may target universal values. Groups with communal values focus on ethnicity or religion, whereas groups with universal values identify with liberty or equality, for instance. What we have here are two different types of fraternity or brotherhood, one identifying with their concrete surrounding neighbourhood in terms of ethnic characteristics or religious belief and the other identifying with the abstract ideals of mankind. Table I.1 contains the cross-tabulation of these two dimensions, and also gives examples of all the four possible types.

In relation to Table I.1 and the classification of various kinds of groups, we must state that we are not referring to clear-cut distinctions. Some of these groups could perhaps be classified slightly differently, as these distinctions are more a matter of degree than black versus white. Nevertheless the table offers a conceptual lens from which to view the world of communities. Cultures offering people cultural identities appear around the world in the form of ethnicity, religion or universal values. Nations or ethnic groups as well as civilizations or religions, make up two types of culture, characteristic of specific areas. Universal cultures, on the other hand, are to be found in all societies, but to a very different degree within various groups.

Civilization could be regarded as the broader concept, whereas ethnicity or nationality would be the more narrow concept. Thus, civilizations would comprise different nations in various countries, which in addition could consist of various ethnic groups. Universal cultures, on the other hand, are present in all societies, though to a varying extent. Groups in every society display attitudes or values that may be subsumed under general labels such as egalitarianism or libertarianism. Groups with strong social trust may be contrasted with groups with weak social trust, and their relative occurrence could be measured. Among many groups within the developed countries, postmaterialism occurs in different forms such as social movements, environmental groups, feminist groups and so on. The borderline between political values and political ideologies is anything but clear-cut. However, in the study of new politics in the postmodern society, the emphasis is not on the traditional political ideologies dating back to the great revolutions of the eighteenth century but, instead, on new values, such as the environment or sustainable development.

**Table I.1    Groups and cultural identity**

| Groups | Cultural Identity | |
|---|---|---|
| | Communal values | Universal values |
| Low degree of compactness | Nations, races, churches | Marketeers, egalitarians |
| High degree of compactness | Ethnic groups, sects | Homosexuals, lesbians, new social movements |

Cultural compactness may increase over time, as, for instance, when a group becomes increasingly conscious of its cultural identity. Such a process may involve several generations. Consider, for example, the province of Quebec and the emergence of French separatism in Canada. The growth of national identity in what was called Lower Canada involved more than 200 years of consciousness-raising about the fate of the French-speaking population, left isolated due to the French defeat at the battle of Plains of Abraham in 1760 and the consequent land concession to Great Britain as part of the Treaty of Paris in 1763. It took a long time before the alternatives were clarified – assimilation or recognition of a special community. And it was even longer before a decision was made about which alternative to choose (Dumont, 1996). Culture, therefore, also includes historical traditions as may be illustrated by the persistence of colonial legacies, to take one example.

## Outcomes of Culture

An inquiry into the effects of the occurrence of various cultures is a difficult undertaking. As this is basically a task for causal modelling, one needs to specify not only the set of outcomes that one wants to relate to cultures, but also the other conditions, apart from culture, that may explain these outcomes. Whether one either examines correlations between variables or uses the more complex regression technique, holding certain factors constant, causal analysis always involves empirical tests of explicit models against a set of data.

The distinction between *intrinsic* and *extrinsic* importance is crucial when inquiring into the effects of cultural identities. A culture may offer a source of identity for a person or a group, making it of utmost importance for the people concerned – intrinsic importance. However, while acknowledging the relevance of the intrinsic perspective on culture, we focus exclusively on extrinsic importance: does culture matter for social, economic or political outcomes?

The outcomes of culture can be strictly political as well as socioeconomic. Among the political outcomes, we include both institutional outcomes, such as the protection of human rights, and electoral outcomes, such as the support for ethnic or religious parties. Into the analysis of cultural effects one may also enter political decision-making or policy-making, including policy outputs such as welfare state spending, social spending or other public finance items, when looking at the impact of culture – especially the effects of universal values. Our analysis of electoral outcomes will focus on the fate of political parties that have a distinct ethnic or religious orientation. Such parties tend to attract different levels of support in various regions of a country, depending on the nature of the region in terms of basic population characteristics. Ethnic and religious fragmentation is a typical feature of several countries with ethnic and/or religious cleavages. As a result the party system often reflects this fragmentation through a profound regional variation in election results. In so-called divided societies there are cultural effects in the sense that the political parties fare very differently in the regional voting outcomes. Strong ethnic or religious fragmentation may push divided societies towards a bad performance record on macro outcomes.

We link the non-political importance of cultural identities with socio-economic development, which is a broad enough concept to cover a number of outcomes. First and foremost, we have two economic outcomes, affluence and economic growth, where the first outcome is a measure of the *level of income* and the second is a measure of the *rate of change* in income on a yearly basis. Second, we have social outcomes such as the level of human development according to some index on the quality of life in a country or the extent of equality in the country in question, according to indices on either income distribution or the parity between men and women. Cultures may be oriented towards the promotion of social outcomes or they may focus exclusively on spiritual matters. However, the position that culture matters for outcomes in society and politics increasingly must be confronted with the theme of globalization.

## Globalization

It is increasingly argued that the traditional civilizations and nations are under growing pressure from various global processes which diminish the relevance of cultures. Among the forces of globalization we find economic globalization, regional integration in Europe, the United States and Asia, and the technological revolution in communications. Nonetheless, it is counterclaimed that we can expect culture to become more relevant as people seek identity in communities rather than in individualism. Thus, some scholars argue that national identity is still highly relevant for the politics of a country whereas others claim that we are heading for a clash of civilizations or religions. Yet other scholars speak of a single global marketplace and its consequences for immigration and the elimination of borders and cultural differences (Held *et al.*, 1999; Gilpin, 2000; Lechner and Boli, 2000). Thus, they state that the major civilizations of the world are under increasing pressure from various global processes – all called 'globalization'. Can we find out whether cultures are relevant today and, if so, how?

Distinguishing between three kinds of culture – ethnicity, religion and universal values – we ask whether they are all equally relevant today in the global society. The argument that cultural ties or communal identities are less sustainable than before in a global world ignores the possibility that cultural identities increasingly tend to take the form of adherence to universal values as globalization proceeds. Thus, it has been stated that universal values may account for changes in public policy as well as for the variation in socioeconomic outcomes. Although values such as liberty and equality have had many adherents for a long time, their impact upon political life and society has only increased as the pace of globalization has stepped up. What has decreased in relevance for outcomes is brotherhood or the cultures of ethnic or religious communities – so the argument goes. But is it really true that communities have declined in political relevance alongside the rise of multiculturalism? In fact, globalization has two contrary outcomes, both enhancing materialism and reinforcing communalism. Which force prevails depends on the situation. This argument neglects what has almost amounted to a communal revolution as expressed in the growing relevance of *communal politics*. The emergence of multiculturalism reflects not only the increase in migration promoted by globalization but also the growing power of the previously powerless, such as indigenous peoples.

**The Framework of Analysis**

In examining the relationships between cultural identities and outcomes, our approach is basically a cross-sectional one, targeting the variation in cultures around the world today and the consequences of this variation on outcomes. One must not forget that cultures tend to change slowly, which means that a great deal of longitudinal information is contained in the cross-sectional information. We will analyse at length the consequences of historical legacies, especially colonial traditions, which require a longitudinal perspective on culture, but we will also employ a cross-sectional framework here. We make use of three kinds of information about culture: society (macro) level, regional level and individual (micro) level information.

Cultures are carried by individuals. It is people who identify with, or practise, culture. Information about individuals can be aggregated to various levels. Two relevant levels of aggregation are the society as a whole and the region. Cultural homogeneity versus cultural heterogeneity is a dimension of societies. When a society supports a single culture, then one may pose questions about compactness or the strength of support for groups, as well as how united the population is behind a culture. When a society is fragmented culturally, then ethnic or religious heterogeneity most often takes on a regional dimension with political consequences. Thus, regionally-based political traditions emerge with highly skewed electoral outcomes regionally. It is one thing to describe how cultures correlate with political decisions or social, economic and political outcomes, but it is another thing to show that culture contributes to these decisions or outcomes. A variation in social, economic and political outcomes may attend the differences in culture, but how do we know whether culture really matters from a causal point of view? As shown by social science research, outcomes in politics and society depend on factors other than culture. We use regression analysis to pin down the partial impact of culture, recognizing the influence of other factors such as social structure and institutions.

We will discuss at great length a number of concepts covering quite a few aspects concerning ethnicity, religion, legacies and values. Nevertheless, our focus will be continuously on the impact of culture on society, the economy and the polity, meaning that we will be searching for so-called *cultural effects*. If it is true that culture matters, then we must ask what it matters for? A number of well-known models in social science may be seen as attempts to specify the following proposition more clearly – the cultural thesis (CT) that culture matters.

The CT covers a few ethnicity models claiming that ethnic groups and nations play a major role in human affairs. Furthermore, it includes the Max Weber theory of the economic consequences of the world religions, as it has the same so-called functional form. We may wish to include the political consequences of religious creed under the same format. Finally, a few new cultural models were launched in the 1980s and 1990s, all suggesting that values play a role for macro outcomes or individual behaviour. Our analysis of the CT is based on an elaboration, replacing it with CT' Cultural Item X Matters for Outcome Y, and employing empirical inquiry to determine how X and Y are linked in the world today.

Models linking two or more variables, X and Y, may be analysed for their beauty as well as their internal consistency. The fascinating models are not always the parsimonious ones, or those which have a neat deductive structure or simplicity. Theories with apparently little model elegance, such as Weber's theory of Protestantism and the theory of social trust, have stimulated an immense amount of research and scholarly debate simply because they raise interesting questions about reality. Ultimately, model-building, as well as conceptual investigations, must pay homage to the one and only reality that the social sciences investigate – namely, the real world of human behaviour and interaction. Concepts with no link to this reality are empty and models that cannot be tested or falsified constitute metaphysics. Concepts and models are tools for describing and explaining the world as it exists or has existed (explanation) or will exist (prediction). This is why we emphasize the empirical test of explicitly stated models right through the examination of various theories or arguments which have the form of (CT). The framework that will guide this book is diagrammatically represented in Figure I.1.

Our focus is culture, and we may label 'culture' our main independent variable. At issue is what impact culture in its various manifestations has on different outcomes. These outcomes may be understood as the dependent variables of this inquiry and they refer to political, social and economic phenomena. Contexts enter this model as a set of exogenous and latent factors. Globalization is such a context, which we understand mainly as a process taking place over time, while culture and outcome will be approached as cross-sectional entities. We will not be able to test directly for any real impact of globalization on culture or outcomes. In short, the data employed for testing this very general model cover three levels: the macro level, the regional level, and the micro level. Table I.2 contains the main independent

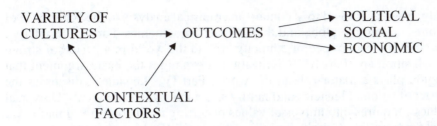

**Figure I.1  Framework for the book: culture, outcomes and contexts**

and dependent variables included in our inquiry into culture and its outcomes. A full list of variables and indicators is presented in Appendix A to C.

Testing models about the impact of culture on outcomes at different levels of social reality strengthens our findings. If we find cultural impacts cross over all data levels, this must increase our confidence in the findings. If, on the other hand, we find that the cultural impact varies between different levels, such a finding would not necessarily weaken the claim that 'culture matters' but it would mean that the claim must be stated in a more qualified manner. Basically this is what we want to find out as we attempt to test the proposition 'culture matters' from various angles, applying a systematic and comparative empirical analysis of real-world data.

## The Structure of the Book

Since our aim is to do a comparative empirical study, the book consists of five main Parts. Part I, 'Culture and Outcomes', is devoted to an overview of theories of culture, pinning down the key ones that have been much discussed

**Table I.2  The key variables at different analytical levels**

| Variables | Macro level | Regional level | Micro level |
|---|---|---|---|
| **Culture** | | | |
| Ethnicity | X | X | X |
| Religion | X | X | X |
| Legacies | X | | |
| Values | X | | X |
| **Outcomes** | | | |
| Political | X | X | X |
| Social | X | | X |
| Economic | X | | |

lately, whereas Parts II to V contain an empirical analysis of the occurrence of cultures around the globe and their impact on outcomes. Part II, 'Ethnicity', describes the occurrence of ethnicity around the world in a period of strong globalization and Part III, 'Civilizations', examines the basic argument that religion plays a major role in the world. Part IV, 'Legacies', discusses the impact of colonial legacies and family structures, whereas Part V, 'Universal Values', inquires into universal values occurring in all countries. Finally, we raise again, in the 'Conclusion', the main issue, 'Does culture matter?'.

Thus, this comprehensive introduction to the new field of cultural studies in political science looks at the main theories of culture from one angle: does culture matter? And it combines theoretical insights into the concept of culture and the various kinds of cultural phenomena – ethnicity, religion and values – with a most thorough empirical inquiry into the role of culture in politics and society, for society as well as for ordinary people.

Part I surveys the various concepts of culture employed in cultural analyses. The question of whether culture matters for politics is, in reality, a whole research programme and it covers a variety of outcomes in society and politics, where the distinction between macro and micro outcomes should be underlined. We suggest, in a new analysis, that culture may be seen as composed of ethnicity, religion, legacies and universal values. Cultural analysis must specify how and for what culture matters. We suggest an analysis of outcomes at three levels. Macro-level outcomes include democracy, quality of life and equality, whereas regional-level outcomes are the electoral support for political parties in a country and individual-level outcomes comprise matters researched by surveys, such as life satisfaction, interest in politics and citizen activity.

Part II examines ethnicity and looks for evidence that various forms of ethnicity matter. Several new findings are reported. Thus, the key ethno-linguistic families of the world are still today associated with macro outcomes such as affluence and democracy. The ethnic effect on voting is apparent in certain countries with traditional ethnic politics, but one needs to examine each country in detail to find out how ethnicity conditions party outcomes. Ethnicity matters a great deal for party support in Spain, Belgium and India, but less so in the USA, Russia and Switzerland. Finally, the ethnic impacts on individual outcomes include both life satisfaction and right-wing political attitudes, but otherwise the role of ethnicity has been overemphasized. Ethnic fragmentation is negative for macro outcomes such as affluence and democracy.

Part III raises the topic of religion, first as a component of civilizations and then as a determinant of party support in elections and also individual outcomes. The macro analysis takes a fresh look at Max Weber's theory of the consequences of the major world religions, pointing out the connections between religion and outcomes that can be found 100 years after Weber suggested that capitalism originated with Protestantism. We find that Protestantism today is more related to human rights than economic development. Islam displays a negative performance on all indicators. In divided countries religion is a major determinant of party support – here we mention the USA, Switzerland and Belgium. In general, religion is a major conservative force in politics although it also motivates individuals to participate in voluntary associations, some of which may harbour a radical message, as was the case in the battle for civil rights in the USA and in the struggle against apartheid in South Africa.

Part IV is devoted to the impact of historical legacies. On the one hand the classical question of the different impact of colonial legacies is examined by a new analysis of outcomes showing that a British colonial legacy has indeed provided a country with a higher probability of performing well than the other colonial traditions. On the other hand, it is shown – again in a new quantitative analysis – that the institutions making up the family structure of a country has a considerable impact upon macro outcomes.

Finally, Part V enters into the field of values research using the well-known world value surveys – both the entire surveys and specific country surveys. We present a critique of the main theories about individual values launched in a couple of famous books in the 1980s and 1990s. Then we show that the strong conclusions drawn about the impact of post-materialism, trust and individualism are most probably exaggerations and that individual values do not matter as much as claimed.

## Conclusion

Culture has developed into a major field of study in political science, especially in the 1990s, where a few key books by Inglehart, Wildavsky, Putnam, Huntington, Kymlicka, Said and van Gunsteren among others, as well as the five-volume study *Beliefs in Government* (Kaase and Newton 1995), have stimulated a lively debate about ethnicity, religion and values. Cultural approaches have become a major challenge to the dominant rational choice framework, where alternative cultural approach frameworks may be further developed by the access to abundant survey information about mass attitudes. We will highlight a few of the new key themes in the study of values in the rapidly expanding culture literature for closer inspection, as well as examining the standard ideas in old culture theory, such as the impact of ethnicity and the world religions.

The objective of this book is distinct as it is devoted to the analysis of the connections between culture and outcomes using a variety of data about the countries of the world. Thus, the focus is distinctly comparative, aiming to explore whether country differences in culture matter. Nevertheless, our approach combines the macro perspective with the micro perspective as we employ data about countries, as well as about individual attitudes, when searching for cultural effects at the societal and individual levels. Our analysis also covers regional outcomes of culture in the form of party electoral support. The selection of countries for analysis depends on the argument to be tested. Thus, the theory that civilization matters may be tested by means of an analysis covering the entire world, but an examination of the role of trust in social life or the impact of libertarianism upon public policies may have to be confined to a more narrow set of countries. The perspective of our book upon culture is best seen as a complement to the prevailing interpretative perspective typical of much of cultural analysis. Instead of penetrating into the meaning(s) of cultures as is done within anthropology and ethnography, we focus on their impact: how important is culture for outcomes? We suggest that one employs the tools of positivistic analysis in order to illuminate whether culture matters. This perspective complements the hermeneutical approach in much of cultural analysis at the same time as it identifies the cultural approach as different from rational choice. We will not go into the attempts to bridge cultural and rational choice perspectives in evolutionary socio-biological analysis (Wilson, 1999).

Our book may be regarded as an attempt to come to grips with the emergence of a multicultural society in the period of globalization. To understand the impact of culture upon politics – how it necessitates a new politics of recognition while preserving the basic principles of liberty and equality under the law – we make an enquiry into three basic aspects of culture, namely ethnicity, religion and values. We hope that this classification of cultural theories and phenomena is helpful in approaching multiculturalism. Whereas we are sceptical about the future relevance of nationalism (or *fraternité*), we do not doubt the future significance of religion, despite the trend towards secularization (Norris and Inglehart, 2004). Value-orientations constitute a new powerful source of cultural politics, as for instance with gender and homosexuality. We remain highly sceptical to the claim of Brian Barry that the post-modern society only requires two concepts: *liberté et egalité* (Barry, 2002). However, the new multicultural society in the advanced world combining democracy with the market economy must be researched with the most powerful empirical methodology available, including e.g. regression and the survey technique.

We now turn first to clarify some of the core concepts used in this book. In Part I we deal with the concepts of culture, the new approaches in cultural analysis and for what culture may matter – that is, outcomes.

# PART I
# CULTURE AND OUTCOMES

# Introduction

Our book is an inquiry into cultural identity and its political and social consequences. When people orientate in terms of a culture, then they may identify with an ethnic group, or they may search for a religious identity and adhere to a world religion or some subsection of such a civilization, or they may adopt universal values that could be present in any nation or within any religion – this is our starting point. Since the fall of communism, the search for belief systems and values has taken on a distinctly cultural tone. Which cultures, then, are relevant for people to adhere to at the beginning of the twenty-first century, when the traditional political ideologies give less and less guidance? And how important are these forms of cultural identity for political affairs?

People search for identity by means of group membership not only with political parties expressing the political ideologies from the Right to the Left, but also increasingly with communities. Communal identities result in ethnic groups, nations, religious sects or world religions when people act on the basis of joining these groups. Other types of community include, for example, new social movements as well as gays, lesbians, environmentalists and vegetarians.

The strong increase in the relevance of communities, together with migration, has created multi-cultural societies almost everywhere. As we enter the twenty-first century it seems as if communities could become just as important as associations, using Ferdinand Tönnies' 1887 classical distinction between culture-based and interest-based groups. Different communities along ethnic and religious lines now exist in most countries, which – we hypothesize – changes the nature of politics. Communal politics is becoming legitimate in rich and poor countries, as communities are increasingly recognized as valid groups.

Culture has always had a connection with civilization. While it is claimed by some that we are heading for a clash of civilizations carried out by a few powerful nations (Huntington, 1996), many others still speak of the peaceful global marketplace with universal cultural attitudes fostered by immigration and the bringing down of borders, national as well as civilizational. Civilization is the broader cultural concept linked especially to the world religions, whereas nation is the more narrow cultural concept. Thus, a civilization could comprise several nations, which in turn could consist of various ethnic groups. In the period of globalization civilizations confront each other, but they need not remain hostile to each other.

The aim of the two chapters making up Part I is to discuss various concepts relating to cultures and outcomes. Here we have a new field in political science in which research is growing at a rapid pace. This makes it an urgent necessity to discuss, and hopefully clarify, key concepts in order to avoid confusion when the basic ideas about cultural effects are put to the necessary empirical tests.

# Chapter 1

# 'Culture' and the Concepts of Culture

## Introduction

The study of culture and cultural variations around the world attracted the interest of the social sciences, as well as anthropology and history, throughout the twentieth century. Only economics has not displayed a major interest in culture, due to its firm adherence to the self-interest axiom of neoclassical economics (Blaug, 1992). Self-interest or egoism is a general and universal motivation among men and women. Cultural identities, on the other hand, vary. But, what is culture, if it is everything that is not materialism or egoism? Consider the following three definitions from major scholars in this field of inquiry:

> Culture is an integral composed of partly autonomous, partly co-ordinated institutions. It is integrated on a series of principles such as the community of blood through procreation; the specialisation in activities; and last but not least, the use of power in political organisation. Each culture owes its completeness and self-sufficiency to the fact that it satisfies the whole range of basic, instrumental and integrative needs. (Malinowski, 1969, p. 40)

> [Culture] denotes an historically transmitted pattern of meanings embodied in symbols, a system of inherited conceptions expressed in symbolic forms by means of which men communicate, perpetuate, and develop their knowledge about and attitudes towards life. (Geertz, 1973, p. 89)

> Political culture is thus the manifestation in aggregate form of the psychological and subjective dimensions of politics. A political culture is the product of both the collective history of a political system and the life histories of the members of that system, and thus it is rooted equally in public events and private experiences. (Pye, 1968, p. 218)

From these three authorities on culture we immediately get a first impression of the immense variety of connotations connected with the term 'culture'. Malinowski relates culture in general to institutions, whereas Geertz links it with symbols. With Pye we have the idea of a special kind of culture – namely, political culture – which comes in addition to general cultures or the cultures of societies.

The more one reflects upon the concepts of culture, the more one realizes that it is a most debated and complex conception. The meaning (connotation) and reference (denotation) of 'culture' are not only essentially contested among scholars, but they also cover a number of factors, which makes it a complicated concept. Before one sets out to carry out empirical research on the occurrence of cultures, one needs to take a stand on some difficult methodological issues concerning the concept of culture. In the conception of *cultural identity*, there is, besides the difficult notion of culture, also the idea of identity. When cultures or cultural factors create the identity of people – their *raison d'être* – then how strongly is this identity creating elements with regard to their personality? The concept of identity or sameness has provoked much philosophical debate and controversy.

Thus, if culture is a problematic concept, then the same applies to the conception of cultural identity. When people today search for personal identity, do they resort to cultural identity as national or ethnic identity, religious identity or identity in the form of universal values? How cultural identities – communal or universal values – occur is a question for empirical research, which has become highly relevant as the traditional political ideologies seem to offer less and less to ordinary people in terms of an identification mechanism.

Below we approach a few key concepts or definitions in cultural theory by means of the classical semantic distinction between connotation (characteristics) and denotation (reference or the set of real objects). In particular, we aim to go beyond the many and often confusing connotations rendered in order to find the denotation – if, indeed, there is only one. Before we inquire into how cultures vary, we must pin down this elusive concept of culture, or at least become aware of its many different guises.

## The Early Meanings of Culture

The history of the usage of a term is often illuminating for an analysis of its present semantics. While it is true that key social science terms change their meanings along with theoretical developments (Sartori, 1984), finding the origin of concepts does allow a certain perspective on the use of the word in question.

The word 'culture' is an English version of the German word *Kultur*, which in turn derives from the Latin word *cultura*, from the verb *colere*, meaning to cultivate. To cultivate something is to handle it or work upon it in such a way that something valuable results. Thus, 'culture' stands for something that has been worked upon, as in agriculture or horticulture. One can immediately see that the word 'culture' and its synonyms in other languages was connected very early on with the term 'civilization' and its synonyms, both meaning attainments by people in the form of positive results or true accomplishments.

The term 'culture' entered into English usage with the publication of E.B. Tylor's text *Primitive Culture* in 1871. The following definition was given in this classic text:

Culture, or civilisation ... is that complex whole which includes knowledge, belief, art, law, morals, customs, and any other capabilities and habits acquired by man as a member of society. (Tylor, 1871, p. 1; cited in Kroeber and Kluckhohn, 1963, p. 81)

If 'culture' denotes all the capabilities and habits of men and women, then 'culture' becomes almost synonymous with 'civilization'. Also 'civilization' has a Latin background, originating in the word *civis* denoting a citizen – that is a civilized person. Thus, having a culture and being civilized was basically the same thing.

The principal German source of inspiration for studies into the culture and civilization of mankind was G.E. Klemm's work, *Allgemeine Kulturgeschichte der Menschheit*, completed in ten volumes in 1852. Some scholars attempted to distinguish between the two concepts of culture and civilization, but with little success. Examining the development of these concepts, Kroeber and Kluckhohn state:

'Culture' is said to be a particular state or stage of advancement in civilization. 'Civilization' is called an advancement or a state of social culture. In both popular and literary English the tendency has been to treat them as near synonyms, though 'civilization' has sometimes been restricted to 'advanced' or 'high' cultures. (Kroeber and Kluckhohn, 1963, p. 19)

We will, however, not accept this equality between culture and civilization. To us, culture is the most general concept, denoting the cultural identity of any community – small or large. A civilization is the culture of an extremely large community, covering many nations or peoples which may have little interaction. Thus, the Greek or Islamic civilizations cover many countries and periods in history, whereas the culture of, for example, the small community of homosexuals in present-day San Francisco is a much more limited phenomenon. Thus, all civilizations are cultures, but not all cultures are civilizations.

Let us first follow the semantic investigation by Kroeber and Kluckhohn (1963) which covers the literature up to the early 1950s. Kroeber and Kluckhohn presented a panorama over the usage of '*Kultur*' or 'culture' since the word entered into scientific discourse with Klemm in Germany and Tylor in England.

The study of culture in the nineteenth century was inspired by a scientific ambition to investigate other aspects of human interaction and societies than the history of great personalities and warfare. A very important text for initiating the study of culture was Voltaire's *Essai sur les Moeurs et l'Esprit des Nations* in 1769, which argued that mankind is better understood if one bypasses the history of kings and their persistent conduct of warfare.

From its usage in history in the nineteenth century, culture entered the emerging social sciences, especially sociology and anthropology. It could be said that the concept of culture became absolutely essential only in anthropology, where it was used by all the early masters of this discipline, mainly for the inquiry into non-occidental societies (Kottak, 2000). It was not until after the Second World War that the concept was applied on a large scale to the study of occidental communities.

Interestingly, the study of culture meant not only a reorientation of the focus from great personalities to the various forms of interaction between anonymous individuals, from the deeds of heroes to the collective achievements of a myriad persons. This new perspective also carried with it the idea of a distinct methodology that could be applied to the understanding of cultures – namely, the methodology of the so-called *Kulturwissenschaften* or *Verstehen*. Perhaps the most well-known work arguing for a radical separation between the methods of the natural sciences and those of the cultural sciences was H. Rickert's *Kulturwissenschaft und Naturwissenschaft* in 1899. Taking an extreme methodological position, Rickert argued for the sharp distinctiveness of the methodology of the cultural sciences, linking it up with the interpretative methods of the discipline of history (Rickert, 1921).

Even among scholars who, like Max Weber, made a less radical separation between the natural sciences and the cultural sciences, there was a belief in a distinct methodology for the cultural sciences (Weber, 1968). Somehow, the understanding of culture required an interpretation of meanings, or the use of what is now considered to be 'hermeneutical' techniques – *Verstehen*. This track of the debate on culture, focusing on the proper methods for understanding cultural phenomena, is highly relevant to the present-day discussion about cultural methodology or the proper approach to be employed for mapping the occurrence of values. While in no way denying the relevance of interpretative methods in cultural research (Geertz, 2001), we wish to show that the ordinary canons of empirical study are capable of providing insights into culture, and especially into how culture matters in practical life.

The results of the Kroeber and Kluckhohn inquiry may be summarized by stating a series of connotations that they were able to distil from the literature up to the early 1950s and which reoccur in the present-day debate about the new cultural approaches. The connotation of a word consists of the characteristics that make up the concept, whereas the denotation of a term is the set of real-life phenomena of which these characteristics are true. Although Kroeber and Kluckhohn did not state the denotation of the various concepts of culture that they were able to retrieve from a large literature, we will hint at the denotation in order to find out how different these concepts really are.

**Connotations of Culture***

As is pointed out in semantic theory, connotations can differ widely while the denotation remains the same. Thus, different concepts may be true of the same phenomenon. There is a strong sense that many of the different definitions of culture really aim at the very same phenomenon – that is, society in general. Below we discuss several connotations and also give examples of definitions suggested under each of them.

*1   Comprehensiveness: 'total', 'sum total', 'complex whole'*   Here, we find several representative definitions, but it is not always the same phenomena that they include in that total or whole. Let us mention a few: 'all the habits acquired by man' (Benedict, 1929), 'the sum total of ideas, conditioned emotional responses and patterns of habitual behaviour' (Linton, 1936), 'that complex whole which includes artefacts, beliefs, art, all the other habits acquired by man' (Kluckhohn and Kelly, 1945), 'the accumulated treasury of human creation' (Kluckhohn and Kelly, 1945). Herskovits (1948) demonstrates how enormously comprehensive the concept of culture can be when he says that culture 'describes the total body of belief, behaviour, knowledge, sanctions, values and goals that mark the way of life of any people'.
      One may wish to remind oneself of the classical phrase 'If a concept C is defined in such a manner that it covers everything, then maybe C covers nothing' (Wildavsky, 1973) when being confronted with these connotations.

*2   Legacy: 'tradition', 'social heritage'*   This connotation adds time to the first connotation above concerning comprehensiveness. However, it is just as vague. Let us quote a few major authorities in the field. These include: 'sum total and organisation of the social heritages' (Park and Burgess, 1921); 'Culture comprises inherited artefacts, goods, technical processes, ideas, habits and values' (Malinowski, 1931); and culture as 'the process by which in a given social group or social class language, beliefs, ideas, aesthetic tastes, knowledge, skills…' are inherited (Radcliffe-Brown, 1949). But is not this connotation also too inclusive? If culture is all that societies inherit, then perhaps culture is nothing? However, there are more specific connotations available in the literature, which we can examine.

*3   Norms: 'folkways', 'accepted ways of thinking and acting', 'way of life'*
Speaking of culture as norms raises the problem of what is a norm. Whether these norms also have to be obeyed or followed, and to what extent, in actual behaviour is crucial. Thus, focusing on norms could be much more specific, but it could also be equally inclusive as connotation 1. Almost all the

---

*   All quotations in this section stem from Kroeber and Kluckhohn (1963).

definitions in this connotation focus on culture as a way of life – that is, as a normative order of some kind. Thus, we have:

> The culture of a society is the way of life of its members, the collection of ideas and habits which they learn, share, and transmit from generation to generation. (Linton, 1945)

> A culture is any given people's way of life, as distinct from the life-ways of other peoples. (Kluckhohn and Leighton, 1946)

> A culture 'refers to a distinctive way of life of a group of people, their complete' design for living. (Kluckhohn, 1951)

> *La culture, c'est la manière de vivre du groupe.* (Maquet, 1949)

This expression 'ways of life' occurs consistently in much of the cultural literature. One may ask whether it stands for the *prescribed* ways of life (that is, norms or directives) or the *actual* ways of life (that is, regular or 'normal' behaviour). The counterargument is that norms which lack any correspondence to reality would sooner or later become completely obsolete. Yet, accepting this counterargument means that we are back to zero or connotations 1 or 2 which are really too inclusive. Let us try another direction.

*4  Psychological characteristics: 'learning', 'habit', 'sublimations'*  One often encounters this connotation in the cultural literature. It is based on the presumption that one knows what kinds of phenomena psychological characteristics are. Yet, this is far from evident. As can be seen from the following definition that falls under connotation 4:

> The sum of men's adjustments to their life-conditions is their culture, or civilization. These adjustments … are attained only through the combined action of variation, selection, and transmission. (Sumner and Keller, 1927)

People adjust primarily through their behaviour. But are physical behaviour reactions to be labelled 'psychological' phenomena? Or are we are more referring to mind phenomena such as the 'process of inventing and transmitting symbols and symbolic systems and technologies' (Lundberg, 1939)? This connotation 4 does not seem to take us anywhere, as so many different phenomena (behaviour, mind) may qualify as 'psychological'. Let us try another connotation that is frequently used.

*5  Structural: 'system', 'integrated', 'patterned'*  This connotation precludes that a culture could be just any random collection of cultural items, whatever they may be composed of. Random pieces of cultural items do not constitute a culture, so states this requirement. But what creates the relationships or ties between cultural items so that a system or a whole emerges? The various definitions found under this connotation are extremely vague as to how much pattern there must be among cultural items and what it is that creates this pattern. Let us quote one authority:

A culture is the configuration of learned behaviour and results of behaviour whose component elements are shared and transmitted by the members of a particular society. (Linton, 1945)

It may be asked how much restriction on the cultural items to be included in a culture is involved in a 'configuration'. It is a matter for debate not only whether or not cultures tend to be integrated but also whether there is a consistent pattern behind cultural items. The amount of cultural consistency or coherence is an empirical matter which cannot be decided by definitional consideration. Why could not a culture be all the past items of behaviour that are somehow transmitted to the future generation whatever the degree of coherence in their configuration? Somehow, we seem never to go beyond connotation 1. A further possibility is discussed below.

6  *Genesis: 'creation', 'man-made', 'transmissible'*  This connotation requires that a cultural item have two characteristics. First, it is something that is created. Second, what has been thus created can be transmitted from one generation to another. Here, we have a connotation that really restricts what is to be included under the concept of culture or a cultural item, and it is the requirement of transmission that is more restricting than the requirement of man-made.

What is man-made? One possible answer could be 'tools, weapons, shelter, and other material goods'. Another equally feasible answer is 'attitudes and beliefs, ideas and judgements, codes and institutions, arts and sciences, philosophy and social organisation' (Reuter, 1939). The following is a somewhat different response, stating that man-made is anything: 'whether a material object, overt behaviour, symbolic behaviour, or social organisation' (Bernard, 1942). Again, we are returned to the problem of comprehensiveness – namely, connotation 1.

Perhaps the requirement of transmission restricts? If culture is 'every object, habit, idea, institution, and mode of thought, or action' that is 'passed on to others', then many things which happen only once and are not communicated further on or accepted by other generations could not constitute culture. However, arguably, it is still too wide a conception, especially if behaviour can be considered as man-made and transmissible as tradition. One would perhaps have expected more of an emphasis on symbols when speaking of transmission.

Yet, this definition also raises another fascinating question, namely: could there be dead cultures – that is, cultures that can no longer be transferred to new generations? Of course, dead cultures could have been of tremendous importance, although we know little of them, given that we have so little concrete information about their ways of life, as, for example, several Indian civilizations before the Incas and the Aztecs.

## The Ambiguity of Culture

It is difficult not to arrive at the disturbing conclusion that all these different connotations of 'culture' mean little in reality, as the references under them is too wide. Basically, from the classical semantic investigation by Kroeber and Kluckhohn (1963) we learn that 'culture' denotes more or less the same set of phenomena under all the various connotations – that is, human interactions in all its aspects. What, then, about the concept of culture in more recent literature? Looking at the most recent literature, we find a number of interesting attempts at making the concept of culture more specific.

Interestingly, in a very popular textbook, published in 2000 and surveying the various fields of study in anthropology one can retrieve all the different meanings of 'culture' identified above. C.P. Kottak argues that culture is 'learned', 'shared', 'symbolic', 'nature', 'all-encompassing', 'integrated', 'activity', 'adaptive or maladaptive' (Kottak, 2000, pp. 60–110). He states:

> Cultural traditions take natural phenomena, including biologically based urges, and channel them in particular directions. Everyone is cultured, not just people with elite educations. Cultures are integrated and patterned through their dominant economic forces, social patterns, key symbols, and core values. (Kottak, 2000, p. 61)

Yet one still does not really know what a culture is, despite all the phenomena that cluster round it. What is meant by these statements that culture channels things in various directions?

Kottak argues that, in today's world, the distinctions between different levels of culture – international, national, and subcultural – are highly important. By 'national culture' he refers to the beliefs, learned behaviour patterns, values and institutions shared by citizens of the same nation. 'International culture' stands for cultural traditions that extend beyond and across national boundaries. 'Subcultures' are 'different symbol-based patterns and traditions associated with particular groups in the same complex society' (Kottak, 2000, p. 68). Kottak has the following to say about these subcultures:

> In a large nation like the United States or Canada, subcultures originate in region, ethnicity, language, class, and religion. The religious backgrounds of Jews, Baptists, and Roman Catholics create subcultural differences between them. While sharing a common national culture, U.S. northerners and southerners also differ in aspects of their beliefs, values, and customary behavior as a result of regional variation. French-speaking Canadians contrast with English-speaking people in the same country. Italian Americans have ethnic traditions different from those of Irish, Polish, and African-Americans. (Kottak, 2000, p. 69)

We believe that our concepts cover the distinctions made by Kottak, although they cut the material in a different kind of slice, as we approach cultures as either ethnic, religious or universal values. To us, subcultures would correspond to ethnic or religious fragmentation.

A civilization is a special type of culture. As stated above, we regard civilization as a broader concept than that of a nation, ethnic group or community. Thus, we need to elaborate the concept of a civilization so that we may identify one main civilization for each country on the globe. To define 'civilization' merely as all that which has been accomplished, or as a refinement, would entail a definition that is as vague as the concept of culture. What is critical is the denotation and not the connotation of 'civilization'. This means that we must identify the main civilizations of humankind and inquire into their social consequences – the outcomes.

As a consequence of the emphasis upon denotation, we focus on the question: how many civilizations are there today? Evidently there is no single correct answer to this question, as civilizations can be identified in various ways. We argue that there are at least two relevant criteria for arriving at a specific conception of a civilization – namely, religion and historical legacy.

Clearly, a civilization may be based on a religion. Whether a civilization may be linked with merely geopolitical circumstances is more doubtful. Thus there is a great deal of documentation about Buddhist or Muslim civilizations, whereas the existence of a new Asiatic civilisation is more debatable. We know what the former two are, but the latter is less familiar or 'real'.

If a civilization is closely connected with a historical heritage of domination, then one would seek information about the Spanish culture or the Anglo-Saxon culture as civilizations. The long period of colonialism and its vast consequences give credence to such an approach. But is historical legacy always distinct from religion? Sometimes the distinction between historical legacy and religion can be made, but in other cases it fails due to the closeness between the two as, for instance, in relation to Spanish, Portuguese and Belgian colonialism which display a close connection with Catholicism.

We will argue that religion is the chief critical factor in identifying the major civilizations of the world. We start out from a classification of the three chief religious civilizations:

1   *The Muslim world*: all countries with a majority of their population adhering to the Qu'ranic system of belief.
2   *The Hinduist/Buddhist worlds*: India, which is Hinduist, and all the countries where Buddhism has a strong position, often in combination with another religion such as Confucianism or Shintoism.
3   *The Christian world*: Protestant, Catholic and Greek Orthodox countries.

Then we proceed to examine the variation within each civilization in order to find out how compact they are, taking into account not only the variety of creeds within the world religions, but also the number of non-believers in the countries with one dominant religion.

Nevertheless, it is also worth pursuing the other perspective on civilizations – that is, to approach this concept by means of historical legacies. In the Weberian tradition of civilizational analysis there is not only the idea that the world religions have different implications for society but also that historical legacies, especially in the form of occidental and oriental heritages, matter crucially for political and economic outcomes. A recent example of this perspective is the hypothesis that Anglo-Saxon and Spanish cultures have quite different consequences for economic affluence and growth due to their impact on transaction costs – the former diminishing and the latter increasing these costs (North, 1990).

But it is questionable whether one can speak of the occidental or oriental civilizations without committing oneself to a value bias, as these concepts are highly value-loaded (Myrdal, 1967). And would it not have to be admitted that both the Occident and the Orient consist of so many various nations that there is almost no cultural compactness within both legacies? Instead of employing Weber's conceptual pair, Occident versus Orient, one could inquire into all the major colonial legacies and penetrate their consequences. Thus, one would speak of, for instance, the British, French, Spanish or Portuguese and Dutch legacies. Does such a perspective on legacies help us understand present-day outcomes?

The problems involved in identifying the major civilizations of the world is evident from Huntington's (1996) classification, in which he uses eight categories in an ad hoc fashion and in which it is obvious that he basically relies on the world religions and geography. So, when asking 'What is the political relevance of the conception of a civilization in the world today?', we need to examine the concept of a civilization closely. Rather than speak of one civilization for each country on the globe, we suggest reducing the number of civilizations, treating civilization as the most encompassing culture covering communities based on ethnicity and nations.

Nations – that is, communities based on national identity – are smaller entities than civilizations but, at the same time, they tend to be large enough to contain a variety of communities with ethnic, religious or other identity bases. Countries, which include sizeable ethnic groups with strong separate identities are spoken of as multi-nation countries or heterogeneous countries. Homogeneous nations have almost become a mere theoretical possibility, at least in so far as all the wealthier countries today are multicultural in one sense or another – even, for instance, the Gulf states. For instance, in Qatar the foreign population is roughly twice as large as the native one. Heterogeneous countries or multicultural societies may also comprise different compact religious groups.

Both the concept of a civilization and the concept of a nation have tended to look upon culture as compact entities, being shaped by their historical pattern of evolution, involving possibly coalescence, diffusion and division. Compact nation-states appear today to be merely a figment of the imagination. And civilizations were perhaps never highly monolithic in the past and are even less so today.

Yet a civilization and a nation represent distinct cultural identities of special kinds in that they are both identities of a particularistic nature, as they always carry proper names. In terms of nations, people are Kurds, Serbs, Argentinians or Norwegians or Finns. In terms of religion, people could be Buddhists, Hindus, Greek Orthodox, Lutherans or Calvinists.

## New Cultural Theory

Recent cultural theory continues to speak of culture as values and beliefs, social relations and ways of life – in other words, 'culture' denotes almost everything. Thus, for instance Thompson and his colleagues speak of 'cultural biases, social relations, and ways of life' as distinct entities, but hasten to add that they are interlinked: 'When we wish to designate a viable combination of social relations and cultural bias we speak of a *way of life*' (Thompson *et al.*, 1990, p. 1).

Let us give a few examples of these specific cultural concepts and how they can be employed for understanding politics.

### The Backward Society

When describing Italy, writers often focus on the so-called *mezzogiorno*, or the differences between northern and southern Italy in terms of economics and politics. Banfield (1958) suggested that the determining factor was not history or legacy – a longitudinal entity – but that what permeates southern Italian society was a set of attitudes which were absent in northern Italy. Banfield studied this culture in detail, discovering despair, distrust, pessimism and resignation in an unpredictable world governed by randomness. And such a fatalistic culture would, one could argue, promote the politics of authoritarianism or clientelism.

### The Dual Society

Sometimes political systems undergo immense and rapid changes in a short period of time. Culture may help to understand how such processes as, for example, the Chinese Cultural Revolution are possible. Pye (1988) viewed Chinese politics as reflecting two major, but opposing, cultures – hierarchy and authority as with Confucianism and radical egalitarianism as with socialism/Marxism. Occasionally, the balance between these cultures is upset and one of them becomes predominant, as was the case with egalitarianism during the Cultural Revolution in the late 1960s and early 1970s, causing political havoc. One may note here that Ogden (1999) saw three factors –

socialism, Chineseness and development – as three competing values in modern China at about the same time. It is often arbitrary to describe a society as having a dual or triple culture.

*The Triadic Society*

Once one admits the possibility that cultures are not compact, then one may wish to identify more than two subcultures. Elazar (1966, 1986) suggested three major subcultures in the USA in order to account for differences in the politics of various states – namely, individualism, traditionalism and moralism. Much effort has gone into validating this triadic construction, both with regard to attitudes among people and with regard to the political consequences imputed to these three subcultures. Who is to say that Elazar was right with three subcultures as opposed to other breakdowns, such as white versus non-white, Protestant versus Catholic and so on.

There are two questions involved. First, how are three, and only three, subcultures identified? Second, can these concepts be applied in such a manner that reality becomes better understood? It could well be the case that more than two or three types of cultures need to be distinguished or that real-life phenomena cannot be classified in accordance with only these three concepts. The great difficulty with specific culture concepts is that one needs to know how many such concepts one can use as well as how one is to apply them.

Individualism embraces the market and the democratic regime, as both stem from open competition where anyone can win. Competitive individualism rejects state intervention if its purpose is not to enhance self-regulation. Individualists handle their lives best through their capacity to make agreements and profit from them. In the USA this type of culture has been carried by both the industrialists and the people living in the frontier society. Traditionalism occurred in both New England and in the deep South, as traditionalism expresses a commitment to hierarchy. The functioning of markets and government must be bent towards the interests of the elite who owe their position to their natural superiority in terms of capacities and values. Thus, regulation is acceptable if it solidifies the inherited order. Finally, moralism occurs with groups that adhere to a communitarian ethic. This would be the most clear opposite to individualism, as it conceives of social life as a commonwealth in which all should participate. Moralism is to be found with groups who intensively seek government regulation in order to rectify what is wrong, as for example, with the Abolitionists, Mormons and Populists in the USA.

*The Culture Quartet*

Suppose that we accept the critique of Thompson *et al.* that Elazar's category moralism is inadequate, because all cultures include, or are based on, morals.

|  | Hierarchy | Equality |
|---|---|---|
| **Individualism** | I | II |
| **Communalism** | III | IV |

**Figure 1.1  Four types of culture**

One way to develop the triadic typology would be to move to four types by crossing the individualism – communitarian distinction with the hierarchy – equality distinction. Figure 1.1 shows the possibilities.

Perhaps one could point out that this typology is as close as one could come to the scheme suggested by Douglas and Wildavsky (1983). New Culture Theory (NCT) modifies Figure 1.1, arguing that fatalism (I), individualism (II), hierarchy (III) and egalitarianism (IV) are to be regarded as the four principal and basic types of culture (Thompson *et al.*, 1990). Figure 1.2, to compare with Figure 1.1, contains the two dimensions of each and every culture – grid and group – and the four resulting types of culture.

The four types of cultural orientation introduced in Figure 1.2 have been employed extensively in various applications of NCT on to quite different behaviour: modern mass behaviour, the activities of historical elites, political action programmes, culture shifts and so on. Evidently, these four categories constitute highly useful tools of social or cultural analysis, but are they more than tools of analysis? One may claim, as does NCT, that they constitute the only possible values that human interaction or behaviour may express.

NCT contains this claim that these four types of cultural orientation are the only, or the most basic kinds of, culture conceivable (Thompson *et al.*, 1990). Allowing for the possibility of a fifth type (autonomy) – that is, a mixture in the centre of Figure 1.2 – can it be demonstrated somehow that these orientations are the only possible or the most universal that one might be conceived of?

The group dimension refers to whether there is a clear separation between those inside and those outside the group or whether group boundaries are

|  | Weak group | Strong group |
|---|---|---|
| **Strong grid** | Fatalism | Hierarchy |
| **Weak grid** | Individualism | Egalitarianism |

*Source*: Thompson *et al.*, 1990, p. 8. The fifth cultural type is labelled 'autonomy' and is placed in the centre of the matrix.

**Figure 1.2  The typology of New Culture Theory (NCT)**

malleable: 'the extent to which an individual is incorporated into bounded units' (Thompson *et al.*, 1990, p. 5). Strong groups differentiate themselves from their environments, whereas weak groups do not make such clear distinctions between 'we' and 'them'. The group dimension, referring to external distinctions, has a long standing in the literature.

The grid dimension refers to whether a group makes distinctions between its members resulting in an internal stratification: 'the degree to which an individual's life is circumscribed by externally imposed prescriptions' (Thompson *et al.*, 1990, p. 5). A strong grid occurs when people are distinguished on the basis of status criteria of some kind. Weak grid is typical of groups where internal group distinctions hardly occur, or when they are not sharp or transparent. The grid dimension also has a long standing in the literature.

What is unique to NCT is the combination of the external and internal distinctions about how the individuals relate to the group into a most comprehensive typology. Unlike most typologies, which have been dualist, stating only two major alternatives, it allows for plural ways of life. If one also takes into account the possibility that societies may harbour competing subcultures, then NCT makes possible a much richer analysis of the occurrence of various cultures or universal values today.

The above is about typology, or the choice of concepts. However, NCT also claims to state fundamental truths about all existing, or previously existing, cultures. But can all prior cultures be analysed with these four concepts, as if all cultures were only variations on these four values or consist of combinations of these four value orientations or cultures? NCT argues not only that its typology is logically coherent 'generating a mutually exclusive and jointly exhaustive set of categories for the domain of social life' (Thompson *et al.*, 1990, p. 14), but also states that these four or five kinds of culture are the only ones, or at least the basic ones, that are viable. This is a most interesting claim which should be scrutinized.

Cultures may be analysed in so many ways. The NCT classification into hierarchy, egalitarianism, fatalism, individualism and autonomy is one way of approaching the variety of cultural phenomena. In future culture research it may become the standard taxonomy, but that depends on whether it allows one to cover most forms of cultural diversity and whether it captures the most essential features of various cultures. A number of cultures that differ substantially spring to mind: the variety of nationalism, the myriad religions, the immense set of attitudes and values. We need to discuss whether or not they are all reducible to the four or five basic cultural categories of NCT. What is involved in this reduction of all cultural phenomena to five basic forms of culture? The five cultures of NCT may be said to 'exist' in two different ways. People may be aware of being egalitarians, individualists or fatalists, referring to themselves as belonging to those categories and also describing their group or other groups with these labels or the entailed conception and terms. Thus, people in different cultures would speak of equality, liberty and destiny in ways which would permit their classification as egalitarians, individualists and fatalists. They may even use these labels to refer to themselves.

Yet cultures which display little in terms of self-reference to the concepts of equality, liberty and destiny, may nonetheless be considered as egalitarian or individualist or fatalist in spirit. Thus, a world religion like Islam can be characterized as fatalist or egalitarian, although people practising Islam would perhaps hardly ever use such labels in self-designation.

There is no doubt that the popularity of NCT derives from its great applicability. It has been used to analyse groups, focusing attention on equality, hierarchy and liberty. But it has also been employed to characterize behaviour without any kind of reference to these labels. The abstract nature of the two basic concepts of NCT – grid and group – implies that its cultural types are highly general. Perhaps they are so general that they can be applied to almost all kinds of social phenomenon? Yet, the five cultures are not empty categories. At the same time, they do not permit a detailed analysis of cultural attitudes, stating, for instance, what is the difference between two cultures which both emphasize hierarchy – for example, Roman Catholicism and Greek Orthodoxy – or between two cultures which are egalitarian – for example, communism and postmaterialism.

When NCT is applied in the analysis of present-day attitudes and value conflicts where the actors themselves are oriented in terms of these cultures, then NCT offers new insights into the nature of the political struggle that surrounds groups with opposing cultures (Wildavsky, 1991). However, when NCT is employed to draw broad historical pictures, then the results appear far more trivial.

## Political Culture

'Political culture' may stand for any belief system or set of values that play a role in the political life of a country. According to this conceptualization, any culture or cultural item could constitute a political culture. This would be a thin concept of political culture, accepting many forms of culture as political culture. More specifically, however, 'political culture' could denote the attitudes and values that orient citizens or elites predominantly towards the political institutions of a country. Pye gives the following 'thick' definition of 'political culture':

> Political culture is the set of attitudes, beliefs, and sentiments, which give order and meaning to a political process and which provide the underlying assumptions and rules that govern behavior in the political system. (Pye, 1968, p. 218)

Pye explains that cultures that specifically structure the political process encompass 'both the political ideals and the operating norms of a polity' (Pye,

1968, p. 218). It is not only a nationalist ideology or the political ideologies in general that Pye has in mind. Political cultures could also include the prevailing constitutional theory of a country. However, the concept of a political culture can be developed in a much more specific manner, as we will discuss below.

The most well-known theory of political culture is that of Almond and Verba. In *The Civic Culture* (1965) they suggested that the political culture of the countries of the world vary in terms of the following categories: alienated or allegiant cultures on the one hand, and deferential or participatory cultures on the other. These concepts were intended just as much for historical inquiry as for contemporary exploration, as the authors wished to explain why the democratic regime prevailed in the Anglo-Saxon world but not in Continental Europe during the interwar years.

Let us reconstruct how these four political cultures were generated. Figure 1.3 has the combinations for a matrix, crossing two distinctions that represent the two basic dimensions in each and every political culture and which were introduced above.

So, now, which of these four combinations, I–IV, most encourage democracy? Almond and Verba pose this question in terms of congruence/incongruence between political orientations on the one hand and political institutions on the other hand.

Given the neatness of the four categories I–IV derived in Figure 1.3, one would expect the four basic political cultures of Almond and Verba to correspond exactly to them. However, this is not the case. They first distinguish between the following three cultures: parochial, subject and participant political cultures, all involving 'the specifically political orientations – attitudes toward the political system and its various parts and attitudes towards the role of the self in the system' (Almond and Verba, 1965, p. 12). However, they thereafter introduce a fourth type, the civic culture, which in their view is the type most congruent with democracy.

None of these types of political culture – parochial, subject, participant and civic – corresponds precisely to the categories derived in Figure 1.3. Instead, Almond and Verba mix the basic dimensions of political cultures, which remain participation/deference as well as alienation/allegiance. The civic culture seems somehow to place itself in the middle of Figure 1.3, combining all four dimensions in a mixture that supports democratic stability.

|  | Alienation | Allegiance |
|---|---|---|
| Deference | I | II |
| Participation | III | IV |

**Figure 1.3   Political cultures**

Often 'political culture' is used only descriptively, as when the totality of values and norms surrounding the political institutions of a country are singled out as the political culture of the country in question. Thus, each state would, in a trivial sense, have its special political culture. However, the theory of political culture has attempted to generalize about the prevailing political values of a country, identifying a few abstract dimensions which could account for much of the variation.

A more recent example of a political culture model is contained in Putnam's (1993) analysis of Italian democracy. He introduced culture in order to explain the classical difference between the northern and southern Italy – *mezzogiorno*. Civic involvement, argues Putnam, explains how democratic institutions work themselves out in practice. And the attitude towards civic involvement entails a value that is not forthcoming automatically, but is to be found in a society with plenty of social trust, which Putnam equates with a broad carpet of associations – for example, in a vibrant civil society, as suggested in 1840 by Tocqueville (1990). Civic involvement is the cultural item that accounts for why participation in politics varies, as well as why democracy works differently in northern and southern Italy (Putnam, 1993).

Behind involvement there is social and political trust, which became a major research topic in the 1990s (see Newton, 1999; Newton and Norris, 2000). It has been argued that trust is an important background factor for stable democracy as well as for the the way in which economic institutions operate. Fukuyama (1995a) focused first and foremost on the consequences of social trust for economic growth, facilitating transactions in the economy. Social trust, he maintained, may be related to either the guarantee of economic rights or to reduction of corruption.

Trust, as analysed by Coleman (1990), like many other items in political cultures, belongs to the set of universal cultures. Although the theme of political culture is an interesting one, it seems unnecessarily restrictive to focus only on political cultures in the narrow sense of concept. Culture in general could play a major role in politics. Thus, the analysis of culture and politics should cover ethnicity, religion and civilizations in addition to universal values.

## Gertz and Cultural Anthropology: A 'Cul de Sac'?

Anthropology has for a long time had a dominant position in the study of culture. World famous anthropologists studied so-called primitive cultures in order to reveal their hidden meaning of behaviour and artefacts. We can mention only a few of these major scholars here, for instance following C. Geertz in his *Works and Lives: The Anthropologist as Author* (1990): However, the conclusion of Geertz, himself a towering anthropologist, is extremely negative: Cultural anthropology no longer has any primitive cultures to study and it never developed an established methodology for doing so. It seems as if the study of the *meaning* of human behaviour is more difficult than the analysis of the *rationality* of human conduct. Whereas the rational choice approach in the social science mushrooms not only in economics but also in political science and sociology, the cultural approach (although spreading) faces more hesitation and criticism.

In *Available Light: Anthropological Reflections on Philosophical Topics* (2001), Geertz widens his scepticism from cultural anthropology to the social sciences in general. The diverse and fluid social sciences are constantly defining and defending its borders, skirmishing with science while the tenured generals snipe at each other. These manoeuvres pass over the most important question of what is at stake in the study of society and culture. This question was central to cultural anthropology, characterized by a self-reflexive intimacy between philosophy and methodology, as exemplified in Geertz' well-known 1973 book, *The Interpretation of Cultures*. The anthropologist can only experience what are always only partial truths in the light available at the moment of encounter, as in Geertz's pursuit of the role of ideas in behaviour through Javanese religion, Balinese states and Moroccan bazaars, modernization, Islam, kinship, law, art and ethnicity. The moral anxieties of fieldwork is triggered by cultural diversity opening up issues pertinent to all intellectual pursuits. For anyone involved or interested in the social sciences, Geertz underlines the importance and value of social study, because the impact of the social sciences upon society will be determined more by what sort of moral experience they turn out to embody than by their merely technical effects or by how much money they are permitted to spend.

If one accepts the argument by Geertz, then one ends up with the following dilemma. Either one pursues the rational choice approach with its scienticism, or one is forced to accept relativism with the cultural approach. However, this dilemma is not inevitable and it should be avoided if possible. The study of culture has its own logic, but it does not necessarily entail relativism. One can study culture with the ordinary canons of scientific methodology.

Rational choice has been elaborated tremendously after the Second World War with the triumph of game theory in both mathematics and the social sciences. As a whole, rational choice with decision-making under risk (Bayes' theory), 2-person game theory (Nash's equilibrium) and N-person game theory (Banzhaf's power index and the core) offers a formidable set of tools for analysing social reality. However, it does not cover the essential aspects of human interaction which pertain to the meaning of behaviour and the social elements of motivation such as community. One does not need to engage in an intellectual war on rational choice (Etzioni, 1990, 1998) in order to reject the imperialist claims of scholars like e.g. Gary Becker (Becker, 1995). It suffices to state that the cultural approach is a most important addition to the rational choice approach covering other aspects of social interaction than calculation, self interests, associations and means-end rationality.

The meaningful aspects of human behaviour have always been a source of puzzles in methodology. To study reasons and motivation has always been a challenge to a positivistic approach to the social sciences, underlining causality and verification through intersubjectively available evidence. Yet, human behaviour is not merely physical movements in space but includes also the meanings that people attach to behaviour, whether in the form of intention or through interpretation. The cultural approach is the major framework for mapping this domain of social interaction consisting of the sense that human beings link up with behaviour and which may also propel interaction. In principle, the study of culture is not more prone to relativism than other approaches to human behaviour. It is true that there is in this field of study more contention among scholars and less of established results than in rational choice for instance. However, also the cultural approach with experience some cumulative findings.

One may interpret the negativism of Geertz as a realisation that cultural anthropology is no longer the only or major arena for cultural studies. The burden of developing this new approach rests more with sociology and political science than with anthropology. We suggest that the cultural approach today comprises three major areas of study: ethnicity, religion and values. And within each of these domains there are some interesting and highly relevant results, besides all criticism and dispute among scholars. Each of these areas may be analysed with the standard canons of scientific research combing model building with the explorative and confirmatory use of empirical investigation. It is when meanings exist in a social context that they become the object of scientific study.

What drives human beings besides the utility maximization studies in rational choice is the search for meaning and community, which tends to be an ethnic, religious or values based endeavour. Ethnicity deals with meanings derived from an ethnie or people, religion offers a basis for action inspired by the world religions and values covering the foundation of behaviour in secular and universal meaning. This is not an exhaustive list, as one can easily add more domains of cultural analysis, such as e.g. historical legacies, homosexuality, etc. Yet, our three part division covers a lot of interesting phenomena that fall outside of rational choice.

## Conclusion

'Culture' is, today, a key term in the social sciences. Introduced before the twentieth century, it has played a large role during the twentieth century in anthropology, sociology and political science. However, it remains a most vague concept. Either it refers to almost all kinds of human endeavours or it stands specifically for symbols.

Cultural theory has become very topical in political science, reflecting a surge of interest in the politics of ethnicity, religion and values – that is, themes relating to how people search for identity by adhering to social groups with various belief systems. This surge of interest in cultural approaches to politics can be seen as a way of counterbalancing the rational choice approach which is focused on the maximization of self-interest. The rational choice framework appears to neglect the cultural setting of preference formation (Wildavsky, 1987). During the 1980s and 1990s the rational choice approach rose to a dominant position in political science. This, however, caused a strong counterreaction calling for the employment of other approaches that do not model human behaviour as being driven by merely self-interest, especially the cultural approaches.

The anti rational choice movement is a very broad one, covering a variety of approaches. They all share the basic methodological commitment that rational choice is not suitable for analysing those aspects of human interaction where values are involved. New Cultural Theory (NCT) is one of the challengers of the rational choice framework, arguing that cultural identities exist and cannot be understood by means of a postulate that people maximize their egoistic interests. The search for cultural identity goes beyond the domain of rational choice. Communities and their group loyalties or cultural identities constitute the domain of analysis of cultural theory.

Adherents of cultural approaches tend to be highly critical of rational choice, especially with regard to its usefulness in understanding those forms of human behaviour that are not merely narrow self-interest maximization. However, one can maintain a balance between cultural approaches and rational choice. Cultural analysis needs, we argue, to accept the methodological belief, so strong in rational choice, that theories have to be confronted in a systematic fashion with a systematic body of data. Different cultural approach models should be put to test and the results should be made intersubjectively available to the community of scholars.

From NCT we take that culture may be understood as values – in particular, universal values. From Old Cultural Theory we borrow the approach that culture is ethnicity, civilization and religion as well as legacies. These are the dimensions of culture that we will employ in the coming chapters. Our framework of analysis – see Figure I.1 (p. 9) – identifies culture as the main independent variable and outcomes as the dependent variable. The next chapter will take a closer look at what culture may matter for – namely, outcomes.

The cultures of a society may be identified in several different ways; there is no one single valid classification. For the purpose of this study, we will look at four bases of culture – ethnicity, religion, historical legacy and value orientations. The aim behind this classification is to inquire into the impact of culture on society and politics. Other classifications might have been more appropriate had our purpose been to analyse in depth the elements of a culture without looking at its social impact. One advantage with our classification is that not only does it capture some of the main theories of culture that are discussed widely today, but it also allows us to test predictions from these models against a body of systematic empirical information. These tests may be replicable by other scholars. The set of outcomes employed to test whether culture matters are, it is true, close to what is often called the occidental or Western idea of development. We wish to emphasize that other studies of cultural impact should focus on entirely different outcomes in order to balance out bias.

The cultural approach in the social sciences answers the key question in the critique against the rational choice approach, namely: Where do the preferences come from? If preferences are not merely assumed to be around before the search for a strategy that maximizes the expected value of alternatives, then one needs to explain where they come from and whether they are called 'interests', 'needs' or 'priorities'. As preferences cannot be random, they may have only one of two possible sources: self-interests or social interests. Culture belongs to the social preferences and below we will examine three kinds of cultural preferences: ethnicity, religion and values. Whereas the first two have occupied a given place in cultural analysis for a long time, the latter type is a newly emerging subdiscipline of cultural analysis, based upon survey research. It has not yet reached the same degree of empirical firmness or confirmation as the study of ethnicity or religion.

One may suggest that institutional analysis is a third major approach in the social sciences besides the rational choice approach and the cultural approach. One can regard institutional analysis as an extension of the rational choice approach or as an independent framework. Be that as it may, the analysis of impact of historical institutions is close to one research on legacies within cultural analysis. Cultural analysis offers an understanding of ways of life and their consequences. It may be conducted with or without a time dimension. In a cross-sectional framework one looks for the variation in cultural patterns searching for their different outcomes. In a longitudinal perspective one traces the emergence of a culture analysing its changes and outcomes. We see cultural analysis as the main alternative to the rational choice approach and it targets the missing element in rational choice, which is to give an account of where preferences come from as well as how selfish preferences are mixed with social preferences: attitudes, beliefs and values.

# Chapter 2

# What Culture Matters For: Outcomes

## Introduction

Cultural analysis is, it must be pointed out, an immense field of research. The five parts of this volume cannot do justice to the immense variety of arguments launched concerning the importance of culture. Consequently, we only approach all these cultural phenomena through one looking glass – namely, the occurrence of a cultural effect. Can we substantiate the claim that culture really matters for society and politics? First we discuss the key theories and then we proceed to an empirical analysis, based on the testing of models derived from the essential theories.

There are several separate bodies of literature that attribute a major role to culture. First, in the study of civilizations, culture in the form of religion is claimed to influence overall political, social and economic outcomes. Second, ethnic studies, especially the analysis of nations and nationalism, similarly argue that culture in the form of ethnic identities may be highly important for the politics and economics of a country, resulting in nation-building processes in some countries or in sharp ethnic conflicts in other countries. Finally, we have the micro studies concerning values occurring among individual attitudes. Here, values are the organizing principle that reveals how the myriad attitudes cluster on to a few major value categories. Furthermore, while it has been said that individual value orientations have an impact primarily on individual behaviour such as voting and party choice, it has also been argued that public policies and macro outcomes are related to these values.

What, then, has culture been said to have a specific impact on, or for what does culture matter? Culture, we argue, may matter for *macro outcomes* as well as for *micro outcomes*. In the former (macro) sense culture impacts on political development as well as on economic and social development, where political development is stable democracy, social development stands for equality and economic development refers to affluence or economic growth. In the latter (micro) sense culture plays a significant role in shaping the individuals' attitudes, which cluster around the values of a culture.

In addition, we examine *regional outcomes* – that is, whether culture impacts on the variation in electoral support for political parties across provinces in a country. To show more precisely that culture matters for outcomes is, however, a task for causal analysis. In all kinds of cultural analysis, one encounters statements to the effect that culture is important for other phenomena besides culture itself – it is extrinsically important. Yet, the evidence is often merely co-existence in time – that is, the simultaneous occurrence of cultural items and outcomes. Whether culture impacts on society or vice versa can only be settled in relation to a specific model stating a cultural effect and tested against a set of data about social reality. Whether the model is true or not depends finally on whether the empirical evidence supports or falsifies the model. General statements about the importance of culture and values need to be reformulated into testable models which link various kinds of cultural phenomena with different outcomes, either by means of correlations or through the use of regression.

The purpose of this chapter is to discuss the outcomes which have been connected with culture. As we map the variation in the dependent variables (outcomes) we also attempt, at the same time, to survey some more specific theories relating culture and outcomes.

## Culture as an Explanatory Factor

In order to explain phenomena in society – why events occur or why people behave or act in this or that way – social scientists have referred to social structure, preferences and institutions. In our view, cultural explanations are derived from preferences. However, in a cultural explanation the preferences are not the standard individual preferences of the rational choice approach – that is, self-interest – but rather group preferences or social preferences comprising elements of ethnicity or religion or universal values as well as the accompanying belief systems.

The real-world consequences of cultural preferences have been researched in a set of social science theories which have received much attention. We classify this set of cultural approach theories, which have always been outside the rational choice framework, into three subsets:

1  *ethnicity theory*, comprising ethnic groups, as well as nations and nationalism;
2  *the sociology of religions*, including all religious beliefs from sects to civilizations; and
3  *universal values*, or certain configurations of attitudes including, for example, postmaterialism, individualism and trust.

The dominance of the rational choice framework within political science has contributed to a neglect of the impact of cultural and altruistic preferences on society and politics, which the cultural approach framework targets.

Several theories of ethnicity and religion highlight the relevance of cultural preferences for explaining macro outcomes. Thus, in relation to macro outcomes, culture has been claimed to have importance – this is a major theme in the analysis of civilizations and nations, aiming at the explanation of developmental differences. The world today is made up of the First World and the Third World, the Second World of communist countries having almost completely disappeared. The First World comprises countries that are stable democracies and have advanced economics, whereas the Third World is characterized by democratic instability and extensive poverty. A few major social science theories state that culture is a major explanatory factor of these differences (Horowitz, 1985; Huntington, 1996; Weber, 1904; North, 1990; Todd, 1983; Inglehart, 1997).

Since culture is itself changing only slowly over time, it can only have an impact in the long term. At least in relation to macro outcomes, there is little reason to expect that the variation in short-term phenomena may be due to any variation in culture. Therefore, one may employ a cross-sectional approach to the explanation of the variation in macro outcomes, using cultural preferences as one explanatory factor. Cultural analysis has typically taken the form of longitudinal analyses, following the development of a culture over a long time. However, understanding stable macro outcomes by means of stable cultural preferences is an alternative cross-sectional approach that we believe is worth trying.

Cultural preferences may be analysed for their own sake – intrinsic importance. They are interesting in themselves as manifestations of people's efforts to come to grips with the world that surrounds them. Nationalism and religious belief tend to comprise complex systems of thought, whose intricate web of belief and values require a specific analytical effort at interpretation, although we certainly cannot neglect the social consequences of such systems of thought. The analysis of citizen attitudes by means of modern large-scale surveys has the same twofold objective. On the one hand, these values are considered important merely because they constitute the attitudes of the population in today's democracies. On the other hand, they have been regarded as being of critical importance for explaining and predicting outcomes, both macro and micro.

Although cultural approaches may seem to offer a bewildering set of ideas about what kinds of culture exist, as well as what cultures matter for, this type of analysis is far from totally eclectic, as it contains a core set of ideas, namely:

1   Culture is a vital intrinsic ingredient of societies.
2   Culture matters extrinsically for outcomes.
3   Culture involves ethnicity, religion and legacies.
4   Culture covers universal values.

These four propositions may be considered as the common assumption of all approaches in the cultural approach framework. While they hardly constitute a concise set of assumptions, allowing, as they do, for various interpretations and developments in different directions, they may be put to use in empirical research aiming at the understanding of phenomena from both a macroscopic and microscopic perspective. Our book inquires into certain specific outcomes in society and politics, probing into how far assumption 2 above is valid and testing well-known models of cultural impact. Thus, from various social science theories about culture and the importance of cultural preferences for society and politics (Granato *et al.*, 1996; Jackman and Miller, 1996; Inglehart, 1990, 1997; Harrison and Huntington, 2000; Hermet, 2000), we derive a few models about cultural effects that may be tested by means of data pertaining to the world as it exists today, or in relation to the most recent available data. The choice of dependent and independent variables in these cultural models is influenced by both theoretical expectations and the need for long-term stability as well as variation in space in the data employed for estimating model parameters. Research upon outcomes within the cultural approach framework is basically not different from outcome inquiry within the rational choice approach. One specifies a model which links the variables, find the data on the indicators measuring these variables, and then undertake an analysis of data relating them to the model, primarily using the correlation and regression techniques.

## Macro-level Outcomes

Culture may have an impact on various kinds of macro outcomes. Among the macro-level outcomes attributed to culture we will here deal with democracy and affluence, as well as various social outcomes such as income distribution and gender equality. We also include indicators on the quality of government such as perceived corruption. Macro-level outcomes that tend to remain in place for some period of time are often analysed as differences in the level of development.

### Political Development

In measuring democracy one attempts to summarize how well the political system of a country tends to respect citizen's political rights, as well as their civil liberties and values. From a normative point of view democracy is very much in accordance with what is expected from a good society, at least within a Western perspective. Political systems scoring high on a democracy index therefore have an intrinsic value – legitimacy – not to be found in political systems scoring low on the same index (Huntington, 1991; see also Collier and Adcock, 1999). When measuring democracy we will basically rely on the estimates reported annually in the *Freedom House* indices from 1972 onwards (Freedom House, 2000). We have transformed their scores into one single democracy index ranging from 10 (democracy) to 0 (non-democracy).

The country variation in democracy through this period, 1972–97, is fairly stable. Countries scoring high in 1997 also tend to score high in

1972 (Australia, Austria, Canada, Denmark, Iceland, The Netherlands, New Zealand, Norway, Sweden, Switzerland and the USA) while a number of countries score low at both periods of time (Burundi, China, Iraq, North Korea and Syria). However, a number of countries were democratized during this period, moving from low scores to high scores, as has been the case in Latin America (Chile, Uruguay), in Mediterranean Europe (Greece, Portugal and Spain) as well as in Central and Eastern Europe (Czech Republic, Hungary and Poland). There are also countries in the Third World that have developed in a similar direction (South Africa, South Korea and Taiwan). Few cases exist of a reversed track, but Lebanon would be such a case, going from relatively high scores in the early 1970s to still having low scores in the late 1990s, reflecting its precarious international position as well as its domestic conflicts. Can this country variation be explained, partially at least, by cultural factors?

An index of democratic stability may be calculated by taking the average democracy score in the Freedom House yearly indices for the period 1972–99. This index measures both the nature of the regime and political stability and results in a firm ranking of the countries of the world, some being safe for democracy, some remaining authoritarian and the rest having changed their regime or having failed to stabilize a democratic regime – for example, Venezuela, Peru, Malaysia, Zimbabwe and Tunisia.

In several social science theories culture constitutes a critical factor when accounting for the variation in democratic stability. The types of cultural factor identified in Chapter 1 have all been singled out – namely ethnicity, religion, legacies and values. In the literature on democracy there are a number of different arguments concerning the impact of ethnicity and religion on democracy. Thus, consociational theory focuses on ethnic and religious fragmentation, which would reduce democratic stability or democratic longevity (Lijphart, 1977). In general, strong ethnic or religious fragmentation negatively impacts on democratic stability (Horowitz, 1985). The early introduction of a modern nation-state – modernized leadership – is claimed by modernization theory to contribute positively to democracy (Huntington, 1996; Rokkan *et al.*, 1970, 1999; Harrison and Huntington, 2000). In theories of religion it has been argued that Protestantism, by virtue of its emphasis upon individualism, has a special link with democracy (Hamilton, 1995), whereas the other major world religions tend to be less favourably linked with political development (Lenski, 1965). Finally, one of the new cultural theories claims that the occurrence of universal values such as trust also affects democracy positively (Putnam, 1993), but trust may be measured in different ways which are relevant for the analysis of democratic outcomes (Newton, 1999).

*Affluence and Poverty*

High economic growth will, if sustained in the long-term, result in higher levels of economic affluence, as measured by the aggregate value of the economic production per capita or various indicators on GDP/capita. High levels of economic affluence are a key outcome, since they remain crucial to improvements in the living conditions of the population. The more affluence in a country, the more are the possibilities to allocate resources not only to basic needs such as food provision and housing, but also to needs such as education, health care and social care. The rise and decline of countries in terms of affluence is a most interesting social science research topic (Olson, 1982), where cultural factors may enter the explanatory models.

Thus, economic development – short-term or long-term – presents a country with the resources it needs to alleviate poverty and raise the quality of life for its population (cf. Easterlin, 1974, 1998; Dollar and Kraay, 2000). However, affluence is unevenly distributed among countries, and this is also true of economic growth. The distribution of affluence seems to be rather stable over time as well as in space, as is indicated by correlating the level of GDP/capita in 1950 and in 1990 ($r = .82$; $n = 130$; Kuwait excluded as an outlier in 1950).

Countries that were rich, relatively speaking, in 1950 tend also to belong to the set of rich countries in the early 1990s. Among the rich set of countries we may identify Australia, Canada, Luxembourg, New Zealand, Switzerland and the USA. The really poor countries are mainly to be found in Africa (Burundi, Ethiopia, Guinea, Lesotho and Malawi) but also in parts of Asia (Burma or Myanmar and Vietnam). Although the general pattern is one of stability over time, there are a number of countries that have improved their economic performance quite remarkably during this period (Japan, South Korea and Singapore). Economic development can be negative in both the short term and long term, as some countries have been the victims of a relative, but sharp, decline in their economic position (Argentina and Venezuela).

When setting out to explain this country variation in economic development, one should examine versions of the thesis that cultural factors have an impact on economic performance (Franke *et al.*, 1991; Gray, 1996; Landes, 1998a, 1998b). Short-term economic development, as measured by the rates of economic growth, is determined by factors which fluctuate in time and space. However, cultural factors are possible explanatory factors to be considered when it comes to long-term economic development, such as the average economic growth rate for a decade or two. One may examine the variation in economic growth over a considerable period of time and still find substantial country differences that remain despite the temporary impact of the business cycle or the effects of random events.

Thus, economic development has a short-run and a long-run aspect. The literature on economic growth is quite substantial, harbouring the neoclassical growth model and its refinements, as well as its critiques (Solow, 2000; Scott,

1989; Chaudhuri, 1989). Economic explanations of the change in output tend to focus on economic factors. Thus, the short-run fluctuations in economic growth are connected with the business cycle and the long-run differences in economic output are related to long-term changes in labour, capital and productivity. However, when accounting for the country variation in very long-run differences in economy output, it is necessary to take wider social conditions into account, including cultural differences. Which social, political or cultural sources are growth-enhancing factors? It seems that countries can move up and down in terms of affluence or poverty, at least to some extent; some countries that were rich in 1900 are now no longer so rich and vice versa, relatively speaking. However, the chief finding is that most countries that are rich close to 2000 were already rich around 1900 – again, relatively speaking. Why?

Much theorizing has focused on explaining why countries differ in long-run economic development. One type of argument centres on the contribution of a specific climate that enhances economic development. Although economic growth in the short run will always be driven by economic factors, including among other things investments, money stability, full employment, thrift and exports, it might be asked why some countries manage almost consistently and permanently to create a growth conducive climate while others cannot. This has led to speculation by economists and sociologists on whether culture matters – is it necessary to have a culture that would not only afford political stability but also a work ethic that promotes growth-enhancing behaviour such as making investments.

Again, the type of religion prevailing in a country has been adduced as of critical importance. This is the well-known theory about the economic consequences of the world religions, preliminarily launched in 1904 by Max Weber and developed systematically in his three volumes of a comparative study on the sociology of religion (1963–72). This set off a whole literature on the religious sources of modern capitalism (Hamilton, 1995). Another theory suggests the timing of the economy's take-off is crucial in that the occurrence of this point in time depends on the degree of modernization of the political system or the emergence of a nation-state (Rostow, 1960). Finally, we have the new cultural theory which claims that the spread of values matters for economic activity, especially the occurrence of social trust in all kinds of social interaction facilitating commerce and finance, as suggested by Fukuyama (1995a) when launching a transaction costs saving argument. But it must be pointed out that other scholars have questioned this search for general causes of development, underlining instead the complexity and unique situation of each country (Diamond, 1998).

Economic development is a necessary condition for a high level of human development. Yet, human development is not only economics. The indices on human development also take into account education and health, as for instance the Human Development Index (HDI) developed by the United Nations Development Programme (UNDP) from 1990 onwards (cf. Sen,

1999). The more human development, the better the overall situation for people in a country is expected to be in terms of health care and education (however, see also Castles, 1998; Henderson, 2000; and UNDP, 2000b).

The level of human development also appears to be very stable over time. The countries displaying a low level of human development in the early 1960s tend to occupy the same position in the early 1990s. It is mostly African countries such as: Burkina Faso, Guinea, Mali, Niger and Sierra Leone which belong to this category but Yemen may also be included. Countries scoring high on this index, both in the 1960s and in the 1990s, include: Canada, France, Norway, USA, Iceland, Finland, Netherlands, Australia, New Zealand and Sweden. Japan, South Korea and Singapore belong to the set of countries which have raised their scores on human development considerably over these 30 years. In fact there is a very strong correlation between the HDI measures over time, no matter which time period is selected (cf. UNDP, 2000a).

Quality of life is linked to economic development, but it is not a linear function of affluence. Most countries display increased quality of life between 1960 and 1990, indicating huge advances in the coverage of the population in terms of health care and education. It does not take a very high GDP to achieve a reasonable level of human development. Quality of life tends to be high in countries where affluence is employed to the benefit of the many. Is culture a factor that matters when countries vary in terms of the quality of life? One would expect nation-states to put human development high on the list of their primary objective, due to their commitment to solidarity. Perhaps also religion matters when explaining the substantial country variation in the HDI, as measured by the United Nations, as religions such as Christianity or Islam seem to be more concerned with alleviating poverty than do Hinduism and Buddhism. Yet it is not that Buddhism is not concerned with the poor – for instance, many people in Thailand truly believe that giving alms would gain them 'boon' (good credit) – but poverty is interpreted as a natural phenomenon in the wheel of life.

*Social Development: Equality*

Obviously, even if a country is rich its distribution of its wealth may be very unequal. From a Western normative point of view stressing the importance of justice or fairness, a more equal distribution is to be preferred to grossly unequal distributions of resources (Sen, 1999). The basic model accounting for the country variation in inequality is the Kuznets curve, which links inequality with low affluence and equality with high affluence, but, as the Kuznets model fails to explain all variation (Kuznets, 1966), it prompts one to inquire into whether culture matters. A religious hypothesis focuses, for example, on the positive impact of Islam on income equality linked with the social teachings of the Prophet. Another cultural hypothesis pinpoints the impact of nationalism in fostering a spirit of solidarity, which would be one of the sources of social equality (Miller, 1995). Finally, there is the New Culture Theory with its emphasis upon egalitarianism, or the set of universal values that give equality precedence over liberty, especially equal outcomes (Wildavsky, 1991).

Data on income distributions displaying the degree of inequality stated through the Gini coefficient are not available for a large number of countries, and it is even more difficult to find data allowing for comparison over time. Here, we make use of data collected within the World Bank (Deininger and Squire, 1997). Comparing distributions from the 1970s (GINI70) with distributions from the 1990s (GINI90), we may note a high degree of stability over time. Countries displaying high Gini coefficients – that is characterized by more income inequality – include Chile, Colombia, Mexico, Peru, Senegal and Zimbabwe. Less unequal income distributions are found in countries like Belgium, Canada, Czech Republic, Finland, the Netherlands and Poland. Over time we may note higher Gini coefficients not only in Australia, Chile, Hungary, New Zealand and Thailand, but also in the UK and the USA, while the reversed trend towards lower Gini coefficients is to be found in Canada, Finland, Italy, Jamaica and Portugal.

Some countries display consistently huge income inequalities. Why? The Kuznets effect – affluence trickling down – can only explain to some extent why poor countries tend towards huge inequalities while rich countries tend towards more equality. Perhaps culture, in addition to economic affluence, makes a difference? Egalitarianism in Western Europe has been interpreted as the main source of support for its welfare state. Affluence and large public sector tend to increase equality. Low Gini scores are to be found in the welfare state of the Scandinavian model type. The values of a postmodern society favour income equality and gender equality whereas globalization tends to increase inequalities. This preference for social development is not exclusively derivable from affluence but probably contains a cultural component.

*Gender Equality*

Gender equality, as it may be captured by the Gender Development Index (GDI) or the Gender Empowerment Measure (GEM), may also be expected to be impacted by cultural factors. Gender equality is in itself conducive to human development, not least in Third World countries (UNDP, 1995). But the level of gender equality may also be affected by various religious or cultural traditions which have resulted in the formation of different kinds of patriarchal structure in societies. The two indicators of gender equality (GDI5 GEM) largely tend to go together (UNDP, 1999). We find consistently higher levels of gender equality in the affluent countries of the world such as Canada, Norway, Sweden and the USA, while the lowest levels of gender equality are to be found in poor African countries such as Nigeria, Mauritania, Togo and Sudan but also in Pakistan and Algeria.

Although affluence enhances gender equality, it is highly likely that culture is also a factor. Religion and the position of women is a classical theme when analysing the social consequences of various creed within Christianity, Islam and Hinduism/Buddhism. In principle, nationalism is favourable to gender equality, as social solidarity is given a high priority. In the postmodern society women's issues are much debated with a strong new value preference for the improvement of women rights.

*Corruption*

Corruption is hardly a new phenomenon, but it is only more recently that there have been more systematic attempts to map the variation in corruption worldwide. Corruption involves a kind of transaction cost to society, thereby lowering economic efficiency. And from a normative point of view widespread corruption must be regarded as a negative in any country, as it hurts justice and fairness (Mauro, 1995; Tanzi, 1998; Lipset and Lenz, 2000).

Measures of corruption, it must be stressed, capture perceived corruption as they rely on expert judgements for classifying the extent of corruption in various countries (Transparency International, 1998, 1999). These measures of corruption tend to agree to a considerable extent when comparing the early 1980s (CORR80) and the late 1990s (CORR98). Low corruption (high scores) is to be found in countries like Australia, Canada, Denmark, Finland, Ireland, The Netherlands, New Zealand, Singapore, Sweden and Switzerland, while more corruption (lower scores) is to be found in countries like Bolivia, Egypt, Indonesia, Mexico, Nigeria, Philippines and Thailand.

By using a simple rational choice argument, one may dare to guess that poverty must be a strong determinant of corruption, but it does not explain all the country variation. Other cultural forces might also be involved. One well-known hypothesis claims that the Buddhist–Confucian culture has a great importance for fostering social morality (Fukuyama, 1995b), which may be contrasted with the hypothesis that Protestantism matters again. The general level of trust in politics or social capital in society could, however, play a greater role than religion. The cement of society deriving from the acceptance of republicanism or civic virtues is probably very important, but it is far from evident how this is to be measured (Pettit, 1999).

**Dependent Variables and Control Variables**

The principal dependent variables that we will employ in our macro-level analysis have been presented above, and we have found a stable cross-country variation over time that warrants explanation. Does culture matter? Any inquiry into the impact of culture must be based on the test of models in relation to data. When inquiring into the macro-level impact of cultural factors on the phenomena described above, it is necessary to control for the impact of other potentially important factors. Societies differ in several aspects, not only culture. Of the major explanatory factors in the social science – social structure, preferences and institutions – which matters the most? Culture is to be classified under preferences, but one may wish to distinguish between individual and group preferences. Making causal attribution even more complex, one could also add tradition as a factor. We will use both surface evidence (correlations) and deep structure evidence (regression).

As major control variables, we will employ two variables which capture the general factors of geography and history. Common to both geographical and historical factors is the fact that they are constants over time. Geographical factors have also been recognized as being important in conditioning economic development (Landes, 1998a, ch. 1; Gallup *et al.*, 1999; Masters and McMillan, 2000). Historical factors such as the timing of the institutionalization of a modernized leadership or the introduction of modern institutions has also been addressed in the research literature (Olson, 1982; Choi, 1983; North, 1990). As proxies for these factors our choice is that *geography* could be captured by a variable measuring country distance from the equator in absolute latitudes (space as climate) and *history* by a variable measuring length of time since the introduction of modernized leadership in a country (history as state longevity).

The absolute distance from the equator may be considered as a proxy for measuring the climatic conditions. Although climatic changes certainly do occur on the globe, when referring to the twentieth century it does seem to be reasonable to say that the countries of the world can be grouped into a number of constant climate zones. Admittedly, distance from the equator is a crude indicator when we consider huge countries like the USA and Russia which themselves may contain a number of different climate zones. Nevertheless, we argue that it is a good proxy for measuring a geographical factor. The identification of the exact time for the introduction of modernized leadership or a modern state in a country may be debatable, but once such an introduction has taken place this date will be a constant.

In Table 2.1 we present an overview of how our set of countries is distributed according to our two control variables. The distance from the equator is expressed as the absolute value of the latitude of the country in question (DISEQU), while the variable measuring the time since the introduction of modernized leadership (MODLEAD) simply says how old a state is – that is, the higher the value, the older the state. In the table the absolute distance from the equator and the time of the state for each country group is displayed using mean values.

These two variables – geographical situation and modernization – tend to be connected to a large extent. Thus, countries located at a considerable distance from the equator in the North also tend to have the oldest states, on average, and among them we may count the Scandinavian countries, as well as Russia, Switzerland and Canada. In general, it seems to be the case

*Culture and Politics*

**Table 2.1     Absolute distance from the equator (DISEQU) and time since introduction of modernized leadership (MODLEAD) in years by country regions: means**

| Region | | Absolute distance from equator (DISEQU) | Modernized leadership (MODLEAD) |
|---|---|---|---|
| OECD (N=24) | Mean | .48 | 180 |
| Latin America (N=22) | Mean | .16 | 112 |
| Africa (N=43) | Mean | .14 | 44 |
| Asia (N=34) | Mean | .23 | 59 |
| Postcommunist countries (N=27) | Mean | .47 | 130 |
| Total (N=150) | Mean | .28 | 96 |
| Eta squared | | .72 | .73 |
| Sig. | | .000 | .000 |

*Sources*: See Appendix A.

that countries belonging to the OECD set of countries, as well as the postcommunist set, are both the most distant from the equator and have quite a long experience of modernized leadership as is the case with the United Kingdom, USA, and most countries in Western Europe. On average, the most recent states are to be found in the areas close to the equator – that is, countries experiencing a tropical rainy climate. Here we have countries like Bolivia and Brazil, but also Nigeria, Tanzania, Singapore and Thailand. We may also note that the regional breakdown that we employ in Table 2.1 really captures the variation in these two variables, suggesting that they measure a real cross-country geographical and historical variation.

Earlier research has shown that both space and time matter for political, economic and social outcomes. Thus, the advanced world is largely located in geographical areas with cool temperatures and countries concerned have had a long experience of a modern state. If culture matters for outcomes, then we encounter the following problem: does culture coincide with the impact of space and time? Or is there a cultural effect that is independent of this impact?

## Regional-level Outcomes: Why Does Different Party Support Vary in Different Regions?

Having identified the between-country variation in outcomes, we move to the within-country variation in outcomes. When examining the role of culture within a democracy, we target the support for different political parties or political movements as it is conveyed in national elections for national parliaments or presidents. We limit our inquiry of the regional level to six countries which have so-called divided societies, where the key hypothesis is that we expect to find a variation in party support at the regional level (provinces, states, cantons), reflecting a regional variation in cultural factors such as ethnicity and religion. The six countries are USA, Russia, Switzerland, Spain, Belgium and India – all countries characterized by high cultural heterogeneity. We now present how regional party support varies country by country.

*The USA*

The two major political forces in American politics, manifested in federal political elections, are the Democrats and the Republicans. We will concentrate on the presidential elections, since in the American political system these mobilise more voters than do the elections to the House and the Senate. Our regional level of inquiry in the USA is the state level – that is, the 50 states comprising the USA (cf. Luttbeg, 1999). Let us here take a closer look at the presidential elections of 1972 and 1996. In 1972 the Republican candidate was Richard Nixon who won an overwhelming victory over the Democratic candidate George McGovern: 60.7 per cent against 35.7 per cent of the popular vote. In the 1996 election Bill Clinton, as the Democratic candidate had a plurality of the popular vote (49.2 per cent) winning over the Republican Robert Dole (40.7 per cent) and the independent Ross Perot (8.4 per cent). However, the relative strength of Republicans is quite stable in time over these two elections at the regional and state levels. Why?

In regions where the Republicans are strong in 1996, they were also strong in 1972 – this is at least the major tendency. The electoral support for the Republican Party from state to state varies from a low of 25 per cent to a high of 55 per cent, roughly speaking. Since this regional variation is stable from one election to another, it cannot be merely accidental or random. The correlation pattern is similar with respect to the support for the Democrats at the same elections (r = .60; n = 50; Washington DC excluded).

The same trend may be observed in the election results for the Democrats, where electoral outcomes range between 30 and 65 per cent. The regional variation in support at both elections appears to be quite substantial, for both parties. Given the nature of a two-party system, where Republicans are strong the Democrats are weak, and vice versa. Republican strongholds at these elections include Mississippi, Nebraska, Alabama, Georgia, Utah and

Kansas. If the District of Columbia is excepted, then the weakest states for the Republicans were Massachusetts, Rhode Island, Minnesota, New York and Oregon. Replacing Oregon with Illinois, then we have these same states as the strongholds of the Democratic Party at these two presidential elections.

Our interest is to inquire into any impact of culture on the distribution of votes for the two parties in the 1990s. In order to verify the impact of culture it is necessary also to include other controlling factors. The choice here is gross state product (GSPC94) per capita as an indicator for wealth in the USA. GSP per capita also tends to be rather stable over time, meaning that states scoring high in the 1970s also score high in the 1990s. The affluent states in the 1990s include Delaware, Alaska, Connecticut, Wyoming, New Jersey and New York, while Mississippi, West Virginia, Montana, Oklahoma, Arkansas and Alabama were among those scoring low on affluence, relatively speaking. We also employ data on unemployment at the state level from 1996 (UNEM96), and the basic data source that we rely on is the US Department of Commerce's *Statistical Abstracts of the United States*.

*Russia*

The demise of the Soviet Union gave Russia the opportunity to democratize (Sakwa, 1996). The first free parliamentary election in Russia after the USSR experience took place in December 1993. A second election took place two years later in December 1995 – the first normal election – and a third election to the Duma was held in December 1999. The major political force in Russia has been the Communist Party (CP), while the Yabloko bloc may be seen as the party that most resembles a liberal party (White *et al.*, 1997). There is a remarkable variation in the regional support for this party. Considering the fact that Russia is a political system with only a weakly developed party system, one may in fact wish to emphasize the stable regional pattern.

Since the Communist Party receives very different amounts of support in various regions of Russia, one may search for an ethnic factor determining this variation. In some regions the party takes more than 40 per cent of the votes, but in other regions the support is as low as 10 per cent. Why? We may establish a similar variation in the support for the Yabloko bloc; indeed the support for the Yabloko bloc in the state Duma elections in 1993 and in 1995 was quite stable over time ($r = .78$; $n = 88$). The ethnic composition of the population in the region in question may matter for the understanding of party support – this is exactly what we wish to find out. The Communist Party has its strongest support in such regions as Kemerovo, Dagestan, Orel and Tambov, many of them located in the central parts of Russia; the weakest support is to be found in regions such as Koryak, Murmansk and Perm, many of them located in the northern part of the country. The Yabloko bloc has its strongest support in St Petersburg, Moscow and Murmansk, but also in far-eastern Kamtchtka.

As a control variable we will, in the Russian case, use estimates of the gross regional product per capita (GRPCAP). These estimates suggest that the relatively wealthiest regions of Russia in the mid-1990s are to be found in Siberia (Tyumen, Yakutiya), in the north (Komi, Murmansk) and, of course, also in Moscow. The very poor regions are to be found in areas around the Caucasus: Adygeya, Dagestan, North Ossetiya and Kalmykia. In addition, we also use variables capturing the variation in life expectancy for men (MALEXP) as well as for women (FEMEXP). The regional data we employ stems mainly from the Centre for Russian Studies Database at The Norwegian Institute for International Affairs (NUPI) in Oslo and The Russian Regional Database at The Centre for the Study of Public Policy (CSPP) in Glasgow.

## Spain

Spanish politics and the Spanish party system operates with strong ethnic cleavages. The principal political party in Spain since the fall of General Franco in 1975 has been the socialist party (PSOE). In addition to the PSOE one may wish to consider the regional parties of Spain (REG), because these play a large political role, at least in comparison with other Western countries (Heywood, 1995; Montero, 1998). Comparing the support over time for these two sets of parties, it is striking that the spatial pattern is relatively stable. The PSOE tends to be strongest in 1996 in those provinces where they were already strong in 1979. The same is true for the regional parties, although one may establish that these are stronger on an aggregate Spanish level in 1996 than they were in 1979. This is partly because regional parties were totally absent in 18 provinces in 1979 but only in three provinces in 1996. Among the political parties classified as regional parties, are the following: Partido Andalucista, Chunta Aragonesista, Nacionalistes de Mallorca, Coalición Canaria, Convergència i Unió, Unió Valenciana, Bloque Nacionalista Galego and Partido Nacionalista Vasco. Thus, there is a profound variation in the voter support for the PSOE among Spanish provinces, hovering between a low 20 per cent and a high 50 per cent.

With regard to the immense difference in support for the PSOE between regions, one may ask an ecological question: does region matter? If so, what is region composed of? The regional variation in voter support for the ethnic parties in Spain is both stable and highly diverse, but not as extended as that of the PSOE; looking at the bivariate relation we may establish that support for the regional parties in the parliamentary elections in 1979 and in 1996 is quite strong (r = .87; n = 50). The regional variation ranges from 50 per cent support to 0 per cent support. Whereas the PSOE contests in each region, the regional parties refrain from putting up candidates in all regions. The PSOE's strongholds are to be found in mainly two regions: Andalucia (Huelva, Sevilla and Jaén) and Extremadura (Badajoz and Cáceres). They have the weakest support in some of the peripheral parts of Spain, namely in the Canary Islands and in the Basque provinces. These are regions where the regional parties are very strong. Other regions where regional parties have strongholds are Catalonia, in particular Girona, but also in Galicia (Pontevedra). Given the ethnic heterogeneity of Spain, one should pose the additional question: does culture matter for the regional differences in party support?

In order to estimate the effect of cultural factors on the variation in support for the political parties we include regional wealth (REGINC95) as one major controlling variable. In the Spanish case, it is also obvious that the regional wealth tends to be rather stable over time. In the 1990s the wealthy regions are the Balearic Islands, Catalonia, Madrid and the Basque country, while the poor ones are to be found in the south: Andalucia and Extremadura.

*Switzerland*

Switzerland scores high on social fragmentation involving both ethnic and religious cleavages. It has a special system of government, which means that over the last 30 to 40 years the same set of parties has taken part in a permanent Grand Coalition (Klöti *et al.*, 1999). At the 1995 election these four parties received the following popular support at the national level: SPS (social democrats) 21.8 per cent, FDP (liberals) 20.2 per cent, CVP (Christian Democrats) 16.8 per cent and SVP (the people's party) 14.9 per cent. In this context we will focus on the social democrats (SPS) and the Christian democrats (CVP), whose electoral support varies widely from one canton to another. The election system employed in Switzerland at elections to the National Council varies between the cantons. Most cantons have a proportional system, while in some of the smaller cantons majority election systems are employed. This creates some problems when comparing electoral outcomes for certain parties, if all 26 cantons are included.

For the CVP in particular, we may note a strong regional stability over time; this is equally true whether all cantons are included or whether those with a majoritarian election system are excluded ($r = .95$ in both instances). The regional support for the SPS varies more over time, although a correlation of $r = .67$ ($n = 19$; cases where SPS did not stand for election excluded) indicates a relatively stable support for this party.

The cantonal variation in the support for the CVP (christian democrats) is so extensive that only culture – such as religion, or the proportion of Roman Catholics – could, it seems, afford an explanation. It cannot be due to randomness. The CVP has its strongest support in the small cantons Obwalden and Appenzell I.-Rh. (majoritarian systems), but they also have a strong backing in Luzern, St Gallen, Valais and Jura. Their weakest support is to be found in Bern, Zurich and Vaud. The picture concerning the SPS is hardly less dispersed. The support for the SPS is more evenly distributed, if we exclude those cantons which have majoritarian systems. They tend to be strongest in Schaffhausen, Basel-Stadt, Jura and Genève, while their support is relatively weaker in Ticino, Valais and Luzern.

The control variable to be employed in the Swiss case is a variable measuring the distribution of cantonal incomes per capita (Volkseinkommen der Kantonen/Revenu cantonal; VOLKS90). Among the extremely rich cantons, one may mention Zug, Zurich and Genève, while among the relatively less wealthy cantons we find Jura, Valais and Appenzell I.-Rh.

*Belgium*

Cultural fragmentation has come to dominate Belgian politics, despite the efforts to accommodate ethnic diversity by extensive state reform. In the Belgian case we look at two party families (cf. Delwit and De Waele, 1997; Delwit *et al.*, 1999). First, we have the ethnic party family comprising both Flemish nationalist and Francophone parties. Here we include Volksunie (VU) and the Flemish Block (VB) in the Flemish nationalist group and the Francophone Democratic Front (FDF) and Walloon Rally (RW) among the Francophone parties. Nationwide, the support for the Flemish parties was 11.0 per cent in 1981 and 12.5 per cent in 1991; the support for the Francophone nationalist parties decreased from 4.2 per cent in 1981 to 1.6 per cent in 1991. These four parties thus comprise the ethnic party family in Belgium, and it is obvious that it is mainly a Flemish phenomenon. Second, we have the christian democratic party family with one Flemish party – the Christian People's Party (CVP), and one French party – the Christian Social Party (PSC). Together these two parties received 26.4 per cent of the vote in 1981 and 24.9 per cent in the 1991 election. Again, the Flemish party surpasses the French party. Looking at the electoral support for the Belgian ethnic parties in the 1981 and in 1991 elections at the level of arrondissement (N = 30), it can be seen that the regional variation is considerable, even when taking into account that these parties did not contest in all regions at the two elections.

The ethnic parties are typically strong in Flemish regions such as Anvers and Saint-Nicolas but also in Bruxelles. Their standing is weakest in Wallon regions such as Tournai-Ath-Mouscron but also in the province of Luxembourg. The regional variation in the support for this party family seems to be quite stable over time. Correlating the regional variation in support for the Christian Democratic parties in Belgium for the two elections in 1981 and in 1991 we find that it is no less pronounced (r = .80; N = 30).

The regional support for Christian Democratic parties in Belgium also seems to be stable over time. Among their strongholds we may count Ypres (F), Verviers (W), Roulers-Tielt (F) and Arlon-Marche-en-Famenne-Bastogne (W). Although this party family is stronger in the Flemish part, we must point out that some of their strongholds are to be found in Walloon regions. They have their weakest support in the larger cities such as Anwers, Bruxelles and in Liège.

In order to control for the impact of cultural factors – use of language or religious practice – on the regional variation in party support we will include a variable measuring the regional economic strength (value added per capita; REGECPRO95). The economically strong regions are also the major regions of Belgium, namely Anvers, Bruges and Bruxelles while the weak ones mainly are located in the Wallon part of the country: Thuin (W), Soignies (W) and Dinant-Philippeville (W).

*India*

The largest democracy in the world rests on a social structure with ethnic and religious cleavages. The analysis of regional patterns in support for Indian parties is based upon the 25 Indian states and seven union territories, all together arriving at 32 regional units (Das Gupta, 1989; Kohli, 1990; Brass, 1996; Khilnani, 1997). The two parties that we will examine more closely for the 1980 and the 1996 elections are first the Bharatiya Janata Party (BJP) and its predecessor the Janata Party (JNP) and, second, the Indican Congress Party. For the 1980 election we add the votes for the competing factions within the Congress Party – namely, the Indian National Congress (Indira) (INCI) and the Indian National Congress (Urs) (INCU). In 1980 the JNP received 19 per cent of the vote which the BJP was able to increase to 20.3 per cent in 1996. The added INC vote in 1980 was 48.0 per cent, which decreased to 28.8 per cent in 1996.

Among the Indian states, the BJP received its strongest support in Gujarat, Rajasthan, Madya Pradesh and Himachal Pradesh while its support was quite weak in Andra Pradesh, Kerala and West Bengal. Among the union territories, its strongest support came from Dehli. The BJP is strong in the same regions as the JNP was strong in at the 1980 election. The corresponding support for the Indian Congress Party in 1980 and in 1996 as displayed by a correlation coefficient ($r = .52$; $N = 32$) indicates that there is more of variation in the support for the Indian Congress party when comparing the outcomes for 1980 and 1996. Assam was a stronghold in 1980 but less so in 1996. Strong states at both elections were Andhra Pradesh, Himachal Pradesh and Meghalaya. The weakest support for the INC in 1996 was to be found in the states of Uttar Pradesh, Bihar and Tamil Nadu.

In order to control for the impact of religion (Hinduism) or language (use of Hindi), we employ as a control variable the level of urbanization (URBAN91) of the different states as it was estimated at the 1991 Census of India. The most urban regions are to be found among the union territories (Delhi, Chandigarh) while the level of urbanization is lower among the states. Gujarat and Tamil Nadu belongs to the set of more urbanized states while the opposite is true of Himachal Pradesh, Sikkim and Assam. In addition, we also employ a variable measuring the sex ratio between men and women among the Indian states. What is remarkable with the regional distribution of the sex ratio is that it is only in Kerala where females are more numerous than males. The Indian data we employ mostly stems from the Indian Election Commission as well as the Census of India – both available on the Internet.

*Summary*

Examining electoral outcomes in six countries with a divided society, we are confronted with a huge regional variation in party support, the region being the province or the state (canton). At the same time we may also note that there tends to be a relatively stable pattern of regional variation over time, which makes it relevant to inquire into the sources of this regional variation. Is there a cultural effect here? In other words, does the ethnic or religious distribution of the population matter? In some of these examples, we have the possibility of double cultural effects, both ethnicity and religion, playing a role at the same time. Posing the question about a relationship between the regional variation in party outcomes and the regional composition of the population entails the ecological approach, but the inquiry into the sources of party support in elections increasingly requires the survey approach. The survey approach has the advantage over the ecological approach in that it bypasses the risk of a so-called ecological fallacy, focusing directly on individuals and their characteristics instead of using aggregate level information. Let us now move to individual-level data.

**Micro-level Data: Individual Values**

At the micro-level we find a wealth of ideas about individual attitudes, launched by the new cultural theories. The basic idea is that the attitudes of an individual are extremely multifaceted, but they do tend to exhibit structure or system, deriving from values. These values that constrain individual attitudes may be researched by means of survey techniques, using grand-scale questionnaires like such as, for example, the World Values Surveys. What could 'culture matters' entail at the individual level? Actually, a number of hypotheses about the impact of culture as individual values have been suggested in social science research from the 1990s. The emphasis on the importance of values for individual behaviour is combined with the idea from postmodernist philosophy about a fundamental heterogeneity of opinion. This has produced an immense interest in the inquiry into how different groups perceive the world and evaluate it. Cultural analyses conducted by means of surveys or through interpretative methods have become highly fashionable, focusing upon value heterogeneity.

The individual level data that we will rely on are based on the World Values Surveys, one from the early 1980s, supplemented by the recently available WVS from the early 1990s and the mid-1990s (Inglehart *et al.*, 2000). These surveys have mapped so-called value orientations among citizens from some 65 societies by means of a large-scale questionnaire tapping individual attitudes on culture, society and politics. Before we discuss theories of culture which target individual attitudes and present our choice of individual level outcomes, we will briefly describe the survey tradition for studying values, as it has evolved since the interwar period.

*The Survey Approach to Values*

In order to map the attitudes of the ordinary citizen or the mass public in the modern society, it was necessary to develop techniques for sampling, as well as to train personnel how to formulate interview schedules and handle questionnaires. Before the Second World War, there were few attempts to use these techniques for studying mass beliefs. In their path-breaking study of the unemployed in Marienthal in the early 1930s, Jahoda *et al.* (1975) employed a number of data sources such as life stories, diaries, protocols and official statistics but no questionnaires. In a similar vein, Tingsten (1937) relied on official election statistics in his imaginative exploration of political behaviour.

One of the first attempts to employ an extensive questionnaire to map mass political attitudes was undertaken by Erich Fromm in a study of the working class in Weimar Germany (Fromm, 1984). It was conducted during his stay at the Frankfurt Institute for Social Research, initiated in 1929 but never completed. More than 3000 questionnaires containing some 600 questions were distributed, but only about 1100 were returned and only 584 could be saved when he fled to the USA. The distribution of these questionnaires did not apply any of the procedures later developed in sampling theory.

In the USA, we find a few instances before 1940 where proper sampling procedures were employed, together with interview schedules and/or mail questionnaires (Cantril, 1951). Here, we could mention polling in advance of the presidential elections but also an increased use of these techniques among market researchers.

After 1945 we may identify at least three fields where survey research techniques have been employed in order to inquire into attitudes and values among the mass publics in modern society. First, we have the studies of presidential elections in the USA, pioneered by Lazarsfeld *et al.* (1968 [1944]) in their study of the presidential campaign of 1940 in the Eire County in Ohio. It was followed up by the study of the 1948 election by Berelson *et al.* (1954). The regular national election studies conducted from the University of Michigan started with the 1952 election, which was reported in Campbell *et al.* (1954). The American research program was then followed by similar research programs in most West European countries like in Sweden, Norway and Britain, but later also in Germany, the Netherlands and France.

In these studies, where more refined techniques were introduced, the focus was clearly upon the voters' intentions at elections, but broader questions were also examined about, for instance, trust in politicians and the political system, as well the degree of identification with political parties. The employment of the very same questions, or wording of questions, has made it possible to arrive at long time-series data concerning certain items of public opinion or attitudes on political matters.

Second, in the evolution of survey research a number of market research organizations emerged around the time of the Second World War. They started to conduct survey studies with an interest in values or the attitudes of the mass public. Outside of the USA, we have the establishment of IFOP (Institut Français de l'Opinion Publique) in 1938 and the foundation in 1948 of a World Association for Public Opinion Research (WAPOR). These organizations conducted their own research, given their foci of interest, but their methods have been employed as research tools by academic researchers as well as in official research financed by the US Information Agency and the European Commission (Scheuch, 1990).

Third, we may single out academic research aiming at mapping and comparing attitudes among mass publics cross-nationally. Such undertakings need large resources of funding and it was only in the late 1950s and the early 1960s that this research begun. One starting point may have been the study of politics of despair conducted by Cantril *et al.* (1958), but the major impact on this research field came from the Almond and Verba (1965) study on political culture. This was a five-nation study, where samples, numbering some 1000 respondents from each nation, were interviewed. The questions were related to their typology of political culture, aiming at the identification of four types of political culture. Almond's and Verba's main finding was that there existed a political culture that was conducive to democratic stability, which they called the 'civic culture'.

Following up on *The Civic Culture* and its idea of a political culture, a number of cross-national survey studies involving less than ten countries, with similar designs but somewhat different foci were undertaken. The Cross-National Program in Political and Social Change was based on a seven-nation comparison, reported on in Verba *et al.* (1978). Similarly, an eight-nation study analysing political action was conducted under the direction of Barnes and Kaase between 1973 and 1978, partly reported on in Barnes, Kaase *et al.* (1979).

Surveys conducted by the European Commission (EC) from 1970 have delivered the database for studies of public opinion in Western Europe. These surveys were employed by Inglehart (1977) in his analysis of value changes in general and of the rise of postmaterialism in particular. Besides the Eurobarometer data, which has been used by the EC to inform itself on the opinions of the public on the EC/EU, a European Value Systems Study Group was formed in the late 1970s. It was responsible for the first European Value Study conducted in 1981 (Stoetzel, 1983). This European Value Study was incorporated into the first World Value Survey covering 25 countries between 1981 and 1982 (Inglehart, 1990). Which was followed up by a second wave in 1990–91 (Inglehart, 1997) and a third one in 1995, which was released in early 2000 (Inglehart *et al.*, 2000); a fourth wave was conducted in 1999–2000, covering some 87 countries, but has not yet been released.

All these data sources – Eurobarometers, World Value Surveys and national election surveys – formed the core data base for the survey analyses reported on in the major research programme on beliefs in government (Kaase and Newton, 1995).

The US national election studies have constituted a model for most other national election studies. Here, the focus is on the motivation of the voter to vote and to choose one candidate/party – that is, electoral decisions – but these studies also had an interest in questions concerning party identification, issue orientation and candidate orientation. In addition, questions are asked about membership of different organizations as well as whether people can be trusted or not (Campbell *et al.*, 1954, p. 225). Similar items reoccur in many of the small cross-national surveys. Thus, the question about trust – 'most people can be trusted' – is used in the civic culture as well as in the political action study.

The Eurobarometer questionnaires are mainly oriented towards EC/EU related topics, but there are also several questions ranging from overall life satisfaction and happiness to attitudes about national pride, frequency of media use, frequency of church attendance, strength of political party attachment as well as trust in people from other countries, interest in politics and the materialistic/postmaterialistic values. Thus, these surveys are very broad in their coverage of topics. The same applies to the European Values Studies as well as the World Values Surveys, although these studies focus more specifically on moral and religious values than on political values.

## Micro-level Outcomes

The World Values Surveys, in their different versions, contain an immense variety of information concerning attitudes of representative samples of people from a variety of different countries. Approaching this massive volume of data entails the risk of naive empiricism, because of the temptation to examine question after question just to find out the distribution of answers which may be interesting in itself. Culture research, as a new field in the social sciences, has been driven largely by sheer curiosity to find out how ordinary citizens look upon their situation, including their government. However, there is no end to the amount of information one may wish to retrieve from these world surveys. From these databases, we will attempt to use questions which shed light on our theme that culture matters.

When approaching these World Values Surveys from the angle of culture being important, we need to clarify the X and Y in the following cultural equation:

Culture X results in outcome Y.                                          (CE)

This basic proposition must be specified with regard to both X and Y, which can be done using either macro (aggregate-level data) and micro information (individual-level data). One may state that the macro interpretation of (CE) is not only more frequent in cultural arguments than the micro interpretation but appears to be much more easily done, as it is quite obvious what X and Y can stand for in the macro interpretations. When it comes to the micro interpretations, the reference of X and Y is far less self-evident. Let us explain why.

The statement (CE) could, in a macro argument about cultural importance, involve the postmaterialist thesis that the stronger the adherence to postmaterialist values in a society, the more emphasis public policy will place upon environmental concerns. This is an aggregate-level association, which does not tell whether it is people with postmaterialist values who occupy key positions in policy-making and implementation. In a micro-level argument about cultural importance the connection between culture and outcomes must make sense at the individual level, as when postmaterialist values are carried by new parties who come to power as a result of electoral successes or bargaining strength in parliament.

We have examined a number of macro-level arguments of the form of (CE) in previous sections, which we will test in subsequent chapters. What we need to discuss now is the micro-level arguments of the form (CE). What could be the range of things that X and Y stand for in micro-level arguments adhering to the form (CE), using the World Values Surveys as the principal source of information?

Concerning the entities to be put into the place of X in (CE), we will turn to the individual attitudes that figure prominently in the above-mentioned theories of values – namely, postmaterialism, trust theory and individualism–collectivism. In the place of Y we will put individual-level outcomes to be found in the World Values Surveys information.

According to the philosophy of communitarianism, culture often gives the impression of embedding the individual in a setting that is pervasively dominant – framing the individual completely. This is especially true of ethnic or religious cultures. One may cite as examples the Arab or Hindi cultures or the Muslim and Mosaic religions. The individual acceptance of these cultures shows up in almost all aspects of individual behaviour – for example, clothing or eating. With regard to values, the argument for strong embeddedness appears much weaker, but what, then, are the outcomes of individuals adhering to one set of values and not another? We are going to limit ourselves to four broad items that may capture individual level attitudes outcomes that are politically relevant.

1  *Interest in politics.* The World Values Surveys contain a number of questions concerning attitudes to politics in general, including whether an individual discusses political matters and considers politics important. If an individual displays political apathy, then this is an attitude that

is relevant for political outcomes even though it limits the further involvement of an individual into politics.

2 *Involvement in politics.* An individual may be active in politics in different ways, ranging from merely voting to being a political activist in some organization. The World Values Surveys have a number of questions about the political activities of people, which may be employed to tap political involvement, although it is impossible to check whether people speak truthfully about how active they are in politically relevant organizations or political manifestations. Involvement in politics will be measured with two variables.

3 *Left–right placement.* The ideological scale measuring how a person identifies with the political forces along a left–right spectrum can be used to predict how a person will vote in an election, at least in a roundabout fashion. The World Values Surveys comprise questions about which party people feel close to as well as how the people in question locate themselves along a left–right continuum. This outcome measure taps not only a person's probability of voting for a political party but also his or her propensity to take definitive stands on political questions – for instance, left or rightist positions on policy matters.

4 *Life satisfaction.* The World Values Surveys contain a few questions about how individuals appreciate their life. Although these attitudes about life satisfaction are not, strictly speaking, political outcomes, we will include them in the analysis when inquiring into how values impact on individual-level outcomes.

When reporting the distribution of our five dependent variables at the micro level, values will be shown for four periods: from around 1980; from around 1990; from around 1995; and an average for the period 1990–95. In the Appendix at the end of this chapter we report which countries are part of the different samples.

Let us first look at interest in politics. There are at least three items in the cumulative WVS data file that directly tap this dimension (see Inglehart *et al.*, 2000). One asks if politics is important or not in one's life, while another asks whether or not politics is frequently discussed among friends and a third one asks if the respondent is very interested or not very interested in politics (V117–POLINTR). These three items covary strongly, and it is evident from a factor analysis that the item about 'political interest' loads highest on the common factor. Thus we will use this variable (POLINTR) as the indicator of political interest.

In Table 2.2 the worldwide distribution in political interest for the three waves is displayed. We have recoded the original data so that high scores here indicate more political interest and low scores less interest.

There are no distinctive global trends over time. Political interest was highest in the postcommunist countries immediately after the events in 1989, but decreased substantially from 1990 to 1995. The pattern is somewhat

**Table 2.2   Political interest: macro-regional means (POLINTR)**

| Region | 1980 | 1990 | 1995 | 1990–95 |
|---|---|---|---|---|
| OECD | | | | |
| Mean | .410 | .470 | .504 | .470 |
| N | 16 | 20 | 10 | 21 |
| Latin-America | | | | |
| Mean | .377 | .371 | .344 | .351 |
| N | 2 | 4 | 9 | 9 |
| Africa | | | | |
| Mean | .325 | .453 | .461 | .466 |
| N | 1 | 2 | 3 | 3 |
| Asia | | | | |
| Mean | .448 | .519 | .455 | .483 |
| N | 1 | 3 | 5 | 6 |
| Postcommunist countries | | | | |
| Mean | .547 | .587 | .443 | .502 |
| N | 1 | 11 | 16 | 20 |
| Total | | | | |
| Mean | .411 | .495 | .439 | .463 |
| N | 21 | 40 | 43 | 59 |
| Eta squared | .20 | .23 | .38 | .18 |
| Sig. | .447 | .050 | .001 | .028 |

N = number of countries.
*Source*:   See Appendix C.

different among the OECD set of countries, displaying slight increase in political interest between 1980 and 1995. In general, the level of political interest tends to be lower in Latin America than in the other macro regions.

Political interest is one thing; political activity is something else. In order to capture involvement in politics we rely on two sets of items available from the cumulative WVS: first, activity in voluntary organizations (V28 to V36); and, second, attitudes to various forms of political activity (V118 to V122). The voluntary organizations covered are churches, sports, arts, unions, parties, environmental, professional, charitable and other; sports and other organizations were not included in the first wave. A second aspect of involvement in politics is attitudes towards signing petitions, joining boycotts, attending lawful demonstrations, joining unofficial strikes, as well as occupying buildings or factories. Again using a factor analysis we find that the attitudes on these items covary strongly and that the item showing the highest loading is joining boycotts (V119). Therefore we will let this variable capture another aspect of involvement in politics.

**Table 2.3    Political activity: membership of voluntary organizations (VOLORG) – macro-regional percentages – and joining boycotts (JOINBOY) – macro-regional means**

| Region | Membership of voluntary organizations | | | | Joining boycotts | | | |
|---|---|---|---|---|---|---|---|---|
|  | 1980 | 1990 | 1995 | 1990-95 | 1980 | 1990 | 1995 | 1990-95 |
| **OECD** | | | | | | | | |
| Mean | 50.4 | 48.7 | 69.6 | 57.8 | .279 | .313 | .376 | .327 |
| N | 17 | 19 | 10 | 21 | 17 | 19 | 10 | 21 |
| **Latin-America** | | | | | | | | |
| Mean | 35.7 | 29.7 | 65.0 | 65.0 | .115 | .177 | .150 | .155 |
| N | 2 | 4 | 9 | 9 | 2 | 4 | 9 | 9 |
| **Africa** | | | | | | | | |
| Mean | 48.3 | – | 91.3 | 91.3 | .242 | .311 | .238 | .268 |
| N | 1 | – | 2 | 2 | 1 | 2 | 3 | 3 |
| **Asia** | | | | | | | | |
| Mean | 37.9 | 57.1 | 56.1 | 56.0 | .262 | .334 | .306 | .286 |
| N | 1 | 2 | 5 | 6 | 1 | 3 | 5 | 5 |
| **Postcommunist countries** | | | | | | | | |
| Mean | – | 50.3 | 49.8 | 48.2 | – | .235 | .201 | .208 |
| N | – | 8 | 15 | 17 | – | 9 | 16 | 17 |
| **Total** | | | | | | | | |
| Mean | 48.3 | 47.3 | 60.8 | 57.0 | .261 | .280 | .246 | .255 |
| N | 21 | 33 | 41 | 55 | 21 | 36 | 43 | 55 |
| Eta squared | .11 | .14 | .38 | .17 | .42 | .23 | .44 | .35 |
| Sig. | .738 | .362 | .001 | .046 | .057 | .083 | .000 | .000 |

N = number of countries.
*Source:*   See Appendix C.


In Table 2.3 we present percentages of the samples who have stated a membership in any of the voluntary organizations asked for in all three waves. Here, it is important to note that the phrasing of the question in 1995 differs somewhat from how the question was asked in the two previous questionnaires; the format used in the 1995 questionnaire tends to elicit higher levels of membership in voluntary organizations. And it is also only in 1995 that we find distinctive differences in membership of these organizations between different regions. Disregarding the two African cases it seems reasonable to find that membership in voluntary organizations is highest among the OECD countries and lowest among the postcommunist countries. Table 2.3 also has information about the variation in attitudes to joining boycotts for the different regions of the world we are using. Since we have

**Table 2.4    Left–right self-placements (LEFTRIG): macro regional means**

| Region | 1980 | 1990 | 1995 | 1990-95 |
|---|---|---|---|---|
| OECD | | | | |
| Mean | .555 | .557 | .542 | .549 |
| N | 17 | 20 | 10 | 21 |
| Latin American | | | | |
| Mean | .639 | .543 | .602 | .602 |
| N | 2 | 4 | 9 | 9 |
| Africa | | | | |
| Mean | .588 | .540 | .530 | .530 |
| N | 1 | 2 | 2 | 2 |
| Asia | | | | |
| Mean | .611 | .613 | .628 | .628 |
| N | 1 | 2 | 5 | 5 |
| Postcommunist countries | | | | |
| Mean | – | .520 | .539 | .542 |
| N | | 9 | 16 | 20 |
| Total | | | | |
| Mean | .568 | .548 | .564 | .561 |
| N | 21 | 37 | 42 | 57 |
| Eta squared | .19 | .18 | .44 | .36 |
| Sig. | .455 | .168 | .000 | .000 |

N = number of countries.
*Source*:  See Appendix C.

recoded the original variable, the higher the score, the more positive is the attitude towards joining a boycott.

There are some differences between these regions with regard to political activity, but it is only for the 1995 wave that we have significant differences. As may be expected, this propensity is highest among citizens living in the OECD area but lower in Latin America and among the postcommunist countries.

A third aspect of micro-level outcomes refers to individual's self-placement on the right–left dimension. Here we simply stipulate that responses to the question about their views on what is 'right' or 'left' according to a scale goes from 0.1 (left) to 1.0 (right) – that is, we have recoded the original scale to fit it within the 0–1 range. The aggregate means on this scale for the different regions are displayed in Table 2.4.

Again, it is only for the third wave that we can identify distinctive differences between the macro regions with respect to left–right orientations.

The public in Latin America and in Asia seems to lean more to the right than those in the African and the postcommunist sets of countries. The public in the OECD set is located somewhere in between. We may also note that there are apparently no particular trends over time in left–right orientations, as the total mean for 1995 falls just in between these for 1980 and 1990.

Our final micro-level outcome dimension concerns various aspects of satisfaction with life. The cumulative file contains at least four variables relevant for measuring this outcome dimension. Here we include items about whether the respondent is happy (V10), the state of the health (V11), but also financial satisfaction (V64), as well as life satisfaction (V65). By using a factor analysis we may establish that it is the life satisfaction variable which loads highest on this identified outcome dimension. Thus the life satisfaction variable will be used as the indicator capturing life satisfaction in a more general way. This variable has also been recoded to range from the low .1 to the high 1.0.

The aggregated scores for individuals on the life satisfaction variable in different regions of the world are presented in Table 2.5. The higher the mean, the more life satisfaction. Here we may find distinctive trends over time, as well as clear differences between the macro regions. The general trend suggests a decline in life satisfaction over time with somewhat lower total means in 1995 than was the case in 1980, and this trend is particularly true of the postcommunist countries, although one should remember that the mean for 1980 only is based on one case. Life satisfaction seems to be highest among the OECD set of countries and lowest among the postcommunist countries. Latin-America comes out quite highly in between these positions, with the Asian set coming second lowest.

## Conclusion

Following certain of the major themes in the extensive literature on culture, we have, in this chapter, tried to substantiate the claim often made that 'culture matters'. Cultural phenomena may be considered intrinsically or extrinsically important. Several social science theories argue in favour of extrinsic importance, which we interpret as the impact of culture – ethnicity, religion, legacies, and universal values – on political, economic and social outcomes.

Underlining the importance of clarifying what level of social reality one is talking about, we have distinguished between the most general level and the highest level of aggregation – that of society – as well as the regional level and the individual level. Both culture and outcomes fall under this three-category separation. The key outcome variables chosen refer to different aspects of political and socioeconomic development, as well as to political party support and life satisfaction.

Taking into account a number of macro-level outcome variables, we tend to find quite stable patterns of spatial variation over time. Changes do, of course,

**Table 2.5    Life satisfaction (LIFESAT): macro-regional means**

| Region | 1980 | 1990 | 1995 | 1990-95 |
|---|---|---|---|---|
| OECD | | | | |
| Mean | .751 | .746 | .731 | .742 |
| N | 17 | 20 | 10 | 21 |
| Latin American | | | | |
| Mean | .738 | .740 | .714 | .714 |
| N | 2 | 4 | 9 | 9 |
| Africa | | | | |
| Mean | .630 | .634 | .664 | .664 |
| N | 1 | 2 | 3 | 3 |
| Asia | | | | |
| Mean | .533 | .648 | .660 | .662 |
| N | 1 | 2 | 4 | 5 |
| Postcommunist countries | | | | |
| Mean | .693 | .591 | .502 | .524 |
| N | 1 | 12 | 16 | 20 |
| Total | | | | |
| Mean | .732 | .688 | .629 | .651 |
| N | 22 | 40 | 42 | 58 |
| Eta squared | .51 | .69 | .69 | .67 |
| Sig. | .012 | .000 | .000 | .000 |

N = number of countries.
*Source*:   See Appendix C.

occur but, taking a long-run perspective for the last decades of the twentieth century, it is true that, at the macro level, political, economic and social outcomes display a stable pattern of variation which may warrant a search for factors which may have an impact on them. This stability is in itself interesting, considering the fact that the globalization process is taking place at the same time; globalization in itself does not seem to have had much impact on these outcome variables which we have encountered at different levels of aggregation.

Our main focus in the following chapters constituting Part II of this volume will be to make an empirical inquiry into what impact one type of cultural factor – ethnicity – has on these dependent variables. In order to estimate the cultural impact correctly, it is necessary to introduce a number of control variables by means of regression analysis. Our control variables comprise historical and geographical factors at the macro and the regional level, while at the micro level we will employ other control variables capturing, for example, education and income.

**Appendix: Countries Included in our Analysis Based on Different Waves of WVS**

| Region | Country | 1st wave | 2nd wave | 3rd wave | 1990–95 |
|---|---|---|---|---|---|
| OECD | | | | | |
| | Australia | X | | X | X |
| | Austria | | X | | X |
| | Belgium | X | X | | X |
| | Canada | X | X | | X |
| | Denmark | X | X | | X |
| | Finland | X | X | X | X |
| | France | X | X | | X |
| | Germany | X | X | X | X |
| | Iceland | X | X | | X |
| | Ireland | X | X | | X |
| | Italy | X | X | | X |
| | Japan | X | X | X | X |
| | Netherlands | X | X | | X |
| | Norway | X | X | X | X |
| | Portugal | | X | | X |
| | Spain | X | X | X | X |
| | Sweden | X | X | X | X |
| | Switzerland | | X | X | X |
| | Turkey | | X | X | X |
| | United Kingdom | X | X | X | X |
| | United States | X | X | X | X |
| Latin America | | | | | |
| | Argentina | X | X | X | X |
| | Brazil | | X | X | X |
| | Chile | | X | X | X |
| | Colombia | | | X | X |
| | Dominican Republic | | | X | X |
| | Mexico | X | X | X | X |
| | Peru | | | X | X |
| | Uruguay | | | X | X |
| | Venezuela | | | X | X |
| Africa | | | | | |
| | Ghana | | | X | X |
| | Nigeria | | X | X | X |
| | South Africa | X | X | X | X |
| Asia | | | | | |
| | Bangladesh | | | X | X |
| | China | | X | X | X |
| | India | | X | X | X |

| Region | Country | 1st wave | 2nd wave | 3rd wave | 1990–95 |
|---|---|---|---|---|---|
| | Korea, South | X | X | X | X |
| | Pakistan | | | X | X |
| | Philippines | | | X | X |
| | Taiwan | | | X | X |
| Postcommunist countries | | | | | |
| | Armenia | | | X | X |
| | Azerbaijan | | | X | X |
| | Belarus | | X | X | X |
| | Bosnia and Herzegovina | | | X | X |
| | Bulgaria | | X | X | X |
| | Croatia | | | X | X |
| | Czech Republic | | X | | X |
| | Estonia | | X | X | X |
| | Georgia | | | X | X |
| | Hungary | X | X | | X |
| | Latvia | | X | X | X |
| | Lithuania | | X | X | X |
| | Macedonia | | | X | X |
| | Moldova | | | X | X |
| | Poland | | X | X | X |
| | Romania | | X | | X |
| | Russia | | X | X | X |
| | Slovakia | | X | | X |
| | Slovenia | | X | X | X |
| | Ukraine | | | X | X |

*Note*: United Kingdom is a weighted added value for Britain and Northern Ireland (1980 and 1990); Germany is also a weighted added value for West Germany and East Germany (1990 and 1995).

# PART II
# ETHNICITY

# Introduction

We begin our examination of the cultures of the world by discussing various aspects of ethnicity – that is, ethnic identity as culture. As a source of cultural identification, ethnicity is second to none of the cultures of the world. The most fervent versions of ethnicity occur in right-wing nationalism, but strong ethnic identification may also occur in liberation movements, conducted by ethnic groups. Several countries adhere to the ideal of a nation-state, and some states are based on a nation that goes far back in time. Yet it has been argued by several scholars that the concepts of an ethnic group in general and that of a nation in particular are as vague as to be almost useless (see, for example, Hutchinson and Smith, 1994). Moreover the concept of a nation-state appears ill-suited to the needs of a multicultural society. How come, then, that ethnicity is said to matter so much?

The importance of ethnicity for politics, as well as for society, boils down to the role that three kinds of group play: ethnic groups, nations and races. To assess the impact of ethnicity on outcomes, one needs to specify and test a set of models which connect ethnic groups, nations or races with political, economic or social results on the basis of theory which establishes links between ethnicity and outcomes. We will replace the discarded conception of race with the concept of language families.

A basic puzzle in ethnicity concerns the nature of ethnic groups – how real they are. Thus, one may ask the question: is cultural identity in nations and ethnic groups the very same expression of ethnicity, although the groups which carry the ethnic identities are entirely different? Whereas few doubt the reality of ethnic groups, the concept of a nation seems to be much more contestable. On the one hand, the nation-building literature is very much focused on the reality of a nation, whether as actually existing or as a potentiality (Deutsch, 1966). On the other hand, there is the position that nations constitute 'imagined communities' (Anderson, 1983). Interestingly, Weber argued early in the twentieth century that the concepts of nation and ethnic group are so vague that they hardly have any foundation at all (Weber, 1978). Admittedly the concept of race has now almost entirely been discarded, but it may also be pointed out that groups with ethnic identities display varying degrees of compactness, from high with certain ethnic groups to low with races.

Chapter 3 discusses how ethnicity may create cultural identity with groups. The purpose is to show why ethnic identity is such a complex conception, covering very different kinds of group with a low or a high degree of compactness. Chapter 4 is devoted to the analysis of the consequences of ethnic identity when ethnic groups have low compactness (language), as well as when ethnic groups are more compact – that is, it targets the impact of ethnic cleavages and ethnic structure on outcomes, including regional and micro-level outcomes. Recognizing that ethnicity is complex in its various manifestations opens the way for the test of various models that state that ethnicity matters in the political life of a country.

The concept of ethnicity and its subconcepts like clan, tribe, ethnie, nation and race have been much analysed in the social sciences (Mortimer and Fine, 1999; Halliday and Ozkirimli, 2000; Kymlicka, 2001; Smith, 2004), but we believe that Max Weber's position that ethnicity is a flawed conception goes too far. Thus, we will attempt to unpack various notions under this general heading. Ethnic identity may take several expressions, whether real or imagined, and they add to the multicultural nature of societies.

# Chapter 3

# Ethnic Groups and Nations

## Introduction

The basic problem in theories of national identity and ethnic identification is to clarify what these phenomena are. The search for a definition of the key words – 'nation' and 'ethnic group' – has resulted in a bewildering array of approaches to ethnic and national identity (Eriksen, 1993; Renner, 1998). Of all kinds of group, how does one pick the groups with an ethnic or national identity? Thus, we face the question: which are the typical characteristics of nations and ethnic groups?

Ethnicity may be connected with race. However, the concept of race has become almost obsolete in the social sciences due to its value-loaded nature. Racial differences among people, according to racial theory, did not only consist merely of observable characteristics but also contained elements of moral inferiority or superiority. It must be recognized that race only conceived as colour or as a language community is an unmistakable fact of the peoples of the world. But does it matter?

We will approach this labyrinth of conceptual problems connected with national identity and ethnicity by proceeding from the most basic or elementary ethnic group to the most inclusive group, the nation. Ethnic groups may exist side-by-side in the form of so-called multicultural societies. Multiculturalism presents a challenge to nationalism in that it may provoke nationalist responses from groups who feel uneasy with social heterogeneity.

We will argue that the concepts of ethnicity and national identity should be defined without legal characteristics. Thus, ethnic groups or nations are different entities from states; they are groups with a special kind of cultural identity. States constitute legal orders. Thus, the concept of a nation-state is a mixture of two different things – namely, a group concept about a certain type of solidarity and a legal concept about a certain kind of normative order upheld by an organization.

One important question in the research on national identity concerns how homogeneous or heterogeneous states tend to be. Here, we have the critical point where ethnic groups and nations meet, as countries with many and strongly motivated ethnic groups would tend to display a low level of national identity. Another essential question for the state is what national identity amounts to, or should amount to practically – for instance, in the form of citizenship rights.

## Ethnic Groups

The key concept in the study of ethnicity is that of an ethnic group constituting a social group which is orientated in terms of shared language or common historical fate. An ethnic group is a group that could be of any size in terms of the group which supports its culture. Minorities constitute ethnic groups when they have a culture based upon ethnicity. Majorities could also qualify as ethnic groups when, for example, they display a strong national identification. However, the concept of a nation is much more problematic than that of an ethnic group.

A nation could consist of the ethnic group that has a dominant position in a society in terms of numbers. However, a nation could also be the agreement on certain principles that various ethnic groups have arrived at in order to live together in a country. It is an open question whether several countries today really harbour one nation or whether perhaps they are to be seen as being made up of a pattern of ethnic groups, as argued by multiculturalism.

Below we list a few definitions of the concept of an ethnic group in order to identify the characteristics that are most often mentioned in relation to such groups that have an identity based upon ethnicity. An expert on ethnicity, F. Barth, states for instance:

> A group, which perpetuates itself biologically, at least for some generations, shares fundamental cultural values, constitutes a field of communication and interaction, identifies as a distinct group by other groups and by itself. (Barth, 1969, pp. 10–11)

The Barth definition of 'ethnic group' combines several characteristics of a group:

a) biological reproduction over several generations;
b) shared or common values;
c) interaction or communication between the members; and
d) self-identification as well as identification by other groups.

While the characteristics (b) and (c) are trivial in the sense that any real group would satisfy them, the characteristics (a) and (d) are controversial – one objective and the other a subjective criterion.

The criterion (a) would separate ethnic groups entirely from one type of group – namely, associations. It would also single out ethnic groups as unique among communities, as religious groups would have difficulty in satisfying criterion (a). But is really biological reproduction essential to ethnic groups? How many of the members of an ethnic group would have to satisfy this requirement in order for the group to be designated as 'ethnic'? Could not an ethnic group receive considerable new blood from outsiders joining it?

Criterion (d), identification by self or others has been singled out by some scholars as the most important one. Thus, Maget argues that an ethnic group is first and foremost a proper name, a description. The most pertinent criterion, in this opinion, would be that the populations concerned classify themselves under a proper collective name (Maget, 1968, pp. 1326–32). Thus, groups such as the Maronites, the Berbers and the Coptes would be ethnic groups, because they have a proper name designating them in their own eyes and those of others. Yet one may wish to know whether all groups in fact constitute ethnic groups when they are referred to by a proper name. Why could not associations satisfy criterion (d)? Maronites and Coptes are primarily religious groups. Evidently, criterion (d) is too weak. How 'objective' must a criterion be in order to be a valid tool for sorting out the groups that are ethnic groups and those that are not. Furthermore, what is the meaning of 'objective' in this connection?

A.D. Smith focuses almost exclusively upon characteristics – myths of descent and historical memories – that many would argue are subjective. His six characteristics of ethnic groups are as follows:

1  a collective proper name;
2  a myth of common ancestry;
3  shared historical memories;
4  one or more differentiating elements of common culture;
5  an association with a specific 'homeland';
6  a sense of solidarity for significant sectors of the population (Smith, 1991, p. 21).

All characteristics except (1) involve how the members of an ethnic group perceive the world and evaluate it. Thus, an ethnic group seems to be predominantly a so-called subjective phenomenon, or an imagined community.

Stating that ethnic groups are social groups based on imagination (Anderson, 1983) may entail that ethnic groups are merely so-called imagined communities in contradiction to real ones. Further to this interpretation, an ethnic group would be one with an identity that has somehow been constructed, as it is far from natural. An ethnic group may have an identity merely fabricated by political elites for the promotion of its own interests. However, social imagination may be the source of well-established and long-lasting attitudes, which are all but unreal. Not all forms of social imagination lead to unrealistic myths. And myths could have very real consequences.

If multicultural societies include a mixture of groups with different identities, then ethnic groups or social groups held together by a few characteristics taken from the list (1)–(6) above would enter such a multicultural society. Religious groups could also enter a multicultural society, but they would not constitute ethnic groups. However, there are religious groups that come very close to being an ethnic group – for example, the above-mentioned Coptes who mix Christianity with Egyptian ancestry.

Ethnic groups are the social groups in which members identify on the basis of a mixture of identity-forming reasons including ancestry, homeland legacy and common culture in the form of, for instance, a language. Since ethnic groups are basically held together by beliefs, they tend to have shifting fortunes, reflecting the number of people who really share these identity-forming reasons. When ethnic groups decay or perish, either the group that supports the cultural identity in question falls apart, perhaps being destroyed or assimilated into another group, or the group no longer commits itself to this particular ethnic identity.

More specifically, ethnicity is the cultural identity of a people. A people in the sense of the German word *Volk* (for which there is no similar English term) may vary considerably in terms of compactness as well as in historical origin, some peoples dating far back in history (Russians), others having emerged recently (Palestinians), while, finally, some have been severely decimated (American Indians).

## Two Types of Ethnic Groups

There is in ethnic studies an often cited theory of two types of ethnic community: lateral versus vertical ethnic groups (Smith, 1991). This distinction draws heavily upon European history and is based on a theory about how ethnic groups developed into nations in Western and Eastern Europe. According to this theory, there would be a sharp distinction between the following types:

1  *Lateral ethnic groups*: bureaucratic incorporation – aristocratic ethnic groups
2  *Vertical ethnic groups*: vernacular mobilization – native, domestic, homely, or democratic ethnic groups (Smith, 1991).

The distinction between two kinds of ethnic groups, (1) and (2) above also appears in the theory of nationalism and the theory of citizenship. Conception (1) is called the French approach whereas conception (2) is referred to as the German approach. In terms of citizenships the key distinction is the basis of the claim for recognition of citizenship: (a) *jus soli*; (b) *jus sanguinis*. The French approach is considered to be universalistic whereas the German one is said to be particularistic, although French nationalism of the Barres type has also leaned towards particularism.

Are lateral and vertical the only possible types of ethnic groups? This is a relevant question because one may also speak of diaspora ethnic groups which do not fit the above distinction. There is, for example at least one group that has exercised an enormous influence on historical developments and whose members are often characterized by a high degree of awareness – namely the Jewish community. At present, there exist several diasporas. Are diasporas to be regarded as ethnic groups in the country where they currently live or are they parts and pieces of the nation in the country in which they have their homeland? A few countries – for example, Canada and Australia – have become virtual diaspora countries in which heavy immigration has resulted in strong multiculturalism.

The fact that ethnic groups also identify on the basis of religion opens up the possibility that ethnic and religious identities are not really that distinct. A striking example would be the emerging Hindu nationalism mobilizing an ethnic and a religious identity at the same time. Another group is the Maronites in Lebanon who also constitute a diaspora. Ethnic groups are said to be people with certain characteristics, which do not include religious belief. However, it sometimes happens that religious minorities constitute a people.

The theory about lateral and vertical ethnic groups includes hypotheses about how they emerge in the first place and how they develop into nations. This is called nation-building and is a key element into the ambiguous concept of the nation-state.

## Ethnogenesis

The evolution of ethnic groups has been studied in connection with the growth of national identities in a number of countries, especially in European ones. Stated somewhat schematically, the theory of nation-building would comprise at least the following building blocks:

First one makes a distinction between an ethnic category on the one hand and an ethnic community on the other. Ethnic mobilization is the development process through which ethnic categories become ethnic communities, corresponding to the distinction between latent and manifest ethnicity. This distinction is well known from the study of social groups and cleavages.

Second, one separates between lateral and vertical ethnic groups. This separation is far more demanding, as it is based on a historical comparison between Western and Eastern Europe. It is closely connected with the theory which claims that mainly two types of nationalism in Europe have occurred and that these two forms have different political consequences.

The theory of two forms of ethnic mobilization and nation-building is a genuine 'culture matters' argument, as the outcomes are stated to be entirely and systematically different. In principle, this distinction would be applicable outside Europe, but is nationalism in the Third World really of either type? Let us follow the way in which Smith distinguishes between two fundamental types of ethnic group. He states about the aristocratic or lateral ethnic group:

> ... it was at once socially confirmed to the upper strata while being geographically spread out to form often close links with the upper echelons of neighbouring lateral ethnic groups. (Smith, 1991, p. 53)

This historical description of lateral or aristocratic ethnic groups in Western Europe serves as a background to the identification of two systematic properties of such groups: malleability of borders and lack of social depth. In the Smith analysis these two characteristics were highly conducive to the successful emergence of nationalism in Western Europe, as ethnic groups could easily mix and create more or less homogeneous nations, served by true geographical implantation through the interpenetration of ethnic groups or ethnic elites within a determinate area. 'Successful' here means the creation of compact nation-states.

The opposite type of ethnic community, the vertical or democratic type, is characterized by the following properties: popular and compact. Smith describes their genesis as follows:

> ... a distinctive historical culture helped to unite different classes around a common heritage and tradition, especially when the latter were under threat from outside. As a result the ethnic bond was often more intense and exclusive, and barriers to admission were higher. (Smith, 1991, p. 53)

Here, the mechanism of ethno-genetics or ethnic mobilization is not mixture but differentiation. Consequently, when these East European ethnic groups – Czechs, Slovaks and Serbs, for instance – developed ethnocentrism and claimed to be nations, the process became much more divisive and conflict-ridden. Perhaps this theory overemphasizes the difference between Western and Eastern Europe, as one finds also vertical ethnic groups in Western Europe such as, for example, the Basques, Corsicans and Scotts.

What we wish to emphasize here is that the distinction between lateral and vertical ethnic groups is based on a theory of ethnic acculturation, or how such groups relate to each other. Several ethnic groups may unite into a nation or a few may divide an empire into small nation-states. In fact, both processes have occurred in Western and Eastern Europe.

One must ask today how an ethnic group may relate to another when they must coexist in a single society. If an ethnic group does not amalgamate intentionally with the other ethnic groups, or does not assimilate unintentionally with them, then all ethnic groups may perhaps live side-by-side in a multicultural society. Researching the preconditions for peaceful multicultural societies is an urgent task. Throughout history there have been numerous cases of ethnic conflicts, forced ethnic assimilation and even ethnic annihilation.

## Ethnic Cores and Nation-building

In the theory of nation-building one encounters the concept of an ethnic core. However, its meaning and reference is most unclear. Smith uses this concept stating about the links between ethnic group, nation and state: 'a state's ethnic core often shapes the character and boundaries of the nation; for it is very often on the basis of such a core that states coalesce to form nations' (Smith, 1991, p. 39).

We believe that this conventional theory of nation-building is highly questionable in relation to several ongoing processes of nation-building in many Third World countries. It may not even be true in relation to some already accomplished nation-building processes in the First World. To see why we hold this view, we need to discuss the concept of an ethnic core in connection with these two central concepts: state and nation. We strongly argue that one should distinguish between the concept of a nation and that of a state. For instance we claim that the following suggested distinction between the two is scarcely correct:

> By definition the nation is a community of common myths and memories, as in an ethnic group. It is also a territorial community. But whereas in the case of ethnic groups the link with a territory may be only historical and symbolic, in the case of the nation it is physical and actual: nations possess territories. (Smith, 1991, p. 40)

This can hardly be so, we say, as many nations do not possess states today, in the year 2002: consider the Kurds, the Palestinians, the Berbers, the Sikhs, the Tibetans, the Tamils, the Eskimos, the Samis and so on. And many territories are populated by more than one nation: consider India, South Africa, Nigeria, Spain and the UK.

States constitute legal entities, whereas nations are groups with an ethnic identity. They are different kinds of entities all together. Nations are modern phenomena, states Smith, as they tend to have: a legal code of rights; a unified economy; a compact territory; a single political culture, guaranteeing citizen socialization (Smith, 1991, p. 69). We disagree with this statement or proposed definition, because this is the definition of the concept of the modern or European state, and this concept should be kept separate from that of a nation.

The state is a legal order (Kelsen, 1961), whereas the nation is a solid social group, making it compact to some degree. In fact, one should not assume that a nation always stems from a predominant ethnic group, as it is possible to form nations without an antecedent and dominant ethnic group – that is, an ethnic core. As new states that emerged after the Second World War show, the relationship of many nations to any ethnic core is problematic. One may search in vain for the ethnic core in the future South African nation. A question could be raised in relation to Hindu nationalism and the state of India. Which is the ethnic core? One may also question the existence of an ethnic core in old nations: which is the core today in the ethnically mixed USA?

At the same time as one theorizes about how an ethnic group may grow into a nation, one should never forget that most such groups never go through this process of nation-building: they remain minorities in their country. When one speaks about two routes for ethnic communities to become nations and have states, the assimilation route and the vernacular mobilisation avenue, then one has in mind the distinction referred to above – that is, between lateral and vertical ethnic groups. However, today it is more likely that a society will lack any dominant ethnic group or ethnic core, being a multicultural society.

Finally, there is a risk of a Western bias in the entire theory of nation-building. Whether a nation is forged by a dominating ethnic group by means of the power of the state, like the UK, or whether a few nations spring out from the ethnic remnants of an empire, as with the Habsburg Double Monarchy, it remains that these two models of nation-building are simple generalizations from the history of Western and Central Europe. One may wish to develop other models of the interaction between ethnic groups or nations, based on experiences from other continents where separate ethnic cores may live together in a state, which is thus not a nation-state.

## Nation and Ethnic Group

In his *Economy and Society* (1978) Max Weber offered a few observations concerning ethnic groups and nations which are well worth reproducing here, as they are in line with postmodernist ideas. He argued that both concepts were extremely vague ones, suffering from a lack of a set of clear conceptual characteristics, as so many things could constitute the bond of solidarity between people entering into a social group. To him, the difference between an ethnic group and a nation concerned power and the state. He stated:

> The concept of 'nationality' shares with that of the 'people' – in the 'ethnic' sense – the vague connotation that whatever is felt to be distinctly common must derive from a common descent. In reality, of course, persons who consider themselves members of the same nationality are often much less related by common descent than are persons belonging to different and hostile nationalities. (Weber, 1978, p. 395)

This is basically Weber's objection to the concept of an ethnic group, as we have already discussed it. Thus, Weber claims that the concept of an ethnic group 'dissolves if we define our terms exactly', as is also the case with the concept of a nation which is 'one of the most vexing, since emotionally charged concepts' (Weber, 1978, p. 395). The basic difficulty with an ethnic group is that its foundation is so difficult to pin down in something really shared among the people concerned. Weber gave the following definition of an ethnic group:

> We shall call 'ethnic groups' those human groups that entertain a subjective belief in their common descent because of similarities of physical type or of customs or both, or because of memories of colonisation and migration; this belief must be

important for the propagation of group formation; conversely, it does not matter whether or not an objective blood relationship exists. (Weber, 1978, p. 389)

Then Weber went on to show that this subjective component – belief and memories – can consist of very different and confusing identities, making the entire concept of an ethnic group not very useful for social science research. Yet, even if ethnic groups are so-called imagined communities, they do exist as such and they seem to increasingly matter in some countries.

Moreover, Weber takes the often reiterated position that the concept of a nation is intimately connected with that of the chief attribute of the state – namely, power. A nation is that ethnic group which aspires to independence, stated Weber:

> Whatever the 'nation' means beyond a mere 'language group' can be found in the specific objective of its social action, and this can only be the *autonomous polity*. Indeed, 'nation state' has become conceptually identical with 'state' based on common language. (Weber, 1978, p. 395)

When Weber wrote this in the early twentieth century, it was hardly empirically accurate but perhaps morally in tune with many aspirations. Weber correctly pointed out that many countries had several language groups and yet one state, thus implying that the nation-state is not the only format of a modern state. However, the thesis that a nation must strive for state independence is hardly ethically relevant today, as several nations often coexist within one state – the theme of multiculturalism.

In addition, we argue that the concept of a nation has become even less useful due to the globalization process. In any case, we must debate the relevance of this concept for the realities of the twenty-first century. Nations today appear much less compact than they did around 1900 when Weber questioned these concepts of an ethnic group and a nation. But if the existence of nation-states is open to doubt, it does not follow that the existence of nations is equally questionable. Different nations may exist in the USA today without them searching for an independent polity. Yet, nations are more difficult to pin down than ethnic groups. Why? Because, we answer, they tend to lack compactness. The concept of the state also remains relevant when one relinquishes the troublesome notion of a nation-state.

## Nationality and Nationalism

The literature on national identity is very large, no doubt because scholars tend to take different opinions about the nature of national identity. The following key questions may be identified in the debate about nationalism or the general theory about the nation:

1    What is national identity as a group phenomenon?
2    What is the relationship between nation and state?
3    Is nationalism ethically acceptable – that is, in conformity with liberalism?

Whereas question 1 deals with the social bases of national identity, question 2 concerns the problematic concept of a nation-state, while question 3 tackles the moral implications of national identity.

Despite a long debate about the nature of national identity, no consensus has been reached about the characteristics of a nation. Any attempt at formulating a clear concept of the nation that would meet with unanimous agreement would involve answering the following two questions:

1    Can one distinguish between a nation as a social group and the political expressions of nationalism, such as the search for a state?
2    Is a nation a cultural identity or a political community? Or both?

These two questions are clearly interlinked, although one could respond 'No' to the first question and respond 'Yes' to the second. Let us start the examination of national identity by focusing upon the controversy between Kedourie and Gellner, which is relevant to question 2.

The different ways in which the special nature of national identities can be evaluated emerge when one reads the debate between two experts on nationalism, Kedourie and Gellner. This discussion is interesting also because one scholar looks at the content of nationalism as a so-called 'ism' or system of thought, whereas the other bases his argument on the social functions of nationalism.

Kedourie's position rests heavily on the idea of a nation and how this conception emerged after the French Revolution. The argument is that, without the major theoreticians of the nation, there would never have been any nationalism. To understand nationalism we need to go back to how Romanticism conceived of a nation, as with the doctrines of Fichte, Herder and Hegel. However, Kedourie not only interpreted the source of nationalism as a doctrine; he also ventured to predict that it was basically a system of ideas that would lack relevance in a modernized society. Nationalism was an atavism which only created political turmoil and one could, without loss, free oneself from this over-metaphysical doctrine (Kedourie, 1993).

Gellner's argument runs almost exactly opposite, although it focuses much more on the social functions of nationalism than its content as an ideology. To Gellner, nationalism is connected with the emergence of high cultures, which in turn are typical of industrialized and urbanized societies. The search for national identity comes with the growth in education among the entire population, which is only feasible in a society that has left the agrarian stage. Thus, Gellner entirely rejected Kedourie's theory that nationalism is a mythical doctrine, loaded with metaphysics. On the contrary, it is typical of what he calls 'high' cultures (Gellner, 1983a).

'Nationalism' is the ideology of national identity. The term stands for a variety of things connected with this type of identity, including: the process of forming nations; the consciousness of belonging to the nation; the symbolism of the nation; the cultural doctrine attached to a nation; and a social or political movement that mobilizes national identity. Thus, nationalism is both potential and actuality, standing for both the dreams of the adherents to this ideology and the realities accomplished in concrete action.

When nationalism develops into irredentism or fascism, it takes on very strong proportions. However, it is perfectly possible to combine nationalism with liberalism. Smith defines nationalism as:

> ... an ideological movement for attaining and maintaining autonomy, unity and identity on behalf of a population deemed by some of its members to constitute an actual or potential 'nation'. (Smith, 1991, p. 73)

Such a movement for attaining or maintaining national identity may be combined with an adherence to humanitarian values or may be associated with a most aggressive form of aggrandizement or collectivism. Perhaps the most curious combination was that of national socialism in Germany during the interwar years, especially when one considers the different wings of this movement. What is the nature of nationalism as an ideology?

Nationalism may emphasize the state or culture as its core territory. Thus we have:

- nationalism as *Weltanschauung*: the world consisting of nations, because only nation-states are truly viable
- nationalism as *Volksgeist* – that is, a cultural spirit
- nationalism as a territorial *patrie* – a homeland.

In the theory of nationalism, one often encounters a distinction between two types of nationalism. Thus, following Kohn, one can distinguish between Western, civic and territorial nationalism on the one hand and Eastern, ethnic and genealogical nationalism on the other. The former tends to be rational and associational, while the latter tends towards being organic and mystical. Smith presents the two types of nationalism as a matrix, as shown in Figure 3.1.

|                | **Civic** | **Genealogical** |
|----------------|:---------:|:----------------:|
| **Bureaucratic** | I | II |
| **Demotic** | III | IV |

**Figure 3.1   The two types of nationalism**

Types I and IV are the historically given kinds of nationalisms. Type I is portrayed as integration nationalism or territorial nationalism. Type IV is characterized as irredentist. But are these two really the most basic kinds?

This distinction between Western and Eastern nationalism corresponds basically to the two models of French and German nationalism as conceived by Renan and Herder respectively. In relation to nationalism as it occurs outside Europe, this distinction seems to be of little assistance. On the other hand, the two other types of nationalism occur frequently.

There are two elements that must be considered when talking about ethnic nationalisms. First, there is the orientation of a nationalist movement. This can be towards entirely different objects – for instance, traditional political systems, such as empires or feudal systems on the one hand, or modern systems such as states and their colonies on the other. It makes a difference whether nationalism targets an empire or a colony. Second, nationalist movements are associated with one of two principal objectives: unification versus separatism. Again, the objective pursued makes an enormous difference. The French model of nationalism is one of unification, whereas the German model is neutral in relation to these two objectives.

Combining these two dimensions in Figure 3.2, we can derive a spectrum over nationalist movements that is perhaps more informative than the classical distinction between the French and German type of nationalism. It is not difficult to identity several examples under these diverse headings.

- Type I: Western European nation-building
- Type II: the Habsburg Empire, the Russian Czarist Empire, the Ottoman Empire, Japanese nation-building
- Type III: nation-building attempts in Latin America, Africa and Asia
- Type IV: separatist movements in Africa and Asia
- Type V: nation-building efforts in countries such as the United States, Canada or South Africa after 1994
- Type VI: the Basque and Corsican movement and Northern Ireland.

| Object | Objectives | |
|---|---|---|
| | **Unification** | **Separatism** |
| **Feudal system (empire)** | I | II |
| **Former colonial entity** | III | IV |
| **State** | V | VI |

Figure 3.2   Nationalist movements

Ethnic separatism is much less frequent in advanced countries than in postcolonial countries.

Theories of nationalism claim that Western European nationalism tends to differ from Eastern European nationalism, corresponding to the separation between the two types of ethnic groups mentioned above. What, more specifically, would be the characteristics of Western national identity and Eastern national identity, respectively? The distinction that we are speaking of here is that between the civic model of nationalism and the genealogical model in the words of experts in this field. This distinction is somehow related not only to the above-mentioned separation between two kinds of ethnic group, but also to another distinction between two kinds of nation – *Staatsnation* and *Kulturnation* in German terminology.

In order to understand these distinctions that have played a major role in the theory of national identity, we have to examine the so-called Renan model of the nation and citizenship, contrasting it with the so-called Herder approach to nationalism. The distinction between the two corresponds to that between a territorial and a genealogical mode of national identity as well as to the separation between lateral and vertical ethnic groups. Let us begin with Herder's conception, since he was, after all, formulating a conception of the nation and national identity some 50 years before Renan.

## Herder

The Herder conception is referred to as the Romantic model of the nation. It originates in German philosophy around 1800, drawing upon the ideas of such scholars as Schelling, Fichte and Arndt. The key work is that of J.G. von Herder, *Outline of a Philosophy of the History of Man* from 1784–91. The conception of a nation in German philosophy is basically collectivist, organic and historicist rather than individualist, voluntaristic or contractualist. The key idea is that of a national genus or collective spirit – what Herder called '*Volksgeist*' – which follows a path in time – that is, an historical evolution.

A nation is a holistic unit, constituting its individual members. But how and on the basis of what? Historical ancestry, biological affinity, language? Different answers, suggested by various German nationalists, were analysed by Meinecke in the form of the opposition between a humanistic approach connected with Humboldt (*Weltbürgertum*) and an aggressive approach (*Nationalstaat*), as stated by Fichte. Meinecke analysed how the latter historically developed out of the former, which was to him a logical process (Meinecke, 1962).

It has always been argued that Eastern European nationalism has resembled the German model, as it has focused on how historical minorities could break loose and form a state of their own, based on their various Slavic or other genuses. A much discussed remnant of the German model is the citizenship and naturalization laws that were in force until 1999. They connected citizenship with participation in the German historical legacy, giving citizenship to persons with any form of German ancestry but being hesitant to naturalize people from other nations.

*Renan*

Renan outlined his model in a famous article written in 1882. Known as the civic, Western model of the nation, it has its origins in the debate around the French Revolution, especially with Sieyès, who stated in 1788 that the third estate constitutes a complete nation. The French model of nationhood is basically a contractualist one, rejecting each and every biological aspect of the concept. What unites a group with national identity is the will to live together and abide by the same laws, accepted by all in a spirit of brotherhood.

This voluntaristic conception of the nature of the nation, focusing on the will to create and adhere to a national identity, means that people could, in principle, join and leave nations as they wish. Sieyès argued that a nation is a body of associates living under one common law and represented by the same legislature (Sieyès, 1985). In a similar vein, Renan declares that 'the existence of a nation is an everyday plebiscite' (Renan, 1994, p. 17). However, things are not so transparently simple when it comes to defining the concrete borders of a nation, as merely the wish to be included does not suffice. Moreover, under the French interpretation, citizenship regulations have to be introduced. These rules tend to focus on 'droit de sol', meaning that they connect citizenship with residence, not ancestry. However, since no country allows people to enter the country as and when they wish, the French citizenship regulation also implicitly takes ancestry into account, the right to residence being linked indiscriminately and directly to French ancestry or to permission to work in the country, which is highly restricted.

A nation is a social group with specific characteristics. The key problem is to specify those properties that separate the nation as a group from other social groups. The word 'nation' is derived from the Latin *natus*, meaning being born, alluding to the biological aspect of regeneration of groups by its own members. However, the biological aspect is seldom stressed in modern theories of nationalism.

Thus, for instance Smith defines a nation as being characterized by: an historical territory – a homeland; common myths and historical memories; a common, mass public culture; common legal rights and duties for all members; and a common economy with territorial mobility for members (Smith, 1991, p. 14). This is a rather demanding definition of a nation in that it requires a set of five characteristics. Perhaps they need not all be present at the same time? For instance, does the Kurdish nation satisfy all five criteria? Smith claims that this definition of a nation sets it apart from any conception of the state (Smith, 1991, p. 14)

Yet, how could there be legal rights or duties without a state? In Smith's conception, the components of national identity include ethnic, cultural, territorial, economic and legal–political characteristics. We are very sceptical about this definition. It is simply not adequate, because it confuses the nation with the state. In our view, a nation is primarily constituted by the bonds of solidarity among members of communities. Nations do not primarily have external functions such as territorial, economic and political activities: they focus essentially on internal functions such as the socialization of their members as 'nationals' or 'citizens'.

## Beyond Nationalism

It cannot be underlined enough that nationalism stands for widely different phenomena that only have one thing in common – namely, the focus on national identity. Nationalism can harbour almost everything from universal liberal ideas about national identification through strong irredentism to explicit fascism. It may thus enter into numerous combinations with either humanitarian ideas about mankind or with racist and hawkish practices.

Is nationalism nowadays on the rise or has it already peaked? This question is highly relevant from the perspective of this book, focusing as it does, on cultural identity in an age of globalization. Here, the distinction between ethnic groups and nations appears highly relevant.

Whereas the political force of ethnic separatism seems to be clearly on the rise in many countries, it is also true that traditional nationalism is under pressure as evidenced by the electoral development of the parties on the right of the left–right continuum. On the one hand, the traditional right-wing parties face mounting difficulties in mobilizing support. On the other hand, new aggressive nationalist parties have made not insignificant inroads into the electorate.

Traditional nationalism, which focuses not on the needs of a minority ethnic group, but on the all-inclusive aspirations of an ethnic majority, seems to be searching for a new response to a number of tendencies which are increasing in substantive force and political relevance. These include global interdependencies, transnational networks, suprastate organizations, intergovernmentalism and cosmopolitanism. Given these tendencies towards globalization, which do not seem to be diminishing in force, and the creation of a world community, nationalism is seeking to relegitimate its basic idea that national identity is important. The trends towards globalization demand an answer to the question of the moral dimension of nationalism – that is, when is nationalism justifiable?

National identity poses not only questions about how to conceptualize this type of cultural orientation, based on ethnicity, but also problems of how to measure this phenomenon. There is also a huge set of concerns relating to the moral status of nationalism. Although this is not the place to discuss the morality of nationalism, which presents a number of essentially contested issues, we wish to call attention to the argument that nationalism constitutes a bedrock for the welfare state (Miller, 1995).

According to Miller, social equality requires nations to have a certain degree of national integration. This may be interpreted as a hypothesis about the outputs and outcomes of national identity. The Miller argument may seem somewhat surprising, nationalism is not usually associated with equality. But reflecting on the moral dimension of nationalism only serves to emphasise yet again how complex national identity tends to be. Although it may be combined with almost any other political ideology – for instance, social democracy, as with Miller, nationalism today occurs primarily among political movements which reject postmodernity and globalization as with the populist parties in France and Austria. As Smith emphasises, nationalism was indeed a progressive political movement around 1900, but nowadays nationalism among the populist movements resembles an attempt to turn back the clock (Smith, 1998).

Nationalism may also surface when minorities seek global justice. One of the most discussed controversies concerning ethnic groups and justice occurred in Switzerland during the 1990s, when several Jewish organizations sought compensation for the assets placed by victims of the Holocaust in Swiss bank accounts during the 1930s. Although this is not the place to discuss this issue, which dates back to the end of the Second World War, we note the lack of appreciation of the Jewish demand for the assets of Jewish people in a recent book by a Swiss scholar, which we quote from below:

> The aim of this book is to lay bare the mechanics of this crisis that so violently shook and harmed Switzerland's international image ... . The declared and perfectly legitimate cause of the crisis was that of seeing justice done to the victims of the Holocaust. But behind that there was a hidden agenda only a closer look can bring to light. (Braillard, 2000, p. 8)

> Since Spring 1996, but especially during 1997 and the first part of 1998, Switzerland was to be the focus of ever sharper criticism from Senator D'Amato and several Jewish organizations (World Jewish Congress, Jewish Agency, Simson Wiesenthal Center) as well as the U.S. Under Secretary of State, Stuart Eizenstat. Very often their aggressive criticism was based on judgements showing little regard for facts and careful investigation. (Braillard, 2000, p. 42)

> Also, Switzerland and America, the source of most of the criticism and actions against Switzerland, have different (some say opposite) ways of doing things. The Swiss are slow to act. Before taking and implementing decisions they gather all the necessary information. Americans, on the contrary, like to make a show of things, make bold statements and are quick to aggressively turn on the pressure. (Braillard, 2000, p. 41)

The Swiss reluctance to settle this dispute may be compared to the willingness of the German government and industry to undo historical injustices such as the use of Nazi slave labour in German factories during the Second

World War, settled in the sum of $7.5 billion in 1999. However, it must be stressed that, once the US government forced the Swiss to settle this dispute in 1998, the agreement that Switzerland accepted was in accordance with the requirements of global justice ($1.25 billion) – this is at least our position. However, Braillard fails to appreciate both the Swiss and the German settlements:

> All this goes to show that the Swiss crisis was obviously part of a wider strategy now being applied to other countries. This strategy is very efficient over the short term. But the methods used are morally flawed. They focus on financial aspects, thereby doing a disservice to the just and noble cause of Jews around the world. The remembrance of the Holocaust should have taken precedence. Instead, it has been flouted. (Braillard, 2000, p. 173)

To summarise: nationalism may be combined with almost any political ideology, as the experiences from the twentieth century testify, and it is independent of the left–right dimension in politics. Smith is probably correct when he states that nationalism has lost its *avant-garde* position by failing to cope with globalization. We are also very sceptical about Miller's theory which links national identity in a globalized world with egalitarianism and the welfare state (Miller, 2000). In our view, the future of nationalism hinges upon whether it can transform itself towards accepting multiculturalism, as suggested early in the twentieth century by Renan, as well as embracing the global market economy.

## Races

Is there a place for the concept of race in an examination of the relevance of ethnicity today? Perhaps the concept of race has been so badly and permanently compromised by the criticism of a few infamous racial theories launched at the end of the nineteenth and the beginning of the twentieth centuries that we should delete it from our inquiry into ethnicity. However, we wish to argue that, while the concept of a race is not without empirical content, there is no good theory available about the races of mankind today. In particular, we wish to distance ourselves from any talk about racial differences in terms of cognitive or moral capacity.

In fact, there are two kinds of literature about race. One attempts to derive numerous behavioural characteristics from racial traits such as colour, including moral ones; the other is entirely different in tone, focusing on social relations that involve a bias in favour of one race and against another. Whereas the first literature resulted in the claims about racial superiority that discredited the whole race approach, the latter, on the contrary, inspired anti-colonialism and bolstered the self-confidence of those who were exploited (Fanon, 1961).

In the article on 'Race' in the *International Encyclopaedia of the Social Sciences* (1968), an expert states it very well:

> It should be carefully noted that the consensus by which racist explanations in the social sciences have been deprived of all claim to scientific respectability does not diminish the importance of further research concerning the essentially 'creative' relation between biological and cultural traits. (Harris, 1968, p. 267)

We wish to follow up this positive proposal to free the concept of race from a number of unscientific theories about race and yet not deny that human races do exist. A concept of race free from notions of superiority could be employed in the inquiry into ethnicity and its impact on social, economic and political outcomes. After all, race seems to be close to kinship which is also a form of ethnicity.

What, then, is the empirical content of the concept of a race? It might be suggested that ethnic groups could be races or that nations constitute races, but this is hardly correct, as a race is a much broader concept than ethnic group or nation. Thus, only huge groups like Europeans, Arabs, Indians, Africans, Afro-Americans and the Chinese may be considered as constituting various races. What is intended here? 'Race is a recurrent ingredient in the ethnosemantics of group identity and intergroup relations', says Harris in the same article (Harris, 1968, p. 263). This is why the concept is interesting to us; race enters the analysis of ethnicity as a type of group identity. However, we argue that the groups identified by means of the concept of race lack almost all degrees of compactness with the consequence that there is little of group identity within races.

Harris suggests an interesting distinction between social race and biological race: A 'social race' is composed of 'socially defined and significant groups', whereas a 'biological race' is a genetic identity captured by means of skin colour, height and body structure. Harris goes on to suggest that social races need not be the same as biological races:

> Social races encompass both phenotypically similar and phenotypically dissimilar populations; actual gene frequencies, the ultimate goal of infrespecies systematics, are obviously not desiderate in folk taxonomies. (Harris, 1968, p. 263)

According to Harris, the biological race concept is more or less discredited, because it entered into a broad-based theory linking other characteristics with racial differences, not least moral traits. Harris dates the origin of biological race theory to Carl von Linné and follows its various versions up to Darwin, Wallace, Huxley, Haeckel and Spencer. Another key figure was the Frenchman, A. de Gobineau, whose book *The Inequality of Human Races*, first published in 1899, played a major role in the dissemination of racist views around 1900, and came to full fruition in the fascist and Nazi ideologies.

Here, we will focus on what we will call 'linguistic races' and inquire into whether the occurrence of these groups, however loosely composed they may be are in any way related to social, economic and political outcomes in a macroscopic sense. How, then, are races to be identified? It has often been suggested that colour is the essential characteristic of race, as suggested for instance by W.E.B. Dubois in 1903: 'The problem of the Twentieth Century is the problem of the color line' (Pettigrew, 1968, p. 277). However, colour is not enough to constitute a race, as it is a mere biological criterion. A race is a group that is somehow socially constructed from certain characteristics, which may include colour. What needs be underlined here is that the same differences in colour may not translate into the same race relations in two different countries.

When race is approached as constituting an intergroup relation, then it is a matter of conflicts between groups having a high degree of awareness of their racial identity. Thus, race as an intergroup relationship is a manifest interaction process where groups with some degree of compactness tend to interact. But these conflict-ridden race relations need not be the same in countries that have the same races. Thus, the division between whites and blacks may constitute a racial divide in some parts of the USA but not necessarily in all parts. And the confrontation between whites and blacks in the UK may change with the arrival of other races from Asia. When race is connected with intergroup conflict, then race is almost identical with ethnic group. In some societies crossings of races constitute intergroup relations, as in Latin America with its large groups of mestizos.

We wish here to separate race from ethnic groups or group minorities. Although many definitions of 'race' exist, several dictionaries concur on certain hereditary characteristics according to the following properties: colour; form of the head; proportion of blood types; and skin. These traits are only biological ones, meaning that the requirement of race as an intergroup relation is not satisfied. Sets of people who satisfy these biological traits may have no interaction together or even any form of cultural identity. Why would a set of people merely sharing some characteristics on the above properties display any consistent form of behaviour or even an intergroup relation? When sets of people are constituted by the characteristics above, then the groups are often so immensely large that people entering them cannot interact.

The comparative theory of languages suggests that a common language may be the missing link which connects the four characteristics and constitute the albeit weak cement of racial groups. Here we will examine a couple of classifications of the linguistic families of the world, which are useful when examining outcomes. Our deliberations thus end with language being the essential aspect of race, because using a common language involves interaction and identity. We suggest therefore that we should inquire into the outcomes of a few major linguistic families which have often been called 'races'.

## Race: Socially Constructed with Immense Political Consequences

By '*race*' is meant a distinct population of humans distinguished in some way from other humans such as skin color, facial features, and possibly genetics. One has debated at great length whether race is real, biologically speaking (Crick, 1995), Conceptions of race are, however, highly controversial due to their political uses and implications, to say the least. Thus, race would be very real even if only socially constructed. Since the 1940s, evolutionary scientists have rejected the view of race according to which a number of finite lists of essential characteristics could be used to determine a like number of races. By the 1960s, data and models from population genetics called into question taxonomic understandings of race, and many have turned from conceptualizing and analyzing human variation in terms of race to doing so in terms of populations and clines instead. Moreover. since the 1990s, data and models from genomics and cladistics have resulted in a revolution in our understanding of human evolution, which has led some to propose a new 'lineage' definition of race. Races arc to be understood as fuzzy sets, clusters, and race definitions are without taxonomic validity. Race definitions tend to be imprecise and arbitrary, meaning that races vary according to the culture examined (http://en.wikipedia.org/wiki/Race).

Race is thus best understood as socially embedded with clear political implications – see the 'immense debate surrounding the controversial book *The Bell Curve: Intelligence and Class Structure in America* (1996) by Hernstein and Murray 1996. This book tried to show that people are becoming stratified according to intelligence. The authors bent over backwards to try to avoid any hint of racism in their studies, but the issue arises when they report that blacks and Latinos have historically scored lower in IQ tests than have whites, and that Asians have scored higher. At the top of society a cognitive elite forms where the passkey to the best schools and the best jobs is high intelligence, whereas at the bottom the common denominator of the underclass is increasingly low intelligence. Hernstein and Murray pull strong consequences of the stratification of the population according to intelligence for social outcomes including IQ's relationship to crime, unemployment, welfare, child neglect and poverty. One may also wish to consult *Critical Race Theory: The Cutting Edge* (Delgado and Stefanic, 2000), which suggests a fast-growing legal genre. In challenging orthodoxy, the premises of liberalism and sacred wisdoms, critical race theory scholars have indelibly changed the way America looks at race.

Here, we have only given a macro definition of 'race' as a linguistic family, following our emphasis upon ethnicity as first and foremost language. One may speak of a few huge linguistic families and one may connect these with so-called macroscopic developmental outcomes such as affluence, democracy and the overall level of human development. However, these macro differences between linguistic families constitute no evidence what-soever for any micro relationship between race and human characteristics, as envisaged in the debate over *The Bell Curve*. The variation among linguistic families brings us to the analysis of civilisations, which belong more under religion than under ethnicity in the field of cultural studies, The ugly face of racism reappears in the analysis of colonial legacies, as emphasized by Franz Fanon (Gibson, 2003).

## Ethnicity and Society

Ethnicity has replaced the concept of race within the social sciences, as it became discredited by the racist ideologies culminating in the 1930s. Much effort has been devoted to the clarification of what kind of social group an ethnic group or a nation constitutes. The suggested solutions to the problem vary widely, ranging from 'imagined communities' to natural 'organisms'. In real life, however, ethnicity means people sharing certain group characteristics, often of a so-called primordial nature.

Groups based on primordial properties may be distinguished from political and economic organizations which recruit members on the basis of ideological reasons or economic interests. Primordial groups are the groups to which people belong for some natural reason like kinship, historical heritage, ethnic or religious background, race or geographical location. The concept of an ethnic group is sufficiently broad to cover any group having some primordial trait that constitutes a foundation for a cultural identity, making the group what one may call 'a people'.

Generally speaking, ethnicity is most often associated with the use of a language, or set of languages – that is, a language family. However, the racial connotations of ethnicity are far from absent in various classifications of the major ethnic communities. Thus, in the American context, race has been a principal dimension in the analysis of the white, black, Indian, Asian or Hispanic ethnic groups. Similarly in Latin America, where Spanish or Portuguese is the dominant language spoken by all ethnic groups, groups are differentiated on the basis of race, as one speaks of, for instance, mestizos, mulattos and Creoles.

With regard to the role of ethnic identity in society an expert on ethnicity states:

> Ethnicity is a powerful affiliation, both because similarity is valued and because genetic (or putatively genetic) origins and early socialisation are potent sources of similarity or, in any case, of cues that signal similarity: appearance, customs, gestures, language, clothing, tastes, and habits. (Horowitz, 2001, p. 48)

Horowitz points out that ethnicity meets with divergent interpretations: it is primordial, or conjured and wholly instrumental, or it emerges from evolutionary hard-wiring. He explains that it seems so powerfully important to people that it is also powerfully conflict-producing. Why?

Ethnic groups seek advantages that tend to be threatened by the presence of traits, such as diligence, clannishness, intractability or intelligence, that they sense in their adversaries. Where ethnic stereotypes, which also threaten positive group evaluation, are employed, then conflict is probably severe (Horowitz, 2001, p. 52). The emergence of a persistent ethnic cleavage results from a decline in the benefits of cooperation as group size increases, as well as from in-group bias that seeks favourable evaluation through discriminatory action. Horowitz states:

> A clear implication of the view of ethic identity as deriving from human needs for cooperation, affiliation, and reward is that ascriptive groups and group relations are universal. They antedate globalisation, the modern state, the industrial revolution, even the printing press. No doubt, all of these developments can make group relations better or worse, not least by altering the contexts in which they take place, but group formation and what follows from it do not depend on them. (Horowitz, 2001, p. 53)

Thus, Horowitz predicts that ethnic cleavages have negative consequences for society. Many countries in Asia, Africa, Eastern Europe and the former Soviet Union are characterized by a predominant ethnic cleavage in that they have two or three large ethnic agglomerations confronting each other. The tendency towards bifurcation is particularly dangerous in ethnic politics, since it is conducive to zero-sum outcomes whereas greater fluidity of alignments would make variable-sum outcomes more likely. Tripolar conflicts become much more dangerous when the third party is induced to align with one of the other two contestants, according to Horowitz.

Yet, one may counterargue that ethnic fragmentation can also be a positive source of diversity and stimulate a vibrant multicultural society. Cultural progress has often taken place in multicultural societies. In the following chapter we will examine data on ethnic cleavages to find out how negative ethnic fragmentation is.

It is with great interest that one reads *The Antiquity of Nations* (2004) by this world-recognized expert on ethnicity. The cultural approach to understanding behaviour has become at least as relevant as the rational choice framework. And ethnicity is one of the three pillars of culture besides religion and values. How far, then, as the field of ethnic studies advanced since Evans-Pritchard?

The new book by Anthony Smith achieves two things. First, it presents in a very clear and easily accessible argument the main problems in the research on ethnies and nations. The method is to confront the reader with the inherent antinomies of the concepts of an ethnie and a nation. Second, it states the position of the author in a concise way, summarizing his whole writing upon the topic.

There are two limitations with this excellent book though which I point out from the outset. On the one hand, this book contains mostly articles that have been published in journals, some dating back to the 1980s. On the other hand, there are quite substantial repetitions from one chapter to the other. However, despite this the book is eminently worth reading for any student interested in the cultural approach to world events. What, then, is an *ethnie* or a *nation*?

Typical of the academic field of ethnicity, I dare suggest, are the many antimonies, which place scholars in opposition to each other. Schematically the key questions, roughly 10, about ethnies and nations include accepting or rejecting the following models:

1  ethnies and nations are natural – no, ethnicity is artificial;
2  ethnicity is ancient or antique – no, ethnies and nations are new;
3  ethnies and nations enhance modernization – no, ethnicity is not adapted to the post-modern society;
4  ethnicity is merely imagined phenomena – no, ethnies and nations are biologically given;
5  ethnies and nations stem from a *Volksgeist* – no, they are manufactured by political elites or irresponsible philosophers;
6  ethnicity is complex and mixed – no, ethnies and nations are of *two* and only two kinds: West European or East European;
7  ethnies and nations enhance social rationality – no, ethnicity is only emotional at best and irrational at worst;
8  ethnicity is propelled by myths – no, ethnies and nations have adequate and often correct memories;
9  nations will survive globalization and multiculturalism – no, nationalism is a force of the past;
10  there are *ethnic cores*, which develop nations – no, ethnic cores will not exist in the multicultural society.

This is the state of ethnicity theory. How, then, about the empirical finds – what do they confirm and reject? *The Antiquity of Nations* presents a few in depth analyses of ethnies and nations – Egypt, the Hittites, the Jews, England and France as well as the Baltic countries, but the findings are not conclusive, allowing us to decide between the alternative models above. Anthony Smith adheres to a theory of ethnicity that somehow is a balanced mixture of primordialism and high culture, instrumentality and an emphasis upon myths, including as well a strong belief in the future of nations. After reading this new text by the foremost global expert on ethnicity I start to doubt whether these 10 basic models of ethnicity are testable at all against empirical data. The difficulty stems from the use of myths in postmodernist interpretation. If all expressions of ethnicity are myth dependent – past or present, and all myths are created anew without ending, then how can nations be ancient, rational and have cores? To me, ethnicity has one feature which is a not a myth, namely language. This should be the basis of a new theory of ethnicity, which recognizes that nationalism does NOT breath smoothly when all advanced societies increasingly have language minorities.

Smith presents his theory of ethnicity as the 'ethno-symbolic' model of ethnies, as if the two could be separated from each other. Even the definition of 'ethnie' includes with him myths. But if all concepts in the field of ethnicity includes the myth, then perhaps myths are merely any belief, i.e. 'myths' designate nothing? What is a myth? Hastings 1066 or Magna Carta 1215? Gustavus Wasa or Christian IV or Rembrandt and Vermeer? It is the indiscriminate employment of the word 'myth' that is conducive to the troublesome state of ethnicity studies, I dare suggest.

I have only one minor objection to Anthony Smith. When he says that sociologists neglected ethnicity or reduced it to state building or economic and social modernisation, then he does not take into account the major contribution of Stein Rokkan, who like Smith himself did not position himself on any of the extremes in the debate over ethnicity and nations.

## Conclusion

A strong current in ethnic studies argues that the concepts derived from ethnicity are too muddled to be employed in the conduct of the social sciences. However, in real life the importance of ethnic groups has hardly dwindled, meaning that ethnicity must be taken into account and concepts be elaborated to describe and analyse this phenomenon. Nations and nationalism may face difficulties as the process of globalization proceeds almost like a juggernaut, but nationalism is not everywhere a force of the past. Independence movements keep up the struggle for their own polity, and sometimes they claim success.

Perhaps Weber's scepticism concerning the future relevance of ethnic groups was somewhat unimaginative. The twentieth century witnessed many ethnic groups and nations in action. Our key question is: does ethnicity matter? In order to answer this question, in the next chapter we will look at two very different kinds of ethnic groups having altogether different degrees of compactness. First, we examine ethnic groups with very little compactness: races or linguistic families. Then we look at ethnic cleavages and ethnic structure. If ethnic groups matter for outcomes, then which type of ethnic group matters most – those with a low or those with a high degree of compactness?

Language should be recognized as the major source of ethnicity despite the hesitations about the concepts of ethnic group and nation that we have discussed. Identifying oneself with a certain language may be the first, or most important, step towards developing, or accepting, a specific cultural identity. Language is primordial as it is basically inherited, although it is, of course, possible to learn foreign languages. We will connect also race with language or, more specifically, language families. It is true that not all ethnic groups or nations identify on the basis of language, but most do. Ethnicity in the former Yugoslavia would constitute an example of ethnic cleavages between groups despite the fact that they all speak the same language (albeit spelt differently).

The languages of the world may be classified into a few principal language families. Such an approach offers an opportunity to tackle the problematic concept of human races. That races belong to ethnicity and a language family could well be the concept to employ when one examines the performance record of human races at a very high level of aggregation across countries. First, we will examine ethnicity from this aspect of language family, focusing on the basic language families of the world, which is a theme with strong race connotations. We will only ask whether these language families matter for major political, economic and social outcomes, making no assumption about any hidden racial superiority. Second, the regional variation within a country in ethnic identities will be studied. Finally, we will inquire into the role of ethnicity for ordinary people.

# Chapter 4

# Outcomes of Ethnicity

## Introduction

Ethnicity is primarily connected with the use of various languages. Groups using the same language tend to develop cultural identities. These identities can be traced back to common inherited traits or primordial characteristics. Language is one such primordial entity that most often serves as the foundation for the cultural identity of an ethnic group and is, without doubt, one of the principal sources of ethnic identity, if not *the* principal one. Language as the basic means of communication between people is conducive to the creation of cultures of groups. Effective communication can be achieved by groups who have a common language or a common medium of communicating with each other. The use of a common language promotes the formation of attitudes and behaviour common to a people sharing this linguistic identity. Since it is true that language enhances ethnic communities with special cultures, one may wish to inquire whether these cultures are conducive to different outcomes – that is, political, social and economic consequences.

The area where a certain language is used tends to become the carriers of traditions or particular kinds of orientation or behaviour. One would expect to find a variation in traditions corresponding to the presence or absence of different linguistic groups. These traditions could translate into a variation in macro outcomes, if indeed ethnicity matters. This kind of ethnic mechanism, language–tradition–outcomes, would apply at various aggregate levels, from the region with its dialect over the nation with its national language to the main language families, globally speaking. Speaking of ethnic groups as language groups opens up a fascinating perspective in macro research, allowing one to engage in global modelling.

Thus, because of the importance of common identities for developing communications, ethnicity is conducive to the formation of cultures and traditions. These cultural identities may have important political, social and economic consequences. For instance, the Arabs are often said to have developed a major cultural tradition (Hourani, 1991), in many ways different from the Anglo-Saxon culture adhered to by English-speaking countries and based on the Arab language. An Arab culture or tradition involves not only a whole set of specific ways of life, which are very different from Anglo-Saxon folk-ways, but it also consists of patterns of thinking and acting that have implications for major social and political outcomes in the Arab world.

Ethnic groups identified on the basis of language may display varying degrees of compactness. A high degree of cohesiveness is typical of small language communities, focusing on either a separate language or a certain dialect of a language. A low degree of compactness characterizes the so-called language families, or a small set of language families covering all the major kinds of language on the globe. The nation as a national language community is located somewhere in between these two poles.

The importance of the use of language in relation to culture and tradition emerges when one looks at how governments create policies to protect their language areas, even when they state that they are favourable to globalization. When the use of a language – say, French – is believed to be threatened, then much is at stake: cultural traditions, state power and perhaps also certain configurations of outcomes analysed in this book. The recent recognition of the Spanish language in the USA is another telling example, although here it is a matter of anticipation of the future size of the so-called latino community.

One may venture to suggest that changes in patterns of communications are crucial for the strengthening or weakening of ethnic identities. Important in this context today is how the globalization process impacts on different ethnic groups, in some cases weakening them but in other cases strengthening them. Globalization involves extensive migration which is conducive to ethnic heterogeneity in the immigrant countries. Searching for the outcomes of ethnicity we will concentrate on societies with wide ethnic diversity. We start, however, by examining the major language families of the world in order to check whether there is empirical evidence that political, social and economic results differ between language families.

## Grand-scale Ethnicity Worldwide

People belonging to the huge language families of the world have little internal interaction except the use of a common language. Nevertheless, we wish to inquire into whether these traditions of persisting language families may have resulted in different performance records or outcomes. To do so, we will employ a database containing information on language families collected for some 150 countries of the modern world. Each and every one of these countries has been classified according to available criteria of language or language family. In the literature there are alternative ways of identifying linguistic communities, and the variation worldwide using these classifications will be mapped. The aim is to try to test the thesis that various grand-scale ethnic communities display different macro outcomes. We suggest that the concept of language families be employed instead of the troublesome concept of race when studying ethnicity on a global level. Thus, we will not link race with language or language family (Solomos and Back, 1996).

There are various ways of identifying these language families. When searching for a few huge ethnic communities one obvious candidate is the concept of a language family. When listing ethnolinguistic families Barrett (1982, pp. 112–15) identifies, among others, Caucasian, Germanic, Latin, Iranian, Arab and Chinese, while Parker (1997c, p. 4) names ethnic groups such as Indo-Aryan, White, Dravidian, Russian, and Bengali to give just a few examples. If ethnicity has an intimate connection with language, then which are the key languages or language families? The question about how the languages of the world are related systematically has puzzled linguistics ever since the launching of the theory about an Indo-European language family (see Katzner, 1994). We duscuss below five alternative classifications of language families.

## Spoken Languages

The number of languages spoken in the world today varies in different estimates. Ruhlen (1987, p. 277) writes about 'the world's roughly 5,000 languages' and Crystal (1997a, p. 284) puts the figure at 4522 languages, while the comprehensive *Ethnologue: Languages of the World* (Grimes, 1999) lists 6703 living languages. Most of these languages are spoken by very few people, and consequently the principal languages are spoken by many millions of people. One may disagree about whether Chinese – that is, Chinese Mandarin – or English is the major language of today. Table 4.1 lists some different estimates of the number of speakers of the major languages of the world in the late twentieth century.

As can be seen, there are some differences in the estimates of numbers of speakers, as well as in the ranking order. But from these three estimates it is obvious that Chinese is the major language in the world of today in terms of numbers of speakers. English and Spanish constitute the other two major spoken languages. It requires little fantasy to connect these major languages with peoples or cultures and traditions. In fact, the major civilizations of the world have, as one of their bases, one of the languages listed in Table 4.1.

One cannot, however, claim that a language family constitutes a civilization. Both more and less are involved in a civilization than the use of a language that is broad enough to make up a language family. Thus, the Hindi language family is not large enough to identify the Indian civilization. And the Spanish language family covers Spain which has an occidental civilization as well as large parts of Latin America that are made up of Third World countries. Furthermore, the Latin American civilization also includes the Portuguese language family in Brazil.

Another way of mapping the use of languages worldwide is to attempt to classify countries according to which languages are dominant. This entails widening the use of language to include commercial and other uses of languages as well. The big advantage with such a definition is that a small set of languages may cover even more of the world population. If languages are classified according to usage, then it is possible to further narrow down the number of language families and arrive at six major linguistic groups, of

**Table 4.1    Estimates of the number of users of the top ten languages (000s)**

| Language | (a) 1980 | Language | (b) 1990 | Language | (c) 1999 |
|---|---|---|---|---|---|
| Chinese (Mandarin) | 551 000 | Chinese (Mandarin) | 726 000 | Chinese (Mandarin) | 885 000 |
| English | 265 000 | English | 427 000 | Spanish | 332 000 |
| Spanish | 228 000 | Spanish | 266 000 | English | 322 000 |
| Hindi | 168 000 | Hindi | 182 000 | Bengali | 189 000 |
| Arabic | 144 000 | Arabic | 181 000 | Hindi | 182 000 |
| Russian | 143 000 | Portuguese | 165 000 | Portuguese | 170 000 |
| Bengali | 138 000 | Bengali | 162 000 | Russian | 170 000 |
| Portuguese | 136 000 | Russian | 158 000 | Japanese | 125 000 |
| Japanese | 117 000 | Japanese | 124 000 | German | 98 000 |
| German | 90 000 | German | 121 000 | Chinese (Wu) | 77 000 |

*Sources*: (a) Barrett, 1982 (ca 1980); (b) Crystal, 1997a (ca 1990); (c) Grimes, 1999 (ca 1999).

which English and Chinese are the large ones. In addition, we may identify an Iberian (Spanish and Portuguese), Russian, Arabic and a French group, as well as a residual group called simply 'Other'. Table 4.2 shows this distribution of the world population into this classification.

Here we not only have a few huge language families comprising millions of users, but we also clearly have a list of some major cultural traditions of

**Table 4.2    Distribution of the world population according to linguistic groups (LINGGRP)**

| Linguistic group | 1900 (%) | 1950 (%) | 1980 (%) | 1990 (%) | 1997 (%) |
|---|---|---|---|---|---|
| English | 24.7 | 27.5 | 28.1 | 28.6 | 29.2 |
| Chinese | 29.9 | 23.7 | 24.2 | 23.7 | 23.2 |
| Arabic | 2.5 | 3.1 | 3.8 | 4.3 | 4.7 |
| French | 4.6 | 4.1 | 3.9 | 4.1 | 4.2 |
| Iberio | 5.6 | 8.0 | 9.3 | 9.5 | 9.4 |
| Russian | 7.4 | 7.0 | 5.8 | 5.3 | 4.9 |
| Other | 25.1 | 26.7 | 24.9 | 24.6 | 24.5 |

*Sources*: Classification of countries based on reports in Parker (1997b, 1997d); see Appendix A.

**Table 4.3    Estimates of English language usage: first (L1) and second (L2) language in the 1990s: by country ranked according to relative size**

| English: L1 (ENG1) | English: L2 (ENG2) | |
| --- | --- | --- |
| United Kingdom | Ireland | Papua New Guinea |
| Jamaica | New Zealand | Philippines |
| New Zealand | United Kingdom | Cameroon |
| Trinidad and Tobago | USA | Nigeria |
| Ireland | Jamaica | Singapore |
| USA | Australia | Botswana |
| Australia | Sierra Leone | South Africa |
| Canada | Trinidad and Tobago | Hong Kong |
| | Liberia | Malaysia |
| | Canada | Zimbabwe |

*Source*:   Based on data reported in Crystal (1997b, pp. 57–60); see Appendix A.

the world. This list is relevant to the study of civilizations, which we engage in subsequent chapters. However, not even here is there a close parallel between language family and civilization, because these linguistic families do not correspond to the major world religions which are essential in the civilizations. English is apparently the major language if the use of language is measured broadly. And it is also displaying an increase in both use and world coverage. If classified in this way it is more than three times as large in terms of size as the Iberian languages. These figures indicate that the English language has a position in many countries that makes it reasonable to look upon the English language as the *lingua franca* worldwide.

Let us therefore, in Table 4.3, present an overview of the position of the English language as of the mid-1990s. Here we report estimates made by Crystal (1997b) where he makes a distinction between people who use English as a first language, or mother language (L1), and people who have learned a variety of English as a second language, in addition to their mother tongue (L2) (Crystal 1997b, p. 55). In addition one could also identify a third category of countries – namely, those where English is taught as the major foreign language (L3). There are, however, only some crude estimates available for the number of speakers of English understood as L1 and L2.

To a large degree the usage of English as a second language reflects the experience of British colonial (Nigeria) or American neocolonial rule (Philippines). Nevertheless, it has not been possible to estimate the most important aspect of English language usage for the future – namely, the use of English as the major foreign language.

**Table 4.4    Distribution of the world population according to language families (LANGFAM)**

| Language family | 1900 (%) | 1950 (%) | 1980 (%) | 1990 (%) | 1997 (%) |
|---|---|---|---|---|---|
| European | 33.1 | 34.7 | 29.5 | 27.6 | 26.1 |
| Indo-Iranian | 19.2 | 19.3 | 21.5 | 22.6 | 23.5 |
| Altaic etc | 2.5 | 2.4 | 2.7 | 2.7 | 2.7 |
| Sino-Tibetan | 33.6 | 27.9 | 27.5 | 26.7 | 25.9 |
| Austro-Asiatic | 4.5 | 6.3 | 7.5 | 7.8 | 8.0 |
| Afro-Asiatic | 3.0 | 3.8 | 4.6 | 5.2 | 5.7 |
| Niger-Congo | 4.0 | 5.6 | 6.8 | 7.5 | 8.1 |

*Sources*: Classification of countries mainly based on Crystal (1997a); population figures from Encyclopaedia Britannica (1998) and Barrett (1982); see Appendix A.

*Language Families*

Linguists have attempted to classify most of the living languages into taxiomatic language families with various kinds of subgroup. Although there is no perfect consensus, one could say that most linguists agree on the existence of some major language families. The largest one, at least in terms of its geographical extension, would be the Indo-European family, which could be divided into the two major subfamilies – namely the European and Indo-Iranian family respectively. The other major families comprise: the Sino-Tibetan (including Chinese); Austro-Asiatic (Khmer); Afro-Asiatic (Arab); and the Niger-Congo (Shona). A remaining group would be a family consisting of Altaic (that is, Turkish) and Uralic (that is, Finno-Ugric) languages. Having arrived at these seven language families, it is possible to crudely classify all the countries in our data set as belonging to one of these families depending on which language constitutes the major language in a country. In order to simplify, we assume that the classification of countries made for the 1990s is a good proxy for the whole of the twentieth century. Based on this assumption we present, in Table 4.4, the proportions of the world population belonging to these seven major language families in our sample of countries. This classification corresponds in an interesting way to some of the major countries of the world in terms of population size, although the category of Europeans is highly amorphous. It also has relevance for the analysis of civilizations – see a few classifications in Chapter 6.

In terms of size, the three major language families in the 1990s were the European, the Sino-Tibetan and the Indo-Iranian language groups. Over time, the European and Sino-Tibetan family display a relative decline, while the

**Table 4.5    Distribution of the world population according to linguistic groups (LINGR)**

| Linguistic groups | 1900 (%) | 1950 (%) | 1980 (%) | 1990 (%) | 1997 (%) |
|---|---|---|---|---|---|
| Caucasian | 38.6 | 40.5 | 36.2 | 34.9 | 34.0 |
| Indian | 18.1 | 18.3 | 20.2 | 21.2 | 22.0 |
| Asian | 38.6 | 34.7 | 35.7 | 35.2 | 34.7 |
| African | 4.7 | 6.5 | 7.8 | 8.6 | 9.3 |

*Sources*: Classification of countries based on de Blij (1993, 1996); population figures from Encyclopaedia Britannica (1998) and Barrett (1982); see Appendix A.

Indo-Iranian and the Afro-Asiatic as well as the Niger-Congo families tend to have the highest rate of increase.

When identifying blocks of language groups, then it is obvious that one approach – race theory – has employed biological criteria. The scepticism against the employment of the race concept dates back to its usage within physical anthropology, where physical traits of people were used to classify people into various races, with certain characteristics being assumed to covary with racial categories. There are simply no empirical proofs for claims of any genetical, or racial, basis for superiority of one population over another (Cavalli-Sforza *et al.*, 1994, p. 20), but, it is feasible to classify the countries of the modern world into various language blocks and inquire into the outcomes of such blocks without any biological theory or racist bias.

For instance the effort to identify so-called human racial groups should be related to language families. The number of human racial groups is notably quite small and there is a considerable overlap between these groups and linguistic groups. Indeed, they tend to follow each other to a quite large extent, although they are not identical (cf. Cavalli-Sforza *et al.*, 1994, pp. 98–101). Following de Blij (1993, pp. 198–9, 1996, p. 195) we identify the following language groups: Caucasian, Indian, Asian and African. The Caucasian group overlaps with the European and the Iranian language groups, but it also includes people belonging to the Arabic language group. The Asian group covaries with the Sino-Tibetan and Austra-Asiatic language families, while the African group goes together with the Niger-Congo language family. Attempts to estimate the size of these language groups are reported in Table 4.5, again assuming that countries are classified in the same way in 1900 as in 1997.

The Asians and the Caucasians represent the two major linguistic groups in terms of population size. At the same time they display a relative decline in size over time, while the other two groups – that is, the Indian and the African

**Table 4.6    Distribution of the world population according to location (GEO)**

| Geographical linguistic groups | 1900 (%) | 1950 (%) | 1980 (%) | 1990 (%) | 1997 (%) |
|---|---|---|---|---|---|
| European | 30.0 | 29.0 | 22.0 | 19.7 | 18.2 |
| Indo-Iranian | 17.3 | 17.4 | 19.2 | 19.9 | 20.7 |
| Latin-American | 3.9 | 6.5 | 8.2 | 8.5 | 8.5 |
| Middle-Eastern | 3.0 | 3.7 | 4.5 | 5.0 | 5.5 |
| Asian | 41.5 | 37.5 | 39.2 | 39.1 | 38.7 |
| African | 4.2 | 5.8 | 7.0 | 7.8 | 8.4 |

*Sources*: Classification of countries groups based upon Barrett (1982); population figures from EB (1998) and Barrett (1982); see Appendix A.

groups – are on the rise. The classification in Table 4.5 appears less congenial for cultural analysis than the language family typology introduced above. One problem with Table 4.5 is the set called 'Caucasian' which is simply too heterogeneous on account of the fact that the Caucasian peoples cover several different cultures. Thus, Table 4.5 is less useful than Table 4.4 for the inquiry into the outcomes of peoples and their traditions. In fact, all linguistic groups are based on an excessive aggregation of peoples with different cultures or civilizations.

Now, from a macro point of view, linguistic groups may be classified in other ways. One could employ the term 'geographical linguistic group' in order to indicate that the linguistic group in question primarily has a geographical component, meaning location in space. In contrast to Table 4.5, in Table 4.6 the Caucasian group is collapsed into a European, Latin American and a Middle Eastern group while the Indian group is extended to cover an Indo-Iranian group. This system of classifying countries relies heavily on Barrett (1982, pp. 112–15), and the table displays the distribution of population into these groups over time.

The major geographical group in this classification is the Asian group, as it now includes both the Indian and the Chinese peoples. The Indo-Iranian group is increasing in size, while the European group in particular is declining sharply, from close to one-third around 1900 down to less than one-fifth 100 years later. The Middle Eastern group covers the Arabs, the Jews and the Turks. Table 4.6 may be said to contain a universal classification that is more congenial to ethnic analysis than Table 4.5, which is linked more closely to the old and discarded theory of an Indo-European race. It is difficult to see what Indians and Europeans have in common culturally. Yet, Table 4.6 also comprises very broad aggregates that include several different cultures such as, for instance, the Asian group. Broad geographical areas like Asia or Africa or Europe do have their counterparts in terms of broad linguistic groups or families.

The crux of the matter is now that geographical location and linguistic family are closely connected. Thus, ranking geographical language groups and language families into an ordinal scale, we find a very high degree of covariation (rho = .90), indicating that the macro-level ethnicity as language and ethnicity as geographical location go closely together. Mapping ethnicity as language, or language family, worldwide shows that one may arrive at interesting classifications of a grand-scale variation based on language families of various kinds. It may be measured in several ways and it is rather stable over time. The uses of language are certainly not constant over time since the beginning of large-scale human civilizations, but the pattern of usage in the early twentieth century is not that different from the pattern of usage of the late twentieth century. It now remains to be seen whether ethnicity conceived of as grand-scale language families might have an impact on political and socioeconomic development.

*Outcomes of Language Families*

We have arrived at macro classifications of the world's population based on language family. Now, we wish to connect these classifications with some of the main outcomes that the social sciences have focused on – affluence, democracy and social and gender equality. When inquiring into the world-wide impact of ethnicity as language family on these dependent variables we will proceed in two steps: first, we will consider the bivariate relations between the different ethnicity variables and the major dependent variables; and, second, we will attempt to estimate the overall impact of language when controlling for other relevant impact factors. It is a matter of language families and the various ways they may be measured.

We have two kinds of variable measuring ethnicity as language. On the one hand, we use the grouping of countries into language families and linguistic groups (that is, strictly nominal data) and, on the other hand, we use the frequency of the use of English as a first or as a second language (that is, interval-level data). Table 4.7 reports the findings from a one-way analysis of variance (eta squares) as well as correlation analysis (Pearson's r).

We observe that language group is related to several of the outcome variables, at least weakly. The chief finding is that, for countries where the European language family dominates, the rankings score higher than countries where other languages are in use. The low scores of African countries show up in all the correlations. This finding surfaces whatever the classification employed. Thus, the same distinctive pattern is not discernible among the different linguistic groups as, in general, the Chinese group ranks highest while the French or the Russian groups tend to rank lower. But, even here, the African crisis surfaces. As stated above, language family is the classification that appears to be most suited to grand-scale ethnicity analysis.

**Table 4.7   Impact of language group on political and socioeconomic variables: bivariate analysis**

|  |  | DEM97 | GDPCAP 90 | PPP1997 | HDI99 | GDI99 | GEM99 | GINI90 | CORR98 |
|---|---|---|---|---|---|---|---|---|---|
| LANGFAM | eta squared | .40 | .37 | .28 | .61 | .62 | .54 | .34 | .15 |
|  | sig. | .000 | .000 | .000 | .000 | .000 | .000 | .000 | .038 |
| LINGGRP | eta squared | .26 | .09 | .08 | .21 | .22 | .26 | .47 | .12 |
|  | sig. | .000 | .076 | .079 | .000 | .000 | .000 | .000 | .000 |
| ENG1 | r | .29 | .34 | .29 | .27 | .27 | .35 | -.06 | .38 |
|  | sig. | .000 | .000 | .000 | .001 | .001 | .000 | .320 | .000 |
| ENG2 | r | .20 | .22 | .22 | .13 | .18 | .26 | .04 | .33 |
|  | sig. | .006 | .007 | .003 | .062 | .014 | .000 | .386 | .001 |

*Note*: The LANGFAM variable is here treated as a nominal variable, but if recoded into an interval scale, the r coefficients come very close to the eta squared scores.

*Sources*: See Appendix A.

In general, the use of English as a first or a second language also seems to indicate modernity. Here one may ask what the use of English as a second language really stands for. Is it an indicator of modernization, of Western orientation or simply a trace of the old British colonialism? The use of the English language is the foremost expression of an acceptance of occidental values, which go together with political and socioeconomic development, even when controlling for a number of other relevant factors. English is also the instrument of communication in the period of globalization. We turn now to ethnicity as language groups in accordance with the classifications presented above. Both linguistic groups and geographical language groups are coded as nominal variables, and consequently here we will also employ a one-way analysis of variance as displayed in Table 4.8.

These two ethnicity variables covary with the dependent variables. But it is the geographical language group which shows a more distinct association than the linguistic language group. Countries classified as European tend to rank highest on performance indicators, to be followed by countries classified as Latin American and Asian while African countries rank low. What the findings in Table 4.8 clearly indicate is the advantage of the so-called occidentals, especially in relation to the peoples in the southern hemisphere with the exception of Oceania.

Countries where so-called Caucasians or Europeans constitute the dominant language group sometimes, but far from always, display more advanced political, economic and social results. The reverse side of the coin is that life in many countries where the other language groups (African, Indian, Asian) dominate is characterized by dictatorship, poverty and inequality. It is obvious that a single category, like the Caucasians, covers an immense variation of language groups and therefore contains many different countries. Ethnicity in its most extensive sense stands for families of languages, of which one may wish to count only five to ten. Such ethnic groups have little compactness, but they are not merely statistical aggregates. What we have called language families or language groups correspond to huge cultural traditions.

So far, we have considered the bivariate relationship between these huge ethnicity groups and the dependent variables that impact on the outcomes. The next step will be to investigate the impact of ethnicity when controlling for other kinds of variables. Can we still trace an impact from language family or geographical language group when controlling for the general impact of space and time? This step in the inquiry will be conducted with the help of regression analysis. Table 4.9 displays information about different attempts to estimate the impact of ethnicity (LANGFAM, GEO) on the dependent variables (DEM97, HDI99, and GEM99) when controlling for geography (DISEQU) and history (MODLEAD). It is important to remember that the variables LANGFAM and GEO are highly collinear and cannot be employed simultaneously in the regression analyses. Furthermore we have recoded these two variables into what could be called pseudo-interval scales:

**Table 4.8    Impact of language groups on political and socioeconomic variables: bivariate analysis**

|  |  | DEM97 | GDPCAP 90 | PPP1997 | HDI99 | GDI99 | GEM99 | GINI90 | CORR98 |
|---|---|---|---|---|---|---|---|---|---|
| GEO | eta sq. | .45 | .58 | .31 | .63 | .63 | .56 | .60 | .31 |
|  | sig. | .000 | .000 | .000 | .000 | .000 | .000 | .000 | .000 |
| LING | eta sq. | .12 | .23 | .18 | .51 | .48 | .16 | .31 | .10 |
|  | sig. | .000 | .076 | .079 | .000 | .000 | .002 | .000 | .042 |

*Note:*    The GEO variable is here treated as a nominal variable but, if recoded into an interval scale, the r coefficients come very close to the eta squared scores.

*Sources:* See Appendix A.

**Table 4.9    Overall impact of language groups on political and socioeconomic outcomes: regression analysis**

| Independent variables | | Dependent variables | | | | | |
|---|---|---|---|---|---|---|---|
| | | **HDI99** | **HDI99** | **DEM97** | **DEM97** | **GEM99** | **GEM99** |
| GEO | coeff | .003 | – | .017 | – | .001 | – |
| | t-stat | 6.50 | – | 1.67 | – | 2.51 | – |
| | tol | .36 | – | .38 | – | .41 | – |
| LANGFAM | coeff | – | .002 | – | .012 | – | .001 |
| | t-stat | – | 6.53 | – | 1.40 | – | 3.17 |
| | tol | – | .43 | – | .45 | – | .49 |
| MODLEAD | coeff | .000 | .000 | .021 | .021 | .001 | .000 |
| | t-stat | 2.80 | 2.50 | 3.27 | 3.32 | 2.91 | 2.49 |
| | tol | .35 | .33 | .38 | .37 | .37 | .36 |
| DISEQU | coeff | .109 | .202 | .996 | 1.67 | .142 | .191 |
| | t-stat | 1.48 | 2.86 | .52 | .91 | 1.58 | 2.22 |
| | tol | .47 | .51 | .47 | .52 | .56 | .58 |
| Constant | coeff | .433 | .428 | 2.09 | 2.08 | .231 | .223 |
| | t-stat | 24.31 | 23.86 | 4.49 | 4.41 | 8.70 | 8.45 |
| Adjrsq | | .65 | .65 | .30 | .30 | .51 | .53 |
| N | | 143 | 143 | 150 | 150 | 90 | 90 |

*Notes:*  coeff = the unstandardized regression coefficient.
t-stat = t-statistics. Used to test the significance of the regression coefficients; t-stat showing more than ± 2 indicates significance.
tol = tolerance. Used to measure the occurrence of multicollinearity in the model; if tol is higher than .3/.4 there is no danger for multicollinearity.

*Sources:* See Appendix A.

European and Western categories score high whereas the African ones score low (cf. the discussion in Shively, 1998, pp. 33–36, 121–22). As was noted in the notes to the Tables 4.7 and 4.8, such a recoding seems to capture the variation associated within the two variables, GEO and LANGFAM, quite well.

The clear findings in Table 4.9 inform us that macro ethnicity, as measured here by language family and geographical language group, go together with political, economic and social outcomes, even when one controls for other major macro factors. This is at least the case for human development (HDI99) and gender empowerment (GEM99), but it is not quite true for the level of democracy (DEM97). From these regression findings appears the enormous advantage of the so-called occidentals in terms of development. The word 'Occidental' is often employed in cultural analysis, although it has a distinct value bias. The material advantage of the occidentals is often criticised as 'Occidentalism', with the entailed argument that it is a matter of a colonial legacy or an expression of world-system capitalism. What one may observe is that one language family and one geographical language group displays a performance record that is better than that of the other categories, even when the impact of other broad factors is taken into account, especially in terms of the level of human development.

As a matter of fact, the control factors also have partial effects on socioeconomic development, which again strengthens the advance of the occidentals on outcomes. It is state longevity – time (MODLEAD) – as well as geographical location – space (DISEQU) – that each further increases the advantage of the Occidentals. The amount of explained variation in these models is high, especially for the level of human development, but it may well be argued that Table 4.9 simply comprises the well-known developmental gulf between the major parts of the world.

Here we have tried alternative ways of measuring grand-scale ethnicity by means of a few very comprehensive categories, which divide the world population, in different ways, into broad groups that correspond to races. Two classifications – language family and geographical language group – may be employed for the purposes of macro analysis, omitting entirely the concept of race with all its prejudices (Delgado and Stefancic, 1999; Sowell, 1995). We found that, when linguistic family or language groups in space are inquired into, there is ample evidence for a cultural effect. It is quite astonishing how strongly these two categories go together and are connected with macro outcomes. Here we observe the triumph of the so-called Europeans or occidentals, giving them a clear lead on so-called developmental indicators.

## Ethnic Cleavages and Ethnic Structure: Outcomes

Ethnic groups in action are perhaps the most substantial evidence one can have of the importance of ethnicity. When groups engage in collective action, they enter the political arena. Ethnic groups that have some degree of compactness may support political parties which identify with them and attempt to promote their interests by participation in elections. The dividing line between ethnic parties and nationalist parties is all but clear. Sometimes ethnic parties operate as separatist parties targeting a region in the country, while at other times they appeal to the whole country as nationalist parties.

When ethnicity is said to be a constitutive dimension of a society, then it is the distribution of the population onto different ethnic groups within that society which is crucial. This is the ethnic structure of society which may vary considerably. The most important aspect of ethnicity in a society relates to how people are distributed with respect to different ethnic groups as well as how they mobilize their ethnic identities in relation to other groups. The ethnic distribution of a society may be characterized as homogeneous or as heterogeneous. It has been argued that this is a crucial distinction which means that heterogeneity may have strong consequences for the outcomes that will occur in a society.

We will now analyse more compact ethnic groups than races and inquire into the efforts of ethnic groups to become politically important, either nationally or regionally. First, we look at ethnic fragmentation showing how it may be measured cross-sectionally and estimating its impact on macro-level outcomes. Second, we target the regional support for political parties and its ethnic correlates. Third, we inquire into the importance of ethnicity for individual behaviour. Again, we are more specifically searching for cultural effects, this time from ethnicity in its various expressions at different analytical levels.

## Ethnic Cleavages

The occurrence of ethnic cleavages depends first on the size, compactness and the number of ethnic groups that exist in a given country. Thus, the occurrence of latent ethnic cleavages is closely connected with ethnic fragmentation. The more numerous and the more compact these groups are, the more of a heterogeneous structure we may expect. Second, ethnic cleavages depend on the mobilization of these ethnic groups. And the more heterogeneous the ethnic structure is, the larger is the potential for the development of ethnic cleavages that take the form of political action. Ethnic groups existing side-by-side often confront each other and tend to mobilize their forces, which often gives rise to persisting patterns of conflict – that is, manifest cleavages.

When comparing countries worldwide there are a number of indicators available that, one way or another, may be used for mapping the variation in ethnic cleavages. We will here employ three indicators:

1  the number of language or ethnic groups;
2  the size of the dominating ethnic or language group; and
3  a measure of the fragmentation of the ethnic/linguistic structure, where high values stand for heterogeneity and low values for homogeneity.

When measuring more specifically ethnic fragmentation in a country, the link between ethnicity and language is very transparent. On the other hand, the indicators capturing diversity in ethnicity and language dominance tend to go together, illustrating that ethnic identity is in most countries closely linked with language. This means that we can choose, in principle, any one of these variables to map the variation in ethnic structure. Our choice is ELF1, which measures ethnolinguistic fragmentation worldwide around the mid-1990s, and we identify clusters of countries as being highly heterogeneous as well as highly homogeneous. Some of the countries belonging to these two clusters are presented in Table 4.10 in order to yield an indication as to which country is to count as fragmented or not.

It is obvious that many countries displaying a highly heterogeneous ethnic structure are to be found in Africa. The Philippines in the Far East is in fact

**Table 4.10   Clusters of ethnic heterogeneous and homogeneous
              countries (ELF1)**

| Heterogeneous | | Homogeneous | |
|---|---|---|---|
| Tanzania | Mozambique | Cuba | Japan |
| Uganda | Cote d'Ivoire | El Salvador | Madagascar |
| Zambia | South Africa | Haiti | Portugal |
| Liberia | Nigeria | Korea North | Bosnia and |
| Togo | Central African | Korea South | Herzegovina |
| Congo Democratic | Republic | Rwanda | Greece |
| Republic | Mali | Colombia | Hungary |
| Cameroon | Philippines | Egypt | Ireland |
| Kenya | Chad | | Somalia |

*Source*:  See Appendix A.

the only exception in this classification. Generally speaking, countries in
Africa have a higher potential for the development of ethnic cleavages than
may be found in other continents or parts of the world. Two alternative
hypotheses explaining so much fragmentation in Africa may be suggested.
Either it reflects the tribal nature of these societies, or colonialism willingly or
unwillingly reinforced ethnic cleavages. It is tempting to predict political and
social instability as a consequence of ethnic fragmentation (Horowitz, 1985,
2001). But far from all ethnically heterogeneous societies display the typical
signs of political or social instability. Perhaps there is something in addition
to ethnic fragmentation that is conducive to tribal conflict in Africa – for
example, perhaps poverty.

Second, there are a few countries listed as homogeneous in Table 4.10 that
are not usually regarded as such – namely, Rwanda, Bosnia and Herzegovina
and Somalia. It is important to note that, in these countries, language *per se*
is not the criterion of ethnic differentiation but rather the confrontation
between highly compact communities identified either by race (in Rwanda,
Hutu versus Tutsi), religion (in Bosnia and Herzegovina, Muslims versus
orthodox) or tribal attributes (in Somalia, clans against each other). Thus, an
indicator on linguistic diversity may not always be able to capture all aspects
of ethnic diversity.

Ethnicity theory does entail the prediction that when there are several
ethnic groups in a society that tend to be compact, ethnicity has major political
consequences (cf. Allardt, 1980; Jalali and Lipset, 1993; Gurr and Harff,
1994; Vanhanen, 1999; Annett, 2000). In the cleavage theory developed
by Stein Rokkan and his followers, ethnic cleavage is one of the three
fundamental organizing principles in the modern society (Flora and Kuhnle,
1999). However malleable ethnic identity may be or however imagined ethnic
communities may be, when compact ethnic groups collide, then what is really

at stake is the stability of society and the polity this cleavage theory claims (Horowitz, 1985, 2001). How about the empirical evidence?

Inquiring into the impact of ethnic cleavages on social, economic and political outcomes, we will look at how variables measuring dominance of ethnic groups (DOMEG), linguistic groups (DOMLG2) and ethnolinguistic fragmentation (ELF1) covary with a set of macro outcomes. According to ethnicity theory, a high level of ethnic fragmentation should have a negative impact upon macro outcomes, holding other factors constant. Ethnic cleavages create dissensus in society, which harms economic affluence as well as democratic stability. Often ethnic differences reinforce social inequalities. We must remember, when testing these hypotheses, that it is not only the case that African countries to a large extent belong to the set of highly fragmented countries, but the opposite also holds – that is, homogeneous countries are to be found outside Africa.

Table 4.11 reports a correlation analysis between the various ways in which ethnic diversity may occur and variables measuring outcomes. Is ethnic fragmentation theory corroborated in the findings in Table 4.11 concerning the connections between a few major outcomes and the ethnic fragmentation indices? This is most probably the case. We must ask whether there could be an African effect hidden in these correlations.

The correlations tell us that the more homogeneous a society tends to be in terms of ethnicity, the better the society will perform in terms of political and socioeconomic outcomes. But we should be aware of the fact that the ranking of the African countries is very important for the direction and strength of the coefficients. Table 4.11 thus expresses the 'African problem'; in other words, when a characteristic is chosen that covers many African countries, then it will display a negative impact on several outcomes (cf. Easterly and Levine, 1997). Yet, ethnic cleavages, measured in the form of fragmentation or in terms of language domination, have a negative impact on the level of human development in particular.

*Ethnic Structure: Regions and Party Support*

In order to understand the impact of ethnicity on politics, we will take a closer look at six countries where ethnicity has been highly visible, studying the impact of ethnicity on politics in parliamentary or presidential systems. When the regional support for parties and candidates varies heavily, is there an ethnic effect at work? The six countries chosen – the USA, Russia, Spain, Switzerland, Belgium and India – will be investigated in a similar fashion: we map the regional variation in ethnicity within each country, examine the bivariate relations between ethnicity and support for political parties or candidates regionally and, finally, test any ethnicity impact by controlling for other factors.

**Table 4.11   Impact of language on political and socioeconomic variables: correlation analysis**

|  |  | DEM97 | GDPCAP 90 | PPP1997 | HDI99 | GDI99 | GEM99 | GINI90 | CORR98 |
|---|---|---|---|---|---|---|---|---|---|
| DOMEG | r | .22 | .36 | .31 | .48 | .46 | .28 | -.43 | .40 |
|  | sig. | .004 | .000 | .000 | .000 | .000 | .004 | .320 | .000 |
| DOMLG2 | r | .25 | .39 | .37 | .55 | .57 | .42 | -.29 | .37 |
|  | sig. | .001 | .000 | .000 | .000 | .000 | .000 | .011 | .000 |
| ELF1 | r | -.26 | -.34 | -.31 | -.52 | -.55 | -.40 | .23 | -.32 |
|  | sig. | .001 | .000 | .000 | .000 | .000 | .000 | .037 | .001 |

*Sources*: See Appendix A.

*Ethnicity matters in the USA*  Since the first major analysis of the USA was published in the form of Tocqueville's *Democracy in America I–II* in 1835–40, the USA been regarded as a multi-ethnic country. The *Ethnologue* (13th edition) identifies 176 living languages in the late twentieth century. The *Harvard Encyclopaedia of American Ethnicity* recognizes some 100 ethnic groups. However, here we will focus on race and language as the major indicators of ethnicity (Glazer and Moyniham, 1975). In official American population statistics, race is one distinguishing criterion differentiating between whites, blacks, American Indians and Asians. Furthermore, among the whites, a language distinction between Hispanics and non-Hispanics is employed. These five groups are the large ethnic groups we account for and their distribution throughout the states constitutes the basis for our estimate of ethnic fragmentation on the regional level in the USA (ELF94).

In defining ethnicity in this region-based way, we may note a distinctive variation between the various states. On the one hand, we have highly fragmented states such as California, New Mexico and Texas as well as the District of Columbia, although these states differ with respect to the presence of a large number of Hispanics or blacks. The most homogeneous states are to be found in the New England constituting a region where the proportion of whites exceeds 95 per cent, as in states such as New Hampshire, Vermont and Maine. This means that there is a very high negative correlation between the index of ethnic fragmentation and the proportion of whites living in a state ($r = -.89$ or $-.92$, depending upon whether Washington DC is included or not). It appears that states in the USA differ immensely in homogeneity–heterogeneity and that a few states are truly fragmented (see Table 4.12).

When there is such an immense variation in ethnic heterogeneity or homogeneity between states in a country, one expects an impact of ethnicity on politics. States which are homogeneous should display a different profile from states that are heterogeneous. The proportion of whites, blacks or Hispanics in a state condition political orientations political traditions influencing election results. Since Washington DC is exceptional in a few respects (an outlier) we will estimate the correlation coefficients for two samples, one where Washington DC is included, and one where it is excluded. The standard picture of American politics includes a strong ethnic component: the white Anglo-Saxon majority votes predominantly Republican, whereas the many minorities vote for the Democrats (Miller and Shanks, 1996). Do we find the same pattern if we turn to regression analysis introducing two control variables – namely, the variation in gross state product per capita (GSPC94) and the level of unemployment as of the mid-1990s (UNEM96)? Consider Table 4.13.

The findings indicate that there is more than one ethnic factor behind the regional voting pattern. Ethnicity is almost as relevant as economic factors for the variation in party strength. When ethnicity is operationalized with several indicators, then it is relevant in more than one way for the American elections

**Table 4.12   Ethnic fragmentation in the USA in the 1990s: ranking of states**

| State | ELF94 | WHITE94 | HISP94 | BLACK94 |
|---|---|---|---|---|
| **High Fragmentation** | | | | |
| California | 62.4 | 53.6 | 26.6 | 7.7 |
| New Mexico | 60.2 | 49.9 | 37.5 | 2.4 |
| Texas | 57.1 | 58.6 | 26.5 | 12.2 |
| District of Columbia | 50.8 | 27.7 | 4.8 | 64.2 |
| New York | 50.6 | 67.1 | 10.4 | 17.5 |
| Hawaii | 50.4 | 30.1 | 3.4 | 2.5 |
| Louisiana | 48.0 | 64.8 | 2.0 | 31.6 |
| Mississippi | 47.9 | 62.6 | 0.6 | 35.9 |
| Maryland | 47.7 | 67.2 | 2.6 | 26.4 |
| Arizona | 46.9 | 70.0 | 18.9 | 3.4 |
| **Low fragmentation** | | | | |
| Maine | 4.0 | 98.0 | 0.6 | 0.4 |
| Vermont | 4.1 | 97.9 | 0.7 | 0.3 |
| New Hampshire | 5.5 | 97.2 | 1.1 | 0.6 |
| West Virginia | 8.2 | 95.8 | 0.4 | 3.2 |
| Iowa | 9.0 | 95.3 | 1.4 | 1.9 |
| North Dakota | 11.7 | 93.9 | 0.6 | 0.6 |
| Minnesota | 14.1 | 92.6 | 1.3 | 2.7 |
| Idaho | 15.4 | 91.8 | 5.4 | 0.4 |
| Montana | 15.5 | 91.7 | 1.4 | 0.4 |
| Kentucky | 15.7 | 91.6 | 0.6 | 7.1 |

*Sources*: See Appendix B.

in terms of the regional outcomes of the major parties. Perhaps because the poor vote in theses states is solid, the very rich states go to the Democrats, whose support also depends on the level of unemployment as well as the number of blacks. Interestingly, the Republican vote seems to be higher in states with ethnic fragmentation, ethnic diversity pushing up the vote for the party that is least favourable to the minorities.

*Ethnic diversity in Russia: the heartlands*   Ethnicity in Russia entirely refers to the use of language, as Russia is a multi-ethnic nation with nearly 100 living languages. The principal and dominating language is Russian, estimates suggesting that 86 per cent of the population speaks this language. In comparison, all other languages are minor and the languages which are

**Table 4.13   Ethnicity and party strength at state level in the USA:
regression analysis**

| Independent variables | | DEM96 (1) | DEM96 (2) | REP96 (1) | REP96 (1) | REP96 (2) | REP96 (2) |
|---|---|---|---|---|---|---|---|
| ELF94 | coeff | -.127 | -.139 | .281 | .179 | .339 | .188 |
| | t-stat | -1.64 | -1.48 | 2.08 | 2.61 | 2.21 | 2.59 |
| BLACK94 | coeff | .180 | .197 | – | – | – | – |
| | t-stat | 1.76 | 1.56 | – | – | – | – |
| WHITE94 | coeff | – | – | .140 | – | .192 | – |
| | tstat | – | – | .88 | – | 1.11 | – |
| GSPC94 | coeff | .000 | .000 | -.000 | -.000 | -.000 | -.000 |
| | t-stat | 3.25 | 1.85 | -3.39 | -4.68 | -2.58 | -2.56 |
| UNEM96 | coeff | 2.569 | 2.652 | -2.557 | -2.783 | -2.72 | -2.90 |
| | t-stat | 2.90 | 2.75 | -2.77 | -3.14 | -2.86 | -3.10 |
| Constant | coeff | 26.400 | 25.05 | 46.09 | 63.06 | 44.44 | 65.46 |
| | t-stat | 6.17 | 3.40 | 2.33 | 15.43 | 2.25 | 9.37 |
| Adjrsq | | .46 | .13 | .43 | .43 | .19 | .19 |
| N | | 51 | 50 | 51 | 51 | 50 | 50 |

*Notes:*    (1) refers to models where Washington DC is included while (2) refers to models
where Washington DC is excluded.
coeff = the unstandardized regression coefficient.
t-stat = t-statistics. Used to test the significance of the regression coefficients; t-stat
showing more than ± 2 indicates significance.
*Sources:* See Appendix B.

spoken by more than 1 million people include Tatar, Ukrainian and Chuvash.
Given the predominance of the Russian language, we may expect the
existence of an ethnic structure with a large number of regions being more or
less homogeneously Russian-speaking while a few others might be highly
fragmented. In order to map the variation in Russia, for each of the regions, we
have computed an ethnic fragmentation index (ELFINDEX), which is based
on the number of speakers of different languages, as well as the proportion of
Russian speakers for each region. Table 4.14 presents an overview of the
Russian regions with the most heterogeneous and the most homogeneous
ethnic structures.

The homogeneous regions are to be found mainly in the central regions
of Russia, situated in the European part of the country. The ethnically
heterogeneous regions are situated in the more peripheral parts of Russia,
such as the Caucasus regions, or in the Asian parts. A few of these regions
have become well known for their ongoing armed conflicts (for example,
Dagestan, North-Ossetia and Chechen and Ingush), but the issue that we

**Table 4.14  Ethnic structure in Russia: ranking of regions in terms of homogeneity/heterogeneity (ELFINDEX)**

| Homogeneous regions | Heterogeneous regions |
| --- | --- |
| Liepitsk | Dagestan |
| Tambov | Bashkortostan |
| Kursk | Karachai-Cherkess |
| Orel | Kabardino-Balkarian |
| Kostroma | Kalmyk |
| Vologda | North-Ossetian |
| Yaroslavl | Yakutsk-Sakha |
| Bryansk | Yamolo Nemets |
| Ivanovo | Chechen and Ingush |
| Ryazan | Komi |

*Source*:  See Appendix B.

will focus on here is whether ethnicity has an impact on party politics in Russia.

The regional ethnic pattern is inherited from the past, reflecting the historical evolution of the country. Ethnicity has been a part of Russian history since a Russian identity emerged around 1000 years ago. Our two measures on ethnicity – the ethnolinguistic fragmentation index and the proportion of the Russian-speaking population – are strongly and negatively related with each other ($r = -.91$). Russian history circles around the expansion of its Russian-speaking core towards the ethnically mixed peripheries. We expect ethnicity to have an impact on the variation in the vote for the liberal Yabloko bloc and the Russian Communist Party. Let us turn to the data and see if an ethnicity hypothesis, in which ethnic homogeneity would favour the liberal party, meets with any support. Correlating party support and ethnicity, we find that the support for the Russian Communist Party in 1995 was apparently not affected by ethnicity. The Yabloko bloc, on the other hand, was stronger in 1995 in regions where the Russian speakers were more numerous and weaker in regions where the ethnic structure was more heterogeneous. Does this relation also hold when the impact of other factors is controlled for?

The findings in Table 4.15 indicate a noticeable ethnic effect in the outcomes for the liberal party. The Communist Party did better in regions which are relatively poorer, while the opposite tends to be the case for the Yabloko bloc. The Russian-speaking variable has a distinctive effect on the Yabloko bloc, mirroring the relative strength of this party in areas like Moscow and St Petersburg which have constituted the heartlands of Russian identity and nationalism. It was from here that Russia started to expand in various directions under the Tsars and the Bolsheviks.

**Table 4.15   Impact of ethnicity on party strength at regional level in Russia: regression analysis**

| Independent variables | | Dependent variables | |
| --- | --- | --- | --- |
| | | CP95 | YAB95 |
| ELFINDEX | coeff | −1.233 | – |
| | t-stat | −.25 | – |
| RUSSIAN | coeff | – | .060 |
| | t-stat | – | 3.27 |
| GRPCAP | coeff | −.693 | .169 |
| | t-stat | −3.20 | 1.96 |
| FEMEXP | coeff | – | −.194 |
| | t-stat | – | −1.26 |
| MALEXP | coeff | 1.345 | – |
| | t-stat | 3.40 | – |
| Constant | coeff | −48.529 | 13.322 |
| | t-stat | −2.09 | 1.17 |
| Adjrsq | | .26 | .19 |
| N | | 76 | 76 |

*Notes*:   coeff = the unstandardized regression coefficient.
t-stat = t-statistics. Used to test the significance of the regression coefficients; t-stat showing more than ± 2 indicates significance.
*Sources*: See Appendix B.

*Spain: ethnicity matters strongly*   In heterogeneous Spain there are now some 14 living languages of which Spanish is the major one. Besides the Spanish language (Castilian) the set of major languages comprises Catalan, Galician and Basque (Euskera).

We have no data indicating the use of different languages in the Spanish provinces, so it is not possible to arrive at any measure of ethnic fragmentation at the provincial level. Instead, we have to rely on indicators measuring the presence (or absence) of regional attachments at this level, as they have been estimated from survey research. The data we report on here mainly dates from the late 1970s. In general, these data on sentiments on national unity (NATUN78) as well as its inverse – that is, regional attachments (REGION76, REGION95) – tend to covary, but it is obvious that these attitudes are not exactly identical. Those regions displaying a high degree of regional attachment have been given more institutional autonomy (INSTAUTO) during the regional reforms implemented in Spain in the late 1980s (Heywood, 1995).

More regional attachment and fewer sentiments of national unity are to be found in the provinces of the Basque countries, Catalonia and Galicia, while more national unity and fewer regional attachments characterize Castilia,

**Table 4.16   Impact of ethnicity on party strength at the provincial level in Spain: regression analyses**

| Independent variables | | Dependent variables | |
|---|---|---|---|
| | | PSOE96 | REG96 |
| NATUN78 | coeff | .234 | – |
| | t-stat | 3.90 | – |
| | tol | .59 | – |
| REGION76 | coeff | – | .218 |
| | t-stat | – | 2.61 |
| | tol | – | .72 |
| INSTAUTO | coeff | 3.347 | 11.142 |
| | t-stat | 1.91 | 3.80 |
| | tol | .76 | .73 |
| REGINC95 | coeff | −.004 | .019 |
| | t-stat | −1.54 | 5.69 |
| | tol | .74 | .97 |
| Constant | coeff | 28.94 | −38.653 |
| | t-stat | 4.44 | −6.10 |
| Adjrsq | | .37 | .63 |
| N | | 50 | 50 |

*Notes*:   coeff = the unstandardized regression coefficient.
t-stat = t-statistics. Used to test the significance of the regression coefficients; t-stat showing more than ± 2 indicates significance.
tol = tolerance. Used to measure the occurrence of multicollinearity in the model; if tol is higher than .3/.4 there is no risk of multicollinearity.
*Sources*: See Appendix B.

La Mancha and Extremadura – that is, the central parts of Spain. The regional issue has been politicized openly in Spain since the fall of General Franco, and ethnicity has been conducive to the formation of regionalist parties. Yet, ethnicity may also affect national political forces as with large parties, such as the social democrats, operating at the national level as well.

Support for regionalist parties (REG96) is associated with ethnicity as regionalist attachments, whereas the vote for the Partido Socialista Obrero Español (PSOE) has almost the opposite source – that is, the PSOE is strong where the population has fewer regional attachments and more sentiments of national unity as they were expressed in the 1970s. The findings of the regression analyses are portrayed in Table 4.16, indicating that ethnicity has an undeniable impact on Spanish politics.

These findings hold also when we control for the effect of the variation in the distribution of regional wealth (REGINC95). The control variables introduced in the regression analyses capture the relative wealth of the various provinces of Spain.

The ethnicity effect is particularly evident in the case of the support for regionalist parties, but the support for the PSOE also depends on ethnicity. The impact of the control variables indicates that the regionalist parties are to be found in the wealthier parts of Spain, while the PSOE in the 1990s has its strongest support in the poorer regions of the country. What is revealed here is the typical postmodernist image of ethnicity and politics, in wealthy regions where people search for ethnic identity.

*Switzerland: ethnic fragmentation but no ethnic impact*    It is not the number of languages used that account for the occurrence or importance of cleavages but the compactness of the groups engaging in action. The *Ethnologue* (Grimes, 1999) lists ten living languages, but in Swiss everyday life the main languages are only German, French and Italian. Räto-Romansch is only spoken in one canton – Graubünden – and even there only by a minority. In addition there is also a great number of languages spoken by many of the immigrants living in Switzerland. The historical evolution of the Swiss Federation has resulted in Switzerland displaying a high degree of ethnic fragmentation following language lines, but does ethnicity matter politically?

The distribution on to the population of these four major languages forms the basis for our computation of an ethnolinguistic index for the Swiss cantons (ELF90). As this index captures both the number of languages in a canton and the size of the language groups, it is obvious that the canton with the lowest number for a dominating language group has the highest score on the ethnolinguistic index. With the exception of Jura, all other cantons where French is the dominating language come out as the most fragmented cantons. The ethnically most homogeneous cantons are to be found among the German-speaking cantons including Uri, Nidwalden, Obwalden, Appenzell I-R. The ethnically heterogeneous cantons include Valais, Fribourg, Graubünden, Genève and Vaud. The internal fragmentation in these cantons partly explains why the so-called Swiss Romand has never mobilized any ethnic separatism. Switzerland as a country scores high on an ethnic fragmentation index, but most of the cantons are ethnically homogeneous. Even cantons that are ethnically diversified cannot be strictly classified as highly heterogeneous. Could this fact partly explain the almost complete absence of any nationwide politicization of the ethnic issue in Switzerland?

Let us first look into the bivariate relations between ethnic structure and the support for two of the major political parties in Switzerland at the 1995 parliamentary election – the Social Democrats (SPS) and the Christian Democrats (CVP). This analysis is based on the cantons where proportional election is employed; on this basis, five cantons are excluded – Glarus, Appenzell I-R, Obwalden, Nidwalden and Uri. From the correlations we note that the SPS, as well as the CVP, are only weakly connected with ethnicity. For the SPS there is a positive but not significant correlation in relation to French-speaking cantons (FRE90) while the CVP tends to be weaker in cantons where so-called speakers of other languages (OTH90) tend to be more numerous. When we introduce a control variable capturing a variation in wealth among the Swiss cantons (VOLKS90), then this negative finding remains. From the regression analyses conducted we conclude that ethnicity has no impact whatsoever on the support for the SPS. The picture is slightly different for the CVP where the coefficient for other languages (OTH90) is significantly negative. Thus, the Christian Democrats are weak in niches where foreigners are numerous.

Ethnicity, as it occurs at the regional level in Switzerland only has a marginal impact on the variation in support for political parties, especially when compared to Spain. Other factors are more important in the Swiss context for understanding the regional variation in party support. We may conclude that ethnic fragmentation does not automatically translate into ethnic politics. The extremely high level of affluence in Switzerland softens ethnic tensions, we suggest – although, as will be seen below, this is not necessarily so in Belgium.

*Belgium: an ethnic undercurrent*   Ethnicity in Belgium may be associated with language – Flemish-speaking or French-speaking – or citizenship – Belgian citizenship or foreign citizenship (Leton and Miroir, 1999). Data on the distribution of the population at the regional level, according to their use of language, has not been collected at the regional level since the immediate post-Second World War period, due no doubt to the sensitivity of the issue. The distribution changed only marginally from the early to the mid-twentieth century, and there are reasons to believe that no major changes have occurred in this respect in the late twentieth century. Here we rely on data on language distribution from 1947, and even from 1910, to capture this dimension of ethnicity in Belgium, although the data is old. The Flemish-speaking population tends to be particularly strong in Turnhout and St Nicholas but less so in Audenard, Ypres and Courtrai. The region of Brussels is fully heterogeneous. The French-speaking population is strongest in Neufchatel, Dinant and Namur. Foreign citizens are most numerous in Brussels and they have a stronger standing in the Walloon regions than in the Flemish regions, as in the mid-1990s their relative strength was most pronounced in Charleroi, Liège and Mons.

A correlation analysis indicates a connection between the support for the ethnic (ETHNP91) and christian democratic parties (PSCCVP 91) and a number of indicators on ethnicity. The ethnic parties in Belgium are primarily the Flemish parties, but it is also evident that the Christian Democrats have a stronger standing in the Flemish regions than in the Walloon regions. Table 4.17 shows that this impact of ethnicity is still there when controlling for other structural factors in Belgian society.

When controlling for other factors we still find that ethnicity has a major impact, especially for the Flemish parties in Belgium. Ethnic diversity

**Table 4.17    Ethnicity and party support in Belgium: regression analysis**

| Independent variables | | Dependent variables | |
|---|---|---|---|
| | | ETHNP91 | PSCCVP91 |
| FOREIGN81 | coeff | .324 | −.668 |
| | t-stat | 2.52 | −4.02 |
| | tol | .59 | .98 |
| FLEM47 | coeff | .231 | − |
| | t-stat | 10.31 | − |
| | tol | .48 | − |
| ETHNFRA10 | coeff | − | .162 |
| | t-stat | − | 1.86 |
| | tol | − | .66 |
| REGECPRO95 | coeff | .014 | −.010 |
| | t-stat | 3.45 | −1.34 |
| | tol | .78 | .65 |
| Constant | coeff | −10.70 | 32.90 |
| | t-stat | −3.98 | 7.37 |
| Adjrsq | | .89 | .35 |
| N | | 30 | 30 |

*Notes*:    coeff = the unstandardized regression coefficient.
　　　　t-stat = t-statistics. Used to test the significance of the regression coefficients; t-stat showing more than ± 2 indicates significance.
　　　　tol = tolerance. Used to measure the occurrence of multicollinearity in the model; if tol is higher than .3/.4 there is no risk of multicollinearity.
*Sources*: See Appendix B.

(ETHNFRA10) has a negative impact on the christian democratic parties, as their votes decline when there is a large presence of foreign citizens (FOREIGN81). In the Belgium case one may draw the conclusion that ethnicity matter.

*India: ethnicity on a giant scale*    From a global perspective India is the most heterogeneous countries in the world with respect to ethnicity. The number of languages used in India numbers 400, but the official national languages constitute 15 plus English as an associate official language. In fact, the differences between some of the major languages are so radical that English must be employed. The principal language used is Hindi and, if second language users are included, Hindi speakers make up around 50 per cent of the Indian population. Other major languages include Tamil and Bengal. Ethnicity understood as the use of language forms a major cleavage in Indian society: is there, then, evidence of an ethnic impact on the party election outcomes?

Ethnicity may be captured by two variables, the proportion of the population using the Hindi language (HINDI91) and the proportion of the population using the major language of the respective state MAJLAN91), both indices indicating the degree of homogeneity. According to the 1991 census the highest proportions of Hindi-speakers are to be found in Harayana, Uttar Pradesh, Rajastan and Himachal Pradesh – that is, the north-western part of India. Together with Kerala, Punjab and Gujarat they constitute the linguistically most homogeneous states. The more heterogeneous ones include states in the north-east such as Arrunchal Pradesh and Nagaland. Is there an ethnic effect? I other words, do these ethnic cleavages matter for the variation in support for the two major political parties in Indian politics, the Bharatiya Janata Paraty (BJP96) and the Congress Party (INC96)?

A correlation analysis suggests that the use of the Hindi language constitutes a major cleavage. The BJP party is stronger in states where the proportion of Hindi speakers is higher, whereas the reverse applies to the support for the Indian Congress Party. The regression analyses displayed in Table 4.18 below test whether this relationship is still valid when we control for the effect of other structural factors such as urbanization (URBAN91) or the position of women in society as it is expressed by the sex ratio for men and women in the Indian states (SEXRAT91).

We find that the language cleavage is very important for explaining the variation in support for the BJP, even when controlling for other factors. Yet, the support for the Indian Congress Party is no longer equally significantly negatively related to the proportion of the Hindi-speaking population. In the Indian case we may conclude that ethnicity understood as the use of language (Hindi) matters for the regional-level variation in party support, especially the support for the BJP. Thus, ethnicity clearly matters for the main nationalist party.

*Summary*   The analyses undertaken here at the regional level confirm the thesis about the importance of ethnicity. Ethnicity is relevant as an important explanatory factor for the understanding of the operation of political forces at this level of aggregation, in a few countries strongly so. In Spain, as well as in Belgium and in India, ethnicity has a clear political impact. Ethnicity in the USA, Russia and Switzerland does not have the same impact on regional outcomes, however. In fact, what we find is that ethnicity works itself out in various ways when the ethnic structure of a country impacts on its politics. In some countries it is ethnic fragmentation itself that matters whereas in other countries it is the strength of a special ethnic group that matters. Finally, ethnic diversity is important not only for the parties that appeal directly to a special ethnic group, as we have also found that the electoral fortunes of national parties depend on the ethnic structure.

**Table 4.18   Ethnicity and party support in India: regression analysis**

| Independent variables | | Dependent variables | |
|---|---|---|---|
| | | **BJP96** | **INC96** |
| HINDI91 | coeff | .267 | −.124 |
| | t-stat | 4.98 | −1.81 |
| | tol | .77 | .44 |
| MAJLAN91 | coeff | −.164 | − |
| | t-stat | −.70 | − |
| | tol | .88 | − |
| URBAN91 | coeff | .410 | .188 |
| | t-stat | 2.10 | .96 |
| | tol | .86 | .80 |
| SEXRAT91 | coeff | − | .068 |
| | t-stat | − | 1.02 |
| | tol | − | .50 |
| Constant | coeff | 15.287 | −34.95 |
| | t-stat | .78 | −.53 |
| Adjrsq | | .43 | .33 |
| N | | 32 | 32 |

*Notes*:  Data is weighted by population due to the large variation in population size between the various Indian states and union territories.
coeff = the unstandardized regression coefficient.
t-stat = t-statistics. Used to test the significance of the regression coefficients; t-stat showing more than ± 2 indicates significance.
tol = tolerance. Used to measure the occurrence of multicollinearity in the model; if tol is higher than .3/.4 there is no risk of multicollinearity.
*Sources*: See Appendix B.

## Ethnicity and Everyday Life

When inquiring into the importance of ethnicity for individual behaviour, we rely on all three waves of the World Values Survey data set from 1980 to 1995 (Inglehart *et al.*, 2000). Ethnicity may stand for race or ethnic group as well as referring to the use of language. Data are available for the USA (ethnic group = V233 = white), regional location for Belgium (region = V234 = Flemish) and for Spain, Switzerland, India and Russia (use of language = V209 = Spanish, German, Hindi and Russian). Ethnicity may also be measured with a proxy for national sentiments such as national pride, where the question is asked if a person is proud to be of the nationality in question according to a four-grade scale (V205). As control variables we employ the respondent's income, educational level, age and gender.

**Table 4.19   National pride by regions of the world as aggregated percentages**

| Region | NATPR80 | | NATPR90 | | NATPR95 | | NATPR9095 | |
|---|---|---|---|---|---|---|---|---|
| OECD | 43.4 | (16) | 45.6 | (20) | 50.5 | (11) | 47.4 | (21) |
| Latin America | 57.1 | ( 2) | 57.0 | ( 4) | 73.4 | ( 9) | 72.1 | ( 9) |
| Africa | 41.4 | ( 1) | 68.7 | ( 2) | 81.5 | ( 3) | 79.3 | ( 3) |
| Asia | 48.7 | ( 1) | 50.9 | ( 3) | 60.8 | ( 6) | 58.4 | ( 7) |
| Postcommunist countries | 68.0 | ( 1) | 41.5 | (12) | 44.4 | (16) | 44.1 | (20) |
| Total | 46.1 | (21) | 47.0 | (41) | 56.4 | (45) | 52.9 | (60) |
| eta squared | .14 | | .20 | | .33 | | .33 | |
| sig. | .651 | | .089 | | .003 | | .000 | |

*Sources*: See Appendices A and C.


*National Pride*

Let us first take a look national pride worldwide. Table 4.19 has information about the percentages who agree that they are very proud of their national identity.

If we take national pride as a proxy for nationalism, we then find that national pride is stronger in the Third World than in the First World, and that it is weaker in the postcommunist regions than in the OECD area. National pride is especially strong in Latin America and Africa.

What is the impact of ethnicity on the five outcome variables that we have identified in Chapter 2: life satisfaction, left–right orientation, interest in politics, membership of voluntary organizations and the propensity to join boycotts? The analyses are presented for eight different sets of data – the six countries selected from the WVS data set (that is, Belgium, Spain, the USA, Switzerland, India and Russia), the aggregates for these six countries and the total sample.

Thus, ethnicity is here national pride as well as ethnic identification or the use of a language. In our sample of countries national pride is highest in the USA (77.4 per cent very proud) and India (68.6 per cent) while people are more lukewarm about nationalism in Switzerland (31.7 per cent), Russia (29.3 per cent) and Belgium (28.3 per cent) with Spain lying somewhere in between (64.3 per cent). The Flemish dominates in the Belgian sample (62.1 per cent) and this is also true for the white ethnic group in the USA (84.6 per cent). We have identified the following major language groups: Hindi speakers in India (52.4 per cent), German speakers in Switzerland (69.0 per cent), Spanish speakers in Spain (83.5 per cent) and Russian speakers in Russia (93.2 per cent).

**Table 4.20 Ethnicity and life satisfaction: regression analysis**

| Indep variable | Coeff | Dependent variable: life satisfaction | | | | | | | |
|---|---|---|---|---|---|---|---|---|---|
| | | Total | Six | Belgium | Spain | USA | Switz. | India | Russia |
| National pride | coeff | .139 | .167 | .079 | .133 | .208 | .098 | .269 | .037 |
| | t-stat | 49.13 | 22.14 | 4.96 | 3.68 | 9.96 | 5.39 | 7.35 | 1.40 |
| Ethnicity* | coeff | – | – | .030 | .025 | .028 | .078 | –.013 | .006 |
| | t-stat | – | – | 3.24 | 1.11 | 2.80 | 6.91 | –.78 | .18 |
| Education | coeff | –.014 | .049 | .001 | .030 | .075 | –.003 | .216 | .007 |
| | t-stat | –4.98 | 6.36 | .04 | .76 | 4.67 | –.08 | 6.58 | .18 |
| Income | coeff | .177 | .164 | .113 | .166 | .049 | .112 | .141 | .247 |
| | t-stat | 56.14 | 19.07 | 5.70 | 3.26 | 3.96 | 6.04 | 3.21 | 7.29 |
| Gender | coeff | –.035 | –.009 | –.014 | .019 | –.001 | .006 | .027 | –.009 |
| | t-stat | –2.27 | –2.25 | –1.62 | 1.16 | –.08 | .61 | 1.63 | –.58 |
| Age | coeff | –.020 | .002 | .002 | –.044 | .048 | .040 | .101 | –.074 |
| | t-stat | –7.94 | .33 | .13 | –1.61 | 4.69 | 2.47 | 3.02 | –2.72 |
| Constant | coeff | .499 | .446 | .627 | .457 | .448 | .606 | .241 | .329 |
| | t-stat | 137.39 | 49.95 | 28.60 | 9.61 | 17.43 | 23.11 | 6.20 | 6.87 |
| Adjrsq | | .056 | .083 | .038 | .042 | .058 | .096 | .136 | .075 |
| N | | 93920 | 11670 | 1674 | 606 | 2892 | 1111 | 924 | 985 |

*Notes:* * Ethnicity is measured in the following way in the models estimated for the different countries: Belgium: Flemish; Spain: Spanish-speaking; USA: white; Switzerland: German-speaking; India: Hindi-speaking; and Russia: Russian-speaking.
coeff = the unstandardized regression coefficient.
t-stat = t-statistics. Used to test the significance of the regression coefficients; t-stat showing more than ± 2 indicates significance.

*Sources:* See Appendix C.

## Life Satisfaction

Life satisfaction is analysed in Table 4.20, where two findings appear – namely that life satisfaction is conditioned by both national pride and material well-being.

The positive connection between life satisfaction and national pride is an ethnicity effect. The expected finding is that income also contributes to life satisfaction: the more income, the more one is satisfied with life. Among the ethnicity variables, national pride has a significant impact on life satisfaction. The other ethnic variables have some impact as life satisfaction is higher in Belgium among people living in the Flemish regions, in the USA life satisfaction is higher among whites than among non-whites, and in Switzerland the same is true for those who are German-speaking. Ethnicity is less important than income, which is hardly surprising.

*Left–Right Orientation*

Left–right orientation is a classical scale in attitude research that allows one to classify both the electorate and political elites (Esaiasson and Holmberg, 1996). Left–right orientation is scaled so that high scores refer to the right while low scores stand for the left. There is, again, an ethnicity impact, as national pride goes together with rightist political orientations. Ethnicity also strengthens political orientations to the right, as is the case with the German speakers in Switzerland and the Hindi speakers in India.

*Interest in Politics*

In the electorate a substantial group of people displays apathy, some scholars claiming that apathy benefits democracy, others saying it is a defect (DiPalma, 1970; Dalton, 2000). On the whole, our models fit well for explaining the variation in interest in politics. It is striking, although not unexpected, to find that education is consistently positively associated with interest in politics, and this is also true for age, while gender (women) is negatively associated with political interest. Ethnicity does not matter much for interest in politics. Only two positive instances may be reported – namely the case of peoples living in the Flemish regions in Belgium and the German-speaking people of Switzerland (see Table 4.21).

*Voluntary Organizations and Political Activity: Joining Boycotts*

The fourth outcome variable to be tested for the impact of ethnicity is membership of voluntary organizations. But there is no consistent explanatory pattern emerging from this analysis. National pride is only associated with membership in the American case while, in India, Hindi speakers seems to be less engaged in voluntary organizations. We conclude that ethnicity has a very limited impact on engagement in voluntary organizations, either positively or negatively, and these estimates are not reported here. The final outcome variable is one form of direct and strong political activity as it may be captured by the propensity of a citizen to join boycott actions. The model tested arrives at an acceptable level of explained variation. The variables that have a significant impact are absence of national pride, high educational level and gender – that is, more males have experiences of this kind of political activity. The plain ethnic variables do not matter much and it is only in India we can find an effect from those not speaking Hindi.

*Summary*

On the one hand, ethnicity in the daily life of people refers to language. Here we have ethnic groups in the USA, as well as language groups in Belgium, Spain, Switzerland, India and Russia. On the other hand, ethnicity is also

**Table 4.21   Ethnicity and interest in politics: regression analysis**

| Indep variable | Coeff | Dependent variable | | | | | | | |
|---|---|---|---|---|---|---|---|---|---|
| | | **Total** | **Six** | **Belgium** | **Spain** | **USA** | **Switz.** | **India** | **Russia** |
| National pride | coeff | −.041 | .029 | −.078 | −.077 | .061 | −.080 | −.063 | .104 |
| | t-stat | −10.82 | 2.87 | −2.94 | −1.45 | 1.79 | −2.81 | −1.40 | 3.57 |
| Ethnicity* | coeff | − | − | .045 | .040 | −.002 | .079 | .015 | −.058 |
| | t-stat | − | − | 2.96 | 1.19 | −.12 | 4.45 | .71 | −1.70 |
| Education | coeff | .255 | .330 | .280 | .248 | .307 | .365 | .256 | .245 |
| | t-stat | 65.48 | 32.02 | 8.94 | 4.29 | 11.75 | 7.38 | 6.32 | 5.51 |
| Income | coeff | .084 | .093 | .199 | .222 | .037 | .043 | −.045 | −.002 |
| | t-stat | 19.75 | 7.98 | 6.01 | 2.94 | 1.84 | 1.46 | −.82 | −.06 |
| Gender | coeff | −.081 | −.086 | −.062 | −.070 | −.057 | −.094 | −.163 | −.087 |
| | t-stat | −39.52 | −15.54 | −4.26 | −2.96 | −5.24 | −5.73 | −8.10 | −4.99 |
| Age | coeff | .124 | .119 | .162 | .099 | .140 | .149 | −.092 | .156 |
| | t-stat | 36.86 | 13.68 | 7.24 | 2.45 | 8.39 | 5.74 | −2.21 | 5.20 |
| Constant | coeff | .287 | .115 | −.010 | .107 | .178 | .210 | .445 | .187 |
| | t-stat | 58.92 | 9.17 | −.29 | 1.51 | 4.21 | 5.07 | 9.29 | 3.58 |
| Adjrsq | | .083 | .130 | .118 | .075 | .072 | .144 | .131 | .067 |
| N | | 90011 | 11661 | 1677 | 602 | 2865 | 1114 | 927 | 990 |

*Notes*:   * The ethnicity variables refer to the following for the models estimated for the different countries: Belgium: Flemish; Spain: Spanish-speaking; USA: white; Switzerland: German-speaking; India: Hindi-speaking; and Russia: Russian-speaking.
coeff = the unstandardized regression coefficient.
t-stat = t-statistics. Used to test the significance of the regression coefficients; t-stat showing more than ± 2 indicates significance.

*Source*:   See Appendix C.

expressed as national pride, and there is no doubt that it is this second aspect of ethnicity that has a stronger impact than the first aspect. Ethnicity as language does not matter as much for individual behaviour as believed. In Table 4.22 we summarize the findings from the micro-level analysis.

National pride has more impact than ethnicity as language. Ethnicity matters a good deal for life satisfaction and left–right orientation and less so for membership in voluntary organizations.

## Conclusion

Ethnicity is a cultural force that has been connected in several social science theories with major outcomes. Do ethnic identities shape not only personal identity but also politics? We have reported much empirical evidence about ethnic effects, but we need to state some important qualifications. It was only

**Table 4.22    Number of significant regression coefficients estimated from the impact of ethnicity by country and dependent variables**

| Values | Distributed by country | | | | | | |
|---|---|---|---|---|---|---|---|
| | Belgium | Spain | USA | Switzer-land | India | Russia | Total |
| National pride | 4 | 1 | 4 | 4 | 3 | 1 | 17 |
| Ethnicity | 2 | 0 | 1 | 3 | 3 | 0 | 9 |
| **Total** | 6 | 1 | 5 | 7 | 6 | 1 | 26 |

| Values | Distributed by dependent variable | | | | | |
|---|---|---|---|---|---|---|
| | Life satisfaction | Left–right orientation | Political interest | Voluntary organiz-ations | Joining boycotts | Total |
| National pride | 5 | 4 | 3 | 1 | 4 | 17 |
| Ethnicity | 3 | 2 | 2 | 1 | 1 | 9 |
| **Total** | 8 | 6 | 5 | 2 | 5 | 26 |

*Note*:    This information is partly based upon a number of estimations not reported in this chapter.

when we employed regional-level data that we could detect very clear and direct impacts of ethnicity. The ethnic impact is particularly strong in certain countries where ethnicity is a regional political force. We have found that, in divided societies, the party system expresses the ethnic regional composition of the population in the form of a strong variation in party election outcomes.

National pride as one of the concerns of ethnicity indeed has an impact on different kinds of individual-level outcome. It is a primary source of life satisfaction. Ethnicity in general has a conservative impact as it fosters right-wing politics. It is true that ethnic diversity presents a country with problems of coordination. In general, ethnic fragmentation has a negative impact on society. The problems currently faced by the African continent to a certain extent concern the high degree of ethnic fragmentation there. In a country like India speaking Hindi has an impact on the political scene both at the regional level (support for the BJP) and the individual level (left–right orientations). Yet, ethnic fragmentation in India has not had the dismal effects that ethnic cleavages have had in Africa.

# PART III
# CIVILIZATIONS

# Introduction

We have examined culture as ethnicity in a few chapters, where ethnic groups were either approached as highly compact or as having a low degree of compactness. Turning now to the analysis of civilization, the key problem is again that of compactness. Since civilizations are typically carried by huge groups, comprising many countries, they can only be coherent if they are founded on some single strong common component. We argue that religion could constitute such a cement. In fact, religion is the critical factor in identifying the major civilizations of the world. Ethnicity is the culture of a people, but, 'people' may stand for very different kinds of groups, which explains to some extent why ethnic theory has delivered controversial results. Let us turn to the other major entity in cultural studies – namely, religion.

Linking civilization with religion is the approach used by Max Weber. If ethnicity is one pillar of culture, then religion is certainly the other foundation. Whereas ethnicity identifies a people living in a certain geographical location, a religion is a belief system which, in principle, may be adhered to by any people wherever they are situated. Religion as culture is more encompassing than ethnicity as culture, although the principal world religions have stable locations or spatial homes. An excellent source for the comparative inquiry into religion is the six volumes edited by Peuch (1970–76). Another source is the set of French *Dictionnaires* published in the 1990s, which cover all the major religions.

It is true that there is an immense variety of religious beliefs, when religion is defined as any kind of non-secular attitude. Yet, if the myriad different religions can be classified into a few world religions, then one may research the outcomes of religious creed in a parsimonious manner. Another approach to the study of civilizations is to link them up with time or the lingering relevance of major historical legacies. The purpose of this chapter is to introduce the analysis of civilizations where we will connect it with religion in particular as the promoter of secular outcomes.

# Chapter 5

# Civilizations and the Major Types of Religion

## Introduction

One of the most well-known social science theories links the type of religion with profound practical consequences. It argues that one of the great world religions has a logic built into its system of beliefs and values which, when put into practice, works itself out in social consequences of huge civilizational significance. In addition, it claims that none of the other world religions has the same core of ideas, which promote economic development *par préférence*. We are, of course, referring to Weber's theory of Protestantism and capitalism (Weber, 1904). Weber's analysis of the major world religions is distributed through several places in his work. On the one hand, there is his general statement of the sociology of religion in *Economy and Society*, but there are also monographs on Protestantism, ancient Judaism, Hinduism and Buddhism as well as Confucianism (but not Islam), as well as brief remarks scattered throughout other works.

In his empirical inquiries Weber relied on the knowledge available about these world religions at that time. Although he read this secondary literature extremely carefully, as time has passed, it has been argued that his empirical descriptions have become partly outdated. Nevertheless, he did set the theoretical focus on which later studies into religions have been conducted. Thus, he had a string of influence on the inquiry into the world religions, with scholars always asking 'Was Weber right or wrong?'. However, we ask, on the contrary: 'How could we evaluate this theory today, making it relevant for understanding not only history but also the present?'

It should be explicitly admitted that the Weber thesis was launched in order to explain historically the occidental advantage in relation to other civilizations. But, we ask, can it be applied to today's differences in outcomes? For instance, economic growth in South-east Asia in the second half of the twentieth century has stimulated a debate about the connections between religion and development. One could obtain a perspective on this question, if one starts from Weber's well-known model which links Protestantism with affluence through the impact of this religion on economic ethics. Examining the evidence about economic outcomes conceived in a broad sense, however, one finds little evidence of the occurrence of the Weberian mechanism today. Instead the religions that Weber rejected – that is, Buddhism and Confucianism – have been very much connected with economic growth. The distinctive characteristic of Protestantism is that it stands strong in countries with human rights – a link that Weber never identified.

One way to inquire into whether 'Culture Matters' is to establish whether there are various configurations of outcomes connected with the persistence of one world religion over another. Weber's model may be interpreted as a theory about a very special connection in history – the joint occurrence of Protestantism and capitalism in Northern Europe and North America. Protestantism gave birth to, or promoted, capitalism, argues Weber, but he never claims that Protestantism will continue to produce economic development, in this part of the world or in any other part, when transplanted into it. Perhaps Protestantism did once have this developmental impact but now, in the early twenty-first century, this connection no longer holds. Either Protestantism may have lost its edge due to secularization or other factors which also stimulate development are at work. Such an interpretation would save the theory but at the cost of limiting it to the understanding of the past. We would, of course, still want to search for a theory about religion and its outcomes that would be sufficiently general to also encompass present conditions.

## The World Religions

Throughout history, religion has been a powerful source of cultural diversity, and it remains today one of the principal vehicles of cultural identification. In the eyes of the *virtuosi*, religion may be seem to be preoccupied with abstract matters with little bearing on day-to-day life – for example, deliverance from sin, salvation and hidden powers. However, to the ordinary man and woman religious behaviour has a practical significance, as it gives very detailed prescriptions about how to act or interact with people. Although secularization has certainly mitigated the relevance of religion, the world religions are still strong enough to give countries or entire subcontinents different cultural identities (cf. Haynes, 1998).

Let us search for ample evidence for the occurrence of religious effects. Macro outcomes may be a function of religious creed – that is, which world religion prevails – but what is the impact of religion within a country when the religious structure is heterogeneous? We wish to elucidate what happens within a country when different religious families meet, as well as examining the social, economic and political consequences of the world religions when they prevail in a country as a dominant creed.

A divided society or religious structure is typical of countries where two or more of the world religions have met and confronted each other without a resolution one way or the other. All the countries of the world are, in one sense, religiously heterogeneous, because even in a country where one of the world religions prevails there is bound to exist a variety of traditions and sects, confronting each other but yet belonging to the same world religion. This is one kind of religious heterogeneity that we will have in mind here. In another sense, however, only countries in which different major religious creeds separate the population into compact groups – be these Muslims, Buddhists or Hindus, Protestants or Catholics, Orthodox or atheists – have a divided religious structure. The ongoing process of secularization will either almost inevitably diminish religious conflict within societies or, conversely, reinforce the tensions between non-religious and religious people. It is only when secularization results in religious indifference that religious tensions cool down, as, for instance, in the Netherlands.

The inquiry into religious heterogeneity or a divided religious structure below will follow the same pattern used in Chapter 4 when dealing with ethnic structure. First, we test the hypothesis that countries with a great deal of religious fragmentation differ in terms of outcomes from countries with little religious fragmentation. Second, we examine regions within one country where the various regions display different religious creed in order to find out what impact religion may have on the support for political parties. Third we will inquire into the impact of religion on micro-level outcomes or individual behaviour.

## Civilizations

From an overview article in the *Encyclopaedia of the Social Sciences* by C. Brinkmann (1930), it is evident that the study of civilizations had already achieved considerable results during the interwar years. In this article a number of features of civilizations are identified and the question of advance and decay of civilizations is raised explicitly – the cycle theory of civilizations. The author places the study of civilizations with cultural history (Alfred Weber) and the new social sciences emerging around 1900.

S. Huntington's *The Clash of Civilisations* (1996) reintroduced the concept of a civilization into political discourse. His argument is that distinct civilizations do exist and that they matter a good deal for politics. Listing nine major civilizations – the occidental, Latin American, the African, the Islamic, the Chinese, the Hindu, the Orthodox, the Buddhist and the Japanese civilizations – he deals mainly with the foreign policy questions that the interaction of these civilizations raises. This is an important, but limited, angle from which to analyse the impact of such cultures as civilizations. Civilizations may matter for more than questions of peace and war; they may also matter, for instance, in relation to democracy and socioeconomic development.

In the Huntington classification religion is obviously one of the criteria for identifying a civilization, but it is combined with other features, such as historical legacy (occidentalism, Latin-Americanism) or nationalism (for example, Japanese civilization) or a mere geographical criterion (for example,

Africa). Once one starts mixing criteria on what is to count as a civilization, then there is hardly any limit to how many civilizations may be identified. Civilizations, as realms of culture, may be identified in different ways but, in our view, they are profoundly associated with the major world religions. Let us first discuss alternative suggested classifications of civilizations before we make use of the Weber system for analysing the major religions of the world and their outcomes.

The concept of a civilization was discussed in Chapter 1. It has a common core, with the concept of culture meaning something that has been accomplished or something developed: 'an advanced stage or system of social development' (*Oxford English Dictionary*). One key feature that separates the concept of civilization from that of an ethnic group is the group or the compactness of the group which carries the civilization. As a civilization is the common property of more than one people, it can never be highly compact. Some civilizations – for example the occidental or Christian civilization comprise more than ten peoples or nations: 'those people of the world regarded as having this (advanced stage)' (*Oxford English Dictionary*). Another important characteristic of civilizations as a kind of community is that they relate somehow to religion and religious identity.

Let us quote from a few definitions in order to see how different scholars have pinned down the characteristics that distinguish these special kinds of community labelled 'civilisations':

> Civilization is generally used so as to include indiscriminately three distinct factors, namely (1) intellectual and technical progress, (2) achievements in the development of community life and of governmental institutions, and (3) cultural expressions of what is traditionally called the 'soul', as distinct from the 'intellect', in religious phenomena, in the arts, or in any other manner. (Brecht, 1967, p. 348)

Brecht's definition qualifies the two features laid down above – namely achievements by a social group – by requiring that a civilization consist not only of technical accomplishments but also of developments in the area of soul. He stresses compactness, requiring not only common community life but also shared governmental institutions, which seems contestable. Civilization and state are different kinds of phenomenon.

Taking a more religious slant, Sorokin presents a list of civilizations that not only have existed but also persist today:

> Let us now turn to a more thorough examination of the types of culture mentality, selecting these not from among individuals and small groups, but largely from the vast and long-enduring psychosocial systems established by the great historical religions: Hinduism, Buddhism, Taoism, Jainism, Judaism, Christianity, Confucianism, and others. (Sorokin, 1957, p. 43)

In line with our approach to civilizations, Sorokin opposes small groups with long-enduring psychosocial systems, defining civilizations as large-scale communities with a medium or low level of compactness, in contradistinction to ethnic communities.

Civilizations may thus be understood as large-scale cultural systems developing over time. This is basically the standpoint of Sorokin who distinguished between ideational, sensate, idealistic and mixed systems of culture. To him, the vast cultural systems consist of language, science, philosophy, religion, the fine arts, ethics and law, as well as the systems of applied technology, economics and politics. But besides these most general cultural systems there are larger cultural unities or cultural supersystems. Each such supersystem is based on certain major premises or certain ultimate principles, the development of which makes up its total so-called ideology (Sorokin, 1966, pp. 22–24).

To us, the general cultural phenomena that Sorokin speaks of do not constitute civilizations in and of themselves, as these aspects of culture enter, in various forms, into civilizations. A civilisation is more concrete than the abstract expressions of culture such as language or technology. Sorokin goes on to state:

> The investigators seem also to agree that these civilisations, or cultural supersystems, like deep cultural undercurrents, largely determine most of the surface ripplings of the sociocultural ocean: the life, organisation, and functions of smaller groups and cultural systems, the mentality and behaviour of individuals, and a multitude of concrete historical events, trends, and processes. (Sorokin, 1966, p. 177)

Sorokin is here advancing a strong 'culture matters' thesis, which needs empirical confirmation.

We here wish to link up with the concept of a civilization as employed in the study of history. Historians such as Toynbee have stressed the relevance of historical legacies for the formation of different civilizations around the world. He originally distinguished 26 civilizations, but identified six types existing in the 1950s: Western, Russian, Islamic, Hindu, Chinese and primitive civilizations. He states:

> Societies of this species are commonly called civilizations, to distinguish them from primitive societies which are also 'intelligible fields of study' and which form another, in fact the other, species within this genus. Our twenty-one societies must, therefore, have one specific feature in common in the fact that they alone are in the process of civilization. (Toynbee, 1987, p. 35)

Anthropologists may not agree with historians about which cultures are civilizations, especially if the latter stress their degree of advancement as the criterion. The study of civilizations among the major anthropologists in the twentieth century concentrated on cultures that historians have labelled 'primitive', but in-depth analyses often showed that a few non-Western civilizations had achieved a high level of development, although not entirely in accordance with the Western criteria (Kuper, 1996; Kottak, 2000). Also, primitive civilizations are, after all, civilizations which call for a cultural approach in order to understand them or their logic.

Geographers have also shown an interest in identifying civilizations or 'culture realms' as they may term them. Common to these culture realms was that they 'all had their elaborate ethical or religious ideologies' (Broek and Webb, 1968, p. 188). Thus, for instance, Broek identifies eight culture realms, based on a mixture of criteria: Occidental, Main Islamic, Indic, East Asian, South-east Asian, Meso-African and Southern Pacific.

Let us here present an overview of these civilization classifications in terms of the population distribution for the twentieth century. Displayed in Table 5.1 are the population distributions for the civilization concepts suggested by Toynbee, Broek and Huntington. As stated above, Huntington identified nine contemporary civilizations as of the late twentieth century, whereas Broek has eight and Toynbee only six civilizations.

We wish to point out two things in respect to Table 5.1 – one conceptual and another empirical. First, the conceptual categories suggested for the major types of modern civilizations are close to each other, as all three identify a Western (occidental), an Islamic, an Indian as well as a Chinese type of civilization. The Indian and Chinese civilizations appear to be ethnically-based, but in reality it is religion (Hinduism, Buddhism–Confucianism) that constitutes the foundation. The same may be said in relation to the Russian civilization (Christian Orthodox). The concepts of a Latin American civilization or an African civilization are interesting, but it is not clear what, besides geographical location, constitutes the characteristics of the culture or civilization in question. Here, historical heritage is probably the relevant consideration. However, it is impossible not to question this classification as harbouring a Western bias. Could one not speak of an Inuit civilization or a Tibetan one, for instance? Furthermore, the standard image of a homogenous 'African' civilization is also questionable, as Northern Africa has a different cultural heritage than Southern or Eastern Africa, or even Central Africa.

Second, it is obvious from these three mappings that various civilizations in many ways converge or overlap empirically, reflecting the fact that the Western/occidental civilizations tend to go together as is also the case with what is called the African/meso-African/primitive civilizations. One observes also that the so-called Western civilization is declining in terms of numbers whereas the Islamic civilization is increasing. The same is true of the Buddhist civilization (declining) when compared with the Hindu civilization (expanding).

Although these three classifications of still existing civilizations converge considerably, the list could easily be expanded. In the Western category one could identify several civilizations such as the French, the British, the German, the Italian and so forth. The same applies to the enormously encompassing categories of Islamic and African civilizations. Why not focus

**Table 5.1     Major civilizations: population distribution in the twentieth century as percentages of total population**

| Civilization | 1900 | Toynbee 1950 | 1980 | 1990 | 1997 |
|---|---|---|---|---|---|
| Primitive | 4.6 | 6.4 | 7.6 | 8.4 | 9.1 |
| Hindu | 20.0 | 21.3 | 23.5 | 24.3 | 24.9 |
| Islamic | 6.3 | 6.9 | 8.5 | 9.5 | 10.3 |
| Chinese | 33.8 | 28.3 | 28.1 | 27.4 | 26.7 |
| Russian | 10.0 | 9.4 | 7.6 | 6.9 | 6.3 |
| Western | 25.2 | 27.7 | 24.7 | 23.5 | 22.7 |

| Civilization | 1900 | Broek 1950 | 1980 | 1990 | 1997 |
|---|---|---|---|---|---|
| Meso-African | 4.1 | 5.6 | 6.7 | 7.5 | 8.0 |
| Indic | 16.5 | 16.7 | 18.3 | 19.0 | 19.6 |
| Islamic | 6.7 | 7.4 | 9.0 | 10.1 | 11.0 |
| South-east Asian | 5.0 | 6.8 | 8.1 | 8.4 | 8.6 |
| East Asian | 32.9 | 27.2 | 26.7 | 25.8 | 25.1 |
| Occidental | 36.0 | 36.3 | 31.2 | 29.2 | 27.7 |

| Civilization | 1900 | Huntington 1950 | 1980 | 1990 | 1997 |
|---|---|---|---|---|---|
| African | 4.6 | 6.4 | 7.7 | 8.5 | 9.2 |
| Hindu | 16.5 | 16.7 | 18.3 | 19.0 | 19.6 |
| Islamic | 9.5 | 10.5 | 12.6 | 13.7 | 14.4 |
| Orthodox | 7.3 | 7.0 | 5.3 | 4.8 | 4.3 |
| Buddhist | 4.2 | 5.4 | 5.1 | 4.9 | 4.8 |
| Sinic | 31.3 | 25.6 | 26.4 | 25.9 | 25.5 |
| Latin American | 3.9 | 6.3 | 8.0 | 8.3 | 8.3 |
| Western | 22.7 | 22.1 | 16.7 | 15.0 | 14.0 |

*Sources*: Based on Toynbee (1987); Broek and Webber (1968, pp. 187, 189); Huntington (1996, pp. 26–27). Some adjustments to the classification of these civilizations have been made. Population figures are from Barrett (1982) and Encyclopaedia Britannica (1998).

directly on the key concept in most of these mentioned civilizations – namely, religion?


## The Weber Approach

Does civilization matter for real-world outcomes? Yes, to a considerable extent, stated Weber in 1904 when inquiring into economic outcomes. When he broadened the analysis to cover the economic outcomes of the world religions, he came to the same conclusion. Let us look at his argument in detail.

The study of the social consequences of religion made its breakthrough with the publication in 1904 of 'The Protestant Ethic and the Spirit of Capitalism'. However, we will extend Weber's focus on the economic consequences of religious beliefs to an analysis of their political implications. In all studies of religious behaviour there are two alternative perspectives which need to be balanced: understanding the main ideas – the content of a religion; and theorizing the practical consequences of a religion for society – their social, economic and political outcomes.

The comparative study of religion has resulted in a few standard distinctions concerning the varieties of religious creed that are almost universally referred to. First, one distinguishes between atheism and the major world religions, although recognizing also the occurrence of animism. Second, one distinguishes between the world religions which may vary in number. The first distinction between non-believers and religious believers has become increasingly problematical, as it is not easy to tell whether an individual is truly a religious practitioner. The second distinction (or distinctions) concerning the number and nature of the world religions is a matter of contention among scholars.

Which religions constitute civilizations? If one wishes to allow for many religions, then there is hardly any limit to the number of religions one may wish to identify. However, if the purpose is to classify religions into families constituting civilizations, then one would at least distinguish between three major religious worlds. Thus, we have the following:

1  *Hindu–Buddhist world*: India, which is Hinduist, and all the countries where Buddhism has a strong position, often in combination with another religion such as Confucianism, Taoism or Shintoism.
2  *Muslim world*: all countries with a majority of the population adhering to the Qur'anic system of belief – whether Sunni or Shia. It may be divided into the Arab world and the non-Arab world – an ethnic dimension.
3  *Christian world*: Catholic, Protestant and Greek Orthodox countries, also including Judaism as the forerunner of Christianity.

This elementary classification says nothing about what separates these three families nor anything about how compact they tend to be – an immense task for various types of research. Let us briefly describe the main differences between these three religious families, although this must be in the form of sketch based on a limited set of sources. The presentation of these three families – the Christian traditions, the Hindu and Buddhist traditions and Islam – is based on the separation between two basic approaches to understanding belief systems: the essentialist and the relativist perspective.

In the *essentialist approach* to religion, the emphasis is placed on its core ideas. The core of a religion is a set of beliefs or values which are in some sense fundamental to the religion in question, at least in the eyes of its *virtuosi*. It may be a controversial task to specify this core, but often religions have key sources from which one may distil its core beliefs or values. However, one may have to be content with laying down a variety of core interpretations of a religion since these will have been interpreted differently at various times. For instance, Christianity received a number of authoritative interpretations when it was established as a state religion, but this did not prevent it from later splitting into several core sets of beliefs and values. The same process has taken place within Islam.

In the *relativist approach* to religion, religion is not seen as a coherent system of beliefs or values but as an active force in social life. This approach models how religion affects, or is affected by, other social systems. Religious beliefs and values are not seen as time-independent responses to the eternal questions of mankind but, instead, as entering into the particular circumstances of time and space, reacting to social forces and also influencing them. Thus, when religion becomes entangled with mundane contingencies, it may be used by individuals in their struggle to maintain power or, under charismatic leaders, may become a revolutionary force, changing major practices.

The interesting thing about Weber's approach to religion is that he combines the two perspectives – the dogmatic and the functionalist. Thus, he claimed immense social consequences from the nature of religious belief, but he also took great pains to understand the logic of a religion.

## Three World Religions: Alternative Classifications

Of course, if one were to name only a few religious families, then one might not necessarily pick the ones mentioned above. Another possible classification would be the following dichotomy derived from Weber's concepts: Hinduism/Zoroastroism. Under Zoroastroism one would then count all the religions which are extra-worldly: Judaism, Christianity and Islam. Under Hinduism one could place all the religions that are inner-worldly: the religions of India and their offsprings in Southern and South-east Asia. Which classification is the correct one depends on the basic criterion or viewpoint that one chooses to apply.

It cannot be overemphasized that a number of different criteria can be employed for the identification of religious families. There is no single best classification. Thus, for instance we have: eschatological religions/non-eschatological religions, depending on whether the religions in question are based on the idea of a paradise, or life after death. Or we might focus on grace: salvation religions/non-salvation religions, reflecting whether a religion concentrates on the deliverance from sin. Or another dichotomy could be: dualistic/non-dualistic religions, depending on whether or not there is a conception of two ultimate forces opposing each other. Finally, one could use a distinction such as: institutional religions/non-institutional religions, as some religions emphasize moral rules more than religious rituals.

These are all doctrinal classifications. From a sociological perspective, religions may also be analysed very differently by various alternative distinctions. All religions have a separation of their adherents. Thus, one finds religious elites or sects on the one hand and the population at large on the other hand. Religious belief may differ tremendously between these two sections, even within one and the same religion. It has been argued that to understand a religion, one needs to focus on a certain group, the ascetic individuals, who drive the inner logic of a religion to its extreme (Weber, 1978) – the *virtuosi*. One may also look at how a religion emerges – that is, its connection with a specific script or the efforts of an actual instigator of religious beliefs – the *prophets*.

There are yet more distinctions involved. How consistent are religious beliefs? Is religion ecstasy or legal prescriptions reflecting extraordinary or ordinary life? Is the core of religion about God or gods, or is the religion a different form of organization – churches? This is not the forum to attempt to answer these difficult questions in the comparative analysis of religion (Hamilton, 1995), so we will restrict ourselves to the question of the impact of religion on politics and socioeconomic development.

According to Weber, religious thought is always somehow linked to the practical problem of personal identity from a cultural point of view (Weber, 1993, 2001). The crucial idea is that of finding the path to a correct way of life – that is, a way of living that is in agreement with the requirements of righteousness. People may change from wrong to right through grace or through work and adherence to the law. All religions have consequences for the conduct of behaviour in daily life by offering an ethical challenge: you live like this, but righteousness entails that!

Despite what has been said about the difficulty in creating typologies which cover the immense variety of religious creeds, we will retain the simple threefold classification above. Let us make a brief overview of the three families without following in detail their historical evolution and mentioning some themes discussed in comparative research from the outcome perspective. The first world religion to emerge is that of Brahmanism, often attributed to the so-called Aryans, said to have conquered Northern India sometime after 2000 BC (Peuch, 1970b; Peuch, 1976a).

*Hinduism and Buddhism*

Analyses of Hinduism have emphasised its social consequences – the legitimation of the Indian caste system with its complex, but immutable, social distinctions between groups and consequent negative consequences for society. It is generally considered as having originated in the needs of a warrior group, the Aryans, to consolidate their grip upon Northern India after the conquest – a functional hypothesis. However, the content of Hinduism as a religion has also attracted much interest, given its very special cosmology and mythology, as well as its intricate rituals.

In its main version, Hinduism is polytheist, including three great gods – Brahman, Vishnu and Shiva – as well as a large number of small gods. There is no one single revelation source, but instead a number of sources in Sanskrit – namely, the Veda texts, dating back to before 1500 BC. The key idea in Hinduism is that of the 'Wheel of Life', which may be interpreted much more deterministically than implied by the polytheism of the religion. The notion of a basic force in the universe – karma – in combination with the idea of reincarnation – samsara – has formed the basis for an entirely different development of Hinduism towards atheism or pantheism. Actually, Hinduism is a religion that covers a broad spectrum of diverse movements, including the non-violence notion or ahimsa. Characteristic for all forms of Hinduism is the idea of a delivery from karma, or blind necessity, by means of some forms of the yoga method as practised by the *virtuosi*.

However, the main version of Hinduism has traditionally focused on the position of the Brahmans, or priests. Very much protecting the survival of the cast-society, the Brahmans provided themselves with the leader positions besides the Kshatriyas (warriors) and the Vaisyas (merchants), whereas the rest of society contained the immense numbers of the casteless, structured hierarchically into various groups down to the lowest of them all, the Pariahs.

One perplexing aspect in Hinduism is not so much the variety of creeds and sects, but the non-existence of a formally instituted church. There are many temples with lots of gods and rituals, sacraments, but there is nothing similar to a priesthood as in Christianity. How are the temples in Hinduism supported? Hinduism seems today to encompass a myriad small gods, worshipped almost in the apotheostic form – that is, by offering small gifts in exchange for personal success. Yet, Hinduism retains its core focus on the collection of myths in its chief texts, dating from almost 1000 years ago. While its mythology describes a world of very active gods and heroes, at the same time there is no master plan for how or to where the wheel of human life moves.

Another startling aspect with Hinduism is the total rejection of all other world religions. There is no apostasy, no proselytism and no heresy, because Hinduism is only a concern for Indians, and Indians who adhere to Hinduism cannot change their religion. This belief in the immense credibility and validity of Hinduism as the only correct way of life for Indians stands in stark contrast to the variability of Hinduism as displayed in all its diverse manifestations. Hinduism is mainly concentrated to India, but there are pockets of Hindu believers in other parts of South-east Asia such as, for instance, Bali in Indonesia.

By far the most important branch to emerge from traditional Hinduism has been Buddhism. This is the export version of Hinduism, conquering a number of countries outside India. Inside India Buddhism was practically wiped out around 1 000 AD, as in 1193 the last stronghold of Buddhism was destroyed in India by forces adhering to traditional Hinduism, who could not accept the basic atheist tone of ancient Buddhism. Whether or not Buddhism involves a principled rejection of the caste system has been much debated but, in any case, members of the casteless groups can also embark upon the road that leads to nirvana – the new idea in Buddhism vis à vis Hinduism.

Buddhism is expressed most visibly in the numerous monks who attempt to live up to the ethics of their Master, Siddhartha, who lived at about 500 BC. Since the monks without a Church (*virtuosi*) are such a dominant feature in Buddhism and all people can become monks, it is easy to overlook another aspect of Buddhism – namely, its strict ethical nature, communicating a way of life to ordinary people participating in society. Mainstream Buddhist ethics is not the ethics of monkhood, but a practical set of maxims about how to live in purity and not to go astray by resorting to artificial solutions such as drinking and so on.

From a doctrinal point of view, Buddhism may be considered to be an atheist Hinduism with the key concept of nirvana, thus emphasizing pessimism or '*Weltschmerz*' – karma being a force of selfishness, greed and endless pursuit. However, the sharp consistency of the message of Siddhartha, as forthcoming in the available sources about his teachings through his life as a vagabond, stands in contrast to the enormous adaptability of Buddhism to other creeds when it expanded outside India and entered into symbiosis with, for example, Confucianism in China and Shintoism in Japan.

Buddhism has spread out over a vast area from Sri Lanka and Tibet to Indonesia, entering into countless alliances with other creeds, diversifying itself to an extent that forces one to raise the question of what remains of its core today. One speaks of two main developmental trends: the 'Little Wagon' and the 'Big Wagon'. When, as in one form of Buddhism, one starts to count so-called Buddhisattvas as some form of godlike phenomena, then Buddhism loses much of its soul and becomes more like a religion of apotheosis. Tibetan Buddhism has retained more of a doctrinal coherence, although its special adherence to the idea of the lamas in the form of a Dalai Lama makes it different from original Buddhism.

Perhaps the socially most important form of Buddhism is its combination with the main Chinese religion, Confucianism. The ethical system introduced by Confucius around 500–400 BC is basically an atheist ethical religion, playing on the opposition between passive versus active: yang and yin. One may even assert that Confucianism is more ethics and less religion, as it regards respect and obedience towards worldly institutions such as the family and the government as the means towards individual harmony. Completely different is Taoism, or the Chinese form of mysticism, created by Lao-Tse. But this has also gone well in combination with Buddhism, testifying to the plasticity of that religion.

Speaking of Hinduism and Buddhism, one must point out the immense difference between the doctrinal core of a religion and the mass beliefs towards that religion. In an essentialist perspective on religion, religion is seen as a more or less coherent system of symbols, being the patrimony of an exclusive group, the religious elite (*virtuosi*). Conversely, in the relativistic perspective, religion becomes a far more diffuse entity, comprising a set of ideas with a minimum of consistency between them.

When one speaks about the consequences for the economy or the polity of religious creed, then it is vital to be clear about whether one is referring to the religion of the ascetics or the religion of the general public. This question is highly relevant in relation to the Weber model, to be evaluated below, for instance with regard to his understanding of the social consequences of Hinduism and Buddhism. Thus, the core of Buddhism, focusing on the notions of karma and nirvana seemed anti-social to Weber, but he did not take into account their teachings for the ordinary man, which emphasize control, frugality and thrift (Weber, 1996).

On the surface, Hinduism and Buddhism seem to be polytheistic religions. They tend to degenerate into an instrumental relationship between the worshipper and a certain deity who brings material advantages against sacrifices. The myriad gods or goddesses in Hinduism, as well as the immense number of Bodhisattvas in Buddhism, might seem reminiscent of Greek and Roman religion with its polytheism and instrumentalism. Yet, in its core beliefs, the Eastern religions are, as Glasenapp stressed, characterized by strict determinism adhering to the idea of life as a wheel portraying the profoundly circular path of events (Glasenapp, 1963). In order to arrive at an evolutionary or teleological conception of life as having a start and an end we have to turn to the Western religions – that is, the religions that somehow seem to have emerged from the teachings of the Iranian prophet Zoroaster, whose actual time of living has not been confirmed, but is thought to be between 1000 and 500 BC.

## Judaism and Christianity

With the religion of Abraham, Moses and the prophets of the Old Testament, we have the first of three religions that adhere to the format of Zoroastrianism. Thus, Judaism, Christianity and Islam have the same basic properties, being eschatological, dualistic, monotheistic, prophetic, messianic and chiliastic (Glasenapp, 1957).

In Judaism, especially during the periods of hardship (Babylonian prison-hood), the ideas of one sole mighty God as creator of the world (Jahweh), of the struggle between good and evil, of the resurrection of the dead, and of the ultimate salvation of the chosen people are developed to the maximum. These ideas entail the problem of predestination, or how to make sure that one will end up in heaven rather than hell (Peuch, 1972a), which tends to be solved by the emphasis on the observation of a large number of behaviour maxims laid down in the Torah and interpreted in the Talmud. Yet, the most distinctive feature in Judaism is the idea that almighty God – Jahweh – is first and foremost the God of a specifically chosen people, the Jewish people.

In the New Testament, according to the interpretation by St Paul, mankind replaces the Jewish people as the end of the drama, the death of Jesus Christ as the son of God being the turning point in the struggle between good and evil, paving the way for an eternal life after death for those who believe in Him. Grace can only be had by belief in Jesus Christ as St Paul laid down in his extremely influential Epistles. With Jesus Christ, the warrior-like features of Jahweh are transformed into Agape or altruism – that is, the Christian love for the miserable, unfortunate and poor (Nygren, 1982). One could perhaps claim that Allah is more reminiscent of Jahweh than of God, according to St Paul. We will speak more of the various types of Christianity, especially the Protestant forms, when we discuss the Weber theory below (Peuch, 1972a, 1972b).

*Islam*

Perhaps more than any other religion, the analysis of Islam has focused on religion and politics. Why is this so? It is often stated that Islam makes no distinction between the secular and the spiritual, but this separation has been problematic in other religions too, as, for instance, in Augustine's theory of *Civitate Dei*. In any case, the strong institutionalization in Sunni Islam suggests that efforts have been made to routinize an extremely dynamic religious creed, creating a kind of boundary between the sacred and the profane (Peuch, 1976a).

Two basic approaches to the analysis of Islam may be distinguished: high culture or essentialist approaches (Gellner, 1983b) and sociological or relativistic approaches (Ayubi, 1991; Zubaida, 1993). In the essentialist approach, one is preoccupied with the contents of the religion – that is, with interpretations based on a hermeneutical understanding. One poses questions sush as the following: 'What kind of religion is Islam?', 'What are its basic beliefs?', 'What is the core of the Koran?' Conversely, in the relativistic approach, one examines either the sources of support for Islam or one researches the social, economic and political consequences of Islam – called its 'functions'. Thus, one ask such questions as: 'Why Islamic fundamentalism?', 'How can Islam be used in political struggles?', 'Which groups endorse what kind of Islam for which reasons?' In relation to the problem of where Islamic fundamentalism comes from doctrinally, as well as why it receives strong backing today, one often sees these two perspectives cross each other. Let us develop the essentialist perspective a little further.

In the essentialist framework there are a few basic sources of Islam: the *Qur'an*; the *Hadith*, or the deeds of the Prophet; the *Ijma* (consensus); the *Qiyas* (analogy), and *Ijtihad* or individual thought or *ra'y* – that is, individual opinion. Together, they form the foundation of Shari'a law as developed by the *figh* (jurisprudence). By the beginning of the tenth century AD 'the gate of *ijtihad* was closed' and the rule of *taqlid* (emulation, imitation, tradition) was formulated so that doctrine might not be derived independently from the original sources (of which the *Hadith* is particularly amorphous), but rather through the teachings of one of the four recognized schools. In the Sunni tradition, one has little or no space of charismatic interpretation by religious leaders.

The Sunni version of Islam may be viewed as both highly political and as a depolitization at the same time. It institutionalizes Islam to a very broad extent, but at the same time it limits the role of religion to the conduct of specific things – namely, the strict observance of a number of behaviour duties. These include the Five Pillars: (1) profession of faith or *shahada*; (2) prayer or *sulat*; (3) almsgiving or *zakat*; (4) fasting or *sanm* and (5) pilgrimage or *haj*. The so-called sacred places and days are clearly laid down, as for instance when to visit the Kaba in Mecca.

Yet, the Sunni version of Islam has been far from the dominant version, as its strictly legalistic tone has provoked a search for other kinds of religious experience. Thus, we find sufism and the dervishes but, more importantly, the challenge from the Shi'a interpretation, which is basically a charismatic version of Islam stressing the role of leaders, so-called imams or, more generally, maddhis.

From the essentialist perspective Shi'a Islam is based on the full recognition of Ali and his descendants. Ali married Fatima (Mohammad's daughter) and was elected as the fourth caliph – as the last true caliph. Shi'a in its principal version recognizes thus far 12 imams, the last (Muhammad) disappearing in the ninth century. The death of Ali in 661 is a key date in the Shi'a version of Islam. Other versions of Shi'a allow for fewer imams than 12 – the Alaouites and the Isma'ilis.

The intersection between religion and politics takes place in Islam at the institution of the caliph, who was both a spiritual and worldly leader. Understandably, there have been numerous conflicts about correct succession – that is, controversies about the election of caliphs – since the death of the Prophet. Changes in the nature and location of the caliphate have reflected the ascension and dethronement of various dynasties in the Arab world. The struggle between groups to control the caliphate as well as the struggle between various caliphates has dominated Arab history right up until the caliphate was more or less abolished under the Ottoman Empire and with the eviction of the Moors in Spain. Today, the Saudi King is the protector of the holy places, but there is nothing corresponding to the caliph. Formally, the caliphate was eliminated by Kemal Atatürk in 1923, resulting in the creation of the Muslim Brotherhood in 1927 as a counterreaction to restore it.

There is a perplexing question concerning Islam: is there a church in this religion? The religious places, the mosques, are state property and are operated by state officials. The Western concept of a church independent from the state is completely outside of the doctrine of Islam. In Islam, all the Muslims are considered as a community, the Umma, which constitutes a body of believers. They are to be served by the mullahs or the religious leaders. The priests are sometimes called sheikhs.

The relativistic perspective on Islam is entirely a different matter. It asks questions about its sources and functions. What are the social, economic, and political origins of Islamic belief? What are the consequences of Islam for democracy, state stability and affluence, as well as income inequalities? Thus, in the relativistic perspective, Islamic fundamentalism is typically seen as a form of alienation or a search for a palliative for counteracting a sense of exclusion in domestic or international politics. Thus, it responds more to a quest for participation than to doctrinal reasons.

The distinction between essentialist and relativist perspectives is highly applicable for the understanding of Islam. We now proceed to examine a theory that argues from an essential perspective to a relativistic perspective, deriving the social consequences of the world religions from their doctrinal core, as understood by religious elites. Strangely enough, Weber did not cover Islam in his grandiose exposé of the world religions, at least not to a considerable extent.

Beverley Milton-Edwards offers a timely introduction to the politics of Islam in *Islam and Politics in the Contemporary World* (2004). She has prepared herself well for a penetrating analysis that is very much up-to-date. The world of Islam and Moslem societies is the major Non-Western civilization today and its immenseness defies any one single comprehension. This book focuses exclusively on the politics of the Koranic countries, covering Islam and the state, protest behaviour, the democracy debate, and the violent processes of change in Moslem societies, including revolutions and counter-revolutions. Milton-Edwards stresses the emergence of Islamic fundamentalism with its dire consequences for the Moslem countries and the rest of the World. She has clearly seen how the teachings of Mawdudi and Qutb offered the solution for people searching for a real and complete alternative to Arab traditionalism, the opportunism of the modernising *élites*, and Anglo-Saxon hegemony. She states: 'In conclusion, there is evidence that the religious fundamentals of Islam are incompatible with modern secular liberal democracy', (p. 116).

I fully agree, if Faraj is the interpreter of the Koranic fundamentals in his Jihad – *The Absent Obligation*. I completely disagree, if giant Averroes is the interpreter in *On the Harmony of Religions and Philosophy*. Islam has many faces: the mujahideen – a religion of warriors, the *waqf* – a religion of monumental architecture, the *fiqh* – jurisprudence and legal order of more than a billion people, the *ulama* – the virtuosi without a clear role limitation, the *umma* – social heterogeneity searching in vain for compactness, and the *caliphe* – the unhappy solution to the problem of charismatic authority.

It is understandable that *Islam and Politics* concentrates upon the Arab world. However, we must not forget that the largest Muslim society is actually in India, with a large minority of almost 300 million Moslems. The status of democracy in the non-Arab part of the Moslem civilisation is not equally contested as in the Arab section. Why? Countries like Malaysia, Mauritius, Bangladesh, Bosnia, and India are more democratic than Arab countries like Tunisia, Syria, and the Emirates. Milton-Edwards offers a lot of information about the nature of Arab politics, but she does not bring out the factor which could be the missing link between religion and retardation in the Moslem world; namely tribalism. This is a phenomenon that is as pervasive in the Moslem world as it is badly understood, even by experts on ethnicity. Theoretically, Islam should undo tribal affinities, constituting a world religion to which any ethnie may belong. In reality, the Moslem societies are organised along tribal sections to an extent that makes legal-rational authority precarious.

The position of women under Islam as well as Arab traditionalism needs to be more researched. Speaking of religion and politics in the Muslim world, one of the riddles of Islam is the place of the clergy in the Koranic state. It remains a puzzle how the *ulama* is paid, recruited, and controlled by government. The titles of the clergy are not the same in the different countries and their autonomy in relation to the state varies, too. What we need is an analysis of the funding and management of the core Koranic institutions, including the mosques, the priests, and the schools and universities.

## Weber's Theory of Religion

Weber's theory about religion comprises several studies, some of which are collected in the three volumes of his *Gesammelte Aufsätze zur Religionssoziologie* (1963–72), which appeared after his death in 1920. It contains numerous fragments of a theory about the economic implications of core religious beliefs, together with extensive comparative historical research, in order to confirm that the actual consequences of long-established religious beliefs are indeed what the theory predicts. Weber limits himself to looking at the economic aspects of the major world religions, in particular whether they further economic growth or economic rationality – that is, '*die Wirtschaftlichen Konsequenzen der Weltreligionen*'.

Weber has a specific perspective when he looks at economic development, namely that of modern capitalism. Sustained processes of economic growth are engineered by capitalist processes, in which the characteristic feature is the means–end rational action on a grand scale, meaning that the capitalist is oriented towards mastering the world by means of huge enterprises that are bent to his or her short-term economic profits which are capitalized long-term in the form of worldly possessions. Thus, modern capitalism is rational and present-minded. Where could such an orientation originate considering the power of traditional modes of thinking in all of the ancient civilisations? Protestantism, suggested Weber in 1904.

His later comparative studies sought to confirm this theory about the developmental implications of Protestantism, when he undertook to examine at great length all the world religions except Islam. Most interestingly, he argued that Buddhism or Confucianism could not bring forward economic growth, at least not in the form of modern capitalism. Let us quote from that examination, because here he states in effect very clearly what is distinctive of puritan or ascetic Protestantism by comparing it with its opposite.

Weber explicitly rejects any positive connection between Buddhism and an ethic of economic behaviour. In fact, he claims that Buddhism as a set of religious beliefs excludes a spirit of capitalism. Examining various forms of Buddhism he states that Buddhism *'wurde eine der grössten Missionsreligionen der Erde'* (Weber, 1972, p. 248), but he fails to see any real rational reason for that. To Weber, Buddhism is basically asocial:

> Assurance of one's state of grace, that is, certain knowledge of one's own salvation is not sought through proving one's self by any inner-worldly or extra-worldly action, by 'work' of any kind, but, in contrast to this, it is sought in a psychic state remote from activity. (Weber, 1996, p. 213)

And after having analysed how '[t]he specific asocial character of all genuine mysticism is here carried to its maximum' (Weber, 1996, p. 213), he concludes that Buddhism is fundamentally *'eine Mönchs-Religion'* and that 'a rational economic ethic could hardly develop in this sort of religious order' (Weber, 1996, p. 216). Considering the enormous economic success of the Buddhist countries in South-east Asia and mainland China after Weber's lifetime, one must ask whether this analysis of Buddhism really covers the whole picture.

In relation to Confucianism Weber acknowledges that it is as rational as Puritanism, displaying *'Nüchternheit'* (prudence) and *'Sparsamkeit'* (thrift). The key difference is the internal drive of Puritanism and the external adaptation of Confucianism. Weber states:

> But only the Puritan rational ethic with its supramundane orientation brought economic rationalism to its consistent conclusion. This happened merely because nothing was further from the conscious puritan intention. It happened because

inner-worldly work was simply expressive of the striving for a transcendental goal. (Weber, 1964, p. 247)

Thus, the inner drive of Puritanism towards 'rationale *Beherrschung der Welt*' reflected its extra-worldly orientation – undoubtedly a complicated, if not paradoxical, explanation. In any case, Weber here identifies the two critical aspects of any religion in so far as they are relevant to his special perspective, namely 'die *Wirtschaftsethik der Weltreligionen*'. In his view, these two dimensions of any religion – rationality versus irrationality and '*Jenseits*' versus '*Diesseits*' – explain why religions have developmental consequences. These two properties – rationality versus irrationality, on the one hand, and what is called '*Diesseits*' (inner-worldliness) versus '*Jenseits*' (extra-worldliness) on the other hand are combined in Figure 5.1 (Weber, 1963, pp. 237–75).

It is not difficult to find examples of all four kinds of religion, arising from combinations of the two critical aspects. Weber's basic model is that a religious orientation of type I brings forward economic growth in the form of modern capitalism, although paradoxically such an '*innerweltlich*' orientation 'an *sich nichts ferner* lag', as Weber admits (Weber, 1963. pp. 235–6). Extra-worldly religions with a so-called '*ausserweltlich* orientation' are typically strongly eschatological, meaning that life on this earth is but a preparation for life after death, which is more real or true. But, even though it may have a rational attitude towards the mechanisms that govern life on earth, how can a religion with a strong *Jenseits* orientation foster something as mundane as economic growth or affluence? Can we make sense of the connection between religion and economic output without making use of Weber's complicated explanation in terms of redemption and double predestination as in Calvinism, Puritanism and other Protestant sects?

Economic growth is the rise in output from production. On a long-term basis, it can only be brought about by savings being channelled into productive investments that increase the capital stock in society. Sustained economic growth is only feasible in a rational environment where people are oriented towards activity in this world. Thus, economic development would prosper from a belief system of type I. Which of the world religions come closest to type I?

Weber's genius was that he knew that religions harbour a variety of beliefs, values and lifestyles. One and the same religion may appear in very different

|  | **Rationality** | **Irrationality** |
|---|---|---|
| **Inner-worldliness** | I | II |
| **Extra-worldliness** | III | IV |

**Figure 5.1  Basic Weber orientations in all religions**

formations. For instance, taking Christianity, what are the core beliefs? Those of the layman or those of the *virtuosi* – for example, the monks or nuns or Aquinas, Luther or Calvin? Various trends can be found in all religions, some moving closer to rationality and *Diesseits* or *Jenseits* than others. Mysticism, asceticism, priesthood, personal piety and religious indifference are to be found in all of the world religions.

Weber in his *Verstehen* focused on the logic of core beliefs and the implications of these beliefs for action. Thus, not only did he show empirically that modern capitalism arose among people who happened to adhere to various branches of Puritanism (ascetic Protestantism) but he also claimed that the logic of Puritanism would entail or promote modern capitalism. However, in accomplishing both these objectives he had to make a transition from rational *Jenseits* to rational *Diesseits* although, admittedly, it does not actually seem to make much sense.

If one dares to make generalizations about the world religions, given their heterogeneity, then, with the exception of countries or regions where Islam is strong, there is one obvious candidate for type I – the combination of Buddhism and Confucianism that dominates South East Asia to-day. Although there are widely different forms of Buddhism, the combination with Confucianism seems to result in a religious belief system with a work ethic that would be eminently suitable for serving as the foundation for economic development.

Hinduism and Catholicism would have to be placed under irrationality, the first with a *Diesseits* bias and the second with a *Jenseits* bias. Islam is clearly rational and *Jenseits*, at least so in both its main orientations, Sunni and Shia, but not under Sufism. Judaism would belong to the same group, as there was always a clear connection between the two, also explicitly recognized in the Torahn. The classification may be expanded to include other religions like Taoism or various types of Protestantism, but the basic model must be that type I fosters economic growth. It has been argued that Weber's thesis about the economic consequences of religious beliefs was merely a historical explanation. It answered the question that had puzzled many for a long time: why capitalism first in Western Europe? However, as Weber always emphasized the general implications of social science arguments, his thesis could be interpreted as a general theory about the social consequences of various religions.

We could apply the Weber theory to the religions of today in order to look for evidence of the effects of religions on economic development. This may not be doing justice to Weber, but the key question is still with us: does religion promote economic development? If so, which religion has the largest impact? Many would argue that Weber's theory of religion concerns only the origins of modern capitalism. However, this leads to the confusing debate about what capitalism is and how modern capitalism differs from ancient or medieval capitalism – see the discussion between Weber and Sombart, for instance. Nevertheless, in whatever manner in which Weber is interpreted, it remains an urgent task to identify or clarify the outcomes of the world religions.

In the proposed new analysis which would also include the profound economic growth processes occurring after the Second World War, it may also be desirable to interpret development more broadly. Thus, we will include not only output or economic development, but also social development and political development, the former meaning quality of life or equality of living standards and the latter the implementation of civil and political rights (that is, democracy) as we have outlined in Chapter 2. But, in the empirical inquiry, we will first classify a number of countries according to the prevailing or dominant religious belief in that country.

## Mapping the Major World Religions

As religious beliefs tend to be stable over time, if religion results in outcomes, then they will sooner or later be discovered. However, these consequences may not be immediately observable as soon as they begin to operate, however, if there are other factors at work which neutralize the development implications of religion, like, for instance, civil war. Thus, one should examine the outcomes of religious belief using long time spans.

Now, religious beliefs are not completely unchangeable. Over very long time periods one may observe fundamental changes in religious creed, including not only secularization but also the shift among broad population groups from one religion to another. The advance of Islam during the twentieth century, not only in terms of its geographical extension but also in terms of a heightened intensity of Islamic belief, is an example of change. What is the relative strength of the major world religions? Table 5.2 shows the number of countries where a majority of the population adheres to one creed in 1900 and 1994. The secularization trend is not well measured in this table though.

Among 150 countries, covering 98 per cent of the population on earth, most countries are either Christian, Muslim or Buddhist. The countries that practise Hinduism are not that numerous, but the number of Hindus is immense considering the size of India. There are far more Roman Catholic countries than Protestant or Orthodox Christian. The advance of Islam in the twentieth century is clearly shown in the table. In relation to some 150 countries of the world today, one may establish that the dominating religion in a country, or the religious creed that a majority of the population adheres to, has been the same one during the twentieth century in as many as 104 of these. The changing countries are those where Christianity has replaced traditionalism – 19 countries – or those where Islam has replaced traditionalism – eight countries – as well as those where Atheism has become dominant, as in communist countries or former communist countries or in countries where secularization has been extensive – five countries all in all. The country

**Table 5.2    World religions: number of countries**

| World Religions | 1900 | 1994 |
|---|---|---|
| Christian | 66 | 78 |
|   Roman Catholic | 38 | 46 |
|   Protestant | 13 | 16 |
|   Orthodox | 12 | 11 |
|   Anglican | 3 | 1 |
| Muslim | 32 | 41 |
| Hindu | 3 | 3 |
| Buddhist | 12 | 13 |
| Jewish | 0 | 1 |
| Other/non-religious | 37 | 14 |

*Notes*:    Other/non-religious covers atheists and non-religious as well as people with animism.
For 1900 our assumption is that the territories of the countries at that time corresponds
roughly with the territories of the countries of the 1990s.
*Sources*: Barrett (1982); Encyclopaedia Britannica (1995).

variation is so substantial that it must be possible to estimate whether various
religions present different outcome configurations and perhaps, in the next
step, test whether religion is the factor that matters for these outcomes.

Table 5.3 gives data on how large the world religions are in terms of the
number of people who practise them. Note that secularization is a powerful
trend in most countries, as the number of atheists/non religious has risen
sharply.

Interestingly, the two expanding world religions are currently Islam and
Roman Catholicism, especially the former. Remarkably, the number of
Buddhists has declined dramatically, relatively speaking, and the Hindus are
now more numerous than the Buddhists, reflecting the immense population
growth in India. Also Protestantism has declined in relative size. The sharp
relative decline of Buddhism reflects the spread of atheism in China and
Japan, which may not be an irreversible trend, given the fact that one of the
principal sources of atheism, namely communism, is losing its attraction
worldwide. It is an open question whether atheism in former communist
countries or communist China will recede to the advantage of religions such
as Greek Orthodoxy (Russia) or Buddhism–Confucianism (China). The
profound process of secularization, so often emphasized in social analysis of
the twentieth century, has not affected two of the world religions, Hinduism
or Islam, as it has mainly concerned Christianity, especially Protestantism, or
Buddhism.

Table 5.4 shows the distribution of the world religions according to
continent. Again, one notes the profound process towards secularization, or

**Table 5.3    Worldwide adherence to the major religions as a percentage of the total population: 1900–98**

| Religion | 1900 | 1970 | 1980 | 1990 | 1994 | 1998 |
|---|---|---|---|---|---|---|
| Christian | 34.4 | 33.7 | 32.8 | 33.3 | 33.6 | 32.8 |
| Roman Catholic | 16.8 | 18.5 | 18.5 | 18.8 | 18.7 | 17.3 |
| Protestant | 7.4 | 7.2 | 6.4 | 6.9 | 6.9 | 5.3 |
| Orthodox | 7.5 | 3.1 | 2.8 | 3.2 | 3.2 | 3.6 |
| Anglican | 2.0 | 1.7 | 1.5 | 1.4 | 1.4 | 1.1 |
| Muslim | 12.4 | 15.3 | 16.5 | 17.7 | 18.3 | 19.6 |
| Hindu | 12.5 | 12.8 | 13.3 | 13.3 | 13.5 | 12.8 |
| Buddhist | 31.7 | 12.5 | 11.0 | 9.3 | 8.8 | 12.5 |
| Jewish | 0.8 | 0.4 | 0.4 | 0.3 | 0.2 | 0.2 |
| Atheist/non-religious | 0.2 | 19.6 | 20.3 | 20.8 | 20.5 | 15.3 |
| Other | 8.0 | 5.7 | 5.7 | 5.3 | 5.1 | 6.8 |

*Sources*: 1900–1980: Barrett (1982); 1990: Barrett (1991); 1994: Barrett (1995); 1998: Barrett (1999).

the increase in atheists/non-religious not only in communist countries but also in Western Europe.

Again, the overwhelming impression is that of variation. No one continent has the same pattern of religious beliefs as any other continent. In Africa it is Christianity versus Islam. On the one hand one can note the immense expansion of Christianity there since 1900, reflecting one aspect of colonialism, and, on the other hand, one can observe the recent heavy expansion of Islam southwards. Religion in Asia is a contest between Buddhism, Hinduism and Islam, although one must take into account at the same time the many atheists in the Far Eastern communist countries, of which numbers are difficult to estimate accurately.

Europe has a totally different religious map, comprising basically Christians of various kinds and atheists/non-religious. The decline of Protestantism is obvious in the data, which reflects the increase in atheism/non-religious. Whereas Hinduism and Buddhism are virtually non-existent in Europe, there is a not insignificant and growing minority of Muslims, or almost 3 per cent. The relative size of the Jewish community is very small in Europe and Russia today due, on the one hand, to the Holocaust and to emigration to Israel on the other. In the UK Anglicanism is the dominant Christian creed, which may be classified dogmatically as somewhere between Protestantism and Catholicism, perhaps closer to the former than to the latter. The number of Anglicans is also large in Oceania. The Americas harbour almost exclusively Christians, while the Roman Catholics prevail completely in Latin America. North America has an almost even distribution of Protestants (who dominated highly around 1900) and Roman Catholics, besides a growing number of atheists/non-religious. The decline of Protestantism in North America has been spectacular during the 100 years since Weber published his first study of religion and development, and it is hardly compensated for by recent advances in Latin America.

According to Table 5.4, the former USSR has a very large proportion of atheists, exceeding the numbers of the Greek Orthodox and Muslims there. It will be most interesting to see whether in future the former communist countries will experience a revitalization of their suppressed religions or whether secularization will continue. As there seems to be little secularization within Islam, constituting a constant warning against the prediction that twentieth-century modernization would soften religious beliefs, one may expect atheism to decline in Russia as well as in the new southern and eastern republics along its borders.

One may establish that the only truly expanding religion today is Islam. This force shows up in turmoil along the borders between Islamic countries and their neighbours. The rejuvenation of Islam also affects the internal affairs of the Muslim countries, causing political instability and civil war in some cases. The only similar trend among the other religions is the occurrence of the fundamental Protestantism as in Brazil, Orthodox Judaism in Israel and Hindu nationalism in India.

Another basic observation in relation to Table 5.4 is that religious structure is very stable over time. Only in Africa and in countries under communist rule do we find profound changes during the twentieth century. The sharp decline in the number of people adhering to Judaism reflects the strong currents of anti-Semitism in the twentieth century. Weber devoted a whole volume to the analysis of ancient Judaism but wrote little systematically about Islam, which today is the most rapidly spreading religion. Before the First World War almost all the Islamic countries were under colonial rule, at least with regard to the Arabs, so it is impossible to explain the revival of Islam or Islamic fundamentalism without taking into account the legacy of colonialism. It is not entirely misplaced perhaps to explain Weber's neglect of Islam as being due to the prevailing Western bias against Arabs.

Although Weber dealt with the chief differences between the world's large religions, he was very much aware of how many different versions of creed each one of them had come to comprise. At all times he is careful to point out that religion is not a homogeneous entity and that Buddhism, for instance, has several faces. The same is true of Protestantism with its various creeds, from Lutheranism to Pietism. One may research how divided a country is in terms of religious beliefs, bypassing whether one or another religion prevails. Some countries in the world are highly heterogeneous, but most tend to be rather homogenous.

Table 5.4 Worldwide adherence to the major religions by continental area as a percentage of the total population: 1900 and 1994

| Religion | Africa | | Asia | | Europe | | Latin America | | North America | | Oceania | | Europe (formerly USSR) | |
|---|---|---|---|---|---|---|---|---|---|---|---|---|---|---|
| | 1900 | 1994 | 1900 | 1994 | 1900 | 1994 | 1900 | 1994 | 1900 | 1994 | 1900 | 1994 | 1900 | 1994 |
| Christian | 9.2 | 48.7 | 2.0 | 9.1 | 96.9 | 82.0 | 95.1 | 85.3 | 96.6 | 85.3 | 77.6 | 81.9 | 83.6 | 38.2 |
| Roman Catholic | 1.9 | 18.3 | 1.1 | 3.9 | 59.8 | 52.1 | 92.3 | 86.8 | 18.8 | 34.8 | 17.3 | 29.7 | 9.2 | 2.0 |
| Protestant | 2.3 | 13.0 | 0.2 | 2.6 | 20.3 | 14.7 | 1.5 | 3.7 | 63.7 | 34.5 | 29.9 | 27.2 | 1.8 | 3.4 |
| Orthodox | 3.3 | 4.2 | 0.3 | 0.1 | 7.9 | 7.2 | 0.0 | 0.4 | 0.6 | 2.2 | 0.1 | 2.1 | 72.6 | 32.8 |
| Anglican | 0.5 | 4.0 | 0.1 | 0.0 | 8.9 | 6.5 | 1.3 | 0.3 | 4.6 | 2.6 | 29.9 | 20.7 | 0.0 | 0.0 |
| Muslim | 32.0 | 40.7 | 15.7 | 20.2 | 1.0 | 2.6 | 0.1 | 0.3 | 0.0 | 1.9 | 0.2 | 0.4 | 11.2 | 15.3 |
| Hindu | 0.3 | 0.2 | 21.4 | 22.7 | 0.0 | 0.1 | 0.3 | 0.2 | 0.0 | 0.5 | 0.2 | 1.3 | 0.0 | 0.0 |
| Buddhist | 0.0 | 0.0 | 54.4 | 14.8 | 0.0 | 0.1 | 0.0 | 0.1 | 0.1 | 0.2 | 0.3 | 0.2 | 0.3 | 0.1 |
| Jewish | 0.4 | 0.0 | 0.0 | 0.1 | 1.6 | 0.3 | 0.0 | 0.1 | 1.9 | 2.0 | 0.3 | 0.3 | 4.2 | 0.3 |
| Atheist/non-religious | 0.0 | 0.5 | 0.0 | 26.9 | 0.5 | 14.5 | 0.6 | 4.8 | 1.2 | 8.7 | 0.7 | 15.2 | 0.2 | 45.8 |
| Other | 58.1 | 9.9 | 6.5 | 6.2 | 0.0 | 0.4 | 3.9 | 5.5 | 0.2 | 1.4 | 20.7 | 0.7 | 0.5 | 0.3 |

*Note:* Other = animist; Buddhist includes Chinese folk religion practitioners, Confucians and Shintoists.
*Sources:* 1900: Barrett (1982); 1994: Encyclopaedia Britannica (1995).

**Conclusion**

Religion is a source of cultural identity all over the world. Religious creed involves an orientation towards a few major systems of thought, constituting the huge civilizations of the world. It must, however, be recognized that atheists no longer constitute a small group, unlike animists who have declined in numbers. We have also been able to show that countries with one religion around 1900 tend to have the same religion 100 years later. Changes have occurred, particularly with respect to the categories atheists/non-religious and others. Picking 1970 as the basic year for the measurement of religious creed would in fact summarize the entire twentieth century. In Chapter 6 we will look at the outcomes of the major world religions of today, using number of adherents as the weight of the religion.

In this chapter we have looked at various conceptual frameworks for classifying the myriad religious phenomena. There is no one single correct scheme, but the Weber approach is worth pursuing on account of its emphasis on outcomes. We will now turn to the analysis of the configuration of outcomes that characterize the various world religions. We will analyse the variation in outcomes during the last few decades, fixing religious structure to 1970. As religious creed changes slowly, its impact on development may be measured by examining information about outcomes after 1970. This amounts to a cross-sectional approach, as one would want to know, first, if countries that differ in terms of their main religion in 1970 also display differences in outcomes between 1970 and 1995 and, second, if any such country differences really can be attributed to religious creed.

We have not been able to find any cross-sectional evidence for the hypothesis about a crucial link between religion and economic activity. On the contrary, we found a strong relationship between religion and human rights. Does this finding reduce the relevance of Weber's thesis about a close connection between religion and modern capitalism?

One may very well argue that Weber's thesis is exclusively a historical argument about the unique rise of modern capitalism in Western Europe. Nothing prevents people in other civilisations to imitate what evolved in Western Europe. And imitation may become so successful that other civilisations become more economically dynamic than the model countries themselves. Such a narrow historical interpretation of the Weber thesis would rescue the argument but it comes with a price. It would undo an effort to employ Weber's typology in a search for a sociological theory of the outcomes of religion in a cross-sectional perspective upon the world religions today and their social, economic and political outcomes. And it also goes against the effort of Weber to present a general sociological theory of the consequences of the different world religions.

Be that as it may, Weber's typology, based upon the concepts rational against irrational as well as inner worldly and outer worldly proved highly fruitful in analysing the preconditions for the rise of capitalism. Let us end here with a note on these concepts pointing out how they could be employed in an almost too flexible manner. One may use the clear exposition in *The Religion of China* (1964) where Weber pins down what he derives his typology from, consisting of two 'yardsticks':

> To judge the level of rationalization a religion represents we may use two primary yardsticks which are in many ways interrelated. One is the degree to which the religion has divested itself of magic; the other is the degree to which it has systematically unified the relationship to the world. (Weber, 1964, p. 226)

One may criticize these concepts as being too imprecise. Is not all religious behaviour in some sense irrational? Even the puritan approaching the world in a rational and systematic manner acts upon beliefs which in the final resort are merely just that: beliefs without any claim to truth. All religions whether primitive or abstract share a basic irrational ambition, namely to master reality by means of the conception of a supra natural entitity(ies) called 'spirit' or 'God'. When some religions are scaled as more rational than others, then it begs the question of what is rationality.

The distinction between inneworldly and outerworldly is even more perplexing. One may certainly make a distinction between life and death, but there is in reality only one world, namely the world as we actually live and perceive it – the innerworldly perspective. All religions add another dimension in the form of a belief in a world that is somehow outside this world here and now. The world religions differ in terms of how they mix these two aspects of religion: innerworldly and outerworldly. Thus, it is somewhat arbitrary to identify one religion as innerworldly and another as outerworldly.

Weber relies heavily upon the distinction between this world here and now on the one hand and a world after death or beyond the senses. And his paradoxical argument amounts to a link between the two, as it is the rational drive within this world which is going to give the puritan his/her ticket to the other world. Thus, innerworldly asceticism promotes the basically irrational search for a place in the outer world. Protestantism was rational by intention rejecting magic but it promoted innerwordly asceticism as a means towards outworldly salvation:

> But only the Puritan rational ethic with its supramundane orientation brought economic rationalism to is conclusion. This happened merely because nothing was further from the conscious Puritan intention. It happened because inner-worldly work was simply expressive of the striving for a transcendental goal. The world, as promised, fell to Puritanism because the Puritans alone "had striven for God and his justice". (Weber, 1964, pp. 247–8)

If the rejection of magic and innerworldly asceticism characterized the Protestantism, then in his *The Religion of India* (1958) Weber pinpoints the absence of exactly these two factors as crucial for the lack of economic development:

It was lacking in precisely that which was decisive for the economics of the Occident: the refraction and rational immersion of the drive character of economic striving and its accompaniments in a system of rational inner-worldly ethic of behaviour, e.g. the 'inner-worldly asceticism' of Protestantism in the West. Asiatic religion could not supply the presuppositions of inner-worldly asceticism. (Weber, 1996, p. 337)

It was the combination of both mysticism and the ascetism of the philosophy of *yoga* and *nirvana* that made modern capitalism impossible in Asia:

Asia's partly purely mystical, partly purely innerworldly aesthetic goal of self-discipline could take no other form than an emptying of experience of the real forces of experience. (Weber, 1996, p. 342)

Weber's thesis is paradoxical, as one religion – Protestantism – is both highly distinct in terms of his two 'yardsticks', but it may just as well be classified as both rational and irrational as well as both innerworldly and outerworldly. How can there be any 'experience of the real forces of experience' with regard to any method of salvation?

# Chapter 6

# Religion and its Outcomes

## Introduction

Religious belief has been the main outlet for the people's search for meaning and identity since the dawn of human civilizations 3000 years before Christ. In the previous chapter we attempted to hint at some of the variety of religious belief, offering different classification schemes or typologies. Here, in this chapter, we concentrate on the impact of religion on society, politics and economics.

The debate over the Weber theory, so lauded in 1904, has focused exclusively on historical interpretation. Here, we will attempt a fresh start by focusing on the relevance of his theory for the comparative analysis of culture and development today, asking: what are the macro effects of the world religions today? The assessment of religion urgently needs to be expanded to include not only economic development, but also social and political development. Since religion tends to be fairly stable over time, one can use average measures on developmental indicators in order to find out whether the different world religions tend to be associated with different developmental outcomes, employing measures for the period after 1945.

When attempting to state the present-day relevance of the famous Weber theory about the Protestantic ethic and its economic consequences, it may be emphasized that Weber's theory was launched in two steps. First, he argued that the rise of modern capitalism as an economic system was influenced by the emergence of Protestantism in Northern Europe and North America. Second, he generalized the finding into a comparative historical assessment of the world religions, examining Hinduism, Buddhism, Confucianism and Judaism in depth, but not Islam, aiming at the conclusion that none of the world religions had the same impact as Protestantism. It is the latter part of the argument that we will investigate through a comparative analysis of the situation today.

## Macro Outcomes: Weber Again

Weber suggested a theory about the economic implications of different world religions, but the idea could be framed more generally. Weber's theory of religion focused exclusively on economic development. The argument was that one of the world religions contained a set of beliefs and values which had ethical implications for the conduct of action in economic affairs that would result in behavioural consequences conducive to economic growth. The creed of Protestantism would contain the seeds of the spirit of capitalism, which would be the foundation for long periods of economic expansion, resulting in the affluence of Northern Europe and North America.

Weber claimed not only that Protestantism constituted a sufficient condition for modern capitalism, but also attempted to show, in his later comparative studies on religion, that Protestantism constituted a necessary condition for capitalism, in the sense that no other world religion contained ideas that could be linked with the spirit of capitalism. We are not only interested in showing that the necessary condition argument is more dubious than the sufficient condition argument, which has been debated extensively in the literature. We also wish to include other aspects of development, because there is really no reason that one should only deal with economic outcomes and bypass political ones. Generalizing Weber's thesis about the economic consequences of religion as a culture can be done in two directions. First, the thesis can be deprived of its historical connotation and transformed into a general social science theory that is not bounded or restricted to a specific evolution in time. Second, it can be broadened to cover other kinds of outcome besides the economic ones such as the political and social aspects of development.

It is somewhat astounding that Weber bypassed the coming of democracy, although perhaps it is unjust to make a critical point out of this, as there is no natural limit to the outcomes that can be included in the study of the consequences of religious beliefs and practice. However, the important point is that had Weber included politics, then he might have seen another connection between Protestantism and macro outcomes.

The basic idea in development theory about a ladder of stages, going from a low to a high level of development is questionable. What do we really mean by a 'developed society'? Whatever the word 'development' may mean, one encounters a country variation in outcomes that call for a social science explanation. Development studies have focused on certain outcomes linked with economic development, on the one hand, and social and political development on the other. We included these outcomes in our discussion of 'What Culture Matters For' in Chapter 2. Thus, we will introduce a number of variables measuring economic growth in various ways in order to inquire into the economic outcomes of religion as culture. What is the impact of the world religions on economic growth during different time periods after the Second World War? The time periods we have selected here are 1960–73, 1973–85, 1985–94 and 1990–98. The key questions to be examined below include:

1    Are the different world religions of the world today attended by different configurations of outcomes, not only economic but also social and political?

If religion matters, then it must matter for at least one of the outcomes specified above – that is, for either social, economic or political outcomes. Perhaps each world religion is attended by a specific outcome configuration, one may guess. If so, then question 2 needs to be raised.

2    When the world religions have different outcome configurations, is religion really a key causal factor in bringing about these outcomes?

Question 2 is more difficult to answer than question 1, since we know that each major outcome has a complex causality. But question 1 may be addressed rather easily by examining the present state of development, classifying the countries according to the religious creed of the majority of their populations and measuring their performance record on outcomes. Below, we undertake a performance analysis of where countries with different creeds stand on key indices on economic, social and political outcomes. Such an overview may provide us with a few clues about whether the world religions are attended by outcomes in a systematic, and not merely historical, fashion.

*Economic Outcomes: Affluence and Economic Growth*

It is a well-known fact that there are enormous differences in affluence or total economic output in the world today. On a per capita basis some countries are ten or even almost 100 times richer than other countries. World Bank statistics classify countries as low-, medium- and high-income countries, but what is the picture like when we group countries according to religion? Table 6.1 has the information about gross domestic product (GDP) per capita in 1990 as well as the data about purchasing power parities (PPP) per capita for 1997, where the countries of the world have been organized according to world religion.

Table 6.1 could be interpreted in a Weberian manner, pointing to the fact that the set of Protestant countries remains the richest in the world almost 100 years after the first publication of the Weberian theory in 1904. But how can we account for a high level of affluence in the set of Buddhist–Confucian countries within a Weberian framework? There are many ways to classify the countries of the world, religion constituting only one possible alternative. The relatively low eta-squared scores suggest that religion capture only part of the country variation in economic wealth, other factors playing a role.

More specifically, the eta-squared scores indicates that the variation within the categories in Table 6.1 is larger than the variation between the categories, meaning that religion is not the critical factor behind the country differences in affluence. Both the set of Roman Catholic and the set of Protestant countries now include Third World countries, which were traditionalist around 1900. These African countries have failed to develop quickly, but this may be due to other reasons than religion. The Muslim countries display low averages, despite the fact that several of the rich Gulf states enter here.

**Table 6.1     Affluence and religion: GDP per capita 1990 and PPP per capita 1997 in US$**

| Major religion | GDPCAP90 | | PPP97 | |
|---|---|---|---|---|
| Roman Catholic | 6 712 | (N=43) | 9 010 | (N=47) |
| Protestant | 11 535 | (N=14) | 13 087 | (N=16) |
| Orthodox | 6 320 | (N= 5) | 4 110 | (N=10) |
| Muslim | 2 843 | (N=34) | 4 119 | (N=38) |
| Hindu | 3 119 | (N= 3) | 3 993 | (N= 3) |
| Buddhist | 6 522 | (N=13) | 9 058 | (N=12) |
| Atheist/non-religious | 6 598 | (N= 5) | 7 746 | (N= 5) |
| Other | 1 059 | (N=13) | 1 716 | (N=12) |
| eta squared | .24 | | .22 | |
| sig. | .000 | | .000 | |

*Note*:     The classification of countries according to religious adherence basically follows the one in Table 5.2.
*Sources*: See Appendix A.

Table 6.1 also presents another indicator on affluence, the purchasing power parities (PPP) for 1997. Here, we note, even more strikingly, the ascent of the Buddhist/Confucian culture in terms of economic development during the twentieth century. Again, the eta-squared statistic is low, meaning that countries vary more within the categories than between the categories. Yet, the finding is crystal clear – namely that Buddhist countries are now almost on a par with Roman Catholic countries and not far off from the Protestant countries.

Economic development has not been impressive in the Hindu or Muslim world, nor also in the Orthodox world. Islam as religion combines rationality with an extreme outer-worldly orientation, which is more conducive to belligerent behaviour – at least in Weber's view – than to the peaceful conduct which promotes slow but continuous economic development. The Roman Catholic countries include the former Spanish and Portuguese empires covering large parts of the Third World. Perhaps it is not so much religion that matters here as the Spanish state heritage, and some scholars at least have argued to this effect – see Chapter 9. These sets of countries, classified with religion as basis, cover both rich and poor countries, with the result that the average scores hide a considerable variation. Yet, religion shows up somehow in these numbers, and this requires further research.

Looking, in addition, at data on economic growth substantiates the overall finding here, which is that Buddhism/Confucianism is the religion with the outstanding economic development record in the second half of the twentieth century. Table 6.2 displays four series with average economic growth data for which the eta squares are on par with affluence, meaning that the various sets

**Table 6.2    Affluence and religion: economic growth 1960–73, 1973–85, 1985–94 and 1990–98 – average annual growth by major religion**

| Major religion | GRO6073 | GRO7385 | GRO8594 | GRO9098 |
|---|---|---|---|---|
| Roman Catholic | 2.9 (N=40) | 0.6 (N=40) | 0.4 (N=45) | 1.0 (N=47) |
| Protestant | 3.4 (N=13) | 0.8 (N=14) | −0.3 (N=16) | 0.9 (N=16) |
| Orthodox | 5.4 (N= 3) | 2.1 (N= 2) | −6.4 (N= 8) | −4.9 (N=10) |
| Muslim | 2.7 (N=27) | 1.3 (N=28) | −1.3 (N=35) | −0.8 (N=35) |
| Hindu | 0.9 (N= 2) | 1.4 (N= 3) | 3.6 (N= 3) | 3.5 (N= 3) |
| Buddhist | 3.5 (N=13) | 4.7 (N= 7) | 4.1 (N= 8) | 3.3 (N=12) |
| Jewish | 5.6 (N= 1) | 0.4 (N= 1) | 2.5 (N= 1) | 2.2 (N= 1) |
| Atheist/non-religious | 2.3 (N= 4) | 3.2 (N= 2) | 2.2 (N= 3) | 3.8 (N= 3) |
| Other | 1.5 (N=11) | −0.1 (N=12) | −0.2 (N=12) | 0.4 (N=12) |
| eta squared | .12 | .22 | .27 | .24 |
| sig. | .093 | .001 | .000 | .000 |

*Note*:    The classification of countries according to religious adherence basically follows the one in Table 5.2.
*Sources*: See Appendix A.

of world religions contain countries with both low and high average growth rates. Economic growth is, after all, also a function of several factors.

It has been argued (Krugman, 1994) that the economic miracle in Southeast Asia was built upon special circumstances (state control, forced inexpensive labour) which, when it started to disappear during the 1990s, would limit the growth potential in this part of the world. Sometimes the recession in 1996–98 is regarded as a validation of this argument about the superficial nature of economic development in South-east Asia. We believe that this is erroneous and amounts to a too negative view of economic growth in this part of the world. Once the overheating process in 1996 has worked itself out, we predict that economic growth will resume. Indeed, recent data seem to confirm that the Asian bubble was a temporary phenomenon. On the other hand, the dismal trend for the Orthodox countries could well continue for some time or until transparent market institutions are put in place instead of the planned economy. The Orthodox countries suffer less from culture than from institutional confusion.

Thus, the countries with a dominant Buddhist/Confucian religion display consistently high growth rates whereas economic growth among the countries with a different religion fluctuates considerably, from periods of sustained growth to periods of zero or even negative growth: indeed, economic growth was negative for several Orthodox and Muslim countries in the 1990s. A long period with high economic growth must result in a doubling or tripling of the

**Table 6.3    Religion and social development: the HDI, GDI, GEM and Gini indicators**

| Major religion | HDI99 | GDI99 | GEM99 | GINI90 |
|---|---|---|---|---|
| Roman Catholic | .732 (N=47) | .757 (N=42) | .517 (N=35) | 40.0 (N=20) |
| Protestant | .792 (N=16) | .789 (N=16) | .612 (N=14) | 40.8 (N= 9) |
| Orthodox | .750 (N=10) | .753 (N= 8) | .404 (N= 4) | 29.0 (N= 9) |
| Muslim | .598 (N=38) | .579 (N=32) | .280 (N=18) | 40.7 (N=11) |
| Hindu | .591 (N= 3) | .573 (N= 3) | .334 (N= 2) | 34.1 (N= 2) |
| Buddhist | .695 (N=12) | .706 (N=11) | .414 (N= 5) | 37.8 (N= 6) |
| Jewish | .883 (N= 1) | .879 (N= 1) | .496 (N= 1) | – |
| Atheist/non religious | .805 (N= 4) | .802 (N= 4) | .568 (N= 4) | 30.7 (N= 3) |
| Other | .445 (N=12) | .434 (N=11) | .341 (N= 7) | 47.3 (N= 7) |
| eta squared | .24 | .39 | .55 | .21 |
| sig. | .000 | .000 | .000 | .098 |

*Note*:    The classification of countries according to religious adherence basically follows the one in Table 5.2.
*Sources*: See Appendix A.

level of affluence. But how is affluence distributed? Let us look at social outcomes.

*Quality of Life, Gender and Income Equality*

The concept of social development is most often seen as being complementary to that of economic development, as it takes into account what economic output means for ordinary people. There are a number of possible indicators on social outcomes, including the Human Development Index (HDI) and income distribution measures (GINI), as well as indicators on gender development (GDI) and gender empowerment (GEM), which will be used below. In the HDI life expectancy at birth, adult literacy rate and combined gross enrolment in education is added to the PPP per capita in order to derive a broader index of quality of life than merely aggregate economic output. The GDI is a Gender-related Development Index that measures particularly the position of women in relation to men and the GEM captures the empowerment of women. Table 6.3 shows how countries adhering to the world religions perform on these social outcome measures.

Despite that a number of Third World countries have been entered into the categories of Catholic and Protestant countries it is clear that Protestant countries score very high on social development, both on the Human Development Index and the Gender-related Development Index. At the other end of these scales we find, as before, countries where animism is still strong or where the dominant religion is Islam, especially when it comes to the GDI and the GEM. One must remember though that these average scores are affected by the number of countries for which data is available; lack of data on many Third World Roman Catholic countries has driven average scores downwards. Buddhist/Confucian countries cannot match the Protestant countries when it comes to social development. Surprisingly, Orthodox countries score higher than Buddhist countries, which cannot be explained by the fact that some traditional Greek Orthodox countries have been placed as atheist. The atheist/non-religious category displays, in some cases, astonishingly high measures. This category covers countries as diverse as China, Cuba, the Czech Republic and the Netherlands.

Table 6.3 also has information about income distribution, although data is not available for as many countries as one would wish to include in the analysis. The eta squared scores indicate that income distribution has less to do with religion in contrast to the eta squared scores for the other above-mentioned social outcomes, namely gender development or especially gender empowerment (GEM). However, it looks as if the income distribution in Muslim countries tends to be much more evenly than that of Catholic countries which are characterized by substantial income inequalities. Buddhist countries are less egalitarian than Protestant countries, if one may judge from such a limited sample of countries. Matters are different with regard to the status of women, where religion seems to matter very much, especially Islam.

*Democracy and Corruption*

There are a couple of scales in the literature which measure the implementation of civil and political rights. The scores on these scales correlate highly with each other and tend to be rather stable over time, except when a major transformation takes place in several countries at the same time, such as the wave of democratization initiated in 1989. If religion is connected with democracy, then it would show up in systematic group differences in the human rights scores, ranging from 0 to 10, when countries are grouped by categories of religious creed. It does not really matter which year of measurement one takes for the 1990s. Table 6.4 has the distribution for democracy for 1997 (DEM97), which is truly comprehensive, covering 150 countries. There is a most interesting finding here, namely that the eta squared score is the second highest one for all the distributions concerning development outcome measures included here. Religion really discriminates when it comes to political development, much more than is the case in relation to economic development. Table 6.4 also has the distribution for another relevant political outcome: corruption (CORR98), where high scores signify low levels of corruption.

There exist today such clear differences between the world religions in relation to democracy that one should reconsider the Weberian perspective

**Table 6.4    Religion and political outcomes: democracy index 1997 and corruption 1998**

| Major religion | DEM97 | | CORR98 | |
| --- | --- | --- | --- | --- |
| Roman Catholic | 6.8 | (N=47) | 4.8 | (N=35) |
| Protestant | 9.1 | (N=16) | 7.1 | (N=14) |
| Orthodox | 5.5 | (N=11) | 3.3 | (N= 7) |
| Muslim | 2.4 | (N=41) | 3.3 | (N=22) |
| Hindu | 7.2 | (N= 3) | 4.0 | (N= 2) |
| Buddhist | 4.2 | (N=13) | 5.4 | (N= 7) |
| Jewish | 8.3 | (N= 1) | 7.1 | (N= 1) |
| Atheist/non-religious | 3.8 | (N= 5) | 5.8 | (N= 3) |
| Other | 5.0 | (N=13) | 4.3 | (N= 4) |
| eta squared | .45 | | .26 | |
| sig. | .000 | | .002 | |

*Note*:    The classification of countries according to religious adherence basically follows the one in Table 5.2.
*Sources*: See Appendix A.

on religion. The Protestant countries are almost exclusively democratic, whereas the opposite is true of Muslim countries. It may be the case that Islam and democracy are not compatible entities (cf. the discussion in Esposito and Voll, 1996), but it may also partly be due to the fact that the measure of democracy is negatively biased against Muslim countries (cf. Bollen and Paxton, 2000). The Catholic countries, whether Roman or Orthodox, are slightly more democratic than authoritarian, while the Buddhist/Confucian countries tend towards dictatorship. The rise in democraticness around the world since 1989 has not changed the basic pattern – that is, Protestantism is associated with democracy, Catholicism is mixed and the other religions tend towards authoritarianism except Hindu India.

A high level of corruption occurs with all the religions except Protestantism. The difference between the three Christian creeds is as striking as the differences between the world religions. Thus, we must ask: does religion matter? On the surface, the connection between religion and political development is much more transparent than the Weber theory about a link between religion and economic development. This calls for further inquiry. Let us use regression analysis in order to test models about religion and outcomes in a more detailed manner. Above we have only looked at countries, classified according to dominant belief. Let us now examine how key variables interact, when we measure more exactly how religious support varies in a country. Here we broaden the analysis to also include political outcomes (democracy, corruption) besides economic and social ones.

**Table 6.5    Religion and outcomes: correlations**

| Outcomes | Estimates | LnPROT70 | LnRC70 | LnMUSL70 | LnBUDD70 |
|---|---|---|---|---|---|
| GDPCAP90 | r | .27 | .07 | −.38 | .04 |
| | sig. | .001 | .199 | .000 | .315 |
| PPP97 | r | .21 | .07 | −.32 | .04 |
| | sig. | .008 | .214 | .000 | .325 |
| GRO6073 | r | −.030 | −.11 | −.11 | .12 |
| | sig. | .363 | .120 | .132 | .105 |
| GRO7385 | r | −.21 | −.33 | .08 | .46 |
| | sig. | .016 | .000 | .208 | .000 |
| GRO8594 | r | −.13 | −.05 | −.17 | .48 |
| | sig. | .077 | .301 | .035 | .000 |
| GRO9098 | r | −.23 | −.07 | −.07 | .37 |
| | sig. | .005 | .232 | .224 | .000 |
| HDI99 | r | .08 | .15 | −.43 | .05 |
| | sig. | .201 | .051 | .000 | .271 |
| GDI99 | r | .14 | .19 | −.50 | .06 |
| | sig. | .068 | .017 | .000 | .275 |
| GEM99 | r | .55 | .32 | −.69 | −.06 |
| | sig. | .000 | .002 | .000 | .307 |
| DEM97 | r | .38 | .39 | −.57 | −.15 |
| | sig. | .000 | .000 | .000 | .037 |
| CORR98 | r | .47 | −.09 | −.36 | .03 |
| | sig. | .000 | .227 | .001 | .409 |

*Note*:    Ln means that the variables in question have been transformed into their natural logarithms, i.e. LnPROT70 has been arrived at in the following way: LnPROT70: Ln (PROT70 + 1) and so on.

*Sources*: See Appendix A.

## *Does Religion Matter?*

The pattern derived above shows that there exist today tremendous differences in macro outcomes between countries when they are classified according to religion. Can we, then, conclude that religion is also the factor that creates these differences? No, because these categories of countries may share many properties other than religion which could account for the configuration of outcomes. It may even be the case that religion merely accompanies more fundamental country differences with regard to outcomes that depend on other factors. To probe deeper into the possible connections between religion and outcomes we resort to the analysis of correlations and the use of regression. Countries may be ranked according to how many believers there are, measured in terms of percentages adhering to a creed out of the entire population. Table 6.5 shows the correlations between religion and outcomes and, following the argument advanced in the conclusion of the previous chapter, we will here rely on religious data referring to 1970.

What emerges from this pattern of correlations in Table 6.5 is the following. Islam tends to be associated with negative developmental outcomes, not only political but also economic. Buddhism is connected with rapid economic growth but with a low level of political development. Roman Catholicism is neutral in terms of economic development but tends, to some extent, to be combined with social and political development. Finally, Protestantism is often, but far from always, associated with economic affluence and democracy but not with rapid economic growth. Corruption is generally low in Protestant countries.

These correlations are at odds with the Weberian theory of religion, if indeed it can be transformed from an historical explanation to a cross-sectional or systematic theory. Buddhism is characterized by extreme economic growth whereas Protestantism seems to have lost its economic growth edge. Islam, which Weber did not examine in a separate volume, tends to occur in countries that do badly on all kinds of developmental outcome except income distribution. What distinguishes Protestantism around the world is the adherence to democracy, more so than Roman Catholicism. Perhaps Protestantism has a deeper connection not so much with economic development, but with other aspects of development – namely, political development interpreted as human rights and low corruption. Using regression models, let us now test whether holding the historical background and the geographical context constant yields a change in the connection between religion and development changes. Thus, we include in the regression model a variable that measures the level of institutional modernization of a country, or the time period that has elapsed since the introduction of modernized leadership (MODLEAD) as well as the distance from the equator (DISEQU). Thus, we regress outcomes onto religion, geography and modernization.

Table 6.6 reports on the impact of religion on affluence (Model (1)) as measured by means of the PPP per capita for 1997 when one holds history and geography constant. The only factors which have an impact when accounting for the country differences in affluence today between more than 100 countries is geography (DISEQU) and modernization (MODLEAD): the further the distance from the equator, the higher the level of affluence; the longer the time since modern institutions were introduced, the higher the level of affluence. Taking these basic factors into account, one may next ask whether religion matters. The answer is that, today, neither Protestantism nor Buddhism has any significant impact on affluence (see Table 6.6).

Let us look at economic growth during the last decade of the twentieth century during which the average growth rates differ considerably between countries. When accounting for economic development in the form of economic growth during a short time interval such as between 1990 and 1998, one needs to take into account other factors than simply religion. Economic growth would be determined by primarily economic factors such as investments, exports and economic stability as well as the business cycle. One way to summarize many such economic factors is to include the level of affluence in the regression modelling economic growth. As model (2) shows in Table 6.6, only one factor – Buddhism – proves significant when regressing growth on affluence and types of religion while Protestantism is accompanied by a negative value. One may hold another factor constant – namely, the level of affluence in 1970 (LnRGDPC70). The inclusion of this factor follows the catch-up theme – that is, rich countries grow more slowly than poor countries simply because increases in production will be larger in percentage terms in small economies. If rich countries naturally grow more slowly than poor countries or medium income countries as a result of a mature economy, then perhaps religion may have no impact at all? There is, however, no indication that the catch-up mechanism operates in the variation in economic growth among countries during the 1990s.

Conversely, there is ample evidence that Buddhism is highly conducive to economic growth. Even when the currently rich economies in South-east Asia mature, they may keep displaying impressive economic growth, because Buddhism/Confucianism harbours the kind of economic ethic that Weber thought he had found in Protestantism but failed to recognize outside the occidental countries. When examining and describing religious creeds, Weber perhaps overemphasized the role of the religious elites – the *virtuosi* – to the neglect of the religious ethics of ordinary men and women. This critique of the Weber model that only Protestantism enhances large-scale capitalist development or rational economic growth is further strengthened when one looks at the country variation in human development as measured by the Human Development Index, shown as model (3) in Table 6.6. In fact, the entire surface impact of Protestantism on economic and social development as measured by the broad HDI is spurious when 128 countries are examined, as the key factors are history and geography. One could argue that Protestantism was the initiator of the process of modernization, but such an interpretation means that the Weber model lacks major relevance for present circumstances. One would, in any case, still want to know whether any of the world religions, as they are practised today, has developmental effects. In Models (4) and (5) we estimate the impact of religion on gender (GEM99) and income distribution (GINI90). Religion has some impact on gender development as Protestantism drives up the empowerment of women, while the opposite is true of the impact of Islam. Religion seems less relevant for understanding the variation across countries for the distribution of income.

Now, we turn to examine the possibility of a connection between religion and political development, which latter concept we interpret as democracy. It was shown above that Protestantism tends to be associated with democracy whereas Buddhism and Islam tend to be accompanied by dictatorship. Can this finding be upheld when we control for other factors?

It is a well-known fact that democracy measured as civil and political rights is to be found in rich countries. There is a persistent and rather high correlation between democracy and affluence, between .60 and .75 depending

**Table 6.6    Religion and outcomes: regression analysis**

| Independent variables | Coeffs | LnPPP 97 | GRO 9098 | HDI 99 | GEM 99 | GINI 90 | DEM 97 | CORR 98 |
|---|---|---|---|---|---|---|---|---|
| Model | | (1) | (2) | (3) | (4) | (5) | (6) | (7) |
| DISEQU | coeff | 2.062 | 1.433 | .342 | .136 | -30.889 | 4.047 | 3.493 |
| | t-stat | 3.46 | .71 | 4.00 | 1.88 | -3.57 | 2.37 | 2.93 |
| | tol | .53 | .45 | .53 | .50 | .42 | .46 | .46 |
| MODLEAD | coeff | .009 | .006 | .001 | .000 | -.052 | .005 | -.004 |
| | t-stat | 4.86 | .97 | 5.45 | .67 | -1.74 | .87 | -.83 |
| | tol | .41 | .33 | .41 | .31 | .26 | .36 | .31 |
| LnRGDPC70 | coeff | – | .092 | – | .074 | 1.166 | .701 | 1.723 |
| | t-stat | – | .26 | – | 4.87 | .56 | 2.32 | 6.04 |
| | tol | – | .45 | – | .37 | .24 | .45 | .32 |
| LnPROT70 | coeff | .022 | -.421 | -.009 | .027 | .231 | .128 | .588 |
| | t-stat | .35 | -2.11 | -.96 | 3.68 | .29 | .76 | 5.09 |
| | tol | .69 | .69 | .68 | .68 | .68 | .70 | .79 |
| LnMUSLl70 | coeff | -.018 | -.046 | -.016 | -.026 | -1.622 | -.771 | .182 |
| | t-stat | -.32 | -.25 | -1.94 | -3.79 | -1.95 | -5.06 | 1.51 |
| | tol | .56 | .55 | .55 | .56 | .52 | .56 | .63 |
| LnBUDD70 | coeff | .117 | .806 | .022 | .012 | -1.637 | -.044 | .434 |
| | t-stat | 1.82 | 3.64 | 2.36 | 1.49 | -1.91 | -.25 | 3.34 |
| | tol | .82 | .88 | .82 | .88 | .80 | .88 | .84 |
| Constant | coeff | 6.909 | .064 | .481 | -.191 | 48.221 | 2.137 | -10.724 |
| | t-stat | 25.66 | .03 | 12.42 | -1.84 | 3.46 | .02 | -5.45 |
| Adjrsq | | .49 | .18 | .60 | .77 | .41 | .56 | .72 |
| N | | 129 | 112 | 128 | 80 | 58 | 117 | 78 |

*Notes*:  coeff = the unstandardized regression coefficient.
t-stat = t-statistics. Used to test the significance of the regression coefficients; t-stat showing more than ± 2 indicates significance.
tol = tolerance. Used to measure the occurrence of multicollinearity in the model; if tol is higher than .3/.4 there is no danger for multicollinearity.
*Sources*: See Appendix A.

on the time period and the countries selected. In Model (6) we regress democracy on types of religion while holding affluence constant. If religion matters for democracy, then it will have an impact upon democracy in addition to the standard association between democracy and affluence. It could be the case that religion has an impact on both affluence and democracy but, as we have seen above, this connection is not large enough to create a problem when estimating partial effects, the problem of multicollinearity not being troublesome. Table 6.6 shows that religion indeed has an impact on democracy today, besides the clear and strongly positive connection between affluence and civil and political rights. It is obvious that Islam impacts negatively upon democracy even when controlling for affluence, history and geography. Interestingly, we note that Protestantism enhances gender empowerment. Yet, when controlling for affluence, Protestantism does not seem to matter for the level of democracy. It is only when we are moving to the analysis of perceived corruption (Model (7)) that we can find a strong positive impact from Protestantism as well as from Buddhism.

Summarizing the findings in Table 6.6 we may say that Buddhism – but not Protestantism – is conducive for economic growth, that Islam is negatively associated with less gender empowerment and democracy, and that Protestantism is associated with more gender empowerment and less corruption.

*Summary*

Religion is today as important as it was in 1904 when Weber launched his thesis. Inquiring into a broad set of outcomes we often notice that religion shows up in, or behind, the outcome measures. At the same time, the causality between religious creed and outcomes is far more complex than envisaged in the Weber thesis. This empirical investigation into outcomes linked with religion has followed an approach that is deliberately non-Weberian. We wished to find out whether religion, as one of the basic types of culture, matters systematically for outcomes in society and the state, bypassing any historical connections. Moreover, we employed a far broader approach to the outcomes of religion, emphasizing both social and political outcomes besides the economic ones with which Weber was concerned.

There are two principal findings in the above analysis of religion and three types of outcome: economic, social and political. First, Protestantism has an impact on one kind of development, but it is not economic development as Weber claimed. Protestantism fosters gender empowerment and low corruption. Second, economic development is enhanced by another world religion, namely Buddhism/Confucianism, which at the same time is not conducive to political development. Development in general is quite problematic in the third major world religion, Islam, as it is associated with low levels of democracy as well as low levels of affluence. Thus we should take up the question posed by Weber and broaden it to include all kinds of consequence of religious beliefs and practices. Then, we have one major new finding – namely that Protestantism is very much linked with human rights.

## Religious Fragmentation and Outcomes: Macro Level

If religion matters when it is the dominant creed in a country, then perhaps religious diversity also matters? Most scholars writing about religious heterogeneity attribute negative outcomes to religious diversity because, like

Table 6.7    **Religious fragmentation 1900–95**

|        | RLF1 1900 | RLF1 1970 | RLF1 1995 | RLF2 1900 | RLF2 1970 | RLF2 1995 |
|--------|-----------|-----------|-----------|-----------|-----------|-----------|
| Mean   | 17.3      | 26.0      | 27.8      | 23.8      | 37.5      | 36.6      |
| Median | 10.0      | 18.9      | 23.1      | 17.5      | 40.7      | 40.0      |
| N      | 139       | 135       | 150       | 139       | 135       | 150       |

*Sources*: See Appendix A.

ethnicity it creates conflict. Religious diversity is conducive to religious cleavages, which creates more risks than opportunities. Religious cleavages could bring a country to the brink of disaster, involving civil disorder or anarchy.

Religious fragmentation will be high in societies where more or less compact social groups adhere to different families of religious creed, or where one part of the population tends towards non-confession whereas the other part adheres to one of the world religions. Below we will use two indices of fragmentation: RFL1, which tracks the adherence to the great world religions, and RFL2, which in addition also comprises the major subgroups within Christianity. Data is available for the entire twentieth century as there are estimations for certain points in time – 1900, 1970 and 1995. This means that one may get a glimpse at whether religious fragmentation tends to increase or decrease. Table 6.7 suggests that religious fragmentation has increased considerably during the twentieth century, which may be interpreted as evidence for the multicultural theory. However, one cannot argue, on the basis of these data, that religious conflict has intensified at the same time. It seems apparent, for instance, that many of the tensions within Christianity and Buddhism have 'cooled down'. Islam and Hinduism constitute the exception to the generalization that the world religions have cooled down internally. But tensions between the world religions remain strong, especially between Christianity and Islam as well as between Islam and Hinduism.

In cleavage theory religion is regarded as equally divisive as ethnicity, and the process of latent cleavages becoming manifest can only be avoided if a mutual understanding is reached concerning the necessity of religious tolerance, often laid down in the constitution or a similar document. Religious heterogeneity will, if left unchecked, sooner or later manifest itself in religious clashes – this is the prevailing generalization in the literature. Consociational theory argues that only one or several mechanisms for the peaceful cooperation between compact religious groups can prevent the divisive implications of religious diversity from spilling over into open confrontation and perhaps civil war. Such conflict resolution devices in deeply divided societies along religious lines may consist of federalism or regionalization, proportional representation or *Proporz*, and the recognition of mutual veto (Nordlinger, 1972; Lijphart, 1977, 1999).

Correlating religious fragmentation and outcomes offers a first view of the nature of negative religious fragmentation from the perspective of social, economic and political outcomes. Correlating the two fragmentation indices for different periods and various outcome variables mostly referring to the 1990s, the major finding is that religious fragmentation has a negative impact on political and economic outcomes, although the relationship is not a strong one. Over time, the relationship becomes weaker and weaker, which may be a consequence of the successful operation of conflict resolution devices. On the other hand, religious fragmentation has little, if any, impact on social outcomes. The weakening of these connections may also be due to growing religious indifference. Although many people still belong to churches, most of them no longer regularly participate in religious ceremonies or services. The process of secularization is proceeding in some countries, whereas in others it is counteracted by religious fundamentalism.

The clash between various Christian creeds has become much less harmful for economic and political development (RLF2). The correlation coefficients show that the negative consequences for democracy and affluence stem largely from the clash between the major world religions (RLF1). We therefore concentrate on the analysis of the religious fragmentation according to the index RLF1 for both the 1970s and the 1990s. Table 6.8 regresses democracy, prosperity and the level of human development, as well as gender equality, on to religious fragmentation while controlling for historical and geographical factors as well as for the election system. Against consociational theory it has been argued that power-sharing mechanisms do not always help. A few countries, such as Lebanon and former Yugoslavia, afford dramatic examples of the failure of institutional conflict devices in relation to religious cleavages.

When one takes the impact of other factors into account, then religious heterogeneity is far less of a threat than, for example, ethnicity. Political, social and economic outcomes are more conditioned by history (time from modernization) and geography (distance from the equator) than religious fragmentation. Note, however, the positive contribution of proportional representation election formulas on democracy – a power-sharing device.

In sum, religious fragmentation has no distinctive impact on macro-level outcomes. For macro-level outcomes, religion in the form of variation in denominations seems to matter more than religion understood as religious fragmentation. In short, it is the type of religion that matters, not religious cleavages.

**Table 6.8    Impact of religious fragmentation: regression analysis**

| Independent variables | Coeffs | DEM 97 | DEM 97 | LnPPP 97 | LnPPP 97 | HDI 99 | HDI 99 | GEM 99 | GEM 99 |
|---|---|---|---|---|---|---|---|---|---|
| RLF195 | coeff | .017 | – | .004 | – | .000 | – | .002 | – |
| | t-stat | 1.48 | – | 1.18 | – | .45 | – | 3.50 | – |
| RLF170 | coeff | – | –.004 | – | –.006 | – | –.001 | – | .001 |
| | t-stat | – | –.32 | – | –1.58 | – | –1.35 | – | .79 |
| MODLEAD | coeff | 3.269 | 3.74 | 1.036 | 1.656 | .225 | .267 | .196 | .212 |
| | t-stat | 1.92 | 2.10 | 1.89 | 3.00 | 2.92 | 3.14 | 2.30 | 2.17 |
| DISEQU | coeff | .018 | .019 | .010 | .009 | .002 | .002 | .001 | .001 |
| | t-stat | 3.26 | 3.45 | 5.74 | 5.58 | 7.29 | 6.32 | 5.09 | 4.34 |
| ELECTSYS | coeff | 2.156 | 1.551 | .449 | .167 | .040 | .025 | .064 | .055 |
| | t-stat | 4.54 | 3.07 | 2.97 | 1.08 | 1.90 | 1.03 | 2.55 | 1.94 |
| Constant | coeff | 1.487 | 2.248 | 6.692 | 7.060 | .418 | .455 | .168 | .221 |
| | t-stat | 2.39 | 3.57 | 33.09 | 35.48 | 14.62 | 14.84 | 5.09 | 5.70 |
| Adjrsq | | .37 | .39 | .49 | .57 | .61 | .62 | .55 | .50 |
| N | | 144 | 129 | 138 | 123 | 137 | 122 | 88 | 83 |

*Notes*:    Ln stands for transforming the variables into its natural logarithm.
coeff = the unstandardized regression coefficient.
t-stat = t-statistics. Used to test the significance of the regression coefficients; t-stat showing more than ± 2 indicates significance.
*Sources*: See Appendix A.

## Religious Structure and Party Support

One way of studying in more detail the consequences of religious fragmentation is to focus on a single country and investigate whether a religiously divided society has consequences for political parties' electoral outcomes. Such an approach seems highly suitable for societies where religious fragmentation has taken on a geographical dimension, with people belonging to different religions living preponderantly in certain areas of the country. How much does religious structure matter for party electoral support in divided societies such as the USA, Spain, Switzerland, Belgium and India?

In most divided societies the regional distribution of the population is highly skewed. Does this carry over into regional disparities in the voters' support for certain parties, as it does in explicitly religious or explicitly non-religious ones? The countries selected are the same as those analysed for ethnic structure in Chapter 4 but excluding Russia – that is, they all are so-called plural societies.

## The USA: Religion Matters

Estimates suggest that around year 2000 Christians comprise some 85 per cent of the American population and that most of them are affiliated to a church. Among the Christians, Protestants amount to roughly one-third of the population and those belonging to the Roman Catholic Church make up around one-fifth of the population, so that the Protestants outnumber the Roman Catholics. Looking at the distribution among the 51 states of the USA, the Roman Catholics are mainly to be found on the East Coast in Rhode Island, Massachusetts, Connecticut, New Jersey and New York. The proportion of Roman Catholics is lowest in southern states such as North and South Carolina as well as in Tennessee, Arkansas, Georgia, Alabama and Mississippi. The Protestants have a stronger presence in the states where the Roman Catholics are weak. Religious fragmentation, taking into account Roman Catholics as well as other Christians and non-Christians, tends to be highest in the states where the Roman Catholics are most numerous. Now, does religion have any impact on the support for the two major parties at the presidential elections? Table 6.9 presents a few regression analyses estimating the impact of religion on party support in the USA. In this analysis we also control for the impact of ethnicity in one of the models estimated. Here we have a confirmation that religion matters.

In the American presidential elections the Democratic vote includes a strong Catholic component, whereas the Republican vote includes the Protestant component. Religious fragmentation *per se* does not matter. Again, we find that there are ethnic and social attributes connected with strong regional support for the Democrats – namely the size of black community and unemployment. Exactly the opposite structure is typical of the Republican strongholds.

## Spain: Anti-clericalism

Spain is a predominantly Catholic society where a high rate of church attendance used to be part of Spanish culture. The religious cleavage in Spanish culture is not between adherents to different denominations, but rather concerns those who adhere to a clerical tradition and those who reject it – the anti-clerical tradition, captured by church attendance. Data from the WVS indicate a continuous decrease from a high of 41 per cent in 1980 to 31 per cent in 1990 to a lower 26 per cent in 1995; these figures covary quite well with similar estimates reported by the Eurobarometer which give 30 per cent in 1990 and 27 per cent in 1995. For the regional level we have data that goes back to the 1970s and we believe that these capture the religious cleavage within Spain. The clerical tradition is strongest in the heartland of Spain or in the Old Castille (León, Zamora, Palencia) but also in the Pais Vasco (Alava, Guipúzcoa), whereas church attendance has traditionally been weak in southern provinces such as Almeria, Huelva, Cádiz and Jaén, but also in

**Table 6.9    Religion and party support at regional level in USA: regression analysis**

| Independent variables | Coeffs | DEM96 | DEM96 | REP96 | REP96 |
|---|---|---|---|---|---|
| CATHOL90 | coeff | .322 | .357 | -.398 | -.388 |
|  | t-stat | 4.46 | 5.16 | -5.56 | -5.66 |
| RELFRAG90 | coeff | -.065 | -.087 | .183 | .172 |
|  | t-stat | -.47 | -.67 | 1.35 | 1.35 |
| GSPC94 | coeff | -.000 | .000 | -.000 | .000 |
|  | t-stat | -.07 | .56 | -.30 | -1.47 |
| UNEM96 | coeff | 1.798 | 2.242 | -1.336 | -2.543 |
|  | t-stat | 2.81 | 3.03 | -2.13 | -3.47 |
| BLACK94 | coeff | – | .292 | – | -.157 |
|  | t-stat | – | 3.01 | – | -1.63 |
| ELF94 | coeff | – | -.125 | – | .201 |
|  | t-stat | – | -1.76 | – | 2.84 |
| Constant | coeff | 35.98 | 32.23 | 47.21 | 54.73 |
|  | t-stat | 3.93 | 3.61 | 5.25 | 6.20 |
| Adjrsq |  | .42 | .50 | .48 | .54 |
| N |  | 50 | 50 | 50 | 50 |

*Notes*:  coeff = the unstandardized regression coefficient.
   t-stat = t-statistics. Used to test the significance of the regression coefficients; t-stat showing more than ± 2 indicates significance.
*Sources*: See Appendix B.

the major cities like Madrid and Barcelona. Has this religious cleavage any impact on the support for political parties at the regional level in Spain in the 1990s? Table 6.10 reports the findings from the regression analysis.

Religious orientation has an impact on the PSOE vote, since the socialist party is stronger in provinces where the anti-clerical tradition is strong. Controlling for the impact of ethnicity we may note a weak positive impact on the regionalist parties while the religious variable becomes even stronger for the socialist party. The Spanish case corroborates the argument that both ethnicity and religion may have an impact on party support at the regional level.

*Switzerland: Strong Religious Effects*

Switzerland is a religiously divided society. A plurality of the population belongs to the Roman Catholic Church (46 per cent), while a large minority adheres to the Protestant creed (40 per cent). A not insignificant part of the

**Table 6.10  Religion and party support at regional level in Spain: regression analysis**

| Independent variables | Coeff | Dependent variables | | | |
|---|---|---|---|---|---|
| | | PSOE96 | PSOE96 | REG96 | REG96 |
| RELPRAT75 | coeff | −.203 | −.203 | −.013 | .179 |
| | t-stat | −4.71 | −5.48 | −.13 | 2.17 |
| REGINC95 | coeff | −.007 | −.003 | .022 | .019 |
| | t-stat | −3.53 | −1.59 | 4.83 | 5.45 |
| INSTAUTO | coeff | − | − | − | 17.295 |
| | t-stat | − | − | − | 6.25 |
| NATUN78 | coeff | − | .179 | − | − |
| | t-stat | − | 4.21 | − | − |
| Constant | coeff | 55.81 | 39.96 | −25.48 | −35.70 |
| | t-stat | 16.78 | 8.45 | −3.21 | −5.83 |
| Adjrsq | | .44 | .59 | .31 | .62 |
| N | | 50 | 50 | 50 | 50 |

*Notes*:  coeff = the unstandardized regression coefficient.
t-stat = t-statistics. Used to test the significance of the regression coefficients; t-stat showing more than ± 2 indicates significance.
*Sources*: See Appendix B.

population may be classified as either non-religious or belonging to another religion (14 per cent). This means that one major religious cleavage in Switzerland is the Roman Catholic –Protestant divide. At the regional level of the cantons the Roman Catholics constitute a majority of around 90 per cent of the population in cantons such as Valais, Obwalden, Uri and Ticino, while the Protestants have their strongest standing in Bern, Schaffhausen, Zürich and Basel-Stadt. Those adhering to no confession are most numerous in Genève, Basel-Stadt and Neuchatel where the religious fragmentation is, in fact, the highest. Which impact does religion have on party support in Switzerland? In the regression analyses undertaken and reported in Table 6.11 we have not included the cantons which employ a majority formula at the elections, and the number of cantons examined thus numbers 21.

Strong religious effects explain much of the support for the Catholic party (CVP) and the socialist party (SPS). The Catholic party is strong where the Roman Catholic Church is strong, while the socialist party has its stronghold in no-confession areas. This finding also remains valid when a control for regional income and ethnicity is made.

**Table 6.11 Religion and party support at regional level in Switzerland: regression analysis**

| Independent variables | Coeff | Dependent variables CVP95 | CVP95 | SPS95 | SPS95 |
|---|---|---|---|---|---|
| CATHOL80 | coeff | .552 | .548 | – | – |
|  | t-stat | 9.50 | 9.02 | – | – |
| NOCONF80 | coeff | – | – | 1.309 | 1.855 |
|  | t-stat | – | – | 4.38 | 5.04 |
| VOLKS90 | coeff | –.000 | –.000 | –.000 | –.000 |
|  | t-stat | –1.60 | –1.21 | –1.57 | –1.32 |
| OTH90 | coeff | – | –.184 | – | –1.134 |
|  | t-stat | – | –.34 | – | –2.20 |
| Constant | coeff | –.42 | .21 | 22.78 | 26.48 |
|  | t-stat | –.05 | .03 | 4.31 | 5.20 |
| Adjrsq |  | .84 | .83 | .47 | .57 |
| N |  | 21 | 21 | 21 | 21 |

*Notes*:   coeff = the unstandardized regression coefficient.
   t-stat = t-statistics. Used to test the significance of the regression coefficients; t-stat showing more than ± 2 indicates significance.
*Sources*: See Appendix B.


*Belgium: Strong Cultural Politics*

In religious terms Belgium is a relatively homogeneous country with nearly 90 per cent of the population being considered to belong to the Roman Catholic Church. The religious cleavage in Belgian society thus follows more the strength of one religious orientation than what kinds of religious denomination people belong to. Again, we use church attendance as an indicator of the cleavage between those who are more religious and those who are more secular in their orientations. Data on church attendance in Belgium reported in the Eurobarometer suggest a sharp decline over time from a high level of a claimed 60 per cent weekly attendance in 1970 to around 20 per cent weekly attendance in 1995. When mapping the regional variation in church attendance we rely on data that capture a tradition of church attendance going back to the 1960s. Here we may distinguish between regions where there is a strong religious tradition and regions with more of a secular tradition. In the first group we count Verviers, Tongeren, Arlon and Neufchateu – all located in the eastern part of the country – but some are part of the Flemish regions and others form parts of the Walloon regions. Among the more secular regions we identify certain Walloon regions such as Charleroi, Mons, Liège and Soignies. The religious–secular cleavage does not strictly follow the ethnic cleavage in Belgium.

**Table 6.12  Religion and party support at regional level in Belgium: regression analysis**

| Independent variables | Coeff | Dependent variables | | | |
|---|---|---|---|---|---|
| | | ETHNP 91 | ETHNP 91 | PSCCVP 91 | PSCCVP 91 |
| RELPRAC68 | coeff | .112 | .000 | .322 | .294 |
| | t-stat | 1.33 | .01 | 7.24 | 5.05 |
| REGECPRO95 | coeff | .035 | .014 | −.003 | −.003 |
| | t-stat | 4.04 | 3.38 | −.56 | −.61 |
| FLEM47 | coeff | − | .231 | − | − |
| | t-stat | − | 10.11 | − | − |
| FOREIGN81 | coeff | − | .325 | − | −.123 |
| | t-stat | − | 2.07 | − | −.76 |
| Constant | coeff | −17.82 | −10.73 | 12.62 | 15.02 |
| | t-stat | −2.65 | −2.75 | 3.53 | 3.13 |
| Adjrsq | | .38 | .88 | .64 | .63 |
| N | | 30 | 30 | 30 | 30 |

*Notes* :  coeff = the unstandardized regression coefficient.
t-stat = t-statistics. Used to test the significance of the regression coefficients; t-stat showing more than ± 2 indicates significance.
*Sources*: See Appendix B.

Table 6.12 displays a regression analysis of the regional variation in voting support for the ethnic parties (ETHNP91) and the Christian-Social Party (PSCCVP91). In addition to the religious variable (RELPRAC68) the model also includes some of the ethnic variables employed in Chapter 4.

In Belgium, astonishingly enough, the religious effect is just as strong as ethnicity. The religious cleavage between religious and secular groups is clearly expressed in the voting for the Catholic Party. The religious effect is not, however, visible for the ethnic parties, since, for them, the ethnic variables clearly outflank all other variables. In the Belgian case both religion, or a religious tradition, and ethnicity matters, depending on whether we look at religious or ethnic parties.

*India: Ethnicity More Than Religion*

Cultural cleavages in the largest democracy in the world, India, include religion. The regional structure of India is particularly interesting from a cultural perspective. From a jurisdictional point of view, the states in the Federal State of India have been identified on the basis of ethnic criteria, especially language. However, the regional structure of India includes more than language, as religion and historical heritage also underlie the division of states.

The complexity of the Indian regional structure makes it impossible to separate ethnicity from religion in relation to the major culture of this giant country, namely Hinduism. The Hindu revival during the 1980s and 1990s was not only a religious phenomenon but also a nationalist endeavour, emphasizing the use of Hindi as the native language of the country. Thus, Hinduism is opposed not only by large groups adhering to a different creed – Muslims and Sikhs – but the nationalist drive also encounters resistance from regions speaking languages other than Hindi, such as, for instance, Bengali or Tamil. Those resisting the dominance of Hindi often favour the use of English as the common language of the country.

A huge majority of the population must be counted as Hindus – about 82 per cent according to the 1991 Census of India. Muslims constitute a large minority of about 12 per cent of the population, which in absolute numbers means more than 100 million people. The Christians and the Sikhs constitute smaller minorities each amounting to around 2 per cent of the population. Data on the regional distribution of religious adherence in India suggest that Hindus are most numerous in the northern and western states of Himachal Pradesh, Madhya Pradesh, Gujarat, Haryana and Rajastan, but also in Orissa in the eastern part of India. Relatively speaking, the Muslims are strongest in the states of Assam, West Bengal (north-east) and in Kerala (south-west).

Let us examine how these cultural cleavages work themselves out in a regional voting pattern. Table 6.13 focuses upon the two major parties that confront each other in the struggle for power in India, the Congress Party (INC) and the nationalist BJP, the latter party having replaced the former as the hegemonic party of India today.

The regional pattern of voting in India involves a religious effect, but it is only visible for the BJP vote. When controlling for ethnicity – the use of the Hindi language – this effect disappears. The ethnic impact is also visible for the Congress Party (INC), but the impact of Hindi language is negative for the INC and positive for the BJP. We conclude that, in India, ethnicity matters more than religion when explaining the variation in party support in India.

*Summary*

Religion matters for the regional variation in party support in divided societies. It plays a larger role in the USA and in Switzerland than in India where ethnicity matters more. Ethnicity has more impact in Spain and in India while the impact of religion and ethnicity is equally strong in Belgium. Religion matters more than ethnicity in the USA and in Switzerland.

**Table 6.13    Religion and party support at regional level in India: regression analysis**

| Independent variables | Coeff | Dependent variables | | | |
|---|---|---|---|---|---|
| | | BJP96 | BJP96 | INC96 | INC96 |
| HINDU91 | coeff | .504 | .261 | −.111 | .073 |
| | t-stat | 2.75 | 1.53 | −.67 | .44 |
| URBAN91 | coeff | .081 | .377 | .345 | .123 |
| | t-stat | .41 | 1.99 | 1.88 | .64 |
| SEXRAT91 | coeff | −.189 | – | .156 | – |
| | t-stat | −3.58 | – | 3.12 | – |
| HINDI91 | coeff | – | .235 | – | −.179 |
| | t-stat | – | 4.66 | – | −3.51 |
| Constant | coeff | 154.34 | −17.80 | −116.20 | 26.21 |
| | t-stat | 3.07 | −1.23 | −2.45 | 1.86 |
| Adjrsq | | .35 | .46 | .27 | .31 |
| N | | 32 | 32 | 32 | 32 |

*Notes*:   Data in these regression analyses have been weighted by population.
coeff = the unstandardized regression coefficient.
t-stat = t-statistics. Used to test the significance of the regression coefficients; t-stat showing more than ± 2 indicates significance.
*Sources*: See Appendix B.


## The Role of Religion for People

In the WVS data collected for individuals in various countries religion is tapped by the employment of two variables, namely the attendance at religious services (RELSERV) and adherence/non-adherence to a religious denomination (DENOM). Attendance at religious services, or church attendance, is interesting from the point of view of globalization and secularization. Church attendance worldwide is portrayed in Table 6.14, where the aggregated means of attendance at least once a week as a percentage of the population are broken down by the major world regions.

The lowest figures for attendance at religious services are to be found in the most secularized countries – that is, the OECD countries and the post-communist societies. The rates are distinctively higher in Latin American, African and Asian countries. Secularization is an ongoing process, especially in rich countries. Church attendance remains high in Catholic countries as well as in Muslim countries, especially if they are not highly affluent. Does religious practice also matter for individual behaviour?

In Table 6.15 high values will stand for more of church attendance and the presence of a religious denomination; in Belgium, Spain, the USA and Switzerland denomination stands for a Roman Catholic creed, while in India

Table 6.14   **Attendance at religious services at least once a week by regions of the world**

| Region | RELSERV 1980 (%) | | RELSERV 1990 (%) | | RELSERV 1995 (%) | | RELSERV 1990–95 (%) | |
|---|---|---|---|---|---|---|---|---|
| OECD | 22.7 | (17) | 22.0 | (20) | 16.8 | (10) | 21.4 | (21) |
| Latin America | 42.4 | ( 2) | 34.0 | ( 4) | 34.3 | ( 9) | 34.5 | ( 9) |
| Africa | 40.3 | ( 1) | 83.9 | ( 1) | 72.1 | ( 3) | 72.4 | ( 3) |
| Asia | 19.1 | ( 1) | 26.7 | ( 3) | 40.2 | ( 5) | 35.6 | ( 6) |
| Postcommunist countries | 11.9 | ( 1) | 18.0 | (10) | 14.4 | (16) | 15.5 | (20) |
| Total | 24.6 | (22) | 24.2 | (38) | 26.1 | (43) | 25.4 | (59) |
| eta squared | .14 | | .27 | | .54 | | .38 | |
| sig. | .607 | | .033 | | .000 | | .000 | |

*Sources*: See Appendix A and C.

it stands for Hinduism and in Russia for Orthodoxy. Church attendance is associated with people's life satisfaction. Identification with the Roman Catholic creed is positively related to life satisfaction in Belgium and Spain but not in the USA and Switzerland. In Russia an Orthodox creed is negatively associated with life satisfaction. Thus religion has a certain impact, but income is more important.

We find a stronger impact of religion on the left–right orientation of people. Religion strengthens rightest orientations in the four western countries included in the sample, while religion has no impact on the left–right orientation neither in India nor in Russia. Religion matters for the basic political orientation of an individual, linking church attendance with right leanings. As a matter of fact, religion matters more than income, which factor is positively related to right orientation.

Religion has a less distinct impact on political interest. Church attendance is positively associated with political interest in Belgium, the USA and Switzerland but negatively in Spain, while there is no impact in India or in Russia. If there is an impact from identification with a denomination, then it is rather negative. Membership in voluntary organizations indicates citizen activity. Religions matter. It is true that church attendance is merely an intense form of membership in one organization, the church. But religious activity has a positive impact on activity in other kinds of organization. The impact of church attendance is quite impressive – roughly the same as we find from education (Table 6.15).

Religion motivates people and drives them towards conservative values. Thus, it is no surprise that religion is negatively associated with radical

**Table 6.15  Religion and membership in voluntary organizations**

| Indep. variables | Coeff | Dependent variable: membership of voluntary organizations | | | | | | | |
| | | Total | Six | Belgium | Spain | USA | Switz. | India | Russia |
|---|---|---|---|---|---|---|---|---|---|
| RELSERV | coeff | .140 | .234 | .257 | .175 | .421 | .148 | -.068 | .135 |
| | t-stat | 28.57 | 18.63 | 7.50 | 6.42 | 19.03 | 4.22 | -1.22 | 2.98 |
| DENOM* | coeff | – | – | -.023 | -.043 | -.021 | -.054 | -.097 | -.141 |
| | t-stat | – | – | -.88 | -1.55 | -1.36 | -2.55 | -2.67 | -5.54 |
| EDUCAT | coeff | .266 | .460 | .285 | .183 | .270 | .366 | .119 | .333 |
| | t-stat | 40.74 | 27.15 | 6.31 | 5.58 | 7.73 | 6.10 | 1.92 | 7.72 |
| INCOME | coeff | .163 | .153 | .201 | -.004 | .144 | .226 | -.047 | .121 |
| | t-stat | 23.58 | 8.20 | 4.15 | -.10 | 5.15 | 5.76 | -.60 | 2.69 |
| GENDER | coeff | -.039 | -.003 | -.078 | -.040 | -.025 | -.074 | -.129 | -.025 |
| | t-stat | -11.35 | -3.82 | -3.67 | -2.23 | -1.69 | -3.48 | -4.14 | -1.23 |
| AGE | coeff | .064 | .099 | .070 | .042 | .113 | .105 | .145 | -.187 |
| | t-stat | 11.44 | 7.11 | 2.11 | 1.38 | 5.01 | 3.16 | 2.38 | -5.70 |
| Constant | coeff | .213 | .041 | .066 | .190 | .177 | .208 | .636 | .426 |
| | t-stat | 32.28 | 2.38 | 1.45 | 5.02 | 4.79 | 4.46 | 9.80 | 9.49 |
| Adjrsq | | .043 | .109 | .075 | .025 | .147 | .059 | .031 | .091 |
| N | | 81520 | 11421 | 2030 | 2924 | 2941 | 2131 | 1055 | 2228 |

*Notes*:  * The denomination variable refers to the following for the different countries: Belgium, Spain, the USA and Switzerland: Roman Catholics; India: Hindus; Russia: Orthodox.
coeff: the unstandardized regression coefficient.
t-stat = t-statistics. Used to test the significance of the regression coefficients; t-stat showing more than ± 2 indicates significance.
*Sources*: See Appendix C.

political activity such as joining boycotts. When there is an impact, church attendance is negatively associated with joining boycotts in Spain, the USA and India. The impact is even stronger if we look at the second religious variable – denominational identification (Table 6.16).

*Summary*

Religion matters for life satisfaction, left–right orientation as well as for various kinds of activity. Religion strengthens rightist orientations and is associated with traditional forms of activity, while the reverse applies to non-traditional forms of political activity. The comparative analysis into the individual outcomes of religious creed confirms the standard image of religion as a conservative force in society reinforcing the established order. Table 6.17 summarizes the findings.

Culture as religion is important for citizens' political orientation and activity. Attendance at religious services appears to be equally important as

**Table 6.16   Religion and joining boycotts**

| Indep. variables | Coeff | \| Dependent variable: propensity to join boycotts | | | | | | | |
|---|---|---|---|---|---|---|---|---|---|
| | | Total | Six | Belgium | Spain | USA | Switz. | India | Russia |
| RELSERV | coeff | −.061 | .043 | .005 | −.080 | −.045 | .010 | −.100 | .020 |
| | t-stat | −19.63 | 5.00 | .23 | −4.28 | −2.37 | .28 | −3.54 | .75 |
| DENOM* | coeff | – | – | −.088 | −.100 | −.042 | .013 | −.067 | −.051 |
| | t-stat | – | – | −5.16 | −5.34 | −3.15 | .62 | −3.30 | −3.48 |
| EDUCAT | coeff | .158 | .201 | .262 | .120 | .397 | .458 | .196 | .113 |
| | t-stat | 37.70 | 17.51 | 8.89 | 5.38 | 13.15 | 7.36 | 4.80 | 4.44 |
| INCOME | coeff | .113 | .064 | .070 | .063 | .079 | .030 | −.079 | −.016 |
| | t-stat | 25.17 | 5.03 | 2.24 | 1.97 | 3.28 | .80 | −1.87 | −.62 |
| GENDER | coeff | −.058 | −.089 | −.077 | −.091 | −.036 | −.001 | −.142 | −.061 |
| | t-stat | −26.15 | −14.46 | −5.53 | −7.56 | −2.81 | −.03 | −8.91 | −5.04 |
| AGE | coeff | −.104 | −.141 | −.032 | −.097 | −.140 | −.230 | −.054 | −.141 |
| | t-stat | −28.48 | −14.68 | −1.49 | −4.63 | −7.20 | −6.84 | −1.92 | −7.34 |
| Constant | coeff | .205 | .195 | .111 | .340 | .157 | .126 | .528 | .216 |
| | t-stat | 47.44 | 16.90 | 3.79 | 13.20 | 4.92 | 2.82 | 15.42 | 8.23 |
| Adjrsq | | .076 | .094 | .116 | .125 | .118 | .112 | .086 | .076 |
| N | | 78841 | 10899 | 1802 | 2535 | 2823 | 1031 | 1816 | 1998 |

*Notes*:    * The denomination variable refers to the following for the different countries: Belgium, Spain, the USA and Switzerland: Roman Catholics; India: Hindus; Russia: Orthodox.
coeff = the unstandardized regression coefficient.
t-stat = t-statistics. Used to test the significance of the regression coefficients; t-stat showing more than ± 2 indicates significance.
*Sources*: See Appendix C.

belonging to a religious denomination. Religion matters more in Belgium, Spain and the USA than in India or Russia.

## Conclusion

Besides ethnicity, religion is one of the major forces in human life. It matters for outcomes on all three levels studied here: society, region and individual behaviour. More specifically, the world religions display different performance profiles. In divided societies political parties mobilize religious or anti-clerical votes. And religion is a conservative force in people's minds. It is impossible to draw a clear-cut distinction between religion and historical tradition. Religious creed or practice changes slowly over time. However, we wish to examine the impact of traditions other than religion and ethnicity, such as, for instance, legacies in the form of colonialism and family traditions. Part IV deals with the impact of legacies.

**Table 6.17  Number of significant regression coefficients estimated from the impact of religion by country and dependent variable**

| Values | Distributed by country | | | | | | |
|---|---|---|---|---|---|---|---|
| | Belgium | Spain | USA | Switzer-land | India | Russia | Total |
| Attending religious services | 3 | 4 | 5 | 4 | 2 | 1 | 19 |
| Denomination | 4 | 3 | 2 | 2 | 2 | 4 | 17 |
| Total | 7 | 7 | 7 | 6 | 4 | 5 | 36 |

| Values | Distributed by dependent variable | | | | | |
|---|---|---|---|---|---|---|
| | Life satisfaction | Left–right orientation | Political interest | Voluntary organiz-ations | Joining boycotts | Total |
| Attending religious services | 3 | 4 | 4 | 5 | 3 | 19 |
| Denomination | 3 | 3 | 3 | 3 | 5 | 17 |
| Total | 6 | 7 | 7 | 8 | 8 | 36 |

*Note*:  This information is partly based upon a number of estimations not reported in this chapter.

# PART IV
# LEGACIES

# Introduction

Culture is a human achievement that is transmitted from one generation to another. Let us deal with the idea of culture as a heritage transmitted over generations. This approach to cultural studies emphasizing the developments that enter into a tradition over time is not in conflict with the other two approaches already employed – namely, culture as ethnicity or culture as religion. In a longitudinal perspective on culture it could well be the ethnic or religious heritage that is at the centre of attention. However, in Part IV we will examine traditions as something in addition to ethnicity and religion.

The past determines the present – at least, so many historians argue. The past can be analysed as a set of legacies that act upon the present. Such an approach would accept the claim that the past matters, but it remains an open question to what extent and how the past conditions the present and the future. In order to research the influence of cultural legacies by means of the ordinary canons of empirical research, we take up the theory that, for many countries, colonialism has played a major role in shaping their developmental paths. It is, in our view, an open question whether colonial legacies are as important as claimed and what impact the various colonial legacies have had. Besides colonialism we also analyse the impact of family structures or family values, which have formed a variety of cultural traditions. If we can show that cultural traditions as colonial legacies or as family patterns matter, then we have established evidence in favour of the thesis that cultural traditions – or legacies – are important.

# Chapter 7

# Historical Legacies and the Colonial Heritage

## Introduction

The approach employed in this volume of ever-increasing comprehensiveness for the identification of cultures may start from a highly particular culture, that occurs, for instance, in a Pacific island, and may end with historical legacies covering whole continents or universal values such as individualism or egalitarianism. Old cultural analysis in the anthropological tradition used to have a highly specific focus on localized cultures – often quite isolated ones such as the Trobriand Islands (Malinowski, 1969). By contrast, new cultural analysis examines universal items that may occur in any society. Whereas the identity of an ethnic group is very much localized to a particular community in a single country (except when ethnicity is identified as race), religious identity may take on a much broader scope as when a world religion identifies an entire civilization. Both ethnicity and religion have been approached cross-sectionally in our inquiry into their impact today. It is now time to inquire into the longitudinal dimension of culture, by examining the effects of a few major historical legacies. It has been claimed that a broad cultural heritage such as the Spanish or Anglo-Saxon culture matters a great deal for outcomes. We link up this theme with a general assessment of colonialism – that is, we investigate the argument that the colonial heritage has meant a huge difference, mainly by hindering the development of countries subjugated to the domination of the Europeans.

Looking at the world as it existed around 1900, Weber could not resist being impressed by occidental superiority in terms of money, resources and power. At that time the most conspicuous feature of occidental domination was the colonial regimes put in place almost all over the world by the so-called Europeans. Only South America had managed to free itself from European rule. Colonialization created colonial cultures, the effects of which have been much discussed. We will investigate whether these different legacies still matter for outcomes around 100 years after Weber searched for the source of occidental superiority in the major world religions.

**The Longitudinal Perspective**

When explaining the variation in political, social and economic outcomes between the countries of the world today, then one may employ either a cross-sectional or a longitudinal approach. Thus far, we have employed a cross-sectional method for understanding why countries differ in terms of outcomes, and especially to find out whether culture plays a role when accounting for these differences. Social scientists tend to favour a cross-sectional approach whereas historians in their focus on the past as an explanation of the present, prefer a longitudinal approach. In order to understand why a country is in a predicament, one must understand where the country comes from. According to the longitudinal approach, it is *time* which contains the forces that account for the situation today. To understand the present one we must follow the path that a country has travelled for a long period of time.

Yet, how can causality operate through time? Social scientists tend to wish to find the forces that act upon outcomes in a country within the present constellation of forces. One could combine a cross-sectional and a longitudinal approach by acknowledging the relevance of the past and at the same time investigating how the past in the form of a legacy operates upon the present. Such a combined cross-sectional and longitudinal research endeavour involves pinning down a variation in legacies over space – that is, throughout the countries of the world. In a pure longitudinal approach to culture one would entirely accept *path-dependency*, meaning that the culture of a country today would be explained totally by the evolution of this culture over time. In a pure cross-sectional approach to culture, it is the country differences today that account for the variation in outcomes. Mixing these two approaches, we employ country differences in historical legacies to understand how countries differ in terms of outcomes.

Let us examine a few theories claiming that certain historical legacies matter – that is, they still act upon a country in such a manner that when a country has had a long experience with such a culture, it shapes the outcomes of the country. One such theory deals with the effects of Spanish culture. Another theory states that British colonial rule was more beneficial for development than French colonial domination. We wish to enlarge this examination of the weight of the past upon the present by including all forms of colonial rule during modern history and assess how the experience of colonialism matters today.

**The Iberian Legacy: The Negative Outcomes of a Spanish Culture**

It is D. North who has given expression of a widely held belief that the decline of the Spanish Empire was due to some basic deficiency in that culture. How was it that the British Empire lasted for such a long time whereas the Spanish

Empire began to decline around 1600? A cultural answer to this question would not focus on specific decisions or actions that may have proved more or less disastrous, such as the silver mine policy in Latin America (Potosi) or the expelling of the thrifty Jewish and Moorish populations in the sixteenth century. Instead, North highlights certain fundamental institutions that he connects with the culture of Spain or Portugal and the countries that were under the Spanish Empire. He states:

> The most telling evidence of the increasing returns feature of the Spanish institutional fabric was the inability of the crown and its bureaucracy to alter the direction of the Spanish path in spite of their awareness of decay and decline overcoming the country. (North, 1990, p. 115)

In fact, the bureaucracy could not change this seminal trend or development path, because it was part of the problem, not the solution. North focuses on the basic set-up of economic institutions, or rules for the economy, which gave a very prominent role to the Crown and its bureaucrats. He argues that the decline resulted from the very institutions that were put into place to counter the decline: 'price controls, tax increases, and repeated confiscations' (North, 1990, p. 114). This entails that there were 'insecure property rights' (North, 1990, p. 116), all resulting from the same activities of the bureaucracy.

Spanish disease has often been equated with red tape and inefficient bureaucracy. What North is attempting to do is to render such vague impressions into a testable theory, focusing on institutions and their effect on economic efficiency or productive output. However, the distinction between institutions and culture is a thin one, as a culture may be considered as comprising a set of basic rules about proper behaviour. Thus, North claims, a Spanish culture would be conducive to the establishment of institutions that were heavy on transaction costs, and this sooner or later brings about economic inefficiency. Interestingly, he advances that this explanation holds for the fate of Latin America, which continuously lagged behind North America. He states: 'Latin American economic history, in contrast, has perpetuated the centralised, the bureaucratic traditions carried over from its Spanish/Portuguese heritage' (North, 1990, p. 116).

Thus, the Spanish or Portuguese disease would have contaminated far larger areas than merely the two mother countries. Are we to conclude that all countries with some form of Spanish or Portuguese legacy tend to perform worse? If so, worse than which countries? How could one evaluate this theory, which entails a general hypothesis about the institutional or cultural conditions for economic prosperity? We should beware of impressionistic evidence concerning the impact of colonial cultures, as it is all too easy to blame the past for the sin of the present without recognizing that several factors are at work besides the legacies from the past.

One may object to North's version of the thesis about Spanish or Portuguese disease on the grounds that it must be an exaggeration to link up the present fate of a number of Third World countries, such as Venezuela, Brazil, Peru and Argentina as well as the Philippines, with the system of governance that Spain employed during the period of colonialism that ended more than 100 years ago. After all, what is the basis of comparison? And have all relevant factors been taken into account?

A few of the former Portuguese colonies – for example, Mozambique and Angola – have suffered dismally, if not fatally in terms of development. Linking up the tragedy of civil war and destruction in these countries after their independence with their specific colonial heritage seems questionable. Here, comparison with other legacies becomes highly relevant. If one compares the outcomes for former Spanish or Portuguese colonies with those of former British or French colonies for instance, can one then state generally that the evaluation is clearly much more favourable for the latter when compared with the former? To make this comparison, we need to know the elements of a successful cultural heritage.

## The British Heritage

North contrasts Spanish and Portuguese culture with what we will call here the Anglo-Saxon culture – that is, the entire set-up of institutions that occurred in England and in one area of its colonies, namely North America or more specifically, what became the USA and Canada. The decline of Spain and Portugal, or the occurrence of Spanish disease, is contrasted with the success of the Anglo-Saxons, especially in terms of their wealth.

Following his institutional interpretation, North argues consistently that the superiority of Great Britain and the USA rests upon their adherence to economic institutions that save on transaction costs. Thus, he compares Anglo-Saxon and Spanish institutions as follows:

> In the former, an institutional framework has evolved that permits the complex impersonal exchange necessary to political stability and to capture the potential economic gains of modern technology. In the latter, personalistic relationships are still the key to much of the political and economic exchange. (North, 1990, p. 117)

This quotation is, in reality, a call for comparative research on the various effects of different cultural heritages, which may cover not only economic outcomes, such as affluence, but also political results, such as democratic stability and corruption. What does a body of systematic evidence say about the causes of macro outcomes in Latin America? The analysis of the outcomes of macro cultures does not need to be confined to the test of a hypothesis about the occurrence of Spanish disease or a hypothesis about Anglo-Saxon excellence. It could cover other cultural heritages as well – for instance, the impact of the French or Russian colonial legacies.

North's theory about the accomplishments of the Anglo-Saxon culture can be interpreted in two ways. Their institutions, promoting 'complex impersonal exchange', are said to result in both political stability and economic affluence. Perhaps North would argue that political stability in its turn further advances economic success, or he may regard these two outcomes, affluence and political stability, as ends in themselves.

Let us do a much more profound analysis of the outcomes of various historical cultures, probing into the causality over time, examining a set of outcomes that is much broader than that of North. As it is far from clear what one means by 'political stability', we suggest one focus on democratic stability or democratic longevity. One may wish to compare the outcomes of a Spanish/Portuguese legacy with the outcomes of other colonial legacies in the Third World. North's comparison with North America could involve a biased perspective from the outset, as few countries in the world could fare well in a comparative assessment with the USA. We use an explicit empirical technique that allows for powerful tests of alternative causal hypotheses, as our conclusions rest upon the regression technique. However, we first make an exhaustive coverage of cultural heritages or the variety of colonial ties.

## Dividing the World According to Colonial Experience

Colonialism is a system of political power under which one country subjugates another country, often with the purpose of obtaining economic power. Colonial rule may be characterized by many different governance structures, ranging from total submission to loose association. Colonialism may also be regarded as the philosophy that rationalized this subjugation of one country by another by overemphasizing the advantages of such ties. In reality, colonialism has been practised throughout the entire history of humankind, but the concept refers more specifically to the various forms of European domination during the last 200–300 years. The principal question is whether this European colonial rule gave the European countries a distinct advantage over the subjugated countries in Latin America, Africa and Asia, whose consequences are still with us today. The secondary question is whether one type of colonial rule was better than all the others – namely, the British system of indirect rule that included the acceptance of local autonomy, especially for the European settlers – was better than all the others.

The first major European power to establish an empire in what is now the Third World was Spain, as a result of its conquest of Central and South America. The Dutch, British and French Empires followed, together with the Portuguese expansion, into all continents. At the same time the Ottoman Empire, which involved a specific system of imperial domination, began to build up. However, it was not long before the imperial ambitions of Istanbul ran up against those of the Western European countries and that of Russia, and the Ottoman Empire did not survive this confrontation. Tsarism involved the continuous penetration of Russia in all directions, subjugating various people in combination with the settlement of large numbers of Russian-speaking populations, especially in Asia.

Some countries – for example, Belgium, Germany and Italy – arrived late in the spread of colonialism. The German Empire in Africa was crushed during the First World War, whereas Belgium managed to hang on to vast territories up until after the Second World War. Italy took possession of territories in East Africa, dominating in a few countries for variable lengths of time. During the 1950s and 1960s, the European colonial powers dismantled their possessions or were forced to do so – Portugal later than all the others. During the same period, however, the imperial ambitions of Russia, under the cover of the Soviet Union, became exorbitant, contributing to a considerable degree to its virtual collapse in 1991.

Empires can only be established by the use of force, often resulting from war, including the threat of large-scale military operations. It has been argued that trade or economic ties may result in a subjugation similar to that of empires, but what we will focus on below is only direct imperial domination, and not the subjugation that may stem from superior economic power manifested only through trade. Thus, China will not be considered as dominated by the Europeans, despite all the concessions that they have pushed China to accept. At the same time, we will regard Greenland and Iceland as a form of foreign rule – that is, the Danish Empire, if this is a legitimate expression. While it is true that Germany managed to subjugate many people during the short period of the Second World War, we are reluctant to include these countries under the label of colonies. However, since the Italian and Japanese occupation of other countries lasted longer than the German military conquests, we have included the colonialism of Italy and Japan in the analysis. There are also cases of double colonial legacies, where one can have different opinions whether countries like Kuwait or Oman should be classified as having an Ottoman legacy or a British legacy. We have opted for the Ottoman legacy in relation to Kuwait and Oman, but a few countries that were under the Ottomans – such as Egypt, for example – have been classified according to their European domination.

Table 7.1 presents a tentative attempt to identify the empirical content of the concept of colonial heritage (COLLEG). It covers all countries of the world with a population larger than 1 million. The classification of countries with respect to their colonial legacies has relied on systematizations presented by de Blij (1996, pp. 496–97) and Derbyshire and Derbyshire (1996, ch. 8). A listing of the Third World countries and their respective colonial legacies is presented in the appendix at the end of this chapter.

It is an astounding finding that few countries (here 13, out of 150) have remained outside the colonial efforts of other countries, especially the colonialization ambitions of the Europeans. These countries are to be found both in Western Europe and in the Third World, where very few countries successfully resisted the penetration of foreigners. In terms of size, five major

**Table 7.1    The colonial legacy: population distribution in percentages around 1950 and 1999**

| COLLEG | Total sample | | | Third world sample | | |
|---|---|---|---|---|---|---|
| | 1950 | 1999 | N | 1950 | 1999 | N |
| No legacy | 28.0 | 25.8 | 13 | 36.2 | 30.0 | 7 |
| British | 33.4 | 37.2 | 38 | 35.8 | 38.2 | 30 |
| French | 5.3 | 6.2 | 24 | 5.5 | 6.6 | 23 |
| Spain | 5.9 | 7.4 | 20 | 7.2 | 8.5 | 19 |
| Portuguese | 2.9 | 3.6 | 4 | 3.8 | 4.2 | 3 |
| Dutch | 3.4 | 3.9 | 2 | 4.5 | 4.5 | 1 |
| Belgian | 1.0 | 1.2 | 4 | 1.0 | 1.4 | 3 |
| Italian | 2.7 | 2.2 | 4 | 1.3 | 1.5 | 3 |
| Turkish | 3.4 | 3.0 | 16 | 1.5 | 2.0 | 5 |
| Russian | 8.9 | 5.8 | 19 | 1.1 | 1.2 | 6 |
| Japanese | 4.9 | 3.6 | 4 | 2.3 | 1.9 | 3 |
| Danish | 0.2 | 0.1 | 2 | – | – | – |
| Total | 100.0 | 100.0 | 150 | 100.0 | 100.0 | 103 |

*Source*:   See Appendix A.

empires may be singled out during this period of classical colonialism – that is, the centuries from the Renaissance up to 1991. The largest of all empires constructed is the British one, covering no less than 39 countries. The French, Spanish, Russian and Turkish Empires never reached that immense size, but they covered some 20 countries – a considerable number. The remaining empires included at most three or four countries each.

## The Impact of Different Colonial Regimes

The question of how the numerous subjugated countries were ruled under a colonial regime has been much researched, particularly in terms of whether the colonial power tolerated already established power structures, whether it developed an elaborate administrative structure reminiscent of that of the home country, and whether it arbitrarily resorted to force when faced with resistance.

The classical regime confrontation was that between the so-called indirect rule of the British model and the prefect model used in territories dominated by France. The willingness of the British to accept more local discretion stemmed not only from the cunning use of the principle of 'Divide and Rule', but also involved a recognition of the fact that the British colonies often included large numbers of European settlers. Naked power seems to have been the method employed in the Spanish, Portuguese, and Dutch Empires, at least to a greater extent than in the French and British Empires. It was not until there was a sufficiently large population of Spanish and Portuguese descendants that Latin America could move towards independence. The British also perhaps pursued a more flexible policy of dismantling colonialism once the demand for independence could no longer be rejected. The French and the Portuguese fiercely resisted claims for independence, resulting in large-scale military defeat (Dien Bien Phu), whereas the Dutch and Belgians, suddenly realising that change was inevitable, hurriedly abandoned their empires, leaving chaos in their wake.

The Ottoman Empire, labelled 'Turkish' in Table 7.1, very early on developed a special mechanism for exercising authority while at the same time providing the subjugated peoples with some degree of self-rule – the famous *Millet* system. *Millet* was a people adhering to a different culture than that of the Ottomans. It could govern itself to some extent, although it had to accept the final authority of Istanbul. The *Millet* system was employed in relation to the many religious and ethnic minorities that were under Ottoman rule, whether Christian or Muslim.

The Russian Empire allowed for local discretion, as for instance in Finland under the tsarist regime or as with Eastern Europe under the Bolshevik system. However, in the territories directly included in the Soviet Union, there was uniform party rule, emanating from Moscow. The Russian Empire under the Bolsheviks took on a world dimension, when the USSR began to support communist regimes in South America, Africa and Asia. We have not included these 'satellites' in our classification of colonies. No doubt the Russian empire overextended itself and depleted its resources quickly when the USSR was asked to help all over the world, economically or militarily, as for example in Egypt, the Middle East, Angola and in Vietnam. The invasion of Afghanistan in 1979 resulted in the definitive exhaustion of the USSR. No foreign country has so far been capable of controlling Afghanistan.

The Italian and Japanese colonies were the result of warfare and did not last long. German colonial rule crumbled when Germany could not defend its territories during the First World War, as, for example, when Namibia (or the former German South West Africa) was invaded from South Africa and later taken over as a Mandate. Entirely different is the Danish rule over Greenland, which still exists, perhaps due to its firm adherence to self-government under a rule of law system. A similar system of government is to be found only in the colonies that were given Dominion status in the British Empire in 1931 (Westminster Statutes) – that is, they comprised a majority of European settler populations.

Most people who were subjugated by the Europeans and the Turks, as well as the Russians and the Japanese would state without much reflection: 'Yes, colonialism matters.' However, what we are looking for are the enduring effects of colonialism, showing up today in the set of present outcomes that we are examining. Even when the colonial systems were being built, the pros

**Table 7.2    Colonial legacies and outcomes: comparing means (total sample N=150 at most)**

| COLLEG | DEM97 | GEM99 | HDI99 | PPP90 | PPP97 | GRO 9098 | CORR98 |
|---|---|---|---|---|---|---|---|
| No legacy | 5.90 | 0.61 | 0.78 | 9721 | 14700 | 2.5 | 7.25 |
| British | 5.53 | 0.43 | 0.64 | 5406 | 7314 | 1.8 | 5.32 |
| French | 3.33 | 0.29 | 0.52 | 2256 | 3027 | 0.7 | 3.67 |
| Spain | 6.79 | 0.49 | 0.75 | 4064 | 6115 | 2.2 | 3.49 |
| Portuguese | 5.83 | 0.46 | 0.58 | 4252 | 5510 | -0.2 | 5.25 |
| Dutch | 5.83 | 0.53 | 0.80 | 9547 | 12345 | 3.1 | 5.50 |
| Belgian | 2.71 | 0.61 | 0.53 | 4651 | 6280 | -4.2 | 5.40 |
| Italian | 3.33 | 0.52 | 0.65 | 4993 | 9099 | 1.8 | 4.60 |
| Turkish | 5.05 | 0.38 | 0.77 | 6832 | 8761 | -0.3 | 3.70 |
| Russian | 5.61 | 0.52 | 0.75 | 7862 | 4587 | -5.3 | 4.49 |
| Japanese | 6.46 | 0.42 | 0.89 | 10027 | 12903 | 3.1 | 5.10 |
| Danish | 10.00 | 0.74 | 0.91 | 17666 | 22973 | 2.1 | 9.65 |
| eta squared | .15 | .36 | .32 | .21 | .22 | .43 | .31 |
| sig. | .020 | .000 | .000 | .002 | .000 | .000 | .003 |

*Sources*: See Appendix A.

and cons of colonial regimes were debated. A critical view argued that colonialism really does not pay off, as the many different costs ultimately outweigh the seemingly tangible benefits of increased trade and access to scarce resources. 'Trade, not Empire' was a position advocated by many during the nineteenth century. The costs and benefits of an empire have been calculated by British historians, among others, without arriving at a conclusive assessment. However, what we wish to assess is not the costs and benefits already incurred by the mother country, but the future impact of colonial rule on the colonized country, especially the outcomes related to their degree of development today. In relation to the Danish rule over Greenland and Iceland there have been complaints about colonial exploitation and the arrogance of power when various measures were employed to modernize an indigenous culture, namely that of the Inuits. Table 7.2 portrays some empirical findings that are relevant for a first picture of the general outcomes of colonialism.

The general finding in Table 7.2, covering all countries, or the total sample, is that countries with no colonial legacy at all come out best on the evaluation criteria, where data pertain to the 1990s only. Countries that were within the British Empire have a slightly better performance profile today than countries that were under French rule. The various colonial legacies in Table 7.2, however, include not only First World and Third World countries but also the respective mother country.

**Table 7.3    Colonial influence: comparing means (Third World sample N=103 at most)**

| COLLEG | DEM97 | GEM99 | HDI99 | PPP90 | PPP97 | GRO 9098 | CORR98 |
|---|---|---|---|---|---|---|---|
| No legacy | 2.50 | 0.39 | 0.62 | 2071 | 3561 | 4.1 | 3.25 |
| British | 4.61 | 0.35 | 0.57 | 2630 | 3722 | 1.6 | 4.05 |
| French | 3.08 | 0.27 | 0.50 | 1581 | 2193 | 0.7 | 3.17 |
| Spain | 6.67 | 0.48 | 0.74 | 3636 | 5610 | 2.3 | 3.33 |
| Portuguese | 4.44 | 0.40 | 0.49 | 2108 | 2620 | -1.0 | 4.00 |
| Dutch | 1.73 | 0.36 | 0.68 | 2525 | 3390 | 4.0 | 2.00 |
| Belgian | 0.56 | – | 0.40 | 599 | 676 | -6.1 | – |
| Italian | 1.39 | – | 0.53 | 1340 | 3598 | 2.6 | – |
| Turkish | 2.33 | 0.29 | 0.77 | 8316 | 14291 | -0.4 | 3.40 |
| Russian | 2.92 | – | 0.69 | 2259 | 2039 | -7.6 | – |
| Japanese | 5.56 | 0.34 | 0.85 | 7186 | 7155 | 4.9 | 4.75 |
| Danish | – | – | – | – | – | – | – |
| eta squared | .31 | .45 | .44 | .37 | .34 | .53 | .11 |
| sig. | .000 | .001 | .000 | .000 | .000 | .000 | .649 |

*Sources*: See Appendix A.

Moreover, countries that have had experience of French, Spanish, Portuguese, Belgian or Russian colonialism appear to do worse than countries that have been under British, Japanese, Dutch, Turkish or Danish rule. To what extent is this a mere accidental finding, reflecting the different country fortunes after the fall of colonialism? One must separate a short-term effect of colonialism from a long-term effect, as the fate of country depends on other factors than colonial experience alone.

Table 7.2 may be compared with Table 7.3, which restricts the evaluation of colonialism to Third World countries. Colonialism was very much directed against countries that today make up the so-called Third World. Western European superiority in terms of military, economic and administrative capacity allowed a few West European states to create long-lasting empires, reducing Third World countries to colonies or protectorates.

Colonialism, or the subjugation of less advanced countries by more advanced countries, was such a violent process that it is quite natural to ask afterwards whether it was worthwhile. There are basically two opinions, one positive and one negative. According to the positive view, the colonial legacy ought to be favourable for the country, on the whole. Despite the political dependency a process of modernization was inevitably put in train, which would make the country capable of self-rule. In the negative view, colonialism benefited the colonizing country alone and held back the colonized country, depriving it especially of its resources. The assessment of the consequences of colonialism is an extremely complex research task, requiring a much more profound analysis than we can offer here. Colonialism always displayed a strange mixture of activities involving assistance on the one hand and extreme contempt on the other. Thus, help and contempt went hand-in-hand when missionaries were sent out to Africa in the face of the continuation of the slave trade that had long been declared illegal. The Belgian treatment of Congo is also very telling: while King Leopold mishandled the population, using the customary practice of cuddling people's hands and feet, numerous monks and nuns sacrificed their lives in the name of 'civilization'.

Table 7.3 indicates how far development – political, economic and social – had proceeded in Third World countries in the 1990s. This information is a better clue to the outcomes of colonialism than Table 7.2.

Now, we find that Third World countries that have remained outside all forms of colonialism do not perform worse than Third World countries that were under colonial rule of one form or another. Again, we find that French colonial experience seems to leave countries worse off than British colonial experience. However, we also note that Russian domination has left many countries at a low level of development. Table 7.3 shows that the level of economic development is not the same as the level of political development. While some countries with a specific colonial experience do rather well economically – the countries under Turkish or Japanese domination – democracy is not firmly entrenched in any of the country sets, whatever the particular colonial experience may have been. The level of economic and social development is extremely low in countries with experience of Russian, French, Belgian and Portuguese colonialism, probably for different reasons. The rather high figures for Spanish colonial legacy are surprising. Perhaps these countries have done better than might have been expected, because colonialism does not determine the path of development? Or maybe the Iberian legacy is not such a devastating experience?

One needs to distinguish between the situation immediately after colonial rule had finished and the situation today. Countries may improve upon their predicament by taking actions that undo, at least to some extent, the negative consequences of colonial legacies. Countries may also perform less well in the long run after colonialism has ended for other reasons than colonialism – factors that may be non-conducive for socioeconomic development.

## Close and Distant Consequences

Most of the colonial systems broke up after the Second World. The Spanish Empire is an exception, as it had already been dismantled during the nineteenth century. Russian colonialism is a phenomenon of the twentieth century, whose dismantling began late, or in 1989. Japanese colonial rule was very short-lived but no less dramatic than other forms of colonial rule (1910–45), including the extreme atrocities in Manchuria in the 1930s.

Colonialism always showed two faces. On the one hand, there was the argument expressed in the formula of 'taking up the white man's burden' or the 'manifest destiny theme', namely of establishing a kind of tutelary regime in order to christianize as well as modernize the country. On the other hand, there was the argument about the 'scramble for colonies', or that the power struggle between advanced countries necessitated the building up of colonial systems of domination of less advanced countries. What is true is that colonialism employed both the sword and the nanny when it expanded and put one territory after another under its rule.

Even when colonialism played the helping card, the native country might still get the impression that it was a disguised form of playing the contempt card. Assistance with modernization often went hand-in-hand with favours for the Christian churches, which was seen as an instrument of domination, at least by some countries. Similarly, such assistance often also resulted in economic favours for foreign merchants or trading companies – in India, the British East India company and, in China, trade commissions, the lease of Hong Kong and Macao to name but two examples. The colonial powers employed the sword and the nanny in various mixes. Japanese colonialism was perhaps the most violent form of colonial expansion, although its time-span was brief. British colonialism, on the other hand, seems to have placed far more emphasis on the developmental goals, and also operated over a long time-span. Yet, the British also used the sword, including the use of concentration camps during the Second Boer War (1899–1902).

Table 7.4 compares the development record in time of four sets of countries with different colonial masters at various points. Can we detect any differences between the outcomes that occurred after the end of colonial rule and the outcomes that characterizes these countries today?

A number of interesting observations may be made in relation to the information contained in Table 7.4. The first finding is that countries that were under British rule perform better than countries that belonged to the French Empire when the colonies became independent. This marked difference remains during the entire postwar period, meaning that the French former colonies do not catch up with the former British colonies, on average. The standard image of British imperial rule as more beneficial than French imperial rule is thus confirmed.

The second finding concerns the Spanish legacy. The former Spanish colonies that became independent more than 100 years ago did display a slight advance in relation to British and French colonies when the final liberation from colonialism arrived after the Second World War, but it was hardly a huge one. At the end of the twentieth century, the former British colonies had not closed this gap. The former French colonies have also been unable to catch up so far in relation to the former Spanish colonies. This hardly indicates the existence of Spanish disease, or the pattern of slow development that is typical of the so-called Iberian legacy. It must be stressed that the data do not support the hypothesis that Spanish culture has a negative impact,

**Table 7.4    Four colonial legacies in the Third World: comparing means**

| Outcomes | British legacy | French legacy | Spanish legacy | Portuguese legacy | eta squared | sig. |
|---|---|---|---|---|---|---|
| DEM00 | 4.8 | 2.8 | 4.8 | 4.0 | .09 | .662 |
| DEM50 | 6.4 | 4.4 | 4.4 | 6.0 | .13 | .240 |
| DEM79 | 4.3 | 2.0 | 5.0 | 1.9 | .21 | .001 |
| DEM89 | 4.1 | 2.0 | 6.4 | 3.1 | .32 | .000 |
| DEM99 | 4.9 | 3.3 | 6.7 | 4.4 | .23 | .000 |
| HDI60 | 0.27 | 0.18 | 0.46 | 0.23 | .42 | .000 |
| HDI92 | 0.49 | 0.39 | 0.71 | 0.43 | .34 | .000 |
| HDI99 | 0.57 | 0.50 | 0.74 | 0.49 | .37 | .000 |
| CORR98 | 4.1 | 3.2 | 3.3 | 4.0 | .06 | .469 |
| GRO6073 | 2.5 | 1.2 | 2.2 | 3.6 | .14 | .031 |
| GRO7385 | 1.4 | 0.8 | −0.3 | 1.5 | .08 | .161 |
| GRO8594 | 1.2 | −1.3 | 1.0 | 0.7 | .15 | .015 |
| GRO9098 | 1.6 | 0.7 | 2.3 | −1.0 | .09 | .077 |
| RGDPC60 | 1277 | 972 | 2206 | 1289 | .18 | .007 |
| PPP90 | 2562 | 1627 | 3366 | 2210 | .08 | .103 |
| PPP97 | 3723 | 2193 | 5611 | 2620 | .10 | .050 |

*Note*:    In this analysis we have only included cases from the Third World which have direct experience of these four colonial legacies.

*Sources*: See Appendix A.

as suggested by North. In fact, the former Spanish colonies score well in comparison with the three other sets of colonies and the Iberian legacy does better than the other legacies included in Table 7.4.

Comparing the performance record of former British and French colonies with that of the former Spanish ones over such a long time-span as the postwar period, it can be noted that the latter were more developed than the former, thereby giving support to the negative view of colonialism as an instrument for the domination of the peoples of the Third World working itself out as a brake upon development. How long does a negative colonial legacy last? Are the fundamental problems with both democracy and economic development in Latin America in the twentieth century a product of the Spanish colonial system put into place after the *Conquista* in the sixteenth century? Or does the relatively high level of democracy and affluence in the former colonies at the end of the twentieth century reflect a positive impact? The concept of a colonial legacy contains no time limit on how long the effect may last. We claim that the data concerning the former British and French colonies indicate the existence of an immediate and negative impact of colonialism, whereas the evidence concerning the Spanish former colonies may be interpreted as a long-lasting and distant impact of colonialism which is not mainly negative. But is a colonial legacy a true explanatory factor?

## Do Colonial Cultures Matter?

We must reflect upon the mechanism at work when a colonial past puts its mark upon a country. It is simply not enough to look at the average performance scores for sets of countries that correspond to a type of colonial rule. Differences between such categories may depend on several other factors besides the colonial legacy. In addition, the mechanism at work when a colonial past is transmitted into the future of an independent country must be clarified. One such measure is the number of years under colonial rule – that is, the period between the establishment of colonial rule and the time of decolonization (COLRULE). However, it is not enough merely to count only the number of years of colonial domination, as what is at stake is the orientation of that system which, in one form or another, is transmitted into either a positive or a negative heritage.

The argument that colonialism matters can be developed in two ways. One can either focus on the mere existence of any form of colonial legacy, when it started and how long it lasted, or one can attempt to find out whether different colonial legacies matter – for instance, whether British colonialism favoured development (to some extent at least) while French and Belgian colonialism disfavoured development, relatively speaking. In order to test the theory that colonial cultures matter, one may use the so-called modernization factor. Thus, we construct a new measure which captures the number of years since decolonization (DECOLYR). It should be pointed out that it is sometimes not entirely clear when a country experienced its first day as a modern independent state, but we will rely on the scores arrived at in the modernization literature.

Now, if colonialism matters, then the average performance record of independent countries must be better than that of countries with any form of colonial experience. Moreover, it must also be the case that the length in time of colonial experience is a negative factor, meaning that the longer a country was subjugated, the worse will be its average performance record on some development indicators. These two measures of colonialism – number of years since independence day of a modern state (DECOLYR) as well as number of years of colonial subjugation (COLRULE) – are not quite the same. In relation to Africa for instance, although many African countries have had independent modern states for only a short time period, Africa was subjugated by the main European powers rather late in the infamous scramble for Africa, ending in the Berlin conference of 1884–85.

Table 7.5 presents a regression analysis estimating a model which tests the argument that the performance record of a country today depends on both the length of colonial experience and the length of time of independence. Is there

**Table 7.5    The impact of the colonial legacy on developmental outcomes – number of years since independence (DECOLYR) and number of years of colonial rule (COLRULE): regression analysis**

| Independent variables | Coeffs | Dependent variables | | | | | | | |
|---|---|---|---|---|---|---|---|---|---|
| | | DEM97 | HDI99 | LnPPP97 | GRO9098 | GINI90 | GEM99 | WOM90 | CORR98 |
| MODLEA | coeff | -.000 | .001 | .002 | -.028 | -.130 | -.000 | -.007 | -.005 |
| | t-stat | -.06 | 2.77 | .57 | -2.35 | -1.65 | -1.06 | -.36 | -.47 |
| | tol | .56 | .54 | .53 | .54 | .31 | .43 | .54 | .31 |
| DISEQU | coeff | -.851 | .323 | 1.606 | -.574 | 3.439 | .061 | 2.584 | 3.751 |
| | t-stat | -.34 | 2.53 | 1.87 | -.16 | .19 | .47 | .50 | 1.61 |
| | tol | .79 | .76 | .75 | .75 | .85 | .76 | .77 | .74 |
| DECOLY | coeff | .008 | .000 | .004 | .028 | .071 | .001 | -.004 | -.003 |
| | t-stat | 1.69 | 1.59 | 2.31 | 4.58 | 1.96 | 2.79 | -.40 | -.60 |
| | tol | .73 | .74 | .74 | .74 | .40 | .51 | .71 | .42 |
| COLRULE | coeff | .009 | .000 | .001 | .001 | .011 | .001 | .019 | .001 |
| | t-stat | 4.00 | 2.30 | 1.60 | .23 | .75 | 4.99 | 4.07 | .42 |
| | tol | .85 | .81 | .80 | .82 | .66 | .68 | .85 | .64 |
| Constant | coeff | 2.340 | .393 | 6.970 | .343 | 44.885 | .244 | 5.240 | 3.456 |
| | t-stat | 3.55 | 12.20 | 31.83 | .39 | 10.50 | 6.77 | 3.83 | 5.93 |
| Adjrsq | | .17 | .35 | .15 | .17 | .01 | .45 | .13 | .00 |
| N | | 103 | 98 | 99 | 94 | 38 | 55 | 95 | 48 |

*Notes:*   Only Third World countries are included in this analysis.
coeff = the unstandardized regression coefficient.
t-stat = t-statistics. Used to test the significance of the regression coefficients; t-stat showing more than ± 2 indicates significance.
tol = tolerance. Used to measure the occurrence of multicollinearity in the model; if tol is higher than .3/.4 there is no risk of multicollinearity.

*Sources:*  See Appendix A.

any empirical evidence for the occurrence of a brutal colonial effect, which would mean that the length of colonization is crucially important? To control for other factors, we also include variables that measure a geographical factor (DISEQU) as well as a historical factor (MODLEAD). In the regression analyses presented in Tables 7.5 and 7.6 we only include the Third World sample of countries.

Interestingly, colonial legacies do have an impact on the developmental outcomes, but the findings deviate from the arguments advanced. Colonialism matters both positively and negatively. Democracy, human development and gender empowerment is positively associated with a longer period of colonial rule while a longer period of independence is associated with affluence and economic growth. In the Third World context this actually equals Latin America, which has a better developmental record than many parts of the Third World contrary to what North suggests. The colonial legacy does not matter at all for the variation in income distribution (GINI90) or perceptions of corruption (CORR98).

These findings suggest that Latin America and a Spanish legacy may actually be conducive to development – at least in a Third World context. The direct impact of different colonial legacies is tested in Table 7.6. with the same set of dependent variables and the same set of control variables. The difference is that colonial legacies here are operationalized by employing three different dummy variables capturing three different legacies: the British, Spanish and French. In a Third World context, is the Spanish legacy an asset or not?

Comparing the impact of the three colonial legacies it is obvious that the Spanish one matters most, and, when they matter, the Spanish and the British legacies have a positive impact on the developmental outcomes that we are inquiring into, while the impact of the French legacy is rather negative. Here we should note, however, that high levels of income differences (GINI90) are associated with the Spanish legacy. Neither female parliamentary representation (WOM90), nor the perceptions of corruption (CORR98) depends on colonial legacies. The amount of explained variance is in no case overwhelming, but the models tested suggest that colonial legacies – particularly the Spanish legacy – are important although, again, we must add in the Third World context. The impact of the Spanish legacy is significant on human development (HDI99) and it is positive.

**Conclusion**

Colonial legacies are relevant for understanding Third World countries. Among the rich countries constituting the OECD set of countries, only four of them have experienced a colonial legacy: the USA, Canada, Australia and New Zealand. When inquiring into whether colonialism, or colonial legacies, do matter, the focus must be on the Third World countries, studying the

**Table 7.6  The impact of the colonial legacy – British, French and Spanish legacies: regression analysis**

| Independent variables | Coeffs | Dependent variables | | | | | | | |
|---|---|---|---|---|---|---|---|---|---|
| | | DEM97 | HD199 | LnPPP97 | GRO9098 | GINI90 | GEM99 | WOM90 | CORR98 |
| MODLEA | coeff | -.000 | .001 | .001 | -.021 | -.196 | -.000 | -.010 | -.005 |
| | t-stat | -.02 | 2.28 | .32 | -1.55 | -2.28 | -.63 | -.48 | -.52 |
| | tol | .49 | .45 | .45 | .43 | .23 | .46 | .47 | .28 |
| DISEQU | coeff | .851 | .325 | 1.801 | 3.546 | 18.906 | -.036 | 1.887 | 3.635 |
| | t-stat | .33 | 2.45 | 1.94 | .90 | 1.06 | -.26 | .33 | 1.60 |
| | tol | .71 | .66 | .65 | .65 | .76 | .80 | .71 | .77 |
| BRITLEG | coeff | 1.967 | -.025 | .005 | 2.872 | 1.211 | -.014 | .644 | .464 |
| | t-stat | 2.78 | -.07 | .02 | 2.72 | .22 | -.38 | .38 | .59 |
| | tol | .63 | .60 | .60 | .58 | .28 | .47 | .57 | .31 |
| SPANLEG | coeff | 4.028 | .092 | .721 | 5.051 | 18.539 | .140 | 3.529 | .084 |
| | t-stat | 4.40 | 1.94 | 2.17 | 3.61 | 3.05 | 3.08 | 1.72 | .11 |
| | tol | .52 | .45 | .450 | .45 | .29 | .36 | .508 | .36 |
| FRENLEG | coeff | .428 | -.086 | -.246 | 2.110 | -1.530 | -.085 | -1.159 | -.503 |
| | t-stat | .58 | -2.34 | -.95 | 1.94 | -.26 | -2.04 | -.67 | -.55 |
| | tol | .68 | .65 | .65 | .63 | .26 | .60 | .623 | .50 |
| Constant | coeff | 2.516 | .474 | 7.363 | -.866 | 50.013 | .382 | 7.529 | 3.252 |
| | t-stat | 3.07 | 11.68 | 25.80 | -.72 | 6.58 | 7.97 | 3.82 | 3.20 |
| Adjrsq | | .21 | .39 | .15 | .11 | .13 | .38 | .01 | .01 |
| N | | 103 | 98 | 99 | 94 | 38 | 55 | 95 | 48 |

*Notes:*  Refer to notes to Table 7.5.
*Sources:*  See Appendix A.

impact of colonial legacies on different developmental outcomes today. The negative hypothesis states that colonialism hindered development, whereas the positive hypothesis claims the opposite. We find that a colonial legacy promotes political development but not economic development.

Contrary to earlier research we show that the Spanish legacy is more of an asset for, than a hindrance to, developmental outcomes. This has partly to do with the fact that the Latin American countries gained independence rather early, and that they also were under a colonial rule for quite a long time. This is at least something that distinguishes the Spanish legacy from the legacies of British and French colonialism. This does not, however, explain the differences in developmental paths for Anglo-America and Latin America. If Latin America is understood to be a part of the Third World, then maybe the Spanish legacy was conducive for development in such a context, while a British legacy would not have the same positive outcomes in the Third World as we find in the Anglo-American world. But, even in such a global context, our findings suggest that the Spanish legacy was more of an asset than a burden. Thus, one must question the North thesis.

Our findings although highly tentative, indicate that colonialism is not such an impossible legacy to live with as Franz Fanon claimed in his classical study *Les damnés de la terre* (1961). Perhaps one may foresee a reassessment of not only the Iberian legacy but also the Apartheid legacy in South Africa or British rule in India, despite their despicable racist tones. One can fully endorse the rejection of Edward Said of all forms of neo-colonialism in his *Culture and Imperialism* (1994) but at the same time argue that colonialism did not result in destruction and merely subjugation everywhere. Said is extremely critical of the British colonial legacy, but its outcomes were in general better than, for instance, the Ottoman legacy. One must differentiate between different colonial pasts. At the same time, Said is correct that anti-colonialism may be a great source of popular mobilization, nationalism and democracy – although not always successfully so. In the following chapter we analyse another legacy in the same manner – namely, the family structure. It is a cultural tradition that structures behaviour in a most fundamental way.

## Appendix: Colonial Legacies in the Third World

| British legacy (N=30) | French legacy (N=23) | Spanish legacy (N=19) | Other legacies |
|---|---|---|---|
| Bangladesh | Algeria | Argentina | No legacy (N=7) |
| Botswana | Benin | Bolivia | Afghanistan |
| Burma | Burkina Faso | Chile | Bhutan |
| Egypt | Cambodia | Colombia | China |
| Ghana | Cameroon | Costa Rica | Iran |
| India | Central African | Cuba | Liberia |
| Iraq | Republic | Dominican | Nepal |
| Jamaica | Chad | Republic | Thailand |
| Jordan | Congo, | Ecuador | Russian (N=6) |
| Kenya | Republic of | El Salvador | Kazakhstan |
| Lesotho | Côte d'Ivoire | Guatemala | Kyrgyzstan |
| Malawi | Gabon | Honduras | Mongolia |
| Malaysia | Guinea | Mexico | Tajikistan |
| Mauritius | Haiti | Nicaragua | Turkmenistan |
| Namibia | Laos | Panama | Uzbekistan |
| Nigeria | Lebanon | Paraguay | Turkish (N=5) |
| Pakistan | Madagascar | Peru | Kuwait |
| Papua New | Mali | Philippines | Oman |
| Guinea | Mauritania | Uruguay | Saudi Arabia |
| Sierra Leone | Morocco | Venezuela | Turkey |
| Singapore | Niger | | United Arab |
| South Africa | Senegal | | Emirates |
| Sri Lanka | Syria | | Portuguese (N=3) |
| Sudan | Tunisia | | Angola |
| Tanzania | Vietnam | | Brazil |
| Togo | | | Mozambique |
| Trinidad and | | | Belgian (N=3) |
| Tobago | | | Burundi |
| Uganda | | | Rwanda |
| Yemen | | | Zaire |
| Zambia | | | Italian (N=3) |
| Zimbabwe | | | Ethiopia |
| | | | Libya |
| | | | Somalia |
| | | | Japanese (N=3) |
| | | | Korea, North |
| | | | Korea, South |
| | | | Taiwan |
| | | | Dutch (N=1) |
| | | | Indonesia |

*Source*:  Based on information in de Blij (1996, pp. 496–97).

# Chapter 8

# Family Structure and Democracy

## Introduction

In this chapter we will examine the empirical support for a well-known theory about the consequences of various family cultures for social outcomes – namely, the theory of E. Todd (1983, 1984). This is a theory about profound cultural variation, outlining a set of major family categories covering the entire world. Todd analyses the family system as a consequence of universal cultural items – namely, equality and liberty – but we will approach it as a set of legacies.

One may broaden the cultural analysis of outcomes by bringing in a major culture that structures the behaviour of individuals – that is, the different norms about the proper family. Since the family structure and cultures of a country change slowly, they may be regarded as a kind of historical heritage whose eventual impact on society and politics would show up after a while. Can we detect any stable and durable effects from the operation over a long time-span of one or another type of family structure? Which outcomes might theoretically be the effects of family structures? Obviously, the family is such a pervasive and omnipresent structure of human behaviour that it must affect the individual in many ways during his or her lifetime and throughout the various family stages, but, here, we must ask more specifically what happens to a variety of concrete outcomes when the family culture shifts from one kind to another. If it is as important whether a country has one or another of these family cultures as Todd claims, then we may wish to know for what political, social and economic outcomes is it important?

One word of caution should be added here. Most recent studies indicate that family behaviour, at least in Europe, is in a process of major transformation, reflecting vast cultural change. The occurrence of divorces has increased dramatically in recent decades, as has the number of single parents. Moreover, parents and their grown-up children tend not to live together any more, not even in Catholic countries. Finally, inheritance laws have changed towards more equality among the heirs, limiting discretion in the form of wills. When we set out to explore Todd's classification we will not be able to take these recent changes fully into account. However, this is not strictly necessary, as we focus on *long-term* effects of legacies of family structures.

## The Different Family Cultures

The family is regarded as the most basic human organization underpinning society. How could there be social life without values guiding the interaction between parents and their children? The reproduction of society requires that children not only be born but also raised, developing into adults. The literature on family sociology and individual psychology constitutes a whole field of research about the socialization of children and the nature of the period of adolescence (Graham, 1998; Nock, 1996). Accepting the thesis about the importance of the family, we may still ask how far-reaching are the consequences of the family for other social systems or for outcomes more distant from the family.

Todd's theory about the family is interesting to us not only because of its emphasis on cultural variation, but also because it claims that the family almost determines other social phenomena:

> One can formulate an absolutely general hypothesis: everywhere, the ideological sphere is the implementation in an intellectual form of the family system, a transformation into the social level of the fundamental values that govern the elementary human relationships: liberty, equality, and their negation for instance. To each type of family there corresponds one ideological type and only one. (Todd, 1983, p. 26)

One would want to know what this parallelism amounts to: ideology/ anthropology or social relations/human relations (Todd, 1983, p. 25). Before we examine the links between various types of family system and their purportedly social consequences, we deal with Todd's various dimensions of basic family cultures, which allow him to construct his typology.

Following a few conceptual distinctions suggested earlier by Frederic Le Play (1806–1882), Todd focuses on liberty within the family – that is, the degree of authority that the parents exercise over their children throughout their whole lives, as well as equality among children in terms of inheritance. Dichotomizing Todd gives us Figure 8.1 which we will call the 'Todd 1983 typology'.

Todd's contribution to the typology of family systems is first and foremost his addition of the family type that combines liberty and inequality, which Le Play did not include – the absolute nuclear family. Second, he develops the basic scheme in Table 8.1 in two ways, recognizing that family cultures vary quite considerably as there are many dimensions to take into account.

On the one hand, Todd recognizes the regulation of incest in the form of institutions that either accept endogamous behaviour (marrying within the same tribe) or favour only exogamous behaviour (marrying outside the tribe) (Todd, 1983). On the other hand, in another volume, he further develops his system of family types by entering the distinction between matrilineal and patrilineal family systems, which determines heritage as either on the female

|            | Liberty                    | Authority               |
|------------|----------------------------|-------------------------|
| **Equality**   | Egalitarian nuclear family | Communitarian family    |
| **Inequality** | Absolute nuclear family    | Authoritarian family    |

*Source*: Todd (1983, p. 18).

**Figure 8.1    Basic family institutions according to Todd (1983)**

or male side (Todd, 1984). To Todd, the variation in fundamental and long-lasting family cultures explains the occurrence of several of the chief mass belief systems in the twentieth century – this is the main argument of *La troisième planète* (1983). This is no doubt a most startling monocausal hypothesis, which opens up truly fascinating research. Yet, there is a clear risk that such a macroscopic research puts the cart before the horse in the sense that one employs the distribution of the outcomes – the spatial occurrence of belief systems – when one attempts to map the geographical spread of the variety of family systems – the overall condition.

It should be fully acknowledged that Todd separates between the horse and the cart, stating that research on the impact of family institutions involve two steps. First, we have the so-called independent variable:

... the elaboration of a logically exhaustive typology over family types, the description of the world in terms of an empirically exhaustive analysis of the occurrence of family structures. (Todd, 1983, p. 26)

Second, we have the so-called dependent variable:

... the establishment of a bivariate correlation between all the family types and the political or ideological types of phenomena. (Todd, 1983, pp. 26–27)

However, the making of this logical distinction between the independent variable (horse) and the dependent variable (cart) does not preclude that Todd has used the cart to find the horse, so to speak. Todd argues that ideological belief systems must have one and only one necessary condition, namely the family. If the occurrence of communism, or the electoral support for communist parties, varies tremendously over the continents, then where except in the family institutions could one find a factor that varies in the same manner? If this is Todd's procedure, then it involves a fallacy. Communism could have a variety of sources or sufficient conditions, some present in some countries and others present in other countries. Why would there have to be one single source of communism? Now that communism has more or less vanished, we cannot really conclude that some similar kind of belief system will take its place in exactly the very same regions around the world.

Todd presents a somewhat different typology of the family systems in *L'enfance du monde* (1984). This typology, which we will call 'the Todd 1984 typology', has two basic dimensions: status of women and degree of authority. Combining them he arrives at a matrix containing six types of family system as displayed in Figure 8.2.

He presents a similar causal argument in his 1984 study. Looking at the variation across countries in terms of development, measured by the literacy rate in the population, he searches for one necessary condition that can explain why some countries score high and other countries score low on modernization. But, we ask, why look for necessary conditions? Perhaps a set of sufficient conditions is enough? Todd bypasses the methodological possibility that the variation in development may have various sources, some conditions being present in some countries while other conditions are operating in others. Searching for one single necessary condition may result in a powerful and encompassing theory, but it may also lead to a neglect of sufficient conditions. Todd states:

> Whether it is a matter of analysing the political ideologies or the cultural development, the anthropological project returns always to one single game of hypotheses. It explains the phenomena that are called 'modernity' by latent unchangeable factors, external to history. (Todd, 1984, p. 15)

Todd is perhaps correct in emphasizing that anthropology favours structural explanations, but it does not follow that only necessary conditions should be identified. Why would family types constitute the main bedrock of such phenomena as the electoral support for radical political ideologies or the extent of literacy or socioeconomic development?

| | Degree of authority | |
|---|---|---|
| **Status of women** | Weak non-verticality | Strong verticality |
| **Patrilinearity** | Patrilineal, non-vertical type (1) | Patrilineal, vertical type (2) |
| **Bilaterality** | Bilateral, non-vertical type (3) | Bilateral, vertical type (4) |
| **Matrilinearity** | Matrilineal, non-vertical type (5) | Matrilineal, vertical type (6) |

*Source*: Todd (1984, p. 36).

**Figure 8.2   Basic family typology according to Todd (1984)**

Perhaps widespread changes have recently occurred in the family systems around the world, and not only in Western Europe as all the evidence indicates. Todd argues that one should not pay too much attention to recent changes in family cultures. The important thing is to capture the structure that has prevailed for a long time, because it is this factor that could result in the effect on society that Todd so much wants to capture. Only if one establishes the long-lasting habits in family behaviour could there be an impact on what Todd calls the prevailing ideology or the occurrence of this link from human relations to social relations.

Todd makes no secret about his claim to have discovered a major explanatory factor – the family – which would, in his opinion, condition major phenomena in aspects of society, such as the political beliefs of ordinary people:

> No theory has until now succeeded in explaining the distribution of ideologies, systems and political forces on the surface of the third planet of the solar system. No one knows why certain regions of the world are dominated by liberal doctrines, others by social-democratic or by catholicism, still others by Islam or the Indian cast system. (Todd, 1983, p. 7)

He asks: why the wide-spread acceptance of an ideology such as communism in some parts of the world and not in other parts? What is, or perhaps one should say was, the common social condition underlying the success of Marxism–Leninism in areas such as Russia, China, Finland, Kerala, Vietnam, Cuba, Tuscany, Arauco, Limousin, Bengal, Serbia or Southern Portugal? Todd's answer is solely that a certain type of family systems, namely collectivism, explains all that.

## Behaviour and Values

The family is a system of interaction between individuals, oriented towards reproduction and sexual intercourse. Family values relate to, or regulate, the ends and means of the behaviour of persons participating in family life. And the values of the family are neither constant over time nor invariable over space. Family values include a variety of norms that structure behaviour and define how the persons involved in a family are to be treated in terms of their bodies, possessions and capacity to decide for themselves. Family norms tend to cover a large set of aspects of interaction, which allow for substantial variation:

1  monogamy or polygamy;
2  equality or inequality in inheritance;
3  degree of parental authority;
4  patrimony or matrimony;

5    length of time of family life;
6    number of restrictions on sexual intercourse.

Family systems tend to change slowly; in other words, the norms that govern family behaviour have the force not only of tradition but also of public sanctions. Analysing how and why different family systems have emerged in history is a major social science research issue. Although religion has no doubt been a major factor when it comes to choosing between the alternative family values as specified above, family values are not identical with religion. Family systems vary across religions and nations in a manner that makes the identification of types of family value a worthwhile effort – and this is the starting point of Todd's model.


## Classifying Family Cultures

There can be little doubt that the Todd classification, following Le Play to a considerable extent, is based on a fascinating theoretical construction. Conceptually speaking, one may combine several clearly distinct dimensions or properties in a typology, but the risk is that it becomes too unwieldy, especially if the properties vary a great deal in relation to each other (Todd, 1983). The requirement of parsimony may not be fulfilled, especially if one adds a fourth dimension such as matrimony or patrimony (Todd, 1984). However, much more problematic than conceptual parsimony in relation to the Todd classification is the empirical reliability of separate country classifications. According to Todd, his eight family types all have real-life counterparts. The crucial question that may be raised in relation to Todd's classification concerns the empirical reliability of the placement of each country into one of the eight categories. Let us look at how Todd places some countries in various continents on to a few key categories as displayed in Table 8.1.

Here, we will not question Todd's entire system for the placement of various parts or regions of a country into the eight different categories although this classification seems most dubious in relation to Western Europe, where the family is regulated in the form of national uniform legislation. What we could question, though, is for example, the placement of countries that Todd refers to as the authoritarian family systems. The Todd 1984 family typology may be displayed in a similar fashion, with a few empirical examples listed, as we have attempted to do in Table 8.2.

We suggest that a concentration upon a few major categories of family cultures – individualist versus collectivist – is a more reliable enterprise than the detailed classification that Todd presents in Table 8.2. What we wish to underline is that the basic concepts employed in the anthropological theory of the family are not easily applied to the real world, not only because family systems are less permanent now than before. In addition to the impact of

**Table 8.1    Family systems worldwide: the Todd 1983 typology with empirical examples**

| Family system | Country examples |
|---|---|
| Communitarian exogamous | Russia, Yugoslavia, Bulgaria, Hungary, Finland, Albania, China, Vietnam, Cuba, Northern India |
| Authoritarian | Germany, Austria, Sweden, Norway, Belgium, Scotland, Ireland, parts of France, Spain, Portugal, Japan, Korea |
| Egalitarian nuclear | parts of France, Italy, Spain, Greece, Romania, Poland, Latin America, Ethiopia |
| Absolute nuclear | Anglo-Saxon countries, the Netherlands, Denmark |
| Communitarian endogamous | Arab countries, Turkey, Iran, Afghanistan, Pakistan, Azerbaijan, Turkmenistan, Uzbekistan, Tajikistan |
| Communitarian asymmetric | southern India |
| Anomic | Burma, Cambodia, Laos, Thailand, Malaysia, Indonesia, the Philippines |
| African systems | the sub-Saharan countries |

*Source*:  Todd (1983, pp. 43–215).

globalization on family systems, spreading the liberal type to countries around the globe, there are more fundamental empirical difficulties involved. Thus, one may critically ask: what is an authoritarian family? What is a vertical bilateral family? Is it really true that Sweden and Norway belong to the set of countries that have the authoritarian type or the vertical bilateral type? Are the differences between Sweden and Norway on the one hand and Finland and Denmark on the other hand so large that the latter two countries enter into two different sets of countries, each separately? According to Todd, authoritarian family systems have three characteristics:

1    inequality in inheritance: 'transfer of the entire fortune to one of the kids';
2    cohabitation of the married heir and his parents;
3    few or no marriages between the children of two brothers (Todd, 1983, p. 67).

**Table 8.2    Family systems worldwide: the Todd 1984 typology with empirical examples**

| Family system | Country examples |
| --- | --- |
| Patrilineal, non-vertical | the Arab countries, Turkey, Iran, Afghanistan, Pakistan, Azerbaijan, Turkmenistan, Uzbekistan, Tajikistan |
| Patrilineal, vertical (matrilineal nuances) | Russia, Yugoslavia, Slovakia, Bulgaria, Hungary, Finland, Albania, China, Vietnam, Cuba, northern India |
| Patrilineal vertical | Bhutan, China, India, Mongolia, Nepal, Taiwan |
| Bilateral non-vertical | parts of France, Italy, Spain, Greece, Romania, Poland, Latin America, Ethiopia |
| Bilateral non-vertical (matrilineal nuances) | Anglo-Saxon countries, the Netherlands, Denmark, Burma, Cambodia, Laos, Thailand, Malaysia, Indonesia, the Philippines |
| Bilateral vertical | Germany, Austria, Sweden, Norway, Belgium, Scotland, Ireland, parts of France, Spain and Portugal, Japan, Korea |
| Matrilineal non-vertical | the sub-Saharan countries |
| Matrilineal vertical | southern India |

*Source*:   Based on Todd (1984, pp. 36–40).

These characteristics (1) and (2) do simply not apply to the countries that Todd enters into this set – for instance Sweden and Norway, nor have they applied during the post-war period, when inheritance has been equally shared among all the children.

This is not the place to engage in a detailed criticism of the first step of Todd's analysis – that is, the mapping of the world's family structures. Instead, we will concentrate on the second step, the analysis of cultural effects, in order to discover whether there is some evidence about an interaction between human relations (family) and social relations (outcomes). We will employ a more transparent and simple scale of family systems, focusing mainly on the distinction between liberal and collectivist family structures. In addition, we concentrate on the evidence for the causal theory that family matters for macro outcomes.

## The Effects of Family Cultures

No one would ever deny that family systems are unimportant. Social life would cease to exist or would suffer from enormous strain, if the rules that guide the most intimate forms of private interaction are ambiguous or lack implementation. Without norms family life could not be instrumental towards reproduction and socialization. Yet, Todd's theory is not an argument about the general functions of the family; it is an entirely different theory than the general functional theory of the family, developed within sociology by so-called structural–functionalism (Parsons, 1967; Parsons *et al.*, 2001; Levy, 1952).

Todd focuses on the variation in family values, claiming not that the family *per se* matters but that alternative structures for the family result in a variation in outcomes. Thus, it is important whether a family has one or the other set of values. 'Importance' now refers not to the general functions of reproduction and socialization – that is, values that are consequences of all kinds of family systems – but to the different social outcomes of alternative family structures. How would one demonstrate that family institutions are important in the Todd sense – in other words, the variation in the family values brings about a variation in political, social or economic outcomes? We suggest employing one of the classical methods of induction in relation to a problem of causality – namely, concomitant variation in the language of John Stuart Mill. Using statistical techniques in relation to data about more than 100 countries, one may inquire into the probability that different types of family structure are important for various outcomes, with 'importance' meaning only causal efficiency.

*If* Todd is right that family systems have an impact on political ideologies such as, for example, the spread of communism, then one would want to test a model that says that the family system has an impact on the occurrence of a democratic regime or democratic longevity. After all, where communism was strong, democracy did not do well. Perhaps one may interpret Todd as saying that a collectivist family system is conducive to authoritarian attitudes in that its belief systems would advance the probability of a non-democratic regime. One could go a step further and examine whether alternative family systems result in socioeconomic outcomes, but we will restrict the analysis below to the link between family values and the probability of democratic stability.

In fact, in 1966, Eckstein suggested a theory precisely along these lines, although he only had evidence from one case study, Norway. Eckstein argued that family institutions and the constitutional institutions of a country must display some level of congruence in order for the country to remain viable. Thus, an authoritarian state would tend to coexist with a similar family structure, whereas a democratic state would require an alternative structure of its family system. The implication is that family institutions could be a source of support for democracy or a hindrance against democracy (Eckstein, 1966).

**Table 8.3    Family systems worldwide: the Todd 1983 and 1984 systems**

| Family system: TODD1983 | Number of cases | Percentage | Individualism score |
|---|---|---|---|
| African family systems | 34 | 22.7 | 1.0 |
| Endogamous community family | 25 | 16.7 | 16.7 |
| Anomic family | 11 | 7.3 | 33.3 |
| Exogamous community family | 28 | 18.7 | 50.0 |
| Egalitarian nuclear family | 30 | 20.0 | 66.7 |
| Authoritarian family | 15 | 10.0 | 83.3 |
| Absolute nuclear family | 7 | 4.7 | 100.0 |

| Family typology: TODD1984 | Number of cases | Percentage | Development potential score |
|---|---|---|---|
| Latent matrilineal non-vertical | 34 | 22.7 | 1.0 |
| Patrilineal non-vertical | 25 | 16.7 | 16.7 |
| Patrilineal vertical | 6 | 4.0 | 33.3 |
| Patrilineal vertical (matri) | 22 | 14.7 | 50.0 |
| Bilateral non-vertical | 30 | 20.0 | 66.7 |
| Bilateral non-vertical (matri) | 18 | 12.0 | 83.3 |
| Bilateral vertical | 15 | 10.0 | 100.0 |

*Sources*: See Tables 8.1 and 8.2.

In order to conduct the statistical analysis, we wish to rearrange Todd's categories slightly so that his sets express an interval scale concerning the nature of family values going from individualism towards collectivism (Todd, 1983) and development potential (Todd, 1984). We thus transform the typologies to an interval scale assuming – admittedly unrealistically – equidistance between the different family systems with respect to their adherence to individualism – collectivism, and how conducive they are for development. Furthermore, we have reduced the number of family systems/typologies to seven by incorporating southern India in the other India classification. The outcome of these deliberations is presented in Table 8.3.

These classifications quite closely follow a Western–African divide with individualist/higher development potential family systems assumed to be

**Table 8.4    Family systems and civilizations: Pearson's correlation coefficients**

|          | TODD1983 | TODD1984 | TOYNBEE | BROEK | HUNTINGT |
|----------|----------|----------|---------|-------|----------|
| TODD1983 | 1.00     |          |         |       |          |
| TODD1984 | .90      | 1.00     |         |       |          |
| TOYNBEE  | .82      | .75      | 1.00    |       |          |
| BROEK    | .82      | .78      | .95     | 1.00  |          |
| HUNTINGT | .87      | .80      | .91     | .90   | 1.00     |

*Note*:    The number of cases = 150, and all correlations are significant at the .000 level.
*Sources*: See Appendix A.

more numerous in Western countries and collectivist/lower development potential family systems in the African countries. Using family values this way divides the world into a few macro regions that tend to match the ones we presented in Chapter 5 on civilizations. The Todd systems (TODD1983 and TODD1984) in fact correlate quite highly with the civilization classifications of Toynbee, Broek and Huntington (see Chapter 6), and this is evident from the correlations we display in Table 8.4.

The explanation for the very high correlation coefficients found is that all these variables identify the same set of countries on the two different poles: the Western–African divide. At a global level this divide is very distinctive. However, at issue in this chapter is, what relationship we can establish at the macro level between the type of family system and one key outcome, namely the level of democracy. Conducting an analysis correlating family structure and democracy we may establish that there is a strong positive relationship. Remembering that the recorded variables (TODD1983 and TODD1984) give high values to individualism/high developmental potential and low values to collectivism/low developmental potential, we find a clear, stable and significant positive correlation between the degree of individualism/ development potential in the family system and the degree of democracy. Can we, then, conclude that it is the family system that matters?

The answer is 'No', because when one looks at the country distribution along the seven categories of family institutions, then one observes that it follows more or less a classical distribution of countries along a dimension such as modernity–traditionalism. Therefore we will introduce factors controlling for history (MODLEAD) and geography (DISEQU) as well as for affluence – that is, logarithmically transformed measures for real GDP per capita expressed in US dollars for 1970 (RGDPC70). Table 8.5 contains a number of tests of the model linking family institutions with democratic stability; here we emphasize the impact of the TODD 1983 family system.

The principal finding from testing the family models is that there is a clear cultural effect. Here, we do have a corroboration of an anthropological theme,

**Table 8.5    Family structures and democracy: regression analysis**

| Independent variables | Coeffs | DEM7281 | | Dependent variables DEM8291 | | DEM9299 | |
|---|---|---|---|---|---|---|---|
| DISEQU | coeff | 1.003 | – | –1.834 | – | .340 | – |
| | t-stat | .00 | – | –1.13 | – | .20 | – |
| | tol | .47 | – | .46 | – | .47 | – |
| MODLEAD | coeff | .001 | – | .006 | – | .002 | – |
| | t-stat | .19 | – | 1.00 | – | .34 | – |
| | tol | .28 | – | .32 | – | .32 | – |
| LnRGDPC70 | coeff | 1.399 | 1.422 | 1.042 | .973 | .764 | .825 |
| | t-stat | 4.34 | 4.96 | 4.07 | 4.19 | 2.70 | 3.33 |
| | tol | .41 | .49 | .32 | .56 | .43 | .56 |
| TODD1983 | coeff | .036 | .037 | .051 | .055 | .044 | .046 |
| | t-stat | 3.34 | 4.36 | 5.13 | 7.44 | 4.17 | 5.39 |
| | tol | .32 | .50 | .32 | .56 | .38 | .56 |
| Constant | coeff | –7.721 | –7.829 | –5.406 | –4.960 | –2.948 | –3.259 |
| | t-stat | –3.66 | –3.98 | –3.08 | –2.99 | –1.53 | –1.82 |
| Adjrsq | | .56 | .57 | .64 | .64 | .43 | .44 |
| N | | 110 | 110 | 116 | 116 | 143 | 143 |

*Notes*:    coeff = the unstandardized regression coefficient.
t-stat = t-statistics. Used to test the significance of the regression coefficients; t-stat showing more than ± 2 indicates significance.
tol = tolerance. Used to measure the occurrence of multicollinearity in the model; if tol is higher than .3/.4 there is no danger of multicollinearity.
*Sources*: See Appendix A.

stating that alternative systems of family matter. Family systems supporting individualist values seem to have a strong and positive impact on the level of democracy. This finding from the correlation analysis still holds when we control for economic and other social factors in Table 8.5. We wish to emphasize that the family system is more important than historical and geographical factors and it is as powerful a predictor of democracy as affluence.

# Conclusion

This chapter has analysed whether politics has a source in the most fundamental culture or social values – that is, the norms that govern the reproduction of human societies and socialize children into their adult roles. Few would reply that it does not, but they would perhaps not be prepared to endorse the strong version of this anthropological theme that Todd has suggested. Todd does not theorize the general importance of the family institution, but has suggested a model about the differential effects on society and politics of a variation in the values that govern family interaction.

We have found ample evidence for a cultural impact when employing the Todd classification of the occurrence of family systems around the world. Whereas Todd dealt with the spread of belief systems like, for example, communism, we have placed the family structure among the conditions for democracy, following the theory about value congruence suggested by Eckstein. It should be pointed out that we have not been able to confirm Todd's strong claims that family values constitute a *necessary* condition for social phenomena such as, for instance, the once widespread belief system of communism. The principal finding here is that family is a strong contributory condition to the successful implementation of human rights. To us, family values constitute a legacy, whereas in Todd's analysis they exemplify universal values. In Part V we turn to a systematic analysis of universal cultural items. First, we inquire into how they occur with various peoples of the world. Second, we examine whether there are cultural effects from these universal values.

# PART V
# UNIVERSAL VALUES

# Introduction

Ethnicity, religion, legacies and universal values – these are the four components in our analysis of culture and its impact on politics and social outcomes. All of them differ in terms of their attachment to locality. Individuals may adhere to a culture that is very specific to a locality or a region or they may identify with the abstract notions of humankind or humanity. Basically, ethnicity as a culture is tied down to a specific geographical place, or the area in which an ethnic group is living.

Religion tends to occur more universally, but historically it has had clear connections with the regions of the civilizations. The world religions do not occur everywhere, although nowadays there are small religious diasporas all over the world due to the huge increase in migration. The world religions, including Judaism, have their core areas where they constitute the dominant belief system among those adhering to religious belief. The borders between the world religions change very slowly. A culture lies somewhere in between truly universal values such as liberty and equality on the one hand and civilizations on the other, namely legacies. Colonial legacies and family structures occur all over the world but in different ways.

Universal values such as culture have no specific connection with a geographical area. Individualism or collectivism is a theme in any country. The same holds true of trust and postmaterialism. However, universal values attract different numbers of adherents in various countries. Since all forms of culture comprise values in one way or another, we identify a few universal values for separate analysis, leading finally to an analysis of cultures that entirely lacks a geographical connotation – an analysis based on what we call 'universal values'. Starting with the cultures of ethnic groups as the most particular form of a culture, one may ascend through the analysis of civilisations and historical traditions towards more and more general types of culture, which may exist at any location. A set of universal values would be a set of attitudes and beliefs which have, in principle, no intrinsic link with a specific location. Such a culture could exist with people in any society around the globe.

Libertarians and egalitarians, for instance, would be the groups who favour liberty and equality respectively, whether they happen to live in New York, Berlin, Bombay or Shanghai. Universal cultures tend to display little compactness with the exception of the movements that are organized on a worldwide scale, such as Greenpeace or Amnesty International. One example of a fraternity that adheres to universal values would be a gay or a lesbian community.

# Chapter 9

# Universal Values: Three Main Theories

## Introduction

Theories of universal values raise the interesting question of whether one really can find common values across countries. To what extent can one and the same set of values be said to occur in the attitudes of people in different countries? There are two possibilities. Either one argues that one and the same value orientation actually occurs in two or more countries with an entirely different background, or one claims that different cultures in various countries express in one way or another the very same values. In the following chapters we will discuss and evaluate only three theories of universal values: postmaterialism; trust theory; and the New Culture theory. They all have in common that they target values which may be designated as universal. It could be said that universal values constitute the cultures of groups that are not primordial.

It should be pointed out that there is no definitive limit to the number of cultural models that one may launch when one speaks of universal values. These three theories attribute great political and social consequences to the spread of universal values, which is the focus of our inquiry. Thus, during the 1990s a number of hypotheses were proposed, attributing important extrinsic consequences to universal values. These cultures matter. Whether these three theories of universal cultural items have identified the most important aspects of people's values is very difficult to tell, but we may at least test the inherent claim about cultural efficacy – that is, the idea that these values matter for outcomes. First, however, we will address a methodological issue. Should value orientations be understood as behaviour or attitudes?

## Value Orientations: Behaviour or Attitudes

The analysis of universal values presents somewhat different methodological problems than the inquiry into ethnicity and religion. Let us start by indicating what is at stake from a methodological point of view, when the survey method is employed as the chief means of acquiring information about values or, more precisely, the value orientations of ordinary people. Two key methodological problems in the inquiry into value orientations or in theories about universal values items include:

1    What is a truly universal value item?
2    How do these occur in various countries and at various times?

The first question is conceptual and concerns the nature of values or value orientations – that is, whether such things really can be said to exist. The second question relates to how one would go about measuring the occurrence of such an item empirically by means of a research strategy.

Before we enter the examination of theories of universal values, we wish to point out an important distinction. Cultural items may be identified as universal ones in two entirely different ways: either through the analysis of behaviour or through the examination of attitudes. Let us exemplify this distinction between universal values as derived from behaviour or as referring to attitudes with reference to a much discussed phenomenon, namely *Mezzogiorno*.

In an early example of cultural analysis, E. Banfield in 1958 suggested that general values are to be found behind the well-known phenomenon of *Mezzogiorno* in Italy. Instead of relating the divide between the northern and the southern Italy to historical legacies – that is, country-specific experiences – Banfield used a battery of survey questions to reveal the general atmosphere of backwardness, which could occur in the same way in other countries. He focused on the attitudes that tend to develop within groups living in a society with a persistently uneven development among regions, especially when disparities in life opportunities emerge (Banfield, 1958). Thus, the culture of a specific backward region such as southern Italy could be an example of a general or universal culture. What is Italian about *Mezzogiorno* could only be a historical accident, as what is really at work is the mechanism of backwardness that occurs in any country that experiences this uneven development, especially when this economic imbalance has lasted for a long time and has taken on more and more social or political attributes.

The so-called New Cultural Theory (NCT) suggests that Banfield in reality analysed a general set of values that may occur in any society – amounting to fatalism (Thompson *et al.*, 1990, pp. 223–32). This is not to say that the people of southern Italy would classify themselves as fatalists, but both Banfield and NCT argue that their attitudes express such a culture, whether they agree or disagree and whether they are conscious or not of it.

R. Putnam suggested in 1993 another cultural theory dealing to a considerable extent with the same phenomenon, although focusing on the difference between northern and southern Italy from the perspective of stable democracy. He derived value differences in behaviour between people in the North and people in the South, involving the occurrence of civil society and the role of social trust. Such a research strategy is entirely different from the derivation of values from attitudes. Below, we develop this difference between values as patterns of attitudes and values as patterns of behaviour or interaction.

*Values as Behaviour: Civic Community*

The two main methodological questions, we emphasize, are: 'What is a value?', and 'How it is to be observed in existing cultures?' In survey research there is more restriction on the attribution of a value to attitudes, the value constituting the common core of, or the dimension underneath, a large set of attitudes (Converse, 1964). The theory of postmaterialism is based on this strict methodology for the attribution of values to people's attitudes (van Deth and Scarborough, 1995b). When one can employ information about either attitudes or behaviour as the foundation for cultural analysis, then which is the best? This puzzle arises in relation to the theory about trust. It is definitely a theory primarily about attitudes and not behaviour, as the key indicator is the question to a respondent whether they have or have not trust in society or in the political institutions of the country or in other people. However, it can also be based on behaviour interpretation alone.

Trust theory was partly inspired by Putnam's analysis of regions in Italian politics from 1993. He argues the following. There exist political differences between the various political regions of Italy, especially those in the North and those in the South. These differences may be tapped by outcome variables or a large set of measures concerning *institutional performance* (Putnam 1993, Table 3.2) including: reform legislation (1978–84), daycare centres (1983), housing and urban development (1979–87), statistical and information services (1981), legislative innovation (1978–84), cabinet stability (1975–85), family clinics (1978), bureaucratic responsiveness (1983), industrial policy instruments (1984), budget promptness (1979–85), local health unit spending (1983) and agricultural spending capacity (1978–80). And the scientific problem is to account for these regional differences covered by a composite index covering the above performance or outcome indicators.

Putnam suggests that the *civic community* explains the variation in this index. Now, what is that? Putnam constructs a composite index measuring the nature of civil society from the following four *behaviour indicators*: preference voting, 1953–79; referendum turnout, 1974–87; newspaper readership, 1975; scarcity of sports and cultural associations, 1981. The basic idea is that the stronger the civic community, the higher is the probability that institutional performance will be different – that is, better. To Putnam, a civic community is a society where there are numerous associations, people read many newspapers and election turnout is high. Moreover, in a civic community there would be little preference voting, because it indicates personal attachments (*la clientela*).

It is debatable whether these four behaviour indicators on the spread as well as depth of civil society are the most appropriate ones. However, here we wish to focus on the additional link that Putnam establishes, when he states that the existence of a strong civic community (civil society) is a form of social capital. This is similar to trust theory, which contains the implication that social trust is a form of social capital, upon which all people may draw, that promotes beneficial outcomes (Coleman, 1990). Putnam states:

> Networks of civic engagement, like the neighbourhood associations, choral societies, cooperatives, sports clubs, mass-based parties, and the like examined in Chapters 4 and 5, represent intense horizontal interaction. Networks of civic engagement are an essential form of social capital: The denser such networks in a community, the more likely that its citizens will be able to cooperate for mutual benefit. (Putnam, 1993, p. 173)

Again, arguably, there are also forms of social capital other than networks between people, but here we ask 'What does Putnam place under "social capital"?'. Let us quote again:

> Social capital here refers to features of social organisation, such as trust, norms and networks, that can improve the efficiency of society by facilitating coordinated actions. (Putnam 1993, p. 167)

Putnam has empirical evidence concerning only one form of social capital, namely networks. Can one draw determinate conclusions about social trust in Italy based solely on networks? It is not difficult to argue the case for the importance of social capital, but it is far more difficult to observe its existence in its various forms. And one cannot take for granted that these various forms – for example, trust and network – all covary considerably.

We have no quarrel with Putnam when he says, 'In communities where people can be confident that trusting will be required, not exploited, exchange is more likely to ensue' (Putnam, 1993, p. 172). Putnam refers to James Coleman, who initiated much of the present debate on social capital on the basis of a concept suggested by Loary (1987, 1995). Coleman suggested a most general characterization of social capital:

> Social capital is defined by its function. It is not a single entity, but a variety of different entities having two characteristics in common. They all consist of some aspect of a social structure, and they facilitate certain actions of individuals who are within the structure. (Coleman, 1990, p. 302)

This is an imprecise definition, as it covers so much. Yet, this is not the place to enter into a long debate about capital – physical, monetary or social – as the focus is on trust and how one goes about establishing whether there is much or little social trust in a society. We can accept the basic idea about social capital – namely that social capital constitutes what Hirschman called 'moral resources', meaning assets whose supply increases rather than decreases through use and which become depleted if not used.

If social capital is of such importance, then how do we know whether or not it exists, or how much of it there is in various regions of Italy for example? To Putnam, the existence of social capital is established through his investigations into the existence of another phenomenon, namely the civic community, which is reduced to the occurrence of four behaviour indicators mentioned above. Putnam has not, it must be emphasized, established the existence of trust or social trust, as he has data about networks or the civic community. Yet, he suddenly states: 'In the civic regions of Italy, by contrast to Naples, social trust has long been a key ingredient in the ethos that has sustained economic dynamism and government performance' (Putnam, 1993, p. 170).

There is a risk of a circularity argument connected with the Putnam analysis of the Italian case, as civic community is seen as the expression of social trust and social trust is later employed in order to explain civic community. Perhaps one should clearly distinguish between a set of behavioural phenomena, like civic community, and a value (that is, attitudes or value orientations) such as trust? In our view, one should employ data on social trust that is independent of data on civic community.

*Values as Attitudes: Trust*

Whether trust is interpreted as one form of social capital or not, it is essential, if at all possible, to measure it directly. If survey data are available, then information about attitudes offers such a direct measurement. One may wish to distinguish between different types of trust and measure them accordingly. Trust is looked upon as being at least two-dimensional in survey research (Newton, 1999), as social trust is not the same as political trust.

Let us again quote from Putnam, when he speaks about the sources of social capital. One can regard social capital as the cause of a civic community, but one could also look upon social capital as resulting from a civic community. He states:

> Social trust in complex modern settings can arise from two related sources – norms of reciprocity and networks of civic engagement. (Putnam, 1993, p. 171)

This is hardly correct. There exist other sources of trust than the civic community. The extent of trust that people have in society or in political institutions can depend on several factors. It has been suggested that civil society, or the amount of free associations, is closely related to trust. The more vibrant civil society is, the stronger is social trust and vice versa – this is the classical position of Tocqueville. But why could not trust reflect other things than the occurrence of associations? When trust is measured directly in the form of survey questions, then one may also search empirically for other sources of social capital than civil society. Newton correctly points out that public sector or third-sector institutions, such as educational institutions or the mass media, are an important source of social capital. Such social capital, says Newton,

> ... may be sustained not so much by intensive personal contacts with family, friends, and neighbours, as by education, the mass media, and an increasingly elaborate array of formal rules and institutionalised means of monitoring their observance and sanctioning their breach. (Newton, 1999, p. 180)

Just as vital a distinction is the one between social and political trust (Newton, 1999), because attitudes towards general social trust or personal trust – that is, confidence in dealing with other people – could have different sources than political trust. In fact, social trust is not strongly associated with attitudes towards the legitimacy or efficacy of political institutions. Research on both social and political trust indicates that trust is a complex phenomenon. These two forms of trust may develop differently. Personal trust, or social capital, may decline in one country, like the USA, but rise in another, as in Western Europe (Putnam, 2000).

It should be pointed out that political trust is more difficult to identify and measure, as it is not easy to separate trust in the institutions of a country from trust in the present government. Newton argues:

> The general conclusion suggested by this is that political distrust is not caused so much by social and economic factors, but by the record and colour of the party in power. (Newton, 1999, pp. 182–83)

If this is true, then one should be careful about concluding that civil society or social capital is at risk when broad groups display negative attitudes towards the present power-holders. The difficulty is to identify the indicators of various types of trust in order to make the connection transparent between trust as a value or a set of attitudes on the one hand, and behaviour on the other.

*Trust in Italy*

Returning to the Putnam approach to Italy, we stress that trust should be measured as a set of attitudes, if one has access to survey data. Table 9.1 presents information about the occurrence of civic community (behaviour) and trust (attitudes) in the 20 Italian regions, collected independently. The chief finding is that the two variables covary only moderately as the bivariate correlation is $r = .33$ (sig. $= .076$).

Since trust, as measured by survey data and civic community and tapped by means of behaviour data, correlate weakly, it cannot be claimed that they constitute the same phenomenon. As a matter of fact, trust appears to be quite substantial in a few regions in the South. Here we obviously have a case where attitudinal data about trust and behavioural data about civic community point in different directions. The attitudinal data about interpersonal trust indicate that there is no longer a deep cleavage between northern and southern Italy as suggested by the civic community index. It is no longer correct to claim that

**Table 9.1    Civic community and interpersonal trust in Italian regions around 1990**

| Region | Civic community | Trust |
|---|---|---|
| Piedmont | 15.0 | 39.1 |
| Valle d'Aosta | 14.0 | 20.0 |
| Lombardy | 17.0 | 44.3 |
| Trentino | 17.0 | 44.8 |
| Veneto | 15.0 | 50.8 |
| Friuli | 17.0 | 42.9 |
| Liguria | 17.0 | 37.7 |
| Emilia | 18.0 | 30.8 |
| Toscana | 17.0 | 35.5 |
| Umbria | 15.5 | 20.3 |
| Marche | 15.0 | 49.3 |
| Lazio | 13.0 | 27.7 |
| Abruzzo | 8.0 | 27.9 |
| Molise | 3.5 | 33.3 |
| Campania | 2.0 | 28.0 |
| Puglia | 2.0 | 29.2 |
| Bascilicata | 4.0 | 33.3 |
| Calabria | 1.0 | 37.3 |
| Sicily | 3.5 | 28.6 |
| Sardinia | 8.5 | 6.3 |

*Sources*: Civic community figures come from Goldberg (1996, p. 10) and Putnam (1993, p. 98); trust figures come from Inglehart *et al*. (2000, the 1990 wave).

social capital as trust is abundant in the northern Italy but almost non-existent in the South.

These methodological reflections entail that the analysis of universal cultures is mainly an empirical enterprise about discovering the main forms of value orientations. They also indicate that values should be measured as attitudes. Let us now examine these three theories to find out what they state about the link between culture and outcomes. Few would state that values are of little importance. But to present evidence of *specific cultural effects* is far more difficult than to claim generally that values matter. We focus on postmaterialism theory, trust theory and New Cultural Theory.

**Postmaterialism Theory**

The theme of postmaterialism is a theory about values tapped more by means of attitudes and less through behaviour interpretation. The concept of postmaterialism today involves considerable self-reference, although when the concept was launched it was completely novel in the sense that people did not think about themselves as postmaterialist. The theory of postmaterialism is a set of hypotheses about changing values in the advanced democracies, involving an intricate argument about the structure of human needs and the occurrence of generational shifts in an affluent society, as well as their political consequences. Ronald Inglehart has argued in favour of postmaterialism as a new dimension in mass politics since 1971 (Inglehart, 1997).

As stated earlier, the values approach to people's attitudes, which attempts to tap the relevance of values to party choice, is based on the methodology of identifying basic value dimensions outlined by Converse. Values are revealed by the constraints on respondents' answers to a whole host of attitudinal questions. Thus, value dimensions can be identified technically with factor solutions stating how items tend to correlate with latent dimensions. The more constraints in respondents' answers to a battery of questions in the survey, the more a value dimension is operative. In the language of factor analysis, one searches for solutions with few factors, each having a high eigenvalue, and which may be interpreted theoretically. The relevance of the theme of postmaterialism has been much strengthened by the use of massive databases – for instance, the one accumulated from the Eurobarometer surveys introduced in 1970 and conducted several times a year since then, or the three waves of the World Values Surveys conducted around 1980, 1990 and 1995 (Inglehart *et al.*, 2000). The first wave covered 24 countries while the second wave covered 42 countries, and the third wave covered 53 countries. In fact, the concept of postmaterialism has been so successful that entire groups of actors have begun to identify themselves as adherents of postmaterialist values.

The theory of postmaterialism is very much an empirical generalization of findings from survey research. The basic theoretical core of assumptions is hardly a very powerful one, consisting mainly of three propositions. First, there is the scarcity hypothesis stating that people turn to new concerns once prior concerns are settled. Second, there is the socialisation hypothesis stating that there is a relationship between formative influences and adult personality (Scarborough, 1995, p. 124; Inglehart, 1990, p. 130). Only by adding a third assumption – namely, the silent revolution assumption – can the postmaterialist revolution, strictly speaking, be derived. This third assumption states that a shift in value priorities between older and younger generations occurred some time after the Second World War. Much of the research inspired by postmaterialist theory is aimed at empirically confirming the occurrence of this shift in values rather than elaborating the theory systematically. After all, the two first assumptions of postmaterialism are very vague, but finding the evidence that either supports or rejects the postmaterialist values change is a task for survey research.

The theory of postmaterialism raises two methodological questions, around which much of the debate has focused (Davis and Davenport, 1999; Inglehart and Abramson, 1999). First, there is the question of identification: what are to count as postmaterialist orientations? One would need to know which standard attitudes indicate the existence of postmaterialist values, at least with a certain probability, since one does not ask individuals whether they consider themselves to be postmaterialists or not. How do we document postmaterialist values in the myriad individual beliefs and attitudes? Second, there is the entirely different question of measuring its impact: how do postmaterialist attitudes matter in the electorate? While we might solve the first problem of finding the proper indicators on postmaterialist values, using these indicators might reveal that these value orientations do not play the dominant role in the politics of the advanced countries that Inglehart, especially, has claimed for them. Both these questions have given rise to a methodological debate about the pros and cons of postmaterialism as an empirical theory. What we wish to investigate here is whether postmaterialist values matter for policy outputs or outcomes. Yet, resolving this question in turn presupposes that the above two questions have been answered.

*What are Postmaterialist Values?*

Perhaps post-materialism has become so well known today that many people could respond 'yes' or 'no' to the question: 'Are you a post-materialist?' However, it should be stressed that the standard surveys do not explicitly refer to the word 'postmaterialism'. Instead, they employ proxies in the form of the respondents' ranking of priority of choice items that are assumed to be related to postmaterialism. Thus, since 1973 the Eurobarometer has contained the following four-item instrument, where the respondent is asked to state which two of these items are most important to them:

(A) maintaining order in the nation;
(B) giving people more say in important government decisions;
(C) fighting rising prices;
(D) protecting freedom of speech.

'Post-materialist' orientations are said to combine (B) and (D), whereas (A) and (C) indicate a 'materialist' orientation. 'All other combinations constitute a mixed value orientation', states Scarborough (1995, p. 129). Inglehart has also used a 12-item instrument parallel to the four-item instrument from 1973 (Inglehart, 1977, 1990, 1997; Abramson and Inglehart, 1995). As a matter of fact the Inglehart 12-item instrument includes the above-mentioned four-item instrument.

Against using the items (A) and (C) as well as (B) and (D) as indicators on materialism and postmaterialism respectively, one could argue that they appear to be related to the distinction between the Right – (A) and (C) – and the Left – (B) and (D). The theory of postmaterialism claims, however, that there is a new value dimension besides the old materialist one. How can we identify this new set of value orientations?

Using the Converse approach, the identification of the materialist dimension has proved relatively easy, as responses to a number of items correlate considerably in different surveys. The materialist value dimension appears to continue to be relevant for party choice in the West European democracies, although its relevance varies from one country to another and also from one party to another. Matters are somewhat different in relation to postmaterialism. The degree of constraint is not that high among responses to questions about postmaterialism, which has led scholars to suggest that it is not unidimensional. Thus, there would be humanist versus instrumental postmodernism (Gibbins and Reimer, 1999), or libertarian versus authoritarian postmodernism (Hellevik, 1993). Often, a 2×2 table is used to show how two types of materialism (Left–Right) interacts with two types of post-materialism (Right–Left).

*The Existence of a Postmaterialist Dimension*

In several studies (1977, 1990, and 1997) Inglehart has been able to identify a postmaterialist dimension among the attitudes of citizens belonging to different cultural realms. Nevertheless, one may ask whether the same patterns of postmaterialist orientations are visible in Western Europe as in Asia, conducting a series of factor analyses employing the same set of items in different contexts (N = 58). From each factor analysis we have extracted information about the explained variance of the first factor as well as the loadings of the 12 items on the first factor on the principal component matrix, following the procedure of Abramson and Inglehart (Abramson and Inglehart, 1995, pp. 103–10) and Inglehart (Inglehart, 1997, p. 100). Let us first look at the distribution of the factor loading for the first factor for the whole sample (total sample), the means for the 58 countries analysed (means), as well as for some of the countries (Nigeria, Poland, Pakistan and Brazil) that deviate most from the mean values (Table 9.2).

Postmaterialist items tend to cluster around the positive pole while materialist items cluster around the negative pole. The ordering of the items is quite close if we compare the loadings from the total sample and the loadings from the means for the 58 countries. There are deviating cases and, in Table 9.2, we have listed some that deviate sharply – Nigeria, Poland, Pakistan and Brazil – indicating that deviating cases are to be found outside the Western contexts. On the whole, though, it is possible to confirm the presence of a stable postmaterialist dimension in advanced countries.

**Table 9.2    Factor loadings on the postmaterialist items: 12-item instrument**

| Items | Total sample | Means | Nigeria | Poland | Pakistan | Brazil |
|---|---|---|---|---|---|---|
| More say at jobs | .614 | .556 | −.296 | .523 | .146 | .655 |
| More humane society | .573 | .532 | .369 | .525 | .379 | .350 |
| More say in government | .444 | .520 | .282 | −.123 | .091 | .719 |
| Ideas count more than money | .518 | .410 | .236 | −.012 | .256 | .299 |
| Protecting freedom of speech | .449 | .285 | .322 | .111 | .272 | .254 |
| Making cities more beautiful | .182 | .085 | .391 | .212 | .388 | −.295 |
| Strong defence forces | −.279 | −.163 | .670 | −.031 | .340 | −.480 |
| Fighting rising prices | −.275 | −.217 | −.207 | .285 | .324 | −.508 |
| Fighting against crime | −.523 | −.281 | .159 | .438 | .315 | −.588 |
| High level of economic growth | −.279 | −.487 | −.708 | −.694 | −.707 | .020 |
| Maintaining order in the nation | −.612 | −.528 | −.295 | −.226 | −.591 | .431 |
| A stable economy | −.594 | −.557 | −.689 | −.776 | −.763 | .019 |

*Note*:    The analysis is based on the variables V104 to V109.
*Source*:    Inglehart *et al.* (2000).

To test the cross-cultural assumption further we report, in Table 9.3, a breakdown of the factor loadings for the 58 countries for a number of regions of the world. First we record the amount of explained variance accounted for by the first factor in the factor analysis, indicating the importance of the postmaterialist dimension in a given society. Second, we present information about the absolute difference in scores in the loading on the first factor for a country compared with the total means for all 58 countries arrived at, where larger differences may indicate different priorities with regard to the postmaterialist orientation. Finally, we report the factor loading on the most postmaterialist items ('more say in the workplace' and 'more humane society') and the most materialist items ('maintaining order in the nation' and 'a stable economy') according to the total means.

Again, we find that there are differences between different regions of the world with respect to what the postmaterialist/materialist dimension stands for. This dimension obviously has a stronger position in the Western world than in other parts of the world (column: first factor explained variance) and

**Table 9.3    The meaning of postmaterialism: factor loading items by world regions**

| Region | First factor explained variance | Absolute differences | More say in the workplace | More humane society | A stable economy | Maintaining order in the nation |
|---|---|---|---|---|---|---|
| OECD (N=21) | 22.7 | .20 | .62 | .58 | -.59 | -.56 |
| Latin America (N=8) | 20.4 | .33 | .58 | .58 | -.54 | -.45 |
| Africa (N=3) | 19.4 | 1.26 | .22 | .18 | -.53 | -.55 |
| Asia (N=6) | 19.2 | .52 | .44 | .47 | -.62 | -.52 |
| Postcommunist countries (N=20) | 18.9 | .39 | .57 | .54 | -.52 | -.52 |
| Total (N=58) | 20.5 | .37 | .56 | .53 | -.56 | -.53 |
| eta squared | .51 | .28 | .37 | .27 | .05 | .11 |
| sig. | .000 | .002 | .000 | .002 | .586 | .173 |

Source:  Inglehart et al. (2000).

the variation in the standing of this dimension seems to be larger in Africa than in other parts of the world (column: absolute differences). It is also the case that there is more variation between the regions in the acceptance of the post-materialist items than what is the case for the materialist items. Thus, the postmaterialist/materialist dimension occurs in different cultural contexts, which is why we say that postmaterialism/materialism belongs to the set of universal values.

*Relevance of Postmaterialist Values*

Measuring the degree to which the citizens display postmaterialist values with various survey instruments, the general finding is that postmaterialist values have increased their attraction among young people in particular. What, then, is the political relevance of postmaterialism, for instance, for party choice. In the research on electoral behaviour and party choice one may broadly distinguish between structural factors, value voting and issue voting (Rose, 1974; Dalton, 1996). Structural factors include class voting (Nieuwbeerta and de Graaf, 1999) or economic sector voting, as well as gender voting (Manza and Brooks, 1998) or generational voting. Value voting comprises value orientations related to religious–secular orientations (Knutsen, 2000), left–right materialism or materialism–postmaterialism. Issue voting occur in relation to certain policy-choices or ratings of party leaders.

Examining the relevance of postmaterialism for party choice one must first consider the relative impact of value voting in comparison to structural and issue voting, and then consider the relative importance of postmaterialism versus religion or the left–right orientation. Relying on research conducted by O. Knutsen on Western Europe we report, in Table 9.4, some findings that are relevant for postmaterialist values and party choice.

The general finding is that values are important for party choice, as value voting today matters more than structural voting. However, when comparing the relative impact of different kinds of values, it is only in Germany that postmaterialism matters more than the left–right orientation for party choice. We conclude that value orientations are probably important for party choice, but it need not always be the postmaterialist orientation that is decisive.

All the evidence in the massive survey research done in Western European countries suggests that values matter for party choice. In the 1980s and 1990s the findings indicate that values play a larger role for the electoral fortunes of parties than social structure or traditional cleavages. One of the key values is no doubt postmaterialism, although there are different views about how strongly postmaterialism affects party choice as well as how consistent postmaterialist values tend to be. However, our focus here will be on the impact of values upon macro outcomes at the societal level. Thus, we need to search for evidence that postmaterialist values matter for how countries differ in terms of policy outputs or macro outcomes, asking whether an increase in

**Table 9.4    Impact on party choice in Western Europe of the 1990s: bivariate relationships**

| Country | Structural voting | Value voting | Religious –secular | Left–right | Post-materialist |
|---|---|---|---|---|---|
| Denmark | 0.10 | 0.28 | 0.35 | 0.55 | 0.46 |
| Norway | 0.12 | 0.28 | 0.41 | 0.44 | 0.34 |
| Sweden | 0.07 | 0.25 | 0.28 | 0.47 | 0.28 |
| Iceland | 0.08 | 0.28 | 0.24 | 0.47 | 0.43 |
| Britain | 0.08 | 0.22 | 0.16 | 0.46 | 0.38 |
| Ireland | 0.09 | 0.09 | 0.25 | 0.21 | 0.20 |
| Belgium | 0.09 | 0.18 | 0.44 | 0.36 | 0.24 |
| Netherlands | 0.13 | 0.17 | 0.51 | 0.45 | 0.44 |
| Germany | 0.07 | 0.17 | 0.34 | 0.30 | 0.41 |
| France | 0.09 | 0.16 | 0.37 | 0.42 | 0.28 |
| Italy | 0.11 | 0.18 | 0.46 | 0.30 | 0.28 |
| Spain | 0.09 | 0.20 | 0.43 | 0.36 | 0.32 |
| Portugal | 0.08 | 0.09 | 0.29 | 0.27 | 0.16 |

*Note*:    In the two first columns the entries are Wilk's lambda, while in the last three columns the entries are eta coefficients.

*Sources*: Knutsen and Scarborough (1995, p. 513); Knutsen (1995, pp. 488–89).

support for postmaterialist values really means a difference for macro outputs or outcomes.

**Trust Theory**

The theory that claims that trust is not only a basic value in society, but also that its spread has huge political, economic and social significance, may be traced back to two sources. First, there is Alexis de Tocqueville's classical civil society theory, stating that a vibrant private sector tends to generate numerous voluntary associations, which stabilize both society and the democratic polity (Tocqueville, 1990). Second, there is the theory of Almond and Verba about the civic culture, where citizens successfully mix a participatory role with a deferential one, resulting in a politics of argument and counterargument, of give and take, with trust emerging between government and opposition (Almond and Verba, 1965, 1989).

Interestingly, according to Almond and Verba, a civic culture is a political culture characterized by trust, which is not restricted to the private sector but includes the public sector too. Long before trust became a major theme in social science research, they stated:

Above all, the political orientations that make up the civic culture are closely related to general social and interpersonal orientations. Within the civic culture the norms of interpersonal relationships, of general trust and confidence in one's environment, penetrate political attitudes and temper them. (Almond and Verba, 1965, p. 360)

One may locate trust within the private sector (social capital) as with Tocqueville, or one may emphasize political trust (trust in government), as with Almond and Verba. But what are the macro consequences of trust? The answer is: economic development (Fukuyama) and democracy (Putnam).

F. Fukuyama argues that social capital is fundamental for understanding economic growth on a long-term basis. Besides emphasizing human capital, including individual skills and knowledge, economists have begun to claim that social capital in the form of the capacity to associate or cooperate matters for economic prosperity. Fukuyama states:

The ability to associate depends, in turn, on the degree to which communities share norms and values and are able to subordinate individual interests to those of larger groups. Out of such shared values comes trust, and trust, as we see, has a large and measurable economic value. (Fukuyama, 1995a, p. 10)

This sounds highly plausible, but such a theory needs empirical confirmation. Fukuyama focuses on the consequences of social capital for economic growth, or the dynamism of the business community of a country. In 1989 Fukuyama argued that mankind had arrived at a consensus on two universal institutions: the market economy and democracy. In 1995 Fukuyma, however, finds a new source of cultural variations, namely social capital. On the one hand, we have the high-trust countries with plenty of social capital. On the other hand, we have the low-trust countries where spontaneous sociability is replaced by familialism. Countries that are high-trust countries minimize transaction costs, as plentiful social trust allows for a large firm size and high economic efficiency as, for example, in the USA, Japan and Germany. Countries with low social capital tend to emphasize the family as the economic unit, as, for instance, China or Chinese communities outside mainland China, and Italy. Could social capital also be a source of political outcomes, such as the implementation of human rights?

Trust theory poses three principal questions for empirical enquiry:

1  Does trust reside with the private or the public sector?
2  Is trust declining or not?
3  Does trust cause or reflect political, social or economic outcomes?

Putnam, referring mainly to the USA, takes the view that trust is on the decline (Putnam, 2000). However, Newton does not find that social capital is running low in Western Europe today, which to some extent contradicts Putnam's argument that personal trust or social capital is declining in all Western countries (Newton, 1999). However, our key question is whether trust matters for outcomes, which raises questions not about the sources of trust but about the macro consequences of trust.

## New Cultural Theory (NCT)

New Cultural Theory or NCT, which we already have dealt with in Chapter 1, is based on the Douglas and Wildavsky-inspired typology concerning four or five basic cultures or values, covering all forms of social interaction. It has stimulated much debate about the impact of culture on politics. This scheme was deliberately conceived as a challenge to the dominant approach in political science during the 1990s, the rational choice framework. At the same time, NCT is an attempt to rejuvenate old culture theory.

NCT harbours two interesting ideas, which may be examined separately. First, NCT claims to generate 'a mutually exclusive and jointly exhaustive set of categories for the domain of social life' (Thompson *et al.*, 1990, p. 14) – that is, the typology of NCT is all-encompassing. Second, it claims that these conceptual categories tend to prevail as cultures in social life: 'the categories of social relations described by cultural theory ... cohere *socially*' (Thompson *et al.*, 1990, p. 14) – that is, NCT entails that culture matters. NCT displays a quasi-deductive structure, as it employs a few basic assumptions about two fundamental dimensions of social reality in order to derive its four or five cultural types. The time-independent categories of individualism, egalitarianism, hierarchy and fatalism appear to be highly suitable for comparative cultural analysis and they also lend themselves to longitudinal studies of how universal cultural characteristics have evolved (Douglas and Wildavsky, 1983; Wildavsky, 1991, 1995). From NCT we may derive the importance of value orientations such as individualism or egalitarianism for outcomes at the micro level as well as at the macro level. To us, these two competing values in advanced societies help us understand why some societies, and not others, have a large public sector.

## The Consequences of Values: Macro or Micro?

It is not difficult to find strong causal claims in favour of values among the adherents of the theories discussed here. However, it is far more problematic to find actual evidence that values matter for outcomes. There is a gulf between causal claim and causal evidence. It is important to remember the distinction between a model which specifies a causal relationship between two factors and the corroboration of such a model by probabilistic evidence. It is not enough to launch an interesting model, as one must also check the model against data by, for instance, running a corresponding regression model. The key distinction among cultural models is that between macro and micro models. Let us quote from Almond and Verba who, when discussing civic culture and democratic stability, state:

> To a considerable extent the future of these nations will be affected by the nature of their political cultures, but other factors will also have important consequences. (Almond and Verba, 1965, p. 365)

This amounts to the formulation of a macro model linking the occurrence of democratic stability with the political culture of a country, conditioned on the caveat that other factors also play a role. Yet, Almond and Verba never estimated a regression model corresponding to that hypothesis. Nor did they ever guard themselves against the objection that a stable democracy could further a specific type of political culture such as the civic culture, meaning that values reflect practices but do not cause them.

In a similar vein Putnam argues that the values he focuses on could be causally relevant. Discussing the importance of social capital, he writes:

> For political stability, for government effectiveness, and even for economic progress social capital may be even more important than physical or human capital. (Putnam, 1993, p. 183)

This is all modalities. No one would deny that social capital could influence the macro outcomes which Putnam mentions. But the crux of the matter is whether it really does so. Causality is not possibility, it is probability. Putnam employs the case of Italy in order to show that regions with high social capital perform differently from regions with low social capital. But this does not prove causality. If social trust is really higher in northern Italy than in southern Italy, then this could be so because of *Mezzogiorno*. One swallow does not make a summer, we argue. Is there any strong evidence that trust can explain country differences in democracy or economic growth when other factors are held constant using a sample of countries?

Inglehart is no less vague. Theorizing the role of political culture for stable democracy, he states:

> There is no question that economic factors are politically important – but they are only part of the story. This chapter argues that different societies are characterized to very different degrees by a specific syndrome of political cultural attitudes; that these cultural differences are relatively enduring, but not immutable; and that they can have major political consequences, one being that they are closely linked to the viability of democratic institutions. (Inglehart, 1990, p. 15)

Again, the argument about the impact of values is framed in terms of modalities. Only probabilities can inform us whether values in fact have 'major political consequences' – for instance, conditioning the vitality of democracy in a country. Such vague claims about the importance of values constitute at best a first step towards the identification of a more precise relationship between specific values and determinate outcomes. At worst, such generalizations are more confusing than illuminating, as what they claim may turn out to be blatantly false. The fact that societies have different political cultures does not prove that values are causally efficient. Even values that receive much attention in a society may reflect that society more than drive it. Alternatively, political culture and society could be independent entities.

Finally, we quote from two adherents of NCT, who asking themselves 'Is this faith in a rigorous science of culture naively optimistic?', state:

> We think not. The promise of cultural theory is attested to by Robert Putnam and his colleagues' (1993) painstakingly careful work on Italian regional governance, the immense body of cross-national survey research that has been spawned by Ronald Inglehart's seminal work on postmaterialism … . Works such as these do not just affirm that 'culture matters' but set themselves to the much more difficult task of specifying the ways in which culture matters, the conditions under which it matters, and how much it matters. (Ellis and Thompson, 1997, p. 18)

To tell the truth, we believe that cultural analysis has not arrived at any definitive findings, supported by strong empirical evidence, concerning cultural causality, at least not in relation to macro outcomes. Much of cultural theory is still suggesting that 'culture matters', but it has not been able to replace this vague message with more specific causal models, confirmed by empirical tests.

In Chapter 10 we will proceed to an empirical test of cultural hypotheses. What is the evidence for specific cultural hypotheses linking the spread of various values with macro outcomes in society, the economy or the polity? Testing hypotheses derived from these cultural theories, one arrives at a more conclusive view about whether and how much culture matters than from reading the many promises about the prospects of cultural analysis. The next chapter will, however, first deal with the relations between the micro and macro levels in values research.

## Conclusion

The analysis of values in the 1980s and 1990s has resulted in a new literature on culture, which should be placed on a par with the traditional concerns of cultural theory, namely ethnicity (race, nation) and religion (civilization, sect). This new literature is not talking about primordial groups, as the communities that carry these values are not identifiable on the basis of ascriptive criteria. However, groups that adhere to these universal values play a role in politics today. The key research question concerns how important they are for society, the economy and the polity – in short, for outcomes.

Cultural theory focusing on values refers either to values in general as with NCT or they deal with a special set of values – that is, the political culture as with civic culture. Values may be investigated through the survey research on attitudes as in postmaterialism or values may be found expressed in behaviour, as in NCT. All theories about values claim that values have an important impact on social, economic and political outcomes, and this claims need empirical corroboration.

To us, values belong first and foremost to the sphere of attitudes, or beliefs and norms. Thus, we wish to restrict our test of theories about universal values to an examination of attitudes and their consequences. One may certainly extend cultural analysis of values into the sphere of behaviour, but it is a somewhat different enterprise. We are interested in the theories about values in so far as they contain hypotheses about cultural effects – in other words, we search for the impact of social and political trust, postmaterialism and the cultures of NCT upon outcomes. Our examination is limited to arguments about cultural impact that can be tested without the danger of a circular definition, deriving values from behaviour, which then are considered to explain the behaviour.

From Fukuyama, we take the hypothesis that trust accounts for affluence and economic growth. However, trust may also be related to political outcomes such as democracy. From NCT, we borrow the argument that the modern society contains a conflict of values between libertarianism and egalitarianism. Finally, postmaterialism implies that mass beliefs in the advanced democracies contain something more than the left–right materialism values or the religious–secular values. But what is that other dimension and does it matter for policy-making?

Values may be researched not only for their macro effects but also for their consequences for micro outcomes. Since individuals adhere to these values, one may ask whether they matter for their behaviour. The distinction between micro and macro effects is essential when the impact of values is researched. Chapter 10 will explain why.

# Chapter 10

# Value Orientations: How Real Are They?

## Introduction

In the previous chapter we looked at values from a methodological point of view, discussing whether behaviour or attitudes afford evidence on, or constitute indicators to, the occurrence of values. Our position is that attitudes are more valid and reliable indicators of the existence of values than behaviour, because behaviour may be interpreted in various ways as the expression of values. Now we wish to discuss the existential question of what a value is, when it is said to exist, and also bring forth certain 'central' value orientations.

In the study of the values that people have, or have had, it is always emphasized that these values are nothing but value orientations, meaning beliefs about values. Thus, the values that cultural analysis aims at researching today are not absolute values, or ends in themselves, but people's conceptions about objectives or norms. Cultural inquiry is not moral investigation, as the former only aims at describing which value orientations exist, whereas moral investigation raises the question whether some values are better than others.

It is not just the distinction between values in themselves and value orientations that is crucial here. When one decides to limit the inquiry into values to the attitudes of people, then one must clarify what kinds of entity these value orientations are. Stating that values are merely value orientations may appear to be a very modest claim, but it remains a huge task to identify which are the main value orientations among citizens in democracies today. Presumably, central value orientations would matter for outcomes.

The purpose of this chapter is to clarify what values are when they exist as well as to indicate how a few values occur with people today. We will discuss Converse's thesis that values as value orientations are merely patterns of attitudes in order to suggest an alternative position. We also deal with the micro and macro relationships between values.

## The Problem with Values and Value Research

The inquiry into values has become a major enterprise within the social sciences during the 1990s. The emergence of value research as a major field in its own right cannot be explained merely by the modern easy access to lots of data about attitudes. There is also the lacunae created by the fall of the Berlin

Wall, which reduced the dominance of ideological politics in the democracies around the world, reinforcing the search for cultural values. If people do no longer position themselves along a one-dimensional left–right continuum of positions linked with parties, then which values are expressed in voting or in policy standpoints? One may wish to distinguish between two kinds of values in politics: ideological values and cultural values. If the former dominated politics between 1945 and1989, then the latter are very much at the forefront today.

'New politics' is the common label for a whole set of new phenomena that cannot be fitted into the image of politics as an ideological struggle between the left and the right. Here, we find, among other things, the green revolution, the feminist movement, the transformation of the extreme parties, the new nationalism, the new centre parties, and the participatory movement, including the social movements. How can we explain these new phenomena?

New politics in all its variety, it is widely agreed, calls for a new approach, supplementing the existing dominant one namely the rational choice framework – which offered the analysis of politics as basically a game or a uni-dimensional exercise (Ordeshook, 1992; Hinich and Munger, 1997). New politics, various scholars argued, could only be understood as the reflection of new values. Thus, a cultural approach of some kind is the appropriate one when setting out to explain new politics, because values did not fit well with the rational choice framework and its emphasis on self-interests. As culture had focused on ethnicity, religion and primitive cultures, a new form of cultural analysis also had to be invented – the cultural approach framework.

The inquiry into values has thus attempted to establish a solid foundation and has been helped enormously by increased access to attitude data. The release of huge quantities of survey data in various forms – Eurobarometers, World Values Surveys and national election surveys – has allowed social science to ask many more questions about the citizens attitudes as well as developing elaborate new techniques for answering these questions with more refined tools of analysis.

## Value Inquiry

Value research faces certain methodological stumbling blocks which are not easily resolved. They include problems concerning the following questions:

- Is the inquiry into value orientations a value-neutral enterprise?
- Is a value orientation a real entity in people's minds?
- Is a value orientation more a way to describe behaviour than a cause of behaviour?
- Is value orientation a micro or macro phenomenon?
- Are certain value orientations more important than others?

The inquiry into value orientations tends to use quantitative methods as a response to the abundantly available data about attitudes. However, it has also been claimed that values require their own methodology of research, focusing on the use of interpretative or qualitative techniques.

We will quote from two leading scholars in the field of value research in order to give an impression of the difficulties in establishing a conceptualization of values suited for research tasks. Thus, we start with:

> Values are seen here as conceptions of the desirable which are not directly observable but are evident in moral discourse and relevant to the formulation of attitudes. For heuristic purposes, we understand these conceptions as hypothetical constructs which constrain attitudes. The claim for the empirical relevance of values, we argue, is demonstrated by evidence of patterning among attitudes. We call these meaningful patterns value orientations. This approach places attitudinal measures at the centre of our empirical work. (van Deth and Scarborough, 1995a, p. 46)

In this quotation the authors are, so to speak, 'all over the place'. Let us explain.

First, values, in the moral sense, are not sharply distinguished from value orientations. Values, it is said, are conceptions of the desirable – but 'to whom?', we must ask. In the moral universe of discourse, the term 'value' could be defined as a conception of the desirable, but this is an essentially contested issue involving so-called meta-ethical issues. The emotive theory of values, for instance, argues that values are expressions of emotions or imperative sentences rather than conceptions of anything. The inquiry into values in cultural analysis always targets value orientations, not questions about what is desirable in itself.

Second, value orientations are looked upon as hypothetical constructs which constrain attitudes. This is, again, a confusion of two interpretations of values. On the one hand, one could say that value orientations are hypothetical constructs, identifying underlying or latent factors, which are not directly observable. Only response items tapping the myriad attitudes are observable directly. On the other hand, one can claim that values are nothing but the observable pattern among attitudes which constrain them – Converse's position. Thus, we have two different theories about what values are: underlying entities; or constraints or patterns. Either value orientations are real phenomena that lie beneath, or cause, the observable phenomena. Or values are merely the way in which many attitudes happen to covary or are constrained into certain patterns. One has to choose between these two positions, as they cannot be combined.

Third, there is no way to separate the evidence for the existence of values from the relevance of the values themselves. One kind of evidence for the occurrence of values is that attitudes form a pattern that either constitutes the value or expresses it. However, the evidence for the operation of values could also be found in data about behaviour. On the other hand, the relevance of value orientations would have to be found in their impact on society and politics. Values could be interesting in themselves (intrinsic importance), but they could also play a major role in influencing other phenomena, being important for micro or macro outcomes (extrinsic importance). Let us discuss the theme of value relevance further.

People hold value orientations, but does it really matter which ones they adhere to? People's attitudes could constitute an interesting area of research, because people's beliefs and fundamental commitments are interesting and often fascinating in themselves. The analysis of culture could easily harbour the inquiry into values as one additional field of research, as the variety of values that people cling to would be as interesting as, say, philosophy or architecture or any traditional concerns of cultural analysis. However, more than intrinsic importance is involved in the emergence of the inquiry into new values during the 1990s.

Fourth, many values could be identified, if behaviour is seen as evidence of the occurrence of a value orientation. Thus, we read:

> In addition to traditional value orientations such as authoritarianism, deference, conservatism, progressiveness, religiosity, and materialism, the last two decades or so have witnessed the rise (and sometimes already the decline) of new orientations such as postmaterialism, environmentalism, postmodernism, ecologism and feminism. (van Deth, 1995a, p. 8)

Given such a diversity of value orientations there is a need to limit the focus of new values inquiry. Here, the idea of central values is being suggested, with the claim that there are certain central value orientations which constitute central trends (van Deth, 1995a, p. 9). But which values are central? Central value orientations are those which explain value change in advanced industrial societies. The survey literature in the past has suggested at least three such central value orientations, namely the following: materialism–postmaterialism, left–right materialism and religious–secular orientations. Now recent value research has added trust and individualism–egalitarianism. These value orientations are central because they make up trends in the development of the electorates in democratic countries. Thus, value centrality entails political importance. But how can we establish the importance of values for society, the economy and the polity? By inquiring into the link between values and outcomes, we suggest.

## The Relevance of Value Orientations

Much of the interest in the value inquiry resulted from the prevailing image that major value changes had occurred since 1970 in the advanced democracies. These shifts in value orientations connected with the new politics were seen as reflecting the major social transition from modernity to postmodernity. They were perceived as impacting on the politics of the postmodern countries (Harvey, 1989; Jameson, 1991). Let us again quote from the same expert in value research saying that 'value orientations are to be thought of not only as the consequences of the modernization process but also as co-determinants of many aspects of advanced industrial societies' (van Deth, 1995b, p. 74). This sounds very plausible, but what does it really mean when one starts pondering about how value change – a micro process – is linked with macro changes in society and in the polity?

Whether value orientations are regarded as accompanying macro social change or as conditioning macro events, it is still the case that there is a micro–macro problem, which creates not only difficulties in research but also potentially much confusion. Figure 10.1 clarifies this double-natured character of value research, or the micro–macro connections.

The four possibilities of micro–macro connections between values and behaviour include: I. micro–micro, or people with certain value orientations engage in specific forms of behaviour; II. macro–micro where, in societies characterized by a certain aggregate distribution of value orientations, individual people are affected in their behaviour, although they need not hold these values themselves; III. micro– macro, or people having certain value orientations found in societies with a specific set of aggregate characteristics, although it need not be the case that these people with these values actually promote these macro traits; IV. macro–macro, where specific macro outcomes tend to occur in societies where certain value orientations prevail at the aggregate level there.

The reason why it is crucial to keep these four possibilities in mind when stating that values matter follows from the all-important circumstance that the nature of causality involved in these four connections between the macro and the micro varies. Two kinds of causal interactions – namely, micro–micro and macro–macro – create few difficulties from a methodological point of view. What are problematic are the combinations across micro and macro.

Micro–micro relationships between values and behaviour can only be established by means of pure individual level research. Any interaction would have to consist of a correlation stating that the same individuals with a certain value orientation display a certain behaviour. Macro–macro relationships

|  |  | Value orientations | |
| --- | --- | --- | --- |
|  |  | Micro | Macro |
| **Behaviour** | Micro | I | II |
|  | Macro | III | IV |

**Figure 10.1    Value change: micro versus macro**

could entirely bypass any such individual level interaction, as it need only be the case that societies with a certain configuration of values also tend to display specific outcomes, whether or not there exists a corresponding micro–micro interaction. What is questionable is the micro–macro relationship or the macro–micro relationship, because it is far from clear what causal mechanism could be at work.

To find out whether values matter we need to test a few major models about values which argue that these values are not only central because they capture changes in values, but also that they matter for outcomes in society, the economy and the polity. To conclude, value orientations may be relevant in two senses:

1   They may be important for the acting individual in the sense that people with certain values tend to behave in specific ways – micro importance.
2   They may be important for society in the sense that aggregates of value orientations tend to be associated with macro outcomes – macro importance.

Confusion may arise when micro and macro relevance is mixed. Thus, the research on the outcomes of universal values has to take a stand on a difficult methodological problem, namely: should one use macro-level or micro-level data? One may examine whether adhering to certain values impacts on the people's behaviour by asking, for example, whether adhering to certain universal values impacts on their appreciation of their life situation. One may also examine how different values combine at the individual level – that is, whether people who adhere to one value, like trust, also adhere to another, like achievement. Any connection found at the individual level between variables derives their meaning from the association that individuals do. Since it is individuals who make these connections between variables, one may assume that there is some internal logic between them. With regard to macro-level associations, it holds true that the association between variables is not made at the individual level, but represents only a relationship between aggregate properties of society.

Inquiring into the macro effects of universal values, one must first aggregate individual-level information into society-level information. Thus, one constructs society-level properties which capture how various values are adhered to by various individuals, meaning the relative frequency of groups which belong to these values as a proportion of all individuals. These society-level properties may or may not be related to other society-level properties, such as political, social and economic outcomes. But whether that is the case or not depends wholly upon whether variables are associated for a set of societies. Thus, one may suggest that postmaterialism finds many adherents in more affluent societies, but it is not implied that rich people in these societies adhere to postmaterialism. There is no individual-level logic to that association.

When one deals with macro-level relationships, then one covers indicators which measure, *inter alia*, as discussed in Chapter 2, the following outcomes:

- Economic development: level of affluence and growth rates;
- Politics: democracy, public sector size, the occurrence of corruption;
- Social development: Income distribution and gender development.

## Central Value Orientations

Now, which are the central value orientations in our times? In our view, value orientations belong to the sphere of attitudes, beliefs and norms. Thus, we wish to restrict the examination of theories about universal values primarily to an examination of value orientations that pertain to attitudes and their consequences at the macro level. One may certainly extend the cultural analysis of values into the sphere of behaviour, but it is a different enterprise. In addition, the micro consequences of values could be included, as per the examples given below.

First, we are interested in trust theory, including its hypotheses about social and political trust. It can be tested without the danger of a circular definition, deriving values from behaviour which are then considered to explain the behaviour. From Fukuyama we take the hypothesis that trust accounts for affluence and economic growth. This is a macro–macro hypothesis, which may be tested in a cross-sectional design. We may also ask, following Putnam, whether trust may also be related to political outcomes such as democracy or corruption. Again, this is a macro–macro hypothesis.

Second, Inglehart's theory of postmaterialism implies that mass beliefs in the advanced democracies contain something more than left–right materialism values or religious–secular values. But how important is this new dimension and does it matter for policy-making as it does with political outputs in the form of welfare state spending?

Third, we take from Douglas and Wildavsky the argument that the postmodern society contains a conflict of values between competitive individualism or the achievement orientation and egalitarianism. Do these competing values in advanced societies help us understand political outputs – for instance, why some societies, and not others, cherish the welfare state?

We may thus pin down which value orientations these cultural theories target in order to try to measure their occurrence today worldwide. Three new clusters of universal values have so far been identified in Chapter 9: trust (Putnam, Fukuyama), the postmaterialist orientation (Inglehart), and individualism and achievement orientation (NCT). In order to describe how they occur, we will below use attitudinal indicators at the aggregate level of society. Thus, the individual-level measures in the form of responses to survey questionnaire items give data that may be aggregated to a society-level measure. We employ data from the World Values Surveys (Inglehart *et al.*, 2000).

The choice of three theories of universal values is, we argue, hardly accidental one or merely arbitrary. The theories of Fukuyama, Putnam, Inglehart, Wildavsky and Douglas deal with the basic attitudes of individuals towards society. In reality, these three theories of values capture various aspects of individualism in the postmodern society in a most encompassing sense. Below, we present the following value orientations as they have been measured by means of survey data as they are available from the cumulative three-wave World Values Survey (Inglehart *et al.*, 2000). Our analyses indicate that they tend to form separate factors, if factor analyses using the separate items are used. Here are the value orientations that we have distilled from the main theories of values in the postmodern society, together with indicators on the attitudes that tap these values. These indicators have all been taken from the World Values Survey and we list them systematically by the question corresponding to the attitude in the WVS. Thus, we have the following values and the corresponding attitude questions:

1   *Individualism (INDIV)*. Individualistic orientations may be identified when combining the following variables: $(V127-(V128+V129))$ – that is, 'people should take more responsibility' (V127); 'competition is harmful' (V128); and 'hard work doesn't generally bring success' (V129). Higher scores on this index means more individualism.
2   *Postmaterialism (POSTMAT)*. Here we rely on the four-item indicator developed by Inglehart *et al.* (V1000MPM) that was discussed earlier in Chapter 9.
3   *Trust or, rather, interpersonal trust (TRUST)*. This is captured by variable V27 measuring whether those interviewed agree with the statement: 'Generally speaking, would you say that most people can be trusted or that you can't be too careful in dealing with people?' Trust occurs when people endorse such a statement.
4   *Achievement orientation (ACHIEVE)*. Inglehart (1997, p. 390) measured this variable as the percentage in a society who stressed 'thrift' and 'determination' as important things for a child to learn, minus the percentage stressing 'obedience' and 'religious faith'. We have, however, chosen a slightly different operationalization replacing 'determination' with 'hard work', thus arriving at the following: $((V20+V16)-(V24+V22))$.

These indicators on the occurrence of individualism, achievement orientation, postmaterialism and trust allows one to carry out both micro and macro research. Thus, one may make aggregations from survey data, constructing average scores for a whole society on the basis of data about the attitudes of single individuals. Consequently, these indicators on individual value orientations, together with available data, allow for the computation of average scores at a very high level of aggregation, which opens up the possibility of employing values when explaining macro outcomes. At the same time, one may search for individual-level associations, if they exist.

In relation to individualism we will also make use of the following indexes that tap a macro variation in individualism across countries. On the one hand, we have survey data aggregated to a societal level and presented by Hofstede (Hofstede, 1994, p. 53), which may be used as an individualism index; on the other hand, we have an expert rating of individualism across nations developed by Triandis and presented by Diener *et al.* (Diener *et al.*, 1995, p. 856; see also Triandis, 1995). Our variable NEWIND is the added mean for the previous two indices. This is partly an attitudes-based and partly an expert-based indicator. Thus, for NEWIND, only the macro-level information is available, which limits its usefulness in the inquiry into value orientations.

These values – individualism, achievement orientation, postmaterialism and trust – have emerged independently from research on culture. The individualism–collectivism theme originated in the Douglas–Wildavsky approach to culture, whereas the trust theme came out of research on regional differences and the civic tradition in Italy as well as the search for the social sources of different business ethos. Inglehart launched the postmaterialism theme in response to the declining relevance of the traditional cleavages for understanding party choice. As a matter of fact, one may find traces of all these different themes in the classical study *The Civic Culture* (Almond and Verba, 1965). It clearly anticipated trust theory, and included individualism as well as personal integrity and deference.

Now, to what extent are these value themes different in the real world? We must start the empirical inquiry into value orientations by finding out how they occur in different societies (macro question) as well as how individuals relate to these values (micro question). If these values are truly central, then one would guess that they are firmly entrenched among citizens. And if each one of them is important in itself, then the very same persons would not adhere to all of them, making them indistinguishable. Let us look at data pertaining to this kind of centrality or intrinsic importance before we examine the evidence about causal impact of values.

## Macro: The Spread of Universal Values

In an effort to describe how these value orientations are spread in the population worldwide, a comparison of means between different parts of the world is displayed below in Table 10.1. In an analysis covering a substantial portion of the countries of the world, placed on all the continents, we may see from the eta-squared coefficients that space – the continent in question – figures prominently in the variation of these values, especially for the occurrence of individualism and collectivism. Our data stemming from the World Values Survey makes use of all three waves (that is, roughly 1980, 1990 and 1995) and, in addition, we have computed a mean value for the two waves of 1990 and 1995. All averages are based on weighted data from the WVS.

**Table 10.1  Individualism (INDIV): means**

| Region | INDIV 90 | INDIV 95 | INDIV 9095 | NEWIND |
|---|---|---|---|---|
| OECD | .621 (N=20) | .598 (N= 9) | .618 (N=21) | 70.5 (N=24) |
| Latin America | .561 (N= 4) | .543 (N= 8) | .552 (N= 8) | 27.8 (N=16) |
| Africa | .607 (N= 2) | .610 (N= 3) | .619 (N= 3) | 33.7 (N= 7) |
| Asia | .642 (N= 4) | .592 (N= 6) | .612 (N= 7) | 29.3 (N=16) |
| Postcommunist countries | .589 (N=12) | .489 (N=16) | .527 (N=20) | 53.4 (N= 4) |
| Total | .608 (N=42) | .546 (N=42) | .578 (N=59) | 45.6 (N=67) |
| eta squared | .14 | .44 | .35 | .67 |
| sig. | .219 | .000 | .000 | .000 |

*Note*:  See the Appendix in Chapter 2 for information about which countries belong to the various regions.
*Sources*: See Appendices A and C.

Consider, first, the occurrence of attitudes along the distinction between individualism and collectivism. First we have the individualism scores based on the WVS data (INDIV) in which the higher the score, the more individualism, the score ranging from a low 0 to a high 1. We have also constructed a new individualism index (NEWIND) which varies between 0 and 100 in which the higher the value, the more individualism. These indexes attempt to capture a cross-country variation in individualism around the 1990s and, at the most, some 60 countries are covered in our sample (Table 10.1).

The two indices on individualism only covary moderately ($r = .36$; $N = 41$). The macro index, NEWIND, gives scores that deviate from the micro index used in relation to WVS data, especially for African and Asian countries. This lack on coherence between the macro index and the micro index could depend on the low number of African and Asian countries covered in the WVS, but it may also testify to the complexity of individualism.

One may observe some clear differences among individualist and collectivist countries. The latter are to be found outside of the so-called Occidental world covering Western Europe and the Anglo-Saxon settlement countries outside of Europe. It is hardly surprising that Africa and Asia display very low scores on NEWIND, when we consider the findings on their family systems in these continents discussed in Chapter 8. However, the low scores for Latin America are astonishing, if indeed these scores can be considered valid.

Despite the fact that the countries in Latin America were settled by West European colonizing states, they display collectivism to an extent that is on par with the postcommunist countries. Is this a legacy of Catholicism? Whatever the explanation, this finding is a surprise. If these data are correct, then the postcommunist countries score about the same on individualism as

**Table 10.2 Achievement orientation (ACHIEVE): percentages scoring high achievement**

| Region | ACHIEVE80 | ACHIEVE90 | ACHIEVE95 | ACHIEVE9095 |
|---|---|---|---|---|
| OECD | 23.4 (N=16) | 30.8 (N=20) | 33.3 (N=11) | 31.3 (N=21) |
| Latin America | 28.5 (N= 2) | 24.3 (N= 4) | 24.6 (N= 9) | 24.6 (N= 9) |
| Africa | 27.7 (N= 1) | 14.2 (N= 2) | 16.3 (N= 2) | 16.3 (N= 2) |
| Asia | 49.9 (N= 1) | 58.7 (N= 3) | 42.9 (N= 7) | 42.9 (N= 7) |
| Postcommunist countries | 37.5 (N= 1) | 63.0 (N=12) | 62.3 (N=15) | 58.9 (N=20) |
| Total | 26.1 (N=21) | 40.8 (N=41) | 42.2 (N=44) | 40.5 (N=59) |
| eta squared | .29 | .56 | .61 | .51 |
| sig. | .208 | .000 | .000 | .000 |

*Note*: See Appendix in Chapter 2 for information about which countries belong to the various regions.

*Sources*: See Appendices A and C.

the Latin American ones, but lower than the African and Asian countries included here – very surprising indeed.

Let us now look at the data on achievement orientation which is, theoretically speaking, close to the individualism factor, at least in some analyses. Table 10.2 indicates the occurrence of the achievement value. The achievement orientation index breaks down to a five-score index with 0 indicating the lowest score and 1 the highest achievement score. In Table 10.2 we report the aggregate percentages of people scoring high on the index – that is, either .75 or 1.

Again, we face a stunning finding made possible through the WVS data. It is among people living in postcommunist and Asian countries that achievement is valued highly. The emphasis on effort and accomplishments meets with strong approval among a majority of the people in these two areas or continents, whereas such a work ethic receives, at best, a lukewarm acceptance in Western countries. The ideals of persistently trying hard and accomplishing results in life are not seen as the most important value by a majority of the populations in Latin America or Africa. Is this a legacy of the *mañana* spirit that is often said to characterize so-called Latinos or those parts of the world that have a tropical climate?

It has been argued that individualism entails an acceptance of the value of achievements as a necessary corollary of its rejection of collectivism. This finding, reported in Table 10.2, that the achievement orientation is not strongly endorsed in the individualist Western countries is again an example of how the survey method reveals new facts by its close examination of massive empirical data. Individualism and achievement orientation are not one and the same thing, nor do they go together.

**Table 10.3    Postmaterialism (POSTMAT): percentages being
                postmaterialist**

| Region | POSTMAT 80 | POSTMAT 90 | POSTMAT 95 | POSTMAT 9095 |
|---|---|---|---|---|
| OECD | 15.5 (N=15) | 21.6 (N=20) | 22.7 (N=11) | 22.3 (N=21) |
| Latin America | 11.3 (N= 2) | 14.5 (N= 4) | 17.0 (N= 9) | 17.0 (N= 9) |
| Africa | 9.4 (N= 1) | 7.8 (N= 2) | 8.5 (N= 3) | 8.5 (N= 3) |
| Asia | 8.6 (N= 1) | 6.5 (N= 3) | 5.3 (N= 6) | 5.2 (N= 7) |
| Postcommunist countries | 2.4 (N= 1) | 8.4 (N=12) | 5.1 (N=16) | 5.7 (N=20) |
| Total | 13.8 (N=20) | 15.2 (N=41) | 12.0 (N=45) | 13.3 (N=60) |
| eta squared | .24 | .59 | .66 | .65 |
| sig. | .371 | .000 | .000 | .000 |

*Note*:    See the Appendix in Chapter 2 for information about which countries belong to the
various regions.
*Sources*: See Appendices A and C.

Let us now see how postmaterialism varies from one continent to another
using average country scores. The figures in Table 10.3 refer to the percentage
of people matching the requirements for being postmaterialists according to
the four-item measure. Here, we find that Latin America is much more similar
to the occidental world than Africa, Asia and the postcommunist countries.
This makes it all the more urgent to find out why Latin America is low on
individualism when it is high on postmaterialism. Evidently countries with a
strong dose of achievement values are hardly postmaterialist countries.

It is always argued that postmaterialism occurs where affluence is high.
Thus, it has been concluded that it is an economic effect. Yet Table 10.3 does
not entirely support such a simplistic view. Affluence is not high in Latin
America, meaning we could expect less postmaterialism, and it is very low
in Africa compared with most of Asia, meaning that postmaterialism should
be much higher in Asia than in Africa. However, the findings in Table 10.3
deviate from these predictions. It is true that postmaterialism stands strong in
a sizable part of the population in the affluent OECD countries. However, it
also receives a considerable, though hardly huge, support in Latin American
countries, whereas the support in Asian countries is much lower.

It should be pointed out that postmaterialism is not a value orientation
that is widespread. According to Inglehart, postmaterialism is the value
syndrome of the young, which could account for the fact that only about 15
per cent of the sample reported upon in Table 10.3 state that they adhere
to postmaterialism. Moreover, it should be emphasized that postmaterialist
values have the weakest support of all the value orientations studied here.
This may have consequences for a test of the argument that this value is the

**Table 10.4    Trust (TRUST): percentages expressing interpersonal trust**

| Region | TRUST80 | TRUST90 | TRUST95 | TRUST9095 |
|---|---|---|---|---|
| OECD | 43.2  (N=17) | 42.6  (N=20) | 39.9  (N=11) | 40.0  (N=21) |
| Latin America | 22.3  (N= 2) | 21.6  (N= 4) | 16.5  (N= 9) | 16.5  (N= 9) |
| Africa | 30.6  (N= 1) | 25.7  (N= 2) | 20.0  (N= 3) | 20.0  (N= 3) |
| Asia | 38.0  (N= 1) | 41.8  (N= 3) | 30.2  (N= 7) | 30.2  (N= 7) |
| Postcommunist countries | 33.1  (N= 1) | 26.4  (N=12) | 22.5  (N=16) | 22.7  (N=20) |
| Total | 40.0  (N=22) | 35.0  (N=41) | 26.5  (N=46) | 28.6  (N=60) |
| eta squared | .29 | .56 | .61 | .42 |
| sig. | .208 | .000 | .000 | .000 |

*Note*:    See the Appendix in Chapter 2 for information about which countries belong to the various regions.

*Sources*: See Appendices A and C.

cause of many changes in the postmodern society, especially the new politics. Postmaterialism has strengthened its position little over time, as a matter of fact.

We may expect from Table 10.4 that the belief in the trust value varies differently from post-materialism, as surely the trust value orientation must be more widespread. If it is indeed true that trust is the principal type of social capital, facilitating human interaction, then a substantial portion of the population must have trust in others. Table 10.4, displaying the occurrence of this value in mass attitudes, confirms our suspicion. In the table we report the aggregated percentages that agree with the statement that most people can be trusted. And it is quite substantial.

Interestingly, trust is high in the occidental world and in Asia, but not in Latin America. The expectation that trust would be low in the postcommunist world as well as in Africa turns out to be well founded. Trust seems to vary with affluence, which has set off the hypothesis that trust is the cause of affluence. It may well be the opposite way around – that is, affluence results in trust.

Trust is a value orientation that roughly one-third of the population adheres to. It is not a high proportion, but it is definitely higher than the support for postmaterialist values. Trust remains firmly entrenched within the Western countries. Could its spread help us understand the occurrence of corruption? This is a hypothesis that is at least as plausible as the one that claims that trust enhances economic growth.

*Summary*

We look upon all these four values reported upon above as aspects of the culture of a postmodern society, dealing with the place of the individual person. These values define the person and help him or her in the search for meaning. There exist clear differences between many of the countries of the world in terms of the occurrence of support for the four values of individualism, achievement, postmaterialism and trust at the mass population level. To a large extent, this country variation can be summarized with the help of the distinction between the continents of the world. Whereas the occidental world scores high on all values except achievement and Africa scores low on all values, the remaining continents score differently on the different values. Surprisingly, Latin America scores low on individualism, but its low scores on trust are in accordance with expectations. Asia scores high on trust but low on individualism and postmaterialism. The post-communist countries score high on achievement but low on individualism and trust. The pattern of regional variation in cultures needs further explanation, as one could investigate separate country scores. However, despite the uncertainties about the data, especially when aggregated at such a high level, it is evident that this regional breakdown is relevant for the variation in universal values cross-nationally.

## The Micro and Macro Relationships Between Values

It may be suspected that the above-mentioned values are all related to modernity or, more accurately, postmodernity. If there is trust within a society, then there may also be individualism and postmaterialism. There may even be a risk that these values are not really distinct, as it is the same groups that adhere to them and the same groups that reject them. Let us therefore examine the micro-level correlations presented in Table 10.5. Here, we encounter some very interesting questions for empirical research that need to be answered before we tackle the problem of whether universal values matter. Thus, we ask, 'Is there empirical evidence to the effect that the very same social groups endorse all these values at the same time?' Table 10.5 suggests that this is not the case.

At the individual level there is some cohesion between the occurrences of various values. Due to the sample size all correlations are significant, but the correlation coefficients are low. Individualism, postmaterialism and trust go together, while the achievement orientation is negatively related to these values. This correlation analysis indicates that these value orientations are rather independent of each other. To test for such a possibility we go further with a factor analysis on these four variables to find out whether they constitute one single dimension or two dimensions. The outcome of such a factor analysis on the total sample is not conclusive. The eigenvalue of the

**Table 10.5   Micro level correlation between values (total sample)**

|         |      | INDIV   | ACHIEVE | POSTMAT | TRUST |
|---------|------|---------|---------|---------|-------|
| INDIV   | r    | 1.00    |         |         |       |
|         | sig. |         |         |         |       |
|         | N    |         |         |         |       |
| ACHIEVE | r    | −.046   | 1.00    |         |       |
|         | sig. | .000    |         |         |       |
|         | N    | 127580  |         |         |       |
| POSTMAT | r    | .061    | −.069   | 1.00    |       |
|         | sig. | .000    | .000    |         |       |
|         | N    | 125956  | 161523  |         |       |
| TRUST   | r    | .075    | −.012   | .100    | 1.00  |
|         | sig. | .000    | .000    | .000    |       |
|         | N    | 124998  | 1663989 | 157905  |       |

*Source*: See Appendix C.

first factor is higher than 1 while the eigenvalue of the second factor comes very close to one, or to be exact, .997. Thus, one could well say that these variables do capture a unique dimension – occidentalism perhaps. However, the empirical analysis suggests that achievement does not fit this picture, as it varies almost oppositely to the other values. Probably, the values of a postmodern society constitute complexity.

When we proceed to examine aggregate measures of the occurrence of values – the macro level – then we may obtain an entirely different finding. It is no longer required that the values be associated with the same individual. The unit of analysis is now the country and it is an open question how these four values occur at this level of aggregation. When we change the focus from the individual and his or her acceptance of values to concentrate on society, the meaning of value coherence or correlations between values is a different one.

Table 10.6 presents the correlations between the occurrence of four value orientations at the country level. Here it is a matter of associations only between aggregate-level scores and not between individual-level attitudes. These correlations only state whether a society as a whole tend to have sizable groups who adhere to these values and not whether one and the same person adheres to all of them. In Table 10.6 the set of units examined is small or, at most, N = 60 societies. The aggregated data from the WVS refers to the period 1990–95. The question for Table 10.6 to answer is whether groups who adhere to these values tend to be of the same size in all societies. It is not a requirement that the group has the same members.

Two findings stand out from Table 10.6. First, the evidence suggests that three of the four cultures investigated have a common source, which is most

**Table 10.6   Macro correlations between the indices on universal values**

|          |      | INDIV | ACHIEVE | POSTMAT | TRUST |
|----------|------|-------|---------|---------|-------|
| INDIV    | r    | 1.00  |         |         |       |
|          | sig. |       |         |         |       |
|          | N    |       |         |         |       |
| ACHIEVE  | r    | −.32  | 1.00    |         |       |
|          | sig. | .007  |         |         |       |
|          | N    | 58    |         |         |       |
| POSTMAT  | r    | .38   | −.45    | 1.00    |       |
|          | sig. | .002  | .000    |         |       |
|          | N    | 59    | 59      |         |       |
| TRUST    | r    | .37   | −.07    | .33     | 1.00  |
|          | sig. | .002  | .306    | .005    |       |
|          | N    | 59    | 59      | 60      |       |

*Source*:  See Appendix A.

probably how advanced a country is, or postmodernity. Achievement orientation is the value that deviates. The correlations for all other values are all positive, meaning that the stronger support there is in a country for individualism, the more likely it is that there will be groups in the country displaying strong support for postmaterialism and acceptance of trust. Thus, we see the same pattern of covariation as we found for the micro level (Table 10.5).

However, and this is the second point, the correlations are not so strong as to lead to the suspicion that these cultures are merely versions of one and the same, more fundamental, culture. On the one hand, the evidence covers only a limited number of countries, most of which are advanced, which increases the likelihood of a strong association between the indices. On the other hand, these correlations hover around 0.5, which is not strong enough to suggest that the countries that score high or low on the three indices are fundamentally the very same ones.

Interestingly, the countries with a high emphasis on the achievement value are not those with a strong backing of postmaterialism or individualism. This again supports the conclusion that these value orientations occur rather independently of each other, not only with single individuals but also as aggregate phenomena. If this independence between the value orientations is a real finding, then it becomes an urgent task to find out whether each of these value orientations has a separate and special impact on society or politics.

It may be pointed out that the Todd index of individualism– collectivism derived from the family structure (Chapter 8) correlates highly with the macro scales of individualism (r = .62 for NEWIND), which supports the hypothesis that this macro dimension is a real one. One the one hand, postmaterialism tends to occur in countries that score high on individualism. On the other hand, trust seems to be rather independent of the other two cultures, which is also true of achievement orientation.

As underlined, these connections in Table 10.6 are all macro relationships, and do not state to what extent the very same social groups at the individual level tend to adhere in the same manner to the three cultures. In this analysis of values, there is the risk of an ecological fallacy – that is, of a wrong conclusion from the macro level to the micro level, meaning that countries may have strong scores on all three cultures but all groups in the same country might not necessarily score high on all three themes.

## Do Values Matter?

There exist clear differences between many of the countries of the world in terms of the occurrence, at the mass population level, of support for four values that figure prominently in the postmodern society: individualism, achievement, postmaterialism and trust. To a large extent, this country variation can be summarized with the help of the distinction between the continents of the world. Whereas the occidental world scores high on all values except achievement and Africa scores low on all values, the remaining continents score differently on the different cultures. Surprisingly, Latin America scores low on individualism, but its low scores on trust are in accordance with expectations. Asia scores high on trust but low on individualism and postmaterialism. The postcommunist countries score high on achievement but low on individualism and trust.

In social science empirical research, it is often necessary to employ measures that do not directly tap the occurrence of a factor or variable, but constitute a so-called proxy – that is, a measure which taps something that is strongly associated with the phenomenon that one wishes to measure. Often, one employs several proxies in order to measure the occurrence of certain phenomena, like, for example, a set of attitudes in relation to values or better value orientations. Value orientations may be identified and described by means of survey research on attitudes. Thus, the responses of individuals may be used as indicators on the existence of value orientations. Alternatively, behaviour may be interpreted as the expression of values, which entails the use of entirely different types of proxies. Here, we have underlined the use of attitude data when constructing indicators on values.

The idea that values matter is a very general or vague one. We have made an effort to replace it with a specification of a few key or central value orientations. Drawing upon new theories of culture we arrive at the following four value orientations for which we have individual-level indicators: individualism, postmaterialism, trust and achievement. It seems clear not only that these value orientations exist but also that these four value orientations are fairly independent of each other, both at the micro and the macro levels. We regard these four value orientations as basic attitudes among citizens. This implies that we see them as not merely the pattern of responses to attitudinal items or proxies; they form a fundamental value commitment that tends to be expressed in various attitudes. Only one task remains: to discuss the idea implicit in all kinds of value research – namely that value orientations are conducive to social, economic and political change, especially when values change or new values spread.

The inquiry into values or value orientations has attracted much attention from social scientists during the last 20 years, replacing the earlier focus on political ideologies. The interest has concentrated on the change in values among ordinary citizens, as scholars have argued that many countries are in the process of moving from one or two dominant value systems to other – new politics. The theory about the growth in postmaterialism is a very well-known example of an idea targeting value change and its consequences (Inglehart, 1990). But one could also mention the hypothesis about a major value shift from individualism to egalitarianism in the politics of Western countries (Wildavsky, 1991). Indeed, here, one may also wish to place the hypothesis about a reduction in social trust among the theories dealing with value change (Putnam, 2000). These themes analysing value change have stimulated research into how one identifies the predominant values which groups of ordinary citizens cling to.

The debate about the occurrence of various kinds of value change has been much driven by the either explicit or implicit hypothesis that culture matters. We now turn to an examination of this hypothesis, which we interpret as linking values with determinate social, economic and political results, policies or outcomes. Yet, even if the intrinsic interest in the values of people is not underestimated, especially if these values are in a process of shifting, the theme of values change seems highly relevant for the analysis of real outputs and outcomes, especially in democracies. Finding out how ordinary people orientate towards the political system of their country, as well as what they feel about their leaders, is interesting in itself, especially in a democracy. Understanding how changes in values condition outcomes comes as an additional advantage with value research, as it throws light upon whether values really matter.

The purpose is now to search for evidence that supports this claim about the extrinsic importance of value change for society and politics. Following our discussion in this Chapter we will deal with survey research data. How can we substantiate the claim about the considerable role played by values in politics? We wish to state explicitly that we believe that the association between values and outcomes is an empirical one, meaning that only empirical tests in relation to (preferably) survey data can corroborate the claim that 'culture matters', implicit in the theories mentioned above. What does the presently existing evidence look like?

## Values Matter for What?

Value orientations cannot be the direct cause of outcomes, as there must be a mechanism that translates values into outcomes. The value orientations of the population are distant from social, economic and political outcomes. One link is the making of public policy that may result in outcomes through its implementation. Ideally, the process works as follows: value changes condition election changes which result in policy changes that bring about changes in outcomes.

Value changes are primarily important for the analysis of policy changes in the advanced democracies. When the value orientations among people are transformed from one set of dominant values to another, then politics will sooner or later reflect these broad-scale changes. First, the electoral support for parties will be affected. Second, the composition of governments is drawn into the implications of changing electoral outcomes. Finally, the new government makes different policies. In the long run, outcomes may also differ due to shifts in value orientations.

Thus, the link between value changes and social, economic and political outcomes involves a long chain of events. A shift from one culture to another could mean not only that many people's beliefs change, but also that political, social and economic policy change consequently. But it would take time before value changes materialize into outcome changes. An analysis of the consequences of value orientations may examine the whole chain of events from value changes to outcomes or it may focus on one or two links in this chain – for instance, between values and policies. The paradigm case of new values giving rise to new politics resulting in new policies changing outcomes through implementation is, of course, environmentalism. In this philosophy we have not only a new way of looking at men and women in relation to Mother Nature, but also a new set of values to guide decision-makers.

If values matter, then what do they matter for? We have here the same methodological predicament as occurred with the argument that religion or ethnicity matter. Just as one cannot rest content with such a general argument that culture is important, one cannot simply claim that values are important. In a scientific analysis of culture or values, one must proceed to ask what it is that culture or value impacts on. One would state a number of models about value effects and test these against empirical data in order to arrive at a conclusion about what culture matters for. These models can be either macro-level or micro-level models. Let us specify a set of models about cultural effects from values, drawing upon the three major theories about universal values presented in Chapter 9.

Values play a role in democratic politics by giving direction to the interaction between voters and political parties/candidates. They provide many of the preferences handled by politics through its institutions. A change in society's values will become reflected in politics through the preferences that struggle against each other in political institutions. Not all political preferences concern values, as self-interest or political egoism must also be recognized. However, values solve much of the classical problem in rational choice analysis: if preferences are not simply to be taken as given, then where do they come from? The cultural approach framework answers: values. When values among people change, then preferences among politicians will also change, which results in different decisions and, finally, in different outcomes. The impact of values on political preferences may be either diffuse or specific. And it may concern micro or macro outcomes. Let us explain these distinctions.

*Specific Value Impacts*

The relevance of values in politics can be very transparent, as when a few new values emerge, changing the preferences of both politicians and the voters. When such new value orientations spread and receive sufficient numerical support in order to count, then they may become accepted as key political preferences among decision-makers. This process may involve the creation of new political parties or the ideological repositioning of old ones. When new political preferences increase in strength, then policy-makers will pay them attention, either by making new ones or remaking old ones.

Take the example of postmaterialism. Postmaterialist value orientations have been said to offer much of the foundation for the emergence of new politics, being linked to new preferences at odds with traditional politics, such as environmentalism, feminism and egalitarianism. On the basis of these preferences new political parties have been introduced and old parties have adapted their programmes. When postmaterialist values become strong in society and government, then they tend to affect policy-making very concretely in the form of a variety of environmental legislation as well as in measures that enhance the quality of life and equality, especially among the sexes. Thus, we predict that countries where postmaterialist values stand strong will also be the countries where the public sector is large, with government correcting market failures or counteracting inequalities. The degree of gender equality would also be high where postmaterialism has gained a firm rooting in political preferences.

Green politics would hardly have had the success that it has enjoyed the last 20 years without a profound value change among ordinary citizens. Although organized action by various environmental groups played a major role in the making of new policies, it may be claimed that value change among the electorate was the *sine qua non*.

*Diffuse Value Impacts*

When new values come forward and shape political preferences, then it may be more the general political climate that changes. Thus, when individualism or achievement orientation receives a more pronounced backing in society, then private sector solutions tend to be preferred over public sector solutions. Or when trust increases, then social interaction is facilitated empowering economic life which in turn pushes up economic growth. Trust may also reduce political conflicts, as they become more manageable through an increased willingness to making compromises, thereby strengthening political stability.

The impact here is a diffuse one, as a change in values affects a set of very broad outcomes, increasing, for example, economic growth or democratic stability. Such a diffuse effect may be difficult to validate as more factors than values condition such broad outcomes. To discover diffuse effects from values one needs to employ research techniques that allow one to identify the partial effects of values while holding other relevant factors constant.

It should be pointed out that a diffuse value impact may be either trivial or profound. No one would deny, for instance, that trust would contribute to a better society. But the theory of trust makes a much bolder claim – namely that it is critically important for major social outcomes such as economic growth and the capacity of a country to withstand corruption. Similarly, the transformation in the predominant values of the population towards individualism or achievement orientation could be seen as a mere change in the social climate. Alternatively, it could be regarded as the cause of major events in politics such as the transformation of the welfare state towards a welfare society – that is, a significant shrinkage of the public sector. Similarly, the shift from competitive individualism towards egalitarianism may be reflected in pop culture or in the arts. We, however, search for its impact on policies, reinforcing, for instance, the welfare state.

The separation between specific and diffuse value impacts can be made in relation to both micro (individual-level) and macro (society-level) outcomes. Actually, one often discussed type of diffuse value impact is when new values are conducive to a different satisfaction with life. Another micro impact is when values play a major role in how people position themselves along the left–right dimension in politics. Such diffuse impacts are not of immediate relevance for political action by elites, but they may certainly have an indirect relevance through the operations of the election channel.

## The Transfer Mechanism: Election Channel and Policy-making

If values are the attitudes people have concerning norms of justice and the good life, then such value orientations should matter primarily for people's behaviour. Political value orientations would be important if they guided people when they become interested in politics and take political action. This is the micro link. From the macro perspective, values matter when they impact on outcomes in society as a whole. The macro link is much more complex than the micro link.

Value orientations condition macro outcomes through two mechanisms which transfer these values from the citizens into politics: namely, via the election channel and policy-making. This process of value change becoming reflected in policy-making is a slow one, except when a landslide election occurs. In order to find outcomes related to value changes, one must, in most cases, allow for a considerable time lag.

Typical of the politics and elections during the latest 20 years has been a steady increase in volatility, as voters in democracies change parties or opt for new ones. An increase in volatility would make it easier for new values to impact on politics and policy-making. When volatility increases, voters no longer remain loyal to the political parties. Instead, they switch from one to another, often on the basis of value considerations. All the while that the electorate is frozen, meaning that voters vote in the same way in election after election, the political ideologies offer values to the voters. These political values in the form of ideologies constrain the voters' choice of party. The rise in volatility has opened up the way for new values to play a political role. Thus, the new value orientations are manifested in the realignment of the electorate behind new parties or behind the old ones in new proportions.

Let us thus now test the key hypotheses derived from the three value theories examined here. We will use the above-mentioned distinctions among value impacts: specific; diffuse; micro; and macro. Micro outcomes may be direct effects from value orientations. They relate how individuals behave, given that they adhere to certain values. When values change people's behaviour – their life situation, their involvement in politics, their self-placement along the left–right scale – then such changes will sooner or later also change politics through the expectations of politicians.

### The Macro-level Consequences of Values

It is now time to look at the empirical evidence supporting various theses about the importance of values for different kinds of outcome. First, we will inquire into the macro-level impact, and then move our focus to the micro-level impact. The macro-level inquiry will deal with the impact of post-materialism, trust, individualism and achievement orientation. Do these universal values have any impact on macro-level outcomes?

The theory of postmaterialism argues that postmaterialist value orientations display associations with so many outcomes that one would be prepared to conclude that all the four kinds of value effects are stated to exist: specific, diffuse, micro and macro. Let us, however, first examine the macro-level evidence.

The gist of the macro effects of postmaterialism is that countries having considerable groups supporting postmaterialism score positively on several standard performance indicators. Postmaterialism is here captured from the

**Table 10.7 Postmaterialism and developmental outcomes: correlations**

| Variables | | POSTMAT 80 | POSTMAT 90 | POSTMAT 95 | POSTMAT 9095 |
|---|---|---|---|---|---|
| GGEXP92 | r | .30 | .37 | .38 | .37 |
| | sig. | .097 | .020 | .028 | .009 |
| | N | 20 | 31 | 26 | 40 |
| GINI90 | r | −.34 | −.09 | .13 | .02 |
| | sig. | .126 | .323 | .271 | .457 |
| | N | 13 | 27 | 23 | 34 |
| HDI99 | r | .38 | .64 | .58 | .62 |
| | sig. | .049 | .000 | .000 | .000 |
| | N | 20 | 41 | 43 | 58 |
| GEM99 | r | .57 | .54 | .61 | .60 |
| | sig. | .005 | .000 | .000 | .000 |
| | N | 19 | 37 | 32 | 47 |
| WOM90 | r | .55 | .38 | .39 | .40 |
| | sig. | .008 | .007 | .004 | .001 |
| | N | 20 | 41 | 44 | 59 |
| GRO9098 | r | .045 | .12 | .47 | .40 |
| | sig. | .426 | .221 | .001 | .001 |
| | N | 20 | 41 | 43 | 58 |
| LnPPP97 | r | .45 | .68 | .69 | .71 |
| | sig. | .024 | .000 | .000 | .000 |
| | N | 20 | 41 | 43 | 58 |
| DEM97 | r | .38 | .45 | .44 | .49 |
| | sig. | .051 | .002 | .001 | .000 |
| | N | 20 | 41 | 45 | 60 |

*Sources*: See Appendix A.

three waves of the WVS – that is, around 1980, 1990 and 1995; estimates of postmaterialism for 1990 and 1995 are averaged and, when data are missing for 1990 or 1995, available data for the other wave is used to calculate the value for 1990–95. Table 10.7 informs us that there are several strong correlations at the macro level. Thus, we find that countries where postmaterialism receives strong mass support are also generally those which score high on affluence, human development, gender equality, democracy, the welfare state and so on. But is there any real causal connection at work? In other words, do postmaterialist values condition these outcomes?

As shown by the table, the values of postmaterialism are strongly adhered to in societies with a postmodern structure – that is, societies which are highly economically advanced emphasize both gender equality and respect for a variety of human rights. It is even the case that postmaterialist values stand stronger among the advanced societies in those countries that have rapid economic growth. But this surely must be merely a coincidence, because economic growth does not hint that such values play any such role.

Interpreting in a general manner the findings reported upon in Table 10.7, we may make the following generalizations: Postmaterialism appears to have the same political and socioeconomic correlates, as it is all a matter of the occidental culture, polity and economy. Where postmaterialism stands strong, society and state display advancedness in terms of affluence, democratic stability and social as well as gender, equality. But what is *cause* and what is *effect*?

Despite the list of positive associations in Table 10.7 between postmaterialism and developmental outcomes one may wish to argue that they are just a coincidence – that is, it just happens to be the case that the occidental countries score high on both postmaterialism and the indicators on modernism. Both phenomena may be regarded as an expression of advancedness, but there would be no causality involved. One could also argue that postmaterialism would be more a reflection of postmodernism than a driving force behind it. However, postmaterialist theory claims that these correlations indicate the importance of these values.

On the contrary, in relation to the positive association between postmaterialism and public sector size in the form of a macro correlation of, at most, .38 one could claim that it is hardly a coincidence. Public policies are not made in a vacuum; they tend to reflect the prevailing opinion about what is expected of government. During the twentieth century, the ideologies along the left–right continuum have provided the main input for policy-making, delineating what is public and private. However, with the declining relevance of the traditional political ideologies, other values may offer guidelines about the size and orientation of the public sector. The positive association between size of government and support for postmaterialist values in Table 10.7 is hardly sensational. It is in the logic of postmaterialist attitudes to endorse a large public sector, as the employment of huge public expenditures enhance equality and quality of life, as well as providing many people with security against adversity.

To support our interpretation of Table 10.7, we examine whether developmental outcomes have any connection with postmaterialism when other relevant factors are taken into account. In Table 10.8 we employ the regression technique in order to find out whether there are spurious correlations involved in the many links between advancedness and postmaterialism. In the table postmaterialism is adapted from the average computed for the 1990–95 period.

Six of the eight regression analyses reported upon in Table 10.8 display the same negative finding. There is no impact whatsoever from postmaterialism on developmental outcomes when other major social factors are taken into account. Likewise, geographical location (DISEQU) and historical legacy or developmental path (MODLEAD) matter more than values, at least the postmaterialist ones. Postmaterialism does not matter much for macro outcomes – this may be interpreted as a major reversal of the Inglehart theory.

**Table 10.8 The impact of postmaterialism (POSTMAT): regression analysis**

| Independent variables | Coeff | Dependent variables | | | | | | | |
|---|---|---|---|---|---|---|---|---|---|
| | | GGEXP92 | GINI90 | HDI99 | GEM99 | WOM90 | GRO9098 | LnPPP97 | DEM97 |
| LnPPP97 | coeff | – | 6.69 | – | .09 | 3.70 | 3.58 | – | 1.77 |
| | t-stat | – | 2.97 | – | 3.87 | 2.01 | 4.69 | – | 4.68 |
| | tol | – | .31 | – | .40 | .33 | .33 | – | .38 |
| DISEQU | coeff | 56.34 | –53.50 | .22 | .23 | 21.97 | –9.15 | 1.27 | 2.57 |
| | t-stat | 5.40 | –5.85 | 3.50 | 2.48 | 2.86 | –2.86 | 2.34 | 1.58 |
| | tol | .75 | .58 | .75 | .76 | .68 | .68 | .75 | .76 |
| MODLEA | coeff | .090 | – | .00 | – | –.056 | –.04 | .01 | – |
| | t-stat | 2.43 | – | 4.43 | – | –1.90 | –3.30 | 2.94 | – |
| | tol | .57 | – | .53 | – | .46 | .46 | .53 | – |
| POSTM | coeff | –.02 | –.29 | .00 | .00 | .24 | .05 | .05 | –.01 |
| | t-stat | –.10 | –1.50 | 3.88 | 1.35 | 1.52 | .81 | 5.37 | –.16 |
| | tol | .68 | .45 | .66 | .49 | .43 | .43 | .66 | .45 |
| Constant | coeff | 2.99 | –.10 | .50 | –.45 | –25.07 | –22.74 | 6.86 | –9.21 |
| | t-stat | .63 | –.01 | 17.44 | –2.44 | –1.93 | –4.20 | 28.03 | –3.29 |
| Adjrsq | | .63 | .50 | .70 | .64 | .32 | .43 | .65 | .54 |
| N | | 40 | 33 | 58 | 47 | 58 | 58 | 58 | 58 |

*Notes:* coeff = the unstandardized regression coefficient.

t-stat = t-statistics. Used to test the significance of the regression coefficients; t-stat showing more than ± 2 indicates significance.

tol = tolerance. Used to measure the occurrence of multicollinearity in the model; if tol is higher than .3/.4 there is no risk of multicollinearity.

*Sources:* See Appendices A and C.

It is only in two regressions that postmaterialism shows significant estimates, and in both cases it is about predicting affluence itself (HDI99 and LnPPP97). However, looking at the analyses presented by Inglehart it is obvious that the impact of postmaterialism is not that strong when increasing the numbers of cases as well as controlling for other contextual factors (cf. Inglehart, 1997, p. 231; Jackman and Miller 1996, p. 652).

Let us now examine the claim that 'trust matters' in the same way. We already know that indicators on trust, especially general social or interpersonal trust, go together with advancedness. And we raise the question whether positive correlations can be taken as indicators of causality. Table 10.9 makes use of the aggregated percentage of the respondents in the different samples who agree with the indicator question – namely, that people can be trusted; here we rely on the averages measured for the period 1990–95. Trust turns spurious in relation to certain outcomes when other major factors such as affluence, geographical location and developmental stage are taken into account. The impact on gender development (GEM99 and WOM90) remains positive, strong and significant. Countries characterized by a high level of social trust tend to promote equality between men and women to a considerable degree. There is also evidence that trust enhances affluence as the partial impact of trust upon LnPP97 is strongly positive. What we find here is a confirmation of Fukuyama's idea that trust enhances economic development. But, as emphasized, the impact of trust on gender development is even stronger.

Third, we turn to individualism, captured for the period 1990–95 by the individualism index we have constructed from the WVS. When controlling for other factors we find that individualism has no significant impact on public sector size, human development, economic growth or democracy. Again, it is with respect to gender development (GEM99 and WOM90) that we find a positive impact from individualism. It is also noteworthy that individualism is strongly positively associated with level of affluence (LnPPP97) – that is, they go together. We must discuss why gender development and affluence is so strongly associated with the spread and acceptance of these values. Individualism is a set of values that emphasizes that each individual is responsible for his or her own life and that people may enjoy the full benefits that derive from their autonomous decision-making. As a consequence, individualism should favour feminism. And indeed it is so. In relation to the connection between individualism and affluence it is far from certain what is cause and what is effect. In Figure 10.2 we have plotted the macro indicator on individualism (NEWIND) against our measure of affluence (LnPPP97).

The close connection between affluence and individualism is one of the major findings in the research into values. When resources are abundant, then men and women opt for personal integrity and individual self-expression. It is hardly possible to turn matters upside down and claim that individualism is the cause of affluence. We believe that affluence is conducive to individualism.

**Table 10.9  The impact of interpersonal trust (TRUST): regression analysis**

| Independent variables | Coeffs | Dependent variables | | | | | | | |
|---|---|---|---|---|---|---|---|---|---|
| | | GGEXP92 | GINI90 | HDI99 | GEM99 | WOM90 | GRO9098 | LnPPP97 | DEM97 |
| LnPPP97 | coeff | — | 4.33 | — | .08 | 3.28 | 3.63 | — | 1.77 |
| | t-stat | — | 2.60 | — | 3.76 | 2.33 | 5.57 | — | 6.40 |
| | tol | — | .61 | — | .43 | .44 | .44 | — | .71 |
| DISEQU | coeff | 55.49 | -47.69 | .11 | .06 | 5.73 | -11.92 | -.16 | 2.93 |
| | t-stat | 4.02 | -5.11 | 1.49 | .59 | .81 | -3.63 | -.23 | 1.72 |
| | tol | .43 | .60 | .64 | .61 | .63 | .63 | .64 | .69 |
| MODLEA | coeff | .09 | — | .00 | .00 | -.04 | -.04 | .01 | — |
| | t-stat | 2.73 | — | 6.98 | 1.27 | -1.42 | -3.09 | 5.79 | — |
| | tol | .75 | — | .76 | .50 | .47 | .47 | .76 | — |
| TRUST | coeff | .01 | -.02 | .00 | .00 | .34 | .05 | .02 | -.01 |
| | t-stat | .08 | -.24 | 1.76 | 3.03 | 4.14 | 1.37 | 2.78 | -.41 |
| | tol | .51 | .66 | .70 | .58 | .61 | .61 | .70 | .62 |
| Constant | coeff | 2.86 | 15.66 | .49 | -.39 | -23.81 | -23.32 | 6.80 | -9.17 |
| | t-stat | .60 | 1.20 | 15.62 | -2.46 | -2.38 | -5.02 | 23.76 | -4.15 |
| Adjrsq | | .63 | .46 | .64 | .69 | .46 | .45 | .54 | .54 |
| N | | 40 | 33 | 58 | 47 | 58 | 58 | 58 | 58 |

*Notes:*   coeff = the unstandardized regression coefficient.
t-stat = t-statistics. Used to test the significance of the regression coefficients; t-stat showing more than ± 2 indicates significance.
tol = tolerance. Used to measure the occurrence of multicollinearity in the model; if tol is higher than .3/.4 there is no risk of multicollinearity.

*Sources:*  See Appendices A and C.

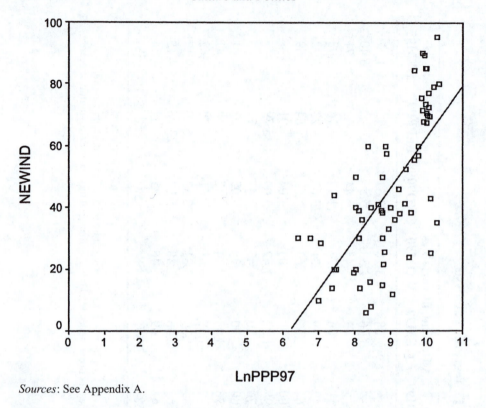

*Sources*: See Appendix A.

**Figure 10.2     Individualism (NEWIND) and affluence (LnPPP97)
(r=.69; N=65)**

*Summary*

When introducing controls for other factors like affluence, geographical
location or historical tradition we find that values no longer have any
significant impact on the macro-level outcome variables, despite the long list
of positive correlations. This is detailed in Table 10.10 where we attempt to
summarize the findings of regression analyses undertaken. In recent research
into value orientations it has been claimed that values strongly influence
macro outcomes. This is wrong.

Trust and individualism seems to matter as much as postmaterialism for the
various macro outcomes. However, we find that many of these universalist
values are obviously strongly associated with affluence. Thus, we propose
that it may be more reasonable to suggest that these values are rather the
consequences of affluence than the conditions of affluence.

**Table 10.10 Number of significant regression coefficients estimated for the impact of macro values by dependent variables**

| Values | GGEXP 92 | GINI 90 | HDI 99 | GEM 99 | WOM 90 | GRO 9098 | LnPPP 97 | DEM 97 | Total |
|---|---|---|---|---|---|---|---|---|---|
| POSTMAT | 0 | 0 | 1 | 0 | 0 | 0 | 1 | 1 | 3 |
| TRUST | 0 | 0 | 0 | 1 | 1 | 0 | 1 | 0 | 3 |
| INDIV | 0 | 0 | 0 | 1 | 1 | 0 | 1 | 0 | 3 |
| NEWIND | 1 | 0 | 1 | 0 | 0 | 1 | 1 | 0 | 4 |
| ACHIEVE | 0 | 0 | 0 | 0 | 1 | 1 | 1 | 0 | 3 |
| Total | 1 | 0 | 2 | 2 | 3 | 2 | 5 | 1 | 16 |

*Note*:    This information is partly based on a number of estimations not reported here.

## The Micro-level Consequences of Values

Several, but probably not all, of the proposed macro effects from values seem to be spurious, and macro research certainly needs to be complemented by micro research on value effects. What is the general finding when looking for a value impact on individual behaviour? Micro effects are not susceptible to the aggregation error that is typical of macro effects. Do values matter? To study the impact of values at the individual level we estimate the simultaneous effect of the four values that we have identified with control for relevant contextual factors such as education and income. We start with life satisfaction and go through all five individual-level dependent variables. The regression analyses are conducted in the same way as in Chapters 5 and 8 – that is, all variables are recoded to values between 0 and 1, and tested against eight different sets of samples. Our analysis of value orientations covers six countries separately as well as the total sample of countries. Do the four universalist values that we have identified have any impact on individual life satisfaction?

We find that life satisfaction at the individual level tends to go hand-in-hand with trust and individualism. Trust displays a significant impact in four of the six countries while individualism displays a significant impact everywhere except in Belgium. Individualism and trust is positively related to life satisfaction while achievement orientation has a negative sign. Postmaterialism does not seem to matter for the level of life satisfaction, whereas high income really is conducive to this outcome. We also find very clearly that postmaterialism is strongly and consistently associated with left orientations while individualism goes together with right orientations. Interpersonal trust has nothing to do with left or right, while achievement orientation, when it has impact, is associated with left orientations. The single strongest predictor appears to be postmaterialism.

Postmaterialism is strongly and consistently positively related with a dependent variable – this time political interest. No other value variable displays any consistent impact on political interest. Together with gender and education, postmaterialist values are good predictors of political interest. Postmaterialist orientations in general have a positive impact on political interest. The same is true for level of education and age. Political interest as it has been operationalized here – 'How interested would you say you are in politics?' – is generally more a matter for men than for women.

There are no distinct patterns to detect when it comes to the impact of value orientations on membership of organizations. We know that old age and more education is conducive to such membership. The same is also true of postmaterialism, but it is not consistently so. If trust values have any importance, it is positive for membership. Individualism, on the other hand, is positively related in some cases and negatively related in others. Therefore, we may draw the conclusion that values do not matter that much for engagement in voluntary organizations.

Trust and postmaterialism are both positively related to joining boycotts. This impact of values on joining boycotts is fairly obvious in Belgium and Spain, while such an impact more or less fails to appear in India and Russia. Joining boycotts as a kind of non-traditional form of political action is probably more accepted in Western countries than in countries like Russia and India. In addition to postmaterialism and trust, education and age also have an impact on this kind of political activity.

*Summary*

Based on the many findings from the regression analyses we may establish that values matter for individual-level outcomes. There is, however, also a variation between countries as well as between values when it comes to the impact of values on the individual-level outcomes. We summarize our findings in Table 10.11 which gives information about the number of significant coefficients estimated when controlling for contextual factors like education, income, gender and age.

Postmaterialist values and individualism matter more than achievement orientation. The direct impact of trust is limited. The various outcome variables are almost equally affected by values. The impact of values also seems to be stronger in Spain than in the other countries, but there is no country where values are irrelevant for individual behaviour like life satisfaction, left–right orientation or political interest.

## Conclusion

Values may impact on macro or micro outcomes. After presenting evidence about the effects of values at both the macro and the micro level we conclude that values do matter but more so on the micro than on the macro level. At the

**Table 10.11    Number of significant regression coefficients estimated for the impact of micro values by country and by dependent variables**

| Values | Distributed by country | | | | | | |
|---|---|---|---|---|---|---|---|
| | Belgium | Spain | USA | Switzer-land | India | Russia | Total |
| Trust | 2 | 3 | 2 | 2 | 1 | 3 | 13 |
| Postmat | 4 | 3 | 3 | 4 | 4 | 3 | 21 |
| Achieve | 0 | 5 | 2 | 1 | 2 | 2 | 11 |
| Indiv | 3 | 5 | 2 | 2 | 3 | 2 | 17 |
| Total | 9 | 16 | 9 | 9 | 10 | 9 | 62 |

| Values | Distributed by dependent variable | | | | | |
|---|---|---|---|---|---|---|
| | Life satisfaction | Left–right orientation | Political Interest | Voluntary organiz-ations | Joining boycotts | Total |
| TRUST | 4 | 0 | 2 | 2 | 5 | 13 |
| POSTMAT | 1 | 6 | 6 | 3 | 5 | 21 |
| ACHIEVE | 3 | 2 | 2 | 3 | 1 | 11 |
| INDIV | 5 | 4 | 3 | 3 | 2 | 17 |
| Total | 13 | 12 | 13 | 11 | 13 | 62 |

*Note*:    This information is based on a number of estimations not reported here.

macro level these universal values are strongly associated with gender equality. But since affluence and values go together, the causal relation is probably from the former to the latter. Postmaterialism is most probably a consequence of affluence.

At the individual level we have stronger evidence in order for the conclusion that values do matter. This is particularly true of value orientations such as postmaterialism or individualism. In comparison with the impact of other factors, the impact of values is less impressive but there are still clear value effects. The micro-level effects are better confirmed than the macro-level impacts. Values are basically part of the mental apparatus of single individuals and they play a role in determining the behaviour of individual persons.

The general finding is thus that values matter since they have impact on micro-level outcomes. Thus, we have further support for the thesis that 'culture matters', although we may not draw any firm conclusion about whether values matter more than ethnicity or religion. So far we are satisfied to have established that values have an impact on outcomes. The concluding chapter will attempt to summarize our findings with respect to the impact of culture on political and socioeconomic outcomes.

# Chapter 11

# Gender (Sex) as a
# Major Cultural Cleavage

## Introduction

Today, the politics of gender as well as the politics of homosexuality constitute a major new cleavage in advanced societies with a post-modern culture. This chapter presents a new analysis of this political cleavage and shows that gender and homosexuality attitudes are linked at the micro level. At the macro level, sex as a cleavage is strongly embedded in culture and civilisation. David Rayside presents his analysis of the politics of achieving gay and lesbian equality under the title *On The Fringe* (1998). Recent events in both Western Europe and the US have shown that the politics of sex is no longer merely a fringe pgenomenon. In order to understand the force of the new politics of gender and homosexuality, one should enquire into the value orientations that support the new public policies and changes in law.

It is often underlined in cultural approaches that sex is socially constructed, at least with post-modernist writers. Some even go so far as to claim that sex is more or less culturally embedded. Although it is a safer bet to say that sex is mainly based upon biology including homosexuality and lesbianism, it still remains an interesting question for social research to look at sex from the perspective of cultural analysis. We will argue that its is the value orientations towards gender equality and recognition of gay and lesbians that are culturally determined.

Sex may be looked upon as a new forthcoming cleavages in the post-modern society. Sex and politics have become intertwined in a few highly salient issues pertaining to gender and homosexuality as well as their recognition in politics. In this chapter we will pose a few elementary questions concerning the occurrence of sex as a cultural cleavage in advanced societies. Politics has responded quickly to issues concerning gender and homosexuality, endorsing the principle of gender equality strongly while reacting to demands for state recognition of homosexuality with much more hesitance.

## Value Orientations Towards Sex as a Cultural Cleavage

Sex becomes culturally defined through citizen attitudes towards gender and homosexuality. A central question for future research is whether these attitudes towards sex merely restate more fundamental value orientations in the post-modern society, such as post-materialism or individualism. Drawing upon the extensive survey research from many countries one may offer some new information about attitudes towards sex, either in the form of macro data or in the form of micro data.

Two questions, one macro and the other a mirco question, figure prominently in the research upon gender, namely first: (Q1) Do countries differ in terms of gender equality? If so, why? This is a macro problem where one would wish to identify the country factors, which are conducive towards a culture of gender equality. Gender equality may be tapped through a host of social indicators and one may theorize that a number of conditions – economic, social and political – play a role for explaining why some countries are characterized by more of gender equality than others. The second question amounts to a micro problem: (Q2) Do individuals who value gender equality have a distinct set of social attitudes? This is a problem for micro research to be answered by means of surveys. The same macro and micro questions may be raised in relation to homosexuality and lesbianism.

We will examine below several aspects of sex as a cultural cleavage, including: (a) Is there a marked difference between men and women when it comes to the attitude towards gender equality? (b) Does the attitude towards gender equality matter for social values? We start with the macro question, probing into a few determinants of the country variation in gender equality. Then we will turn to the micro question where we will employ the same research strategy that was used in the analysis of values above. In the literature there is a number of indicators upon gender development and gender attitude – see *Rising Tide: Gender Equality and Cultural Change Around The World* (2003) by R. Inglehart and P. Norris.

To measure sex as a set of cultural cleavages, we employ the following two types of indicators: (1) *Macro indices*: For measuring gender equality at the macro level across countries we employ: (a) Gender-related development index (GDI) as it has been developed by the UNDP team producing the annual Human Development Report – from 1995 it contains the GDI. Briefly GDI measures the relative position of females to males with respect to life expectancy, education and standard of living. (b) Gender empowerment measure (GEM) was also first presented in 1995 and it is a composite index on gender inequality in relation to 'economic participation and decision-making, political participation and decision-making and power over economic resources' (UNDP 2004 270). (c) Female representation in parliament measured as the percentage of women in parliament (second chamber if a bicameral system) (WOMAN). These three measures will refer to data for the early years of the 21$^{st}$ century, i.e. around 2000 to 2004.

In addition to these three macro based indices, we will also use: (2) *Micro index*: We will use a micro derived index on gender equality, based on aggregated attitudes on gender issues, available from the 3rd and 4th wave of the World Values Studies (Inglehart et al. 2000 and 2004) (Gender Equality Index; GEQ ). The items employed for constructing the index are the following ones: On the whole, men make better political leaders than women do (strongly disagree); When jobs are scarce, men should have more right to a job than women (strongly disagree); A university education is more important for a boy than for a girl (strongly disagree); A woman has to have children in order to be fulfilled (strongly disagree); If a woman wants to have a child as a single parent but she doesn't want to have a stable relationship with a man, do you approve or disapprove? (Strongly approve) (cf Inglehart and Norris 2003b: 69). The variables have been recoded so that a positive value stands for gender equality and then a factor analysis has been employed to arrive at a gender equality index; the same procedure has been applied for the 3rd (1995–97) and 4th (1999–2002) waves of the WVS. Since the scores for the two periods strongly covary predicted scores based on the 3rd wave will be used as the country scores in the forthcoming analysis.

Figure 11.1 gives the size of the groups with different orientations towards gender equality, drawing upon the entire sample from all the countries within the VWS.

Figure 11.1 indicates that in advanced countries there is a cleavage between those who strongly endorse (3 + 4) and those who are hesitant or negative

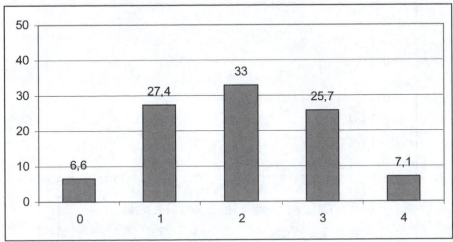

*Note:* The GEQ index has been rescaled in the following way: 0 = lowest thru – 1.5; 1 = – 1.5 thru –0.5; 2 = –0.5 thru 0.5; 3 = 0.5 thru 1.5; and 1.5 thru highest; weighted N = 46 564.

*Sources:* See Appendix 11.1.

**Figure 11.1    Opinions on gender equality (GEQ) (percentages)**

(0 + 1). We assume now that the basic attitude towards acceptance of homosexuality is connected with the gender equality orientation. To validate this assumption about a basic sex cleavage in advanced countries we employ the VWS.

In order to derive an index of value orientation towards homosexuality, we employ a micro based indicator in order to construct macro scores. For attitudes towards homosexuality we employ the following response item from the WVS: Please tell me whether you think it can always be justified, never be justified, or something in between: homosexuality (scores from 1 (=never justifiable) to 10 (=always justifiable). The advantages of the micro based indices on gender and homosexuality is that they allow for both macro and micro enquiries into the sources of such value orientations. Figure 11.2 shows the distribution in the entire sample of respondents in all countries concerning the orientation towards homosexuality.

Let us now enquire into these two value orientations, gender on the one hand and homosexuality on the other hand, and attempt to find some of their determinants, either on the macro level (countries) or with micro data (individuals).

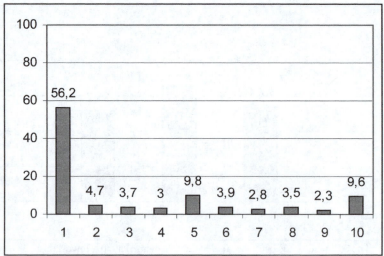

*Note*:     The scale goes from 1 (=never justifiable) to 10 (=always justifiable); weighted
            N = 85 853.
*Sources*: See Appendix 11.1.

**Figure 11.2     Opinion on justifiablity of homosexuality (percentages)**

## Gender

There is available in the literature a few indices, macro or micro based, which all tap the overall position of women in society, especially when compared with men. One may consider them as gender equality indices, which take into account the rights of women from an economic or political point of view. They may measure the position of women in general or the position of women among the elites. These indices all indicate considerable country variation, which calls for an enquiry into the factors, which are conducive to gender differences.

*Gender: The Macro View*

In general, the different measures on gender equality tend to go together. Two figures will illustrate. The first one shows the relation between GEM and GDI, while the second one captures how the WVS-index relates to the GEM. When gender is measured by means of macro-based indices, then one arrives at a picture of considerable country differences – see Figure 11.3.

GEM and GDI take into account a number of aspects of the position of women in society. These two indices show a coherent country variation that

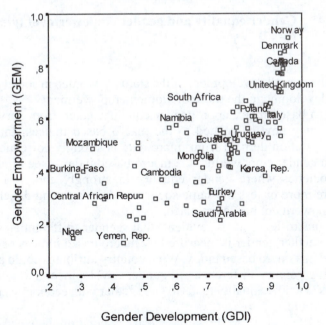

Gender Development (GDI)

*Sources*: See Appendix 11.2.

**Figure 11.3    Gender development and gender empowerment (r=.725; N=102)**

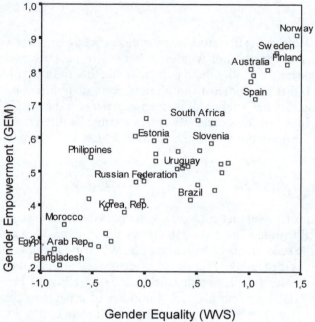

Gender Equality (WVS)

*Sources*: See Appendix 11.2.

**Figure 11.4    Gender equality and gender empowerment (r=.856; N=47)**

expresses the overall development of the status of women in society: the more of gender development, the more of women empowerment.

The micro based index upon gender equality, taken from survey data in the WVS), may now be related to the macro based indices. Interestingly, the macro variation derived from micro data is strongly correlated with the variation in gender empowerment, a macro based index – see Figure 11.4.

Thus, societies where gender equality in strongly endorsed in citizen attitudes are more or less the same societies where a strong development of gender empowerment has taken place.

At the macro-level it is evident that gender differentiates between countries, whether gender is measured by macro based indices or attitudinal data as used in a micro based index. What country attributes could account for these striking country differences in gender development and gender value orientations? Gender equality tends to go together with economic and cultural factors, we argue.

Figures 11.5 and 11.6 show the clear association between economic modernization on the one hand and gender position and gender value orientations on the other hand.

The association between economic affluence (GDP) and gender value

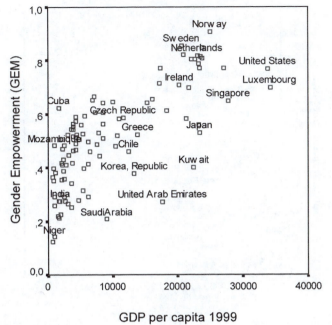

GDP per capita 1999

*Sources*: See Appendix 11.2.

**Figure 11.5      GDP and GEM (r=.725; N=103)**

orientations is somewhat weaker than the association between GDP and gender position – compare Figures 11.5 and 11.6.

We wish to underline that gender equality is not only driven by the requirements of a modern economy. In addition, there is the acceptance of a set of values, which deny the social relevance of gender differences. Thus, the spread of gender values is conditioned by cultural factors, at least to some extent, one would be inclined to argue. Table 11.1 contains the evidence of the test of a number of cultural hypotheses about gender inequalities: religion, historical legacies and family system. Protestant countries support gender equality Muslim countries support gender inequality. Countries with an Iberian (Spain and Portugal and their former colonies) legacy would support gender inequality more than countries with a different cultural tradition. Countries with a collectivist family system would render less support to gender equality than countries with an individualist family structure, all other things equal.

Asking which cultural factor matters most for gender inequality, Table 11.1 reports on the test of a few correlations which link gender equality with culture: Protestantism, Islam, an Iberian legacy and a collectivist family system. The correlation matrix displayed in Table 11.1 suggests that Protestantism tend to be associated with higher scores on gender equality

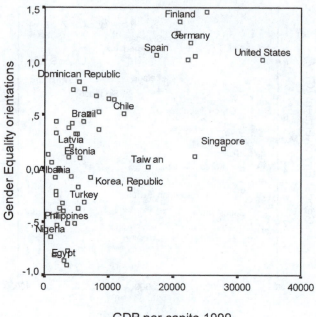

GDP per capita 1999

*Sources*: See Appendix 11.2.

**Figure 11.6    GDP and gender equality (r=.651; N=57)**

**Table 11.1    Gender equality and cultural factors: Pearson's correlation**

| Cultural factors | Correlation | GEM | WOM | GDI | GEQ |
|---|---|---|---|---|---|
| Protestantism (LN) | r | .493 | .344 | .002 | .597 |
| | sig. | .000 | .000 | .978 | .000 |
| | N | 103 | 144 | 137 | 57 |
| Islam (LN) | r | −.591 | −.368 | −.369 | −.620 |
| | sig. | .000 | .000 | .000 | .000 |
| | N | 103 | 144 | 137 | 57 |
| Iberian legacy | r | .106 | .187 | .150 | .398 |
| | sig. | .308 | .031 | .093 | .003 |
| | N | 94 | 132 | 127 | 52 |
| Family system (Todd) | r | .714 | .364 | .772 | .679 |
| | sig. | .000 | .000 | .000 | .000 |
| | N | 103 | 144 | 138 | 57 |

*Sources*: See Appendix 11.2.

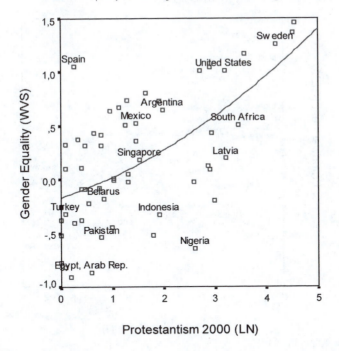

**Figure 11.7   Protestantism and gender equality (GEQ) (r=.597; N=57)**

whereas countries with a high proportion of Muslims tend to score lower on gender equality. Type of family system also covaries strongly with gender equality, while an Iberian colonial legacy *per se* does not tend to correlate with gender inequality.

The findings in Table 11.1 confirm the often-repeated argument that modernisation, expressed in strong gender equality, has cultural sources. Figure 11.7 shows this cultural impact between one world religion and gender and Figure 11.8 shows this cultural impact for another world religion.

Gender inequalities tend to be great in developing countries reflecting a low level of economic development, but the traditional status of women, as reinforced by religion and the family system, also matters. Thus, the strong associations in the figures above come as no surprise. This is all macro analysis. One may wish to complement the macro view with a micro analysis of the sources of gender value orientations. Thus, we rely exclusively upon the WVS data, which may be used for a micro enquiry into which individuals support strong gender equality.

*Gender Orientations: The Micro View*

One may research attitudes towards gender equality by means of data from several surveys Gender equality is considered a basic value in a post-modern

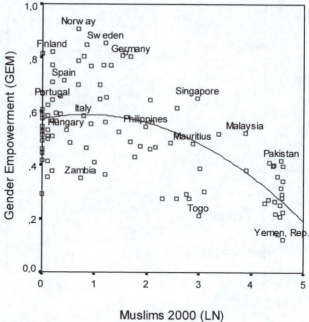

*Sources*: See Appendix 11.2.

**Figure 11.8    Islam and gender empowerment (GEM) (r=-.591; N=103)**

society, advocated by strong pressure groups including the feminist movement. This could give a micro foundation to the macro analysis of gender inequality. In the World Value Surveys a number of questions were asked about attitudes towards gender, where the responses may be employed for the construction of an index covering the individual attitude towards gender equality. Let us first see whether sex itself is related to gender attitudes. Table 11.2 has information about sex and gender attitude. At the individual level we employ the gender equality index constructed from five items of the World Values Survey. Let us first establish how the gender equality orientation is associated with gender, age, education and income. The outcome of a bivariate correlation analysis is reported in Table 11.2 below.

Based on the 4th wave of the VWS it appears that education and gender seems to correlate more with gender orientations than what is the case for income and age.

The next step is to enquire into what impact value orientations may have upon gender orientations. This impact will be estimated through the employment of regression analysis. The gender orientation index will be the dependent variable whereas different value orientations will be captured by variables measuring the survival/self-expression values, traditional/secular

**Table 11.2 Gender orientation and gender, age, education and income: eta correlations**

| Gender | | Age | | Education | | Income | |
|---|---|---|---|---|---|---|---|
| Group | GEQ score | Group | GEQ score | Group | GEQ score | Group | GEQ score |
| Male | -.165 | 15–29 yrs | .052 | Lower | -.292 | Lower | -.160 |
| Female | .165 | 30–49 yrs | -.011 | Middle | .151 | Middle | .035 |
| | | 50+ yrs | -.056 | Upper | .288 | Upper | .127 |
| Eta | .165 | Eta | .042 | Eta | .245 | Eta | .120 |

*Sources*: See Appendix 11.1.

rational values, post-materialist orientations and an autonomy orientation index. The regression model estimated also includes the variables used in the previous correlation analysis: gender, age, education and income. The outcome of the regression analysis is displayed in Table 11.3.

The findings from the regression analysis suggest that value orientations of self-expression and secular rational values go together with gender equality orientations. This is also the case for post-materialism, but to a lesser extent. It is also striking that gender and education matters more than age and income when analysing these value orientations at the individual level.

**Table 11.3 Regression: gender value orientations (GEQ) and value orientations, gender, age, education and income (WVS 4th wave 1999–2002)**

| Independent variables | Regression coefficient | t-stat |
|---|---|---|
| Survival/self-expression | .331 | 58.18 |
| Traditional/secular rational | .319 | 53.79 |
| Gender | .380 | 37.08 |
| Age | -.031 | -4.46 |
| Education | .128 | 17.21 |
| Income | .022 | 3.34 |
| Constant | -.554 | -19.24 |
| R square | .227 | |
| N | 30289 | |

*Sources*: See Appendix 11.1.

**Table 11.4　Attitudes to homosexuals and gender, age, education and income: eta correlations**

| Gender | | Age | | Education | | Income | |
|---|---|---|---|---|---|---|---|
| Group | Homosex. | Group | Homosex. | Group | Homosex. | Group | Homosex. |
| Male | 3.07 | 15–29 yrs | 3.51 | Lower | 2.77 | Lower | 2.85 |
| Female | 3.48 | 30–49 yrs | 3.36 | Middle | 3.370 | Middle | 3.21 |
| | | 50 + yrs | 2.94 | Upper | 4.05 | Upper | 3.60 |
| Eta | .066 | Eta | .072 | Eta | .149 | Eta | .097 |

*Sources*: See Appendix 11.1.

## Homosexuality and Lesbianism

Value orientations condition public policy, at least in the long run. Thus, the growing political saliency of homosexuality would be impossible without value change in the basic attitudes towards sex in the population. Let us look at the support for homosexuality, first with individuals and second at the macro level. The micro sources of a positive evaluation of homosexuality are found in Table 11.4.

*The Micro View*

That culture matters for homosexuality is strongly confirmed in Table 11.5.

**Table 11.5　Regression: attitudes to homosexuals and value orientations, gender, age, education and income (WVS 4th wave 1999–2002)**

| Independent variables | Regression coefficient | t-stat |
|---|---|---|
| Traditional/secular rational | 1.149 | 73.90 |
| Gender Equality orientation (GEQ) | .748 | 52.98 |
| Post-Materialist | .530 | 24.24 |
| Gender | .097 | 3.64 |
| Age | −.067 | −3.98 |
| Education | −.048 | −2.51 |
| Income | .039 | 2.26 |
| Constant | 2.146 | 25.90 |
| R square | .310 | |
| N | 30289 | |

*Sources*: See Appendix 11.1

**Table 11.6   Attitudes to homosexuals and cultural factors: Pearson's correlation**

| Cultural factors | Correlation | Attitudes to homosexuals |
|---|---|---|
| Protestantism (LN) | r | .475 |
| | sig. | .000 |
| | N | 77 |
| Islam (LN) | r | -.484 |
| | sig. | .000 |
| | N | 77 |
| aIberian legacy | r | .109 |
| | sig. | .371 |
| | N | 69 |
| Family system (Todd) | r | .762 |
| | sig. | .000 |
| | N | 77 |

*Sources*: See Appendix 11.2.

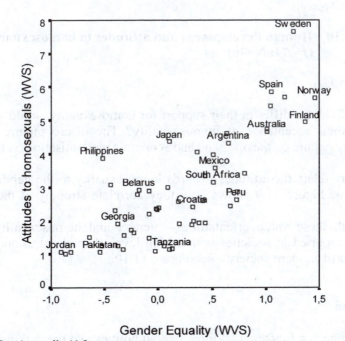

*Sources*: See Appendix 11.2.

**Figure 11.9   Gender equality orientations (GEQ) and attitudes to homosexuals (r=.78; N=56)**

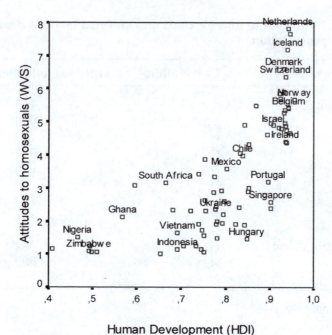

*Sources*: See Appendix 11.2.

**Figure 11.10   Human development and attitudes to homosexuality
              (r=.74; N=76)**

*The Macro View*

Just as individuals differ in their support for homosexuality, so do societies
differ in their acceptance of homosexuality? The macro picture is well
captured by culture on the one hand and economic modernisation on the other
hand.

   One may relate the attitudes towards homosexuality to the gender value
orientations. Figure 11.9 shows how they correlate strongly at the macro
level.

   But both these value orientations – gender and homosexuality – are
strongly supported in societies with a high level of modernization and the
so-called post-modern society – see Figure 11.10.

**Conclusion**

Value change is a fundamental force behind politics and the making of new
public policy. The policies towards women empowerment and the acceptance
of homosexuality in law would not have come about without the powerful
currents of value orientations among citizens supporting these developments.

There is a cleavage in advanced societies between those who endorse the new politics of sex as against those who oppose it. Attitudes towards gender and homosexuality are connected at the micro level. And their occurrence on the macro level is strongly embedded in major cultural aspects of society.

*Appendix 11.1   Micro-level data used in Chapter 11*

| Abbreviation | Description | Variables in Inglehart et al. 2004 |
|---|---|---|
| AGE | Age group; recoded as: 15–29 = 1, 30–49 = 2, 50+ = 3 | V225(x003r2) |
| EDUCATION | Educational level; recoded as: lower = 1, middle = 2, upper = 3 | V226(x025r) |
| GENDER | Gender as a dummy variable; male = 1, female = 2 | V223(x001) |
| GEQ | Gender equality orientation index achieved thru applying a factor analysis on five items | V78(c001(recoded)), V110(d019(recoded)), V112(d023(recoded)), V118(d059), V119(d060) |
| HOMOSEXUALS | Justifiability of homosexuality going from never (=1) to always (=10) | V208(f118) |
| INCOME | Income level; recoded as: lower = 1, middle = 2, upper = 3 | V236(x047r) |
| Post-materialist orientation | Postmaterialism orientation index based on four items | y002 |
| Survival/Self-expression orientation | Index measuring survival vs. self-expression values; see Inglehart and Baker 2000: 24 for the construction of the index | survself |
| Traditional/secular rational orientation | Index measuring traditional vs. secular-rational values; see Inglehart and Baker 2000: 24 for the construction of the index | tradrat5 |

*Appendix 11.2   Macro-level data used in Chapter 11*

| Abbreviation | Description | Sources |
| --- | --- | --- |
| Family system | Classification of countries as belonging to family types according to degree of individualism where the absolute nuclear family scores high and the African family system score low | Based on Todd (1983) |
| GDI | Gender-related development index; based on estimations for different number of years | UNDP (2000–2004) |
| GDP 1999 | GDP per capita expressed as PPP in US$ | CIA (2000) |
| GEM | Gender empowerment measure; based on estimations for different number of years | UNDP (2000–2004) |
| GEQ | Gender equality index; aggregated to the national level, based on both the 3rd and the 4th wave of WVS | Inglehart et al. 2000, 2004 |
| HDI | Human development index; based on estimations for different number of years | UNDP (2000–2004) |
| HOMOSEXUALS | Attitudes to homosexuals aggregated to the national level, based on both 3rd and the 4th wave of WVS | Inglehart et al. 2000, 2004 |
| Iberian legacy | Legacy of Iberian colonial rule as a dummy variable where 1 = Iberian legacy, 0 = no such legacy | Based on de Blij (1996, pp. 496–97) |
| Islam (LN) | Percentage of the population estimated to adhere to the Muslim creed around 2000; natural logarithm | Barrett et al 2001 |
| Protestantism (LN) | Percentage of the population estimated to adhere to the Protestant creed around 2000; natural logarithm | Barrett et al 2001 |

# Chapter 12

# Conclusion:
# The Impact of Culture on Outcomes

## Introduction

It is time to pull together the various arguments in the cultural approach presented in the chapters above. We wish to underline a few of the findings made in these chapters. What does it all add up to? We started out from the often stated claim that 'culture matters'. Our approach was that this assumption or conclusion should be explicitly researched by making it more specific and thus testable by the ordinary canons of scientific discovery. To us, the statement 'culture matters' is incomplete, as one needs to specify which culture impacts on what outcome. Only if rephrased in this manner can the newly emerging cultural approach framework become a competitor to the prevailing rational choice approach.

It is hardly accidental that the cultural approach framework developed strongly in the 1990s. Cultural identity and the role of communities are highly relevant topics in the postmodern age. Nowadays, culture is married to politics to an extent that was not visible during the twentieth century and communities are as important as associations in political life in many countries and even more important in a few. We observe the main manifestations of cultural politics and the communalization of political life in the following trends:

1  the renewed interest in ethnicity and religion;
2  the steadily increase in social heterogeneity – multiculturalism;
3  the surging attention paid to values in life;
4  the growth of diasporas around the world;
5  the increase in the legitimacy of the claims of historical minorities;
6  the efforts at the constitutionalization of the multicultural society.

The communal revolution in politics has been a most vital aspect of the coming of a postmodern age where questions of meaning and identity preoccupy peoples' minds. It goes hand-in-hand with globalization, but these trends have different sources. Paradoxically, globalization both puts brakes upon cultural politics and promotes it through its recognition of minority rights. Globalization is at a stage of development when the interdependencies between the economies of the countries of the world have reached a level at which institutional integration is starting to take place on both a regional or global level. In the first stage of globalization the flows of trade and financial capital take on dramatically increased proportions with the help of the technological revolution in the 'new economy'. In the second stage of globalization, there is a search for institutions to channel these interactions, which requires a common understanding bridging cultural differences. Perhaps the third stage will be the creation of a world culture or a set of world cultures?

## The Findings

Cultural politics has its limits. In order to substantiate how culture matters and for what culture matters, we interpret the new cultural theories according to the following format:

(CT) Culture X matters for outcome Y

where we wish to replace the X and the Y with determinate cultures and outcomes while arriving at the same time at the occurrence of a cultural effect. We have favoured a quantitative approach when testing models in the cultural approach framework, which entails methodologically that the cultural impacts that we establish are confirmed by either correlation or regression evidence.

We have inquired systematically into cultural effects, a cultural effect being said to occur when a different culture displays different outcomes. The cultural thesis (CT) is far more problematic than most cultural theories. Outcomes in society and politics depend on several factors, one of which is culture. The set of cultural factors consists, we suggest, of ethnicity, religion, legacies or values. Any model of a cultural impact must specify both the cultural factor involved and the outcome studied.

The overall finding in this examination and evaluation of the key cultural models suggested in the literature is twofold. On the one hand, there is no general and diffuse cultural determination of behaviour or outcomes. On the other hand, the evidence shows a number of specific cultural effects. Cultural phenomena may be said to be of utmost importance, but this is mainly true from an intrinsic point of view. Extrinsically, a variation in culture far from always brings about a change in outcomes. Let us attempt to present a systematic overview of our specific findings with respect to the cultural thesis. At issue is the impact of cultural factors on different outcomes at different micro or macro outcomes. We start this overview by looking at the impact of cultural factors at the three analytical levels that we have inquired into and then we discuss each cultural factor.

**Table 12.1 The macro level: impact of culture on political and socioeconomic outcome variables – number of significant regression coefficients**

| Culture | Dependent variables | | | | | | |
|---|---|---|---|---|---|---|---|
| | HDI 99 | GEM 99 | GINI 90 | DEM 97 | CORR 98 | LnPPP 97 | GRO 9098 |
| Ethnicity | 2 | 0 | 2 | 0 | 0 | 0 | 0 |
| Religion | 1 | 2 | 1 | 2 | 2 | 0 | 2 |
| Legacies | 0 | 0 | 2 | 1 | 0 | 1 | 0 |
| Values | 1 | 1 | 0 | 0 | 0 | 1 | 0 |
| Contexts | 2 | 2 | 1 | 2 | 2 | 2 | 1 |

*Note*: This information is partly based on a number of estimations not reported here.

*The Macro Level*

The analyses conducted at the macro level have been the broadest in terms of cultural factors covered and the set of outcome variables included. The employment of regression analysis has made it possible to estimate the relative impact of various cultural factors, as well as a number of contextual factors such as history and geography. Admitting that the specification of the models in the analysis is important for the findings and that model specification can be done in different ways, we still find it meaningful to attempt to distinguish between culture and other causal factors with respect to their impact on key outcome variables. Table 12.1 presents an overview of our findings, partly based on what has been previously reported and partly based on model estimations not reported here.

The information on findings in Table 12.1 shows that cultural factors have a certain impact on macro outcomes. Religion matters at this level more than values. Religions and ethnic fragmentation has a negative impact on macro outcomes, which presents multicultural societies with a true challenge in the future. The major linguistic families are still accompanied by differences in socioeconomic performance and democracy. We are very sceptical about the strong claims concerning the macro consequences of values in the literature. Yet, it is also important to note that other contextual factors seem to matter as much as the cultural factors. Thus, culture, and in particular ethnicity and religion, matter, but other factors such as social structure, institutions and time do also have an impact. Religion impacts more on social and political outcomes than on economic outcomes. Had Weber lived today, then he would have seen the link between human rights and Protestantism.

**Table 12.2   The regional level: impact of culture on party support –
number of significant coefficients estimated**

| Culture | Countries where party support is a dependent variable | | | | |
|---|---|---|---|---|---|
| | USA | Spain | Switzerland | Belgium | India |
| Ethnicity | 2 | 2 | 1 | 1 | 2 |
| Religion | 2 | 2 | 2 | 1 | 0 |
| Contexts | 2 | 0 | 0 | 1 | 0 |

*Note*:   This information is partly based upon a number of estimations not reported here.

### The Regional Level

The analyses conducted at the regional level have been narrower in scope, as only one kind of outcome – party support at the regional level – has been addressed. At the same time several variables measuring two kinds of cultural factor – ethnicity and religion – were employed in the analyses. The findings support the idea that culture has an impact on the regional level, according to the overview of the findings presented in Table 12.2.

From Table 12.2 we conclude that cultural factors are highly relevant in explaining the variation in party support at the regional level, especially in so-called divided societies. Ethnicity may be as important as religion, although the impact of these two kinds of culture varies depending on which country the analysis refers to. Thus, religion matters more in the USA than in India. Similarly, religion matters more than ethnicity in Switzerland, while the opposite is true in Russia. Moreover, ethnicity and religion both have a strong impact in Belgium and Spain. Again, we may conclude that culture matters, but that its impact varies between countries.

### The Micro Level

The micro-level analysis, which was very broad in its range, covered a number of different outcomes referring to the political behaviour of citizens. The independent cultural variables employed include ethnicity, religion and values. In order to draw correct conclusions about the impact of various factors on the dependent variables we have controlled for the impact of the contextual variables such as age, gender, education and income. Table 12.3 reports, in a compressed form, the findings for the six countries selected in our sample; they contain information about the number of significant coefficients estimated for the five dependent variables referring to political behaviour – that is, interest in politics, life satisfaction, left–right orientation, membership of organizations and political protest action.

**Table 12.3** **The micro level: impact of the independent variables on the dependent variables – number of significant coefficients when control of other cultural variables has been introduced**

| Independent variables | | Belgium | Spain | USA | Switzer-land | India | Russia |
|---|---|---|---|---|---|---|---|
| Values: | TRUST | 1 | 2 | 2 | 1 | 1 | 1 |
| | POSTMAT | 3 | 0 | 5 | 3 | 2 | 0 |
| | ACHIEVE | 0 | 0 | 0 | 0 | 2 | 0 |
| | INDIV | 3 | 2 | 3 | 2 | 4 | 1 |
| Ethnicity: | NATPRIDE | 3 | 1 | 3 | 4 | 2 | 1 |
| | ETHNIC | 3 | 0 | 1 | 4 | 2 | 0 |
| Religion: | RELSERV | 2 | 2 | 5 | 4 | 0 | 1 |
| | DENOM | 2 | 1 | 1 | 1 | 1 | 0 |
| Contexts: | EDUCAT | 3 | 2 | 4 | 4 | 3 | 3 |
| | INCOME | 3 | 3 | 4 | 3 | 3 | 2 |
| | GENDER | 3 | 1 | 2 | 3 | 3 | 1 |
| | AGE | 3 | 1 | 4 | 2 | 2 | 3 |

*Note*: This information is based on a number of estimations not reported here.

The impact of the value variables is reduced when a control for other independent variables is introduced, but we still have evidence concerning several value effects. Postmaterialism and individualism matter most, while the impact of the achievement orientation is strongly reduced. It is hardly a surprise that the contextual variables seem to matter more than values for these individual-level outcomes. Comparing the outcomes for the six countries we may note that values matter more in countries such as the USA and India than in Russia. Thus, the conclusion from the individual-level analysis is that values matter, but that there are other factors that matter more for life satisfaction, left–right orientation and political activity. Religion remains a powerful conservative force in people's behaviour.

**Comparing the Impact of Cultural Factors**

Let us finally assess the thesis (CT) or 'culture matters' in relation to the four cultural factors that have been covered in our analysis. What is the evidence in favour of the new cultural theories which claim that ethnicity, religion, values and historical legacies, matter a great deal for society and politics?

*Ethnicity*

The old misused concept of a race is not without relevance when examining whether culture matters. The Western language families have a clear lead over other races in terms of development. Having said this, it must immediately be stated that, today, the occidental countries are highly multicultural. Moreover, the advancedness of these countries is a historical advantage that is cumulative.

The ethnic impact is most visible in plural or divided societies where ethnic cleavages take on a regional dimension. In countries like Spain, Belgium and India, ethnic fragmentation surfaces in the regional variation in electoral support for parties, meaning that electoral support is highly skewed for or against a party depending on the region. Ethnicity understood as national pride also matters for the micro level.

*Religion*

We have not been able to confirm the Weber's theory that economic progress can be predicted on the basis of the world religions, with Protestantism being linked with economic growth. On the contrary, we found that Buddhism/ Confucianism had a beneficial effect on economic growth. The advantage with Protestantism appears in relation to human rights. Religion also seems to matter most when there are religious cleavages within a country on a regional basis. Thus, religious fragmentation may destabilize democracy. Religious cleavages show up in regional party outcomes. At the micro level, religion plays a conservative role, as religious orientations matter more than belonging to a religious denomination. Religion is more important in countries like the USA and Switzerland than in India or in Russia.

*Historical Legacies*

Cultural theory has been suggested as a means of accounting for the recent surge in communal politics, as it seems highly applicable to phenomena that have emerged during the last 20 years. However, one could also look at cultures as collective memories of a long narrative which impacts on people today. Perhaps the most debated theory about the impact of cultural tradition is the one which claims that the Spanish heritage has more adverse effects than the Anglo-Saxon one, or at least that it does not promote the same degree of development. We have broadened this interest in how the past weighs upon the present by examining all colonial traditions.

Although traces of historical traditions may be discernable in the present, colonial legacies do not determine the world today. Countries with no colonial experience have a developmental advantage over countries that had to go through the process of colonization and decolonisation. It is also true that British colonial rule had less negative repercussions than the other forms of colonial rule, except the Danish case of Greenland. However, it is not possible to claim that Western domination produced the often dismal predicament in several Third World countries today. And the Spanish legacy seems to be less detrimental than the Soviet heritage, for example.

Family traditions may also be interpreted as a kind of historical legacy. It is only possible to trace them to the macro level and, at that level, family systems impact on a number of macro-level outcomes, especially democracy. Individualism in the family culture is more congruent with constitutional democracy than collectivism.

*Values*

In the last 20 years cultural research has opened up a new gigantic field of inquiry – namely, the value orientations of citizens in democracies, especially the Western ones. The analysis of cultures is no longer confined to historical traditions, ethnicity and religion, as was the case during the years when anthropology was the chief discipline within this area. The access to massive amounts of survey data, the collapse of the ideologies of the twentieth century after the fall of the Berlin Wall, the emergence of postmodernism and its search for meaning – all these things have made values research highly relevant in political science.

Thus far, three major theories of values have been launched in order to account for the many phenomena that are subsumed under the label 'new politics'. To us, they all deal with aspects or facets of the same things – namely, the rise of individualism in the occidental countries. The common core is the loosening grip of inherited belief systems such as nationalism, the world religions as well as the political ideologies that emerged from the French revolution – that is, conservatism, liberalism and socialism. The new value orientations answer questions about the meaning of life in the postindustrial society.

If ways of life constitute the essence of the behaviour of human beings, as culture theory claims, and not the maximization of self-interests as claimed by the rational choice framework, then which are the main ways of life that compete in the postindustrial society for the allegiance of individuals? The cultural approach framework has shown that many aspects of life are related to, or expressed in, values, but it has proven more difficult to give strong evidence for the occurrence of value effects.

The thesis that 'values matter' is much propagated in the cultural theories of postmodernism. But the empirical evidence is not yet sufficient. The distinction between macro and micro evidence is crucial. Whereas it is easy to find macro evidence of the association of values with outputs and outcomes, the general finding is that these associations are accidental when other causal factors are added to the equations. Thus, although postmaterialism may constitute an important new value orientation, it may be the postmodern age that produces postmaterialism and not vice versa. Micro-level evidence constitutes more powerful evidence when verifying that 'values matter', and we have been able to find considerable evidence to the effect that values condition individual behaviour.

## How Much Does Culture Matter?

Has globalization, understood as a process continuing and increasing over time, any impact on culture and outcomes? We have been able to establish that outcomes are fairly stable over time, and we have no clear indications suggesting that the cultural factors into which we have inquired have changed drastically over time. Thus, our tentative conclusion would be that, so far, the impact of globalization on culture and outcomes has probably been relatively weak. There are, however, other contextual factors that we have investigated. Macro contexts, such as historical and geographical factors, seem to be important for explaining the cross-country variation in macro-level outcomes. Micro contexts capturing income, education, age and gender also have a distinctive impact on the micro-level outcomes that we have inquired into. These contextual factors sometimes matters more than culture.

Although we have described all these manifestations of the rise of cultural politics, we have been unable to verify the strong claims that 'culture matters'. If the thesis about the importance of culture amounts to a more specific argument that a variation in culture and values brings about different social, economic and political outcomes, as suggested in CT, then the evidence hardly supports it. One finds specific cultural effects, but they occur less frequently than is claimed by CT.

Culture, it must be remembered, is one of several factors that explain society and politics. Other powerful explanations of outcomes include social structure and institutions. The evidence examined in these inquiries into ethnicity, religion, legacies or values do not suggest that these factors are more fundamental or important than other causes such as social structure or institutions.

Family values is one cultural factor whose effect on outcomes is very significant. Islam, Buddhism and Protestantism cannot be bypassed when the cultural sources of democracy, human development and gender development are investigated. Only corruption seems to be more dependent on social structure than culture, especially the level of affluence. However, it is true that Protestantism matters positively in relation to a low level of perceived corruption. The negative assessment of the Spanish legacy is refuted by our findings. What is clear is that Islam as a civilization scores consistently low on several of these macro outcome measures, whereas Buddhism scores low on democracy.

It may therefore be trivial to conclude that 'culture matters' while recognizing that other factors also have an impact on outcomes. 'Culture matters' does not mean that only 'culture matters'. It implies that 'culture', covering ethnicity, religion, legacies and values, need to be considered when inquiring into social, political and economic outcomes at different analytical levels.

## Muticulturalism – Its Relevance Today

One may look upon multiculturalism as a new social and political theory about the post-modern society in advanced countries, stating the relevance of culture for peoples' allegiances as well as spelling out the implications for the governance of these democracies. At present, it is a vague theory, to say the least, but it holds good promise for the future, as the rich countries of the world are in the process of a development towards more of cultural heterogeneity, as indicated in the declining relevance of nationalism everywhere. A carpet of communities derived from culture is slowly replacing the nation, and it becomes necessary to discuss what this seminal social change entails for democratic governance.

Whereas old culture theory inspired by the great anthropologists enquired into so-called primitive cultures, new culture theory explores the growing saliency of *ethnies*, of religion and of gay and lesbian communities. It maps the increase in so-called *disporans* and *ampersands* all over the post-industrial world. And it struggles with the difficult problem how a politics of mutual recognition among communities and cultures is to be reconciled with liberalism and democracy. 'Culture' is best defined as a way of life, and ways of life are established on the basis of ethnicity, religion and values, we believe. And, as Aaron Wildavsky tirelessly argued, people defend their ways of life and seek to promote their viability. Culture becomes more relevant in a post-modern society, as people search for identity beyond materialism and conventional ideologies of left and right no longer give guidance. Yet, multiculturalism has come under severe attack from various angles. Let us briefly state what is involved.

### The Critique of Multiculturalism

The message of multiculturalism at first received a resounding reception, as it seemed to fill a lacuna after the fall of the Berlin Wall and with the unsatisfactory nature of post-modern theory, overemphasizing methodology at the expense of insights into recent developments of social reality. Understanding culture and communities could benefit from the core methodology of post-modernism, viz hermeneutical interpretation or *Verstehen*, but post-modernism has more to say about subjectivism than about the emerging structure of society, focusing upon communities derived from culture. However, recently there has been forthcoming a sharp critique of multiculturalism from both the right and the left. Multiculturalism also faces the challenge of the growing religious fundamentalism and needs to distance itself from this new phenomenon in all the major world religions.

*Collision with nationalism*   One may employ Huntington's recent book in order to get a grip upon the conservative rebuttal of multiculturalism: *Who Are We? The Challenges to America's National Identity* (2004). Here, it is the tension between multiculturalism and nationalism which is the theme of a virulent attack. Massive immigration on a global scale throws up disporans and ampersands in the thousands, if not millions. And multiculturalism sanctions that these groups of people define a new relationship to the nation, which may weaken it considerably in the future, leading possibly to huge groups of citizens having ambiguous national identity, which could perhaps result in internal political instability. Huntington's fear concerns the rapidly growing Spanish speaking communities, the so-called *Latinos* in the USA.

Huntington's scepticism against diasporans and ampersands is linked with his criticism of globalization in general as producing a click of multicultural intellectuals touring the world and his strong warning against the spread of one culture, Islamic fundamentalism, in particular. It is not clear why Latinos would constitute a similar threat though, as Mexican foreign labour would not go to the US, if it was not needed in the economy. What Huntington's critique of multiculturalism brings out, however, is the fragility of the concept of a nation today. What, then, is a nation and why could *Latinos* not endorse a concept of the nation which is in agreement with their culture?

The concept of nation belongs to the cultural domain of ethnicity, but whereas one may speak without hindrance about *ethnies* it has become increasingly problematic to arrive at a tenable definition of 'nation'. There are basically only three approaches to a definition of the nation:

1   ancestry, heritage, intermarriage, common history;
2   imagined communities; myths;
3   contract, agreement upon principles.

We believe that only the contractual approach to the nation is tenable. And people thus adhere to a nation to the extent that they endorse its key principles. The biological approach founders upon the omnipresence of mulattos in every country. And the mythical approach is simply too indeterminate, as anything could count as a myth. Huntington appears to argue that there can only be one single contract regarding a nation as well as that it must exclude the endorsement of any other allegiances. Thus, disporans and ampersands are suspect people.

There is nothing inherently dangerous to national identity if people attempt to combine a host land conception with a homeland one. Diasporans and ampersands could endorse a contract for the nation and stick to it as well as other groups. It all depends upon how the contract is specified. Countries cannot expect to have one nation today. It may have to face not merely the possibility of a bi-nation society but also a multi-nation structure. To enforce a contract about the nation one need not embark upon an ambitious policy of assimilation, recreating the melting pot of the 19th and 20th centuries. It may not even be feasible, if at all desirable. Dual nationality may become much more prevalent in the 21$^{st}$ century, but its logic must be worked out in terms of law. The rise of the multicultural society is typically attended by lots of problems concerning visa, passports and citizenship. Nationalism is no longer irredentism but dual or multiple citizenship.

*Collision with freedom and equality*    The tension between multiculturalism and liberal egalitarianism or libertarianism has been explored by some critiques of communitarians and the new politics of mutual recognition. Starting from the classical trinity of values from the French Revolution – liberty, equality and fraternity, it is claimed that the latter tends to collide with the former two, especially with equality. Communities and cultures restrict the principles of equality, either equality of opportunity or equality of results. Thus, culture must bend to the priority of equality.

In reality, the tension with liberty may be just as problematic for multiculturalism. Cultures may not only restrict equality but also the freedom of people to choose their community and to debate their culture. One may speak of both external restrictions and internal restriction upon liberty and equality, deriving from community and its culture. In a society with multiple communities, there may emerge strong segmentation, or what is called *zuilen* or the pillarisation of society, resulting in strict *proporz* of opportunities between the various communities. Internally, communities may engage in setting up restrictions upon the liberty of its members, especially if this would threaten the established position of the community and its culture. Multiculturalism here collides with libertarianism, or the kind of liberalism which underlines personal freedom.

Multiculturalism may also collide with another kind of liberalism which underlines equality to the same extent as liberty, namely egalitarian liberalism. An emphasis upon community and culture may serve as an excuse for bypassing the requirements of equal protection under the law as well as due process rights. Under multiculturalism communities may demand derogations from the requirement of equality under the laws, both when it comes to the allocation of opportunities between communities and when it comes to the allocation of opportunities within a community.

*Culture promotes fundamentalism*    In the philosophy underpinning the multicultural society called 'communitarianism' there is one element which collides with any liberal theory of state and society, namely the claim that people are exclusively defined through their culture. If this were true, then multiculturalism could possibly harbour a society where culture would motivate not only segmentation but also violations of the basic precepts of liberalism, namely personal freedom to choose and equality under the laws.

However, radical communitarians are not to be accepted, because it is simply wrong as a theory about people and their cultural allegiances.

Individuals do choose their cultures, sometimes changing it and certainly revising it often. The multicultural society harbouring the following groups

1    historical minorities
2    immigrant groups
3    religious groups
4    gay and lesbian communities
5    secular values: post-materialism, etc.

is not a static society where people are born into a culture and then maintains this culture no matter what. On the contrary, the size and composition of these communities change all the time as people move in and out of cultural allegiances and change the nature of their cultural ties.

## *A Multicultural Regime – The Liberal Restrictions upon Communities*

In stead of speaking of a conflict between liberalism, whether libertarian or egalitarian, and multiculturalism, one needs to spell out how they can be combined. A multicultural society could fulfil the requirements of liberalism, if and only if it endorses the following ideas:

1    Tolerance, or the respect for civil society
2    Rule of Law, or the respect for justice
3    Democracy, or the respect for majority rule

Multiculturalism is a new contract for advanced societies which aims at a different balance between communitarianism on the one hand and libertarianism or egalitarian liberalism on the other hand. If the nation is not a set of common sentiments – a creed – but a contract, then what contract would a multicultural society endorse? The state would not be neutral but could support communities in various. It could not, even if it wanted to. However, the state in a multicultural society must uphold the restrictions upon culture and communities, stated above: 1–3.

## Relevance of Multiculturalism

The recent political mobilisation of communities raises a problem for democracies: How far can the state go in recognising and supporting the various communities that play a major role in civil society? Community based groups whether ethnies, religious groups or groups founded upon values demand increasingly that government pays attention to them by the making of constitutional or public policies. A multi-cultural society needs the politics of mutual recognition, but can it come into conflict with the principle of majority rule in a democracy?

The rising relevance of communal politics in the form of political claims from ethnic and religious minorities, sects and the homosexual collectivities has stimulated to a rather large literature focusing upon communitarianism and democratic theory. The sharp increase in global migration will make these political questions even more urgent. The advanced countries of the world will all be multicultural societies facing pressing governance problems of how to combine majority rule with the existence of several minorities. One need not go so far as C. Taylor in his *The Sources of the Self* (1992), where he claims that communities are highly compact social groups, in order to realize that democracy in multicultural societies faces a governance problem. Even if one agrees with S. Benhabib (2002) that communities are malleable, one would still want to know what political institutions fit a multicultural society best.

The state can never bypass the structure of communities in the society it governs. It comes up in a most visible manner in the laws of citizenship and the rules of work permit and visa. The immense global migration makes the politics of citizenship, work permits and visa a daily reality for many people: How are foreigners to be treated? How many rights can guest workers be given? Can the *sans papiers* be given residence rights? Should citizenship differentiate between inherited *peuples* and recently arrived immigrants? Should historical minorities be compensated for colonialism? Etc. When answering these questions, then one may use either of two approaches:

1  State neutrality: Communal ties are private matters and the state can only enforce universal rules applicable in the same manner to all groups. Example: French republicanism.
2  Communal recognition and support: The state employs a paraphernalia of institutions and support in a politics of mutual respect.

We will discuss these two alternatives by referring to the work of Kymlicka as well as the criticism launched again communitarianism by B. Barry.

## Kymlicka: The Institutions of the Multicultural Society

In his numerous books on the multicultural society Kymlicka and associates present a long list of mechanisms that could constitute the core of a politics of mutual recognition (Kymlicka, 1995). We will simply enumerate these mechanisms here:

1  Exemptions from laws that penalize or burden cultural practices;
2  Assistance to do things the majority (or otherwise privileged group) can do unassisted;
3  Self governance for national minorities and indigenous communities;

4	External rules restricting non-members' liberty in order to protect members' culture;
5	Internal rules for members' conduct that are enforced against ostracism and excommunication;
6	Incorporation and enforcement of traditional or religious legal codes within the dominant legal system;
7	Special representation of groups or their members within governmental institutions;
8	Symbolic recognition of the worth, status, or existence of various groups within the larger state community (Kymlicka and Norman, 2000).

This list of multicultural mechanisms goes beyond the institutions of consociational democracy, recommended in the theory of the plural society. It may be interesting to compare the list of Kymlicka and Norman with the original list of Lijphart from his *Democracy in Plural Societies* (1977):

> Consociational democracy can be defined in terms of four characteristics. The first and most important element is government by a grand coalition of the political leaders of all significant segments of the plural society. This can take several different forms, such as a grand coalition cabinet in a parliamentary system, a 'grand' council or committee with important advisory functions, or a grand coalition of a president and other top officeholders in a presidential system. The other three basic elements of consociational democracy are (1) the mutual veto or 'concurrent majority' rule, which serves as an additional protection of vital minority interests, (2) proportionality as the principal standard of political representation, civil service appointments, and allocation of public funds, and (3) a high degree of autonomy for each segment to run its own internal affairs. (Lijphart, 1977, p. 25)

The politics of mutual respect does not require the most distinctive mechanism of consociational coalition, namely the grand coalition. It shares with consociational democracy the emphasis upon autonomy whether in the form of federalism or home rule in a unitary dispensation, but it differs from it by including a number of mechanisms that officially recognize or promote the interests of communities.

The politics of mutual respect will be expressed in both constitutional policy-making and in public policies. Firstly, constitutional policy may be employed to identify the nations and ethnies of a country. It may pay special attention to historical minorities but also recognize immigrant groups. Constitutional policy-making may provide for both group rights and individual rights. The definition of a citizen is crucial in a constitution, which entails that the rights of ethnies and immigrants will have to be laid down. The territorial dispensation is also a matter for constitutional policy-making where community considerations may play a major role, as for example in the federalism of India.

Secondly, the politics of mutual respect will require a large set of public policies directed towards the support of the cultures of minorities. For instance, when accommodating the large number of Arabs living in France policies may be conducted that support the construction of mosques as well as the education of imams. Or policies may have the objective of systematically compensate historical minorities for the wrong doings of immigrant groups, as in Australia and New Zealand. Language policies are another example of the politics of mutual respect. They can be driven so far as to impose the use of one language, as in French speaking Quebec. Or they may merely amount to a recognition that streets in the capital have two names.

The politics of mutual respect raises two questions, one concerning the guiding principles of the state and the second relating to the economic costs of these policies. We will deal with the first question about a contradiction between the particularism of communitarian politicies and the universalism of the modern state below when examining Barry's rejection of multiculturalism. Here, we will emphasize two things about the potential costs of the politics of mutual respect:

1  Difficult to predict: When governments sets out to give special support to communities, then it may not be able to narrow down what this really entails. Communities may present a never ending list of claims: Who is to test whether one such claim is just or correct? If supporting Islam is a task for governments in Western Europe, then perhaps other religious communities would also wish to have some similar support.

2  Potentially very costly: Supporting communities may comprise huge redistribution claims where minorities demand rectification of old injustices committed long ago. In a sense, there may be no limit to what should be paid to for instance Indians when they lost their entire civilisation. Take the example of supporting Islam in Western Europe again: If the state should help construct mosques and help set up a faculty to teach future imams, then how could the state limit the size of its contribution to such a noble cause which basically knows no spending limit?

The only valid counter-argument is that government in its budget-making always has to trade off various demands against each other and establish priorities. This would be true of communal policy-making just as it has always been true of social and economic policies. When the politics of mutual respect is rejected entirely, then it is not the concerns 1 and 2 which are involved. The argument is entirely different referring to the conflict between multiculturalism and a philosophy of government favouring state neutrality and equal rights and opportunities. Let us employ the Barry argument which contains a most systematic rebuttal of the politics of mutual respect.

## Barry: Moral Universalism Destroying Multiculturalism

It is always recognized that multiculturalism has been advocated by two different groups, one radical and one modest. That the claims of radical multiculturalism are difficult to sustain has been pointed out by several critiques. Thus, Seyla Benhabib launched a successful criticism of radical multiculturalism in *The Claims of Culture* (2002) targeting the uncorroborated implication in much radical culture theory that communities are highly compact groups. It was the argument of Taylor that communities constitute the sources of the self that led to the radical claims concerning communities, such as for instance that people are 'lost' if they do not live within their original community. However, when Barry targeted modest multiculturalism in his *Culture and Equality* (2001) it came as a surprise, especially the complete rejection of all forms of multiculturalism, not only radical but also modest multiculturalism. He stated:

> My target is, rather, those multiculturalists who would be happy to embrace the watch-words of the French Revolution: liberty, equality and (in some appropriately non-sexist rendition) fraternity. What unites them is the claim that, under contemporary conditions of cultural heterogeneity, 'classical' or 'difference-blind' liberal principles fail to deliver on either liberty or equality: only by adopting the tenets of the 'politics of difference', it is said, can we hope to achieve real liberty and equality. Against this, I shall argue that multiculturalist policies are not in general well designed to advance the values of liberty and equality, and that the implementation of such policies tends to mark a retreat from both. Even when there are reasons for introducing group-differentiated rights based on membership in cultural groups, these do not include the advancement of equal liberty that can be supported pragmatically. (Barry, 2002, p. 12)

As Barry himself points out several times, 'multiculturalism' is an ambiguous word. It denotes at least three things:

1  A social structure where communities are important;
2  A set of public policies oriented towards a social structure according to definition 1 above;
3  A political philosophy aimed at replacing culture blind liberalism, or universalist liberalism.

If it is not clear what 'multiculturalism' stands for, then it is perhaps also not evident what Barry wishes to destroy. He definitely does not believe (3) that multiculturalism is a new political philosophy, partly because he rejects (2) that multiculturalism offers a coherent and efficient set of policies for a new politics of recognition. But does Barry also deny (1) that the post-modern society has a social structure where communities play an important role, often increasingly so? He states:

Pursuit of the multiculturalist agenda makes the achievement of broadly based egalitarian policies more difficult in two ways. At the minimum, it diverts political effort away from universalistic goals. But a more serious problem is that multiculturalism may very well destroy the conditions for putting together a coalition in favour of across-the-board equalization of opportunities and resources. (Barry, 2002, p. 325)

Well, this is easily said, but if the society has a structure of communities, then perhaps a politics of culture is necessary, although it may reduce the relevance of universalist principles somewhat? To Barry it is obvious that equality must prevail over culture:

The more severe form of the conflict between group-based and universalistic policies arises where group-based policies split the potential coalition for broad-based egalitarian reform down the middle. (Barry, 2002, pp. 325–6)

Yet, is there not here a *petitio principii*? Why should equality be given such a fundamental place in public policy that it cannot sometimes be overrun? Barry would answer:

The whole thrust of the 'politics of difference', as we have seen in one context after another, is that it seeks to withdraw from individual members of minority groups the protections that are normally offered by liberal states. Where a group qualifies as a national minority within a liberal state, multiculturalists commonly propose that it should be free to make its own laws, perhaps within a decision-making system that gives male elders a monopoly of power. These laws, they suggest, should not have to conform to the norms of 'liberal constitutionalism', and should be able to discriminate with impunity against women or adherents of religions other than that of the majority. (Barry, 2002, p. 326)

This claim by Barry is doubtful. Equality implies two things for communities, it is true. On the one hand, people from various communities must be able to interact on the basis of universalist criteria of competition and achievement, at least in relation to a whole set of opportunities in the economy and in public life. On the other hand, people adhering to one community must be able to count upon a certain treatment by other group members so that their rights are not violated. Modest multiculturalism does not accept that communities become islands with their own law. Nor does it entail that communities do not have to act under certain universalist principles that are community blind.

Modest multiculturalism does not deny the validity of a liberal constitution. It merely adds that such a constitution may not be enough. Modest multiculturalism does not sanction that communities support norms that violate a liberal constitution. But modest multiculturalism outlines a new set of policies that take into account the emergence of a social structure where communities loom large.

How about Barry's own position then? What is egalitarian liberalism? And why would such a political philosophy be against policies which favour the creation of opportunities for disadvantaged groups such as historical communities? Barry would certainly say that Rawls' theory of justice offers a most complete version of egalitarian liberalism. Are we then to conclude that a theory of justice along the universalist line of Rawls, underlining liberty and equality, is in all respects in conflict with all forms of the politics of mutual recognition? No one doubts that there could occur a contradiction between ethical universalism and communitarianism. But what is at stake is not this possibility but its necessity: Is it always the case that any policy adhering to multiculturalism must come into conflict with liberty or equality?

Take the example of affirmative action. It is advocated by both adherents of ethical universalism and of minority rights. Affirmative action is one type of politics of recognition but it is also advocated because of its egalitarian bent or aim. The complete rejection of multiculturalism in *Culture and Equality* seems exaggerated. The real task is to spell out how liberty and equality is to be promoted in a society where communities are on the rise. And liberty and equality may themselves collide. We face a number of goal conflicts between different values: liberty, equality and culture. There is no single solution to how they can be promoted through policy-making.

The contradiction between egalitarians and multiculturalists is pushed to its extreme with Barry. Whereas the first group would underline equal protection under the law meaning state neutrality, fairness and redistribution, the latter group advocates group specific treatment meaning derogations from equal treatment as well as affirmative action programs. According to Barry, multiculturalism as public policy results in parallel universes in a society, which constitutes a threat to civic nationality and liberal institutions. The call for exemptions and affirmative action is based upon a quest for equality of outcomes, but it is equality of opportunity which is the core of liberalism.

Multiculturalism underlines the value of community at the expense of the value of the individual, leading to a theory of group rights which is not in agreement with the liberal principles of freedom of association and freedom to refuse association. Self-governance of communities may result in cultural 'tolerance' or even 'imperialism', if groups are allowed exemptions from law.

Barry goes so far as to reject also multiculturalism in its version 1 above, namely the thesis that the post-modern society faces the challenge from the growing strength and mobilisation of communities. Culture is not a problem in the post-modern society, as what is problematic today is the economic inequalities that characterize the advanced capitalist democracies. Multiculturalist policies would make it more difficult to attack these inequalities through egalitarian policies of redistribution and free public services available for all independently of their community belonging.

The imperatives of ethical universalism take precedence over cultural values, according to Barry. Universalism requires that all be treated in the same way independently of community belonging. Under a universalist philosophy like egalitarian liberalism there can be no separate group rights. Under universalism there is voluntarism meaning that individuals choose the communities they wish to adhere to and all communities are bound to respect the same universal individual rights. Yet, universalism may be given a variety of interpretations and Barry's version of liberalism – egalitarian liberalism – is far from the only one possible or desirable.

The fundamental objection against Barry's *tour de force* is that modest multiculturalism does not entail a complete rejection of liberalism. Its foundation in an analysis of the post-modern society is innovative taking account the rise of communitarian politics and the mobilisation of communitarian demands. Multiculturalism has not yet delivered a final list of policies that accomplish a politics of mutual respect or recognition, but one cannot deny the relevance of such policies in the increasing multicultural social structures in advanced countries – see for instance P. Kelly (ed.) *Multiculturalism Reconsidered* (2002).

# APPENDICES

# Appendix A:
# Macro Data Set: Variable List

| Abbreviation | Description | Sources |
|---|---|---|
| ACHIEV80 | Percentage of a sample in a country displaying an achievement orientation in the WVS first wave ca. 1980 | Inglehart *et al.* (2000) |
| ACHIEV90 | Percentage of a sample in a country displaying an achievement orientation in the WVS second wave ca. 1990 | Inglehart *et al.* (2000) |
| ACHIEV95 | Percentage of a sample in a country displaying an achievement orientation in the WVS third wave ca. 1995 | Inglehart *et al.* (2000) |
| ACHIEV9095 | Percentage of a sample in a country displaying an achievement orientation in the WVS second and third waves | Inglehart *et al.* (2000) |
| BRITLEG | Legacy of British colonial rule as a dummy variable where 1 = British legacy, 0 = no such legacy | Based on de Blij (1996, pp. 496–97) |
| BROEK | Classification of countries as belonging to civilizations suggested by Broek where the occidental one scores high and the Meso-African one scores low | Based on Broek and Webb (1968, p. 189) |
| BUDD70 | Percentage of the population estimated to adhere to the Buddhist creed around 1970 | Barrett (1982) |
| COLLEG | Colonial legacy | Based on de Blij (1996, pp. 496–97) |
| COLRULE | Number of years under colonial rule | Based on Derbyshire and Derbyshire (1996, Ch. 8) |

| Abbreviation | Description | Sources |
|---|---|---|
| CORR80 | Perceived corruption around 1980 | Transparency International (1999) |
| CORR98 | Perceived corruption around 1998 | Transparency International (1999) |
| DECOLYR | Number of years since the year of independence | Based on Derbyshire and Derbyshire (1996, Ch. 8) |
| DEM00 | Democracy score 1900 | Gurr (1990) |
| DEM50 | Democracy score 1950 | Gurr (1990) |
| DEM72 | Democracy score 1972 | Freedom House (2000) |
| DEM7281 | Average value of the democracy score for the years 1972–81 | Freedom House (2000) |
| DEM8291 | Average value of the democracy score for the years 1982–91 | Freedom House (2000) |
| DEM9299 | Average value of the democracy score for the years 1992–99 | Freedom House (2000) |
| DEM97 | Democracy score 1997 | Freedom House (2000) |
| DISEQU | Distance from the equator in absolute degrees – latitudes | CIA (1999) |
| DOMEG | Percentage of the population belonging to the dominating ethnic group in a country | Parker (1997b) |
| DOMLG1 | Percentage of the population belonging to the dominating language group in a country | Encyclopaedia Britannica (1998) |
| DOMLG2 | Percentage of the population belonging to the dominating language group in a country | Parker (1997b) |
| EGNO | Number of ethnic groups in a country | Parker (1997b) |
| ELECTSYS | The electoral system classified as a dummy variable where 1 = proportional systems and 0 = non-proportional systems | Reynolds, Reilly *et al.* (1997) |

| Abbreviation | Description | Sources |
|---|---|---|
| ELF1 | Ethno-linguistic fragmentation index based on the division of the population into different ethno-linguistic groups | Encyclopaedia Britannica (1998) |
| ELF2 | Ethno-linguistic fragmentation index based on the division of the population into different ethno-linguistic groups | Barrett (1982) |
| ENG1 | Percentage of population estimated to use English as a first language | Crystal (1997b) |
| ENG2 | Percentage of population estimated to use English as a second language | Crystal (1997b) |
| FRENLEG | Legacy of French colonial rule as a dummy variable where 1 = French legacy, 0 = no such legacy | Based on de Blij (1996, pp. 496–97) |
| GDI99 | Gender development index ca. 1995 | UNDP (1999) |
| GDPCAP00 | Gross domestic product per capita 1900 | Maddison (1995) |
| GDPCAP50 | Gross domestic product per capita 1950 | Maddison (1995) |
| GDPCAP90 | Gross domestic product per capita 1990 | Maddison (1995) |
| GDPCAP92 | Gross domestic product per capita 1992 | Maddison (1995) |
| GEM99 | Gender empowerment measure ca. 1995 | UNDP (1999) |
| GEORACE | Classification of countries as belonging to geographical location where Europe score high and Africa score low | Based on Barrett (1982, pp. 112–15) |
| GGEX92 | Estimated general government expenditures as a percentage of GDP in the early 1990s | IMF (1994) |
| GINI70 | Gini coefficient measuring inequality of income distribution within countries ca. 1970 | Deininger and Squire (1997) |
| GINI90 | Gini coefficient measuring inequality of income distribution within countries ca. 1990 | Deininger and Squire (1997) |

| Abbreviation | Description | Sources |
|---|---|---|
| GRO6073 | Average of yearly GNP per capita growth 1960–73 | World Bank (1975) |
| GRO7385 | Average of yearly GNP per capita growth 1973–85 | World Bank (1987) |
| GRO8594 | Average of yearly GNP per capita growth 1985–94 | World Bank (1996) |
| GRO9098 | Average of yearly GNP per capita growth 1990–98 | World Bank (2000) |
| HDI60 | Human development index ca. 1960 | UNDP (1994) |
| HDI95 | Human development index ca. 1990 | UNDP (1994) |
| HDI99 | Human development index ca. 1995 | UNDP (1999) |
| HUNTINGT | Classification of countries as belonging to civilizations suggested by Huntington where the Western one scores high and the African one scores low | Based on Huntington (1996, pp. 26–27) |
| INDIV90 | Average score for a sample in a country expressing an individualist orientation in the WVS second wave ca. 1990 | Inglehart *et al.* (2000) |
| INDIV95 | Average score for a sample in a country expressing an individualist orientation in the WVS third wave ca. 1995 | Inglehart *et al.* (2000) |
| INDIV9095 | Average score for a sample in a country expressing an individualist orientation in the WVS second and third waves | Inglehart *et al.* (2000) |
| LANGFAM | Classification of countries as belonging to language families where European ones score high and African ones score low | Based on Grimes (1999) and Crystal (1997a) |
| LGNO | Number of languages groups in a country | Parker (1997b) |
| LINGGRP | Classification of countries as belonging to linguistic groups | Based on Parker (1997a, b) |

| Abbreviation | Description | Sources |
|---|---|---|
| LINGR | Classification of countries as belonging to groups according to linguistic and human criteria | Based on de Blij (1993, pp. 198–99 and 1996, p. 195) |
| MODLEAD | Number of years since the introduction of modernized leadership | Based on Black (1966) |
| MUSL70 | Percentage of the population estimated to adhere to the Muslim creed around 1970 | Barrett (1982) |
| NATPR80 | Percentage of a sample in a country expressing a high national pride in the WVS first wave ca. 1980 | Inglehart *et al.* (2000) |
| NATPR90 | Percentage of a sample in a country expressing a high national pride in the WVS second wave ca. 1990 | Inglehart *et al.* (2000) |
| NATPR95 | Percentage of a sample in a country expressing a high national pride in the WVS third wave ca. 1995 | Inglehart *et al.* (2000) |
| NATPR9095 | Percentage of a sample in a country expressing a high national pride in the WVS second and third waves | Inglehart *et al.* (2000) |
| NEWIND | An individualism index placing countries on a scale where high scores indicate individualism and low scores the opposite | Based on Hofstede (1994, p. 53) and Diener *et al.* (1995, p. 856) |
| POSTM80 | Percentage of a sample in a country displaying a postmaterialist orientation in the WVS first wave ca. 1980 | Inglehart *et al.* (2000) |
| POSTM90 | Percentage of a sample in a country displaying a postmaterialist orientation in the WVS second wave ca. 1990 | Inglehart *et al.* (2000) |
| POSTM95 | Percentage of a sample in a country displaying a postmaterialist orientation in the WVS third wave ca. 1995 | Inglehart *et al.* (2000) |

| Abbreviation | Description | Sources |
|---|---|---|
| POSTM9095 | Percentage of a sample in a country displaying a postmaterialist orientation in the WVS second and third waves | Inglehart *et al.* (2000) |
| PPP97 | Purchase power parities per capita 1997 | World Bank (1999) |
| PROT70 | Percentage of the population estimated to adhere to the Protestant creed around 1970 | Barrett (1982) |
| RC70 | Percentage of the population estimated to adhere to the Roman Catholic creed around 1970 | Barrett (1982) |
| RELSE80 | Percentage of a sample in a country attending a religious service weekly in the WVS first wave ca. 1980 | Inglehart *et al.* (2000) |
| RELSE90 | Percentage of a sample in a country attending a religious service weekly in the WVS second wave ca. 1990 | Inglehart *et al.* (2000) |
| RELSE95 | Percentage of a sample in a country attending a religious service weekly in the WVS third wave ca. 1995 | Inglehart *et al.* (2000) |
| RELSE9095 | Percentage of a sample in a country attending a religious service weekly in the WVS second and third waves | Inglehart *et al.* (2000) |
| RGDPC50 | Real GDP per capita ca. 1950 | Summers and Heston (1994) |
| RGDPC60 | Real GDP per capita ca. 1960 | Summers and Heston (1994) |
| RGDPC70 | Real GDP per capita ca. 1970 | Summers and Heston (1994) |
| RGDPC80 | Real GDP per capita ca. 1980 | Summers and Heston (1994) |
| RGDPC90 | Real GDP per capita ca. 1990 | Summers and Heston (1994) |
| RLF1 1900 | Religious fragmentation index based on the division of the population in the major world religions around 1900 | Barrett (1982) |

| Abbreviation | Description | Sources |
|---|---|---|
| RLF1 1970 | Religious fragmentation index based on the division of the population in the major world religions around 1970 | Barrett (1982) |
| RLF1 1995 | Religious fragmentation index based on the division of the population in the major world religions around 1995 | Encyclopaedia Britannica (1995) |
| RLF2 1900 | Religious fragmentation index based on the division of the population in the major world religions, as well as the major subgroups within Christianity around 1900 | Barrett (1982) |
| RLF2 1970 | Religious fragmentation index based on the division of the population in the major world religions, as well as the major subgroups within Christianity around 1970 | Barrett (1982) |
| RLF2 1995 | Religious fragmentation index based on the division of the population in the major world religions, as well as the major subgroups within Christianity around 1995 | Encyclopaedia Britannica (1995) |
| SPANLEG | Legacy of Spanish colonial rule as a dummy variable where 1 = Spanish legacy, 0 = no such legacy | Based on de Blij (1996, pp. 496–97) |
| TODD1983 | Classification of countries as belonging to family systems according to degree of individualism where the absolute nuclear family scores high and the African family system scores low | Based on Todd (1983) |
| TODD1984 | Classification of countries as belonging to family types according to degree of development potential where the bilateral vertical family scores high and the latent matrilineal non-vertical family scores low | Based on Todd (1984) |

| Abbreviation | Description | Sources |
|---|---|---|
| TOYNBEE | Classification of countries as belonging to civilizations suggested by Toynbee where the Western ones score high and the primitive ones score low | Based on Broek and Webber (1968, p. 185) |
| TRUST80 | Percentage of a sample in a country expressing interpersonal trust in the WVS first wave ca. 1980 | Inglehart *et al.* (2000) |
| TRUST90 | Percentage of a sample in a country expressing interpersonal trust in the WVS second wave ca. 1990 | Inglehart *et al.* (2000) |
| TRUST95 | Percentage of a sample in a country expressing interpersonal trust in the WVS third wave ca. 1995 | Inglehart *et al.* (2000) |
| TRUST9095 | Percentage of a sample in a country expressing interpersonal trust in the WVS second and third waves | Inglehart *et al.* (2000) |
| WOM90 | Percentage of female parliamentarians around 1990 | IPU (1995) |

# Appendix B:
# Regional Data Set: Variable List

| Abbreviation | Description | Sources |
|---|---|---|
| **Belgium** | | |
| ETHNFRA10 | Ethnic fragmentation index based on division into Flemish-speakers, French-speakers, German-speakers, and Flemish- and French-speakers 1910 | Institut National de Statistique (1954) |
| ETHNFRA47 | Ethnic fragmentation index based on division into Flemish-speakers, French-speakers, German-speakers, and Flemish- and French-speakers 1947 | Institut National de Statistique (1954) |
| ETHNP81 | Vote for the ethnic parties (FDF, RW, VLB, VU) at parliamentary elections in 1981 | Institut National de Statistique (1984) |
| ETHNP91 | Vote for the ethnic parties (FDF, RW, VLB, VU) at parliamentary elections in 1991 | Institut National de Statistique (1994) |
| FLEM47 | Percentage of population counted as Flemish-speaking 1947 | Institut National de Statistique (1954) |
| FOREIGN81 | Percentage of the population counted as foreigners in 1981 | Institut National de Statistique (1997) |
| FOREIGN95 | Percentage of the population counted as foreigners in 1995 | Institut National de Statistique (1997) |
| FRE47 | Percentage of population counted as French-speaking 1947 | Institut National de Statistique (1954) |
| PSCCVP91 | Vote for the christian democratic parties (PSC, CVP) at parliamentary elections in 1991 | Institut National de Statistique (1994) |
| REGECPRO95 | Regional economic product per capita in 1995 | Institut National de Statistique (1997) |

| Abbreviation | Description | Sources |
|---|---|---|
| RELPRAC68 | Estimated church attendance around 1968 | CRISP (1974) |
| **India** | | |
| BJP96 | Vote for Bharatiya Janata Party at Lok Sabha elections in 1996: percentages | Election Commission of India (1999) |
| HINDI91 | Percentage of population speaking Hindi in 1991 | Census of India (1999) |
| HINDU91 | Percentage of the population adhering to the Hindu religion 1991 | Census of India (1999) |
| INC96 | Vote for Indian National Congress at Lok Sabha elections in 1996: percentages | Election Commission of India (1999) |
| INCICU80 | Added vote for Indian National Congress (Indira) and Indian National Congress (Urs) at Lok Sabha elections in 1980: percentages | Singh and Bose (1984) |
| JNP80 | Vote for Janata Party at Lok Sabha elections in 1980: percentages | Singh and Bose (1984) |
| MAJLAN91 | Percentage of population speaking the major language in 1991 | Census of India (1999) |
| SEXRAT91 | Ratio of women in relation to men (= 100) 1991 | Census of India (1999) |
| URBAN91 | Percentage urban population in 1991 | Census of India (1999) |
| **Russia** | | |
| CP93 | Vote for the Communist Party at the Duma elections in 1993: percentages | NUPI (1999) |
| CP95 | Vote for the Communist Party at the Duma elections in 1995: percentages | NUPI (1999) |
| ELFINDEX | Ethnic fragmentation index based on divisions made in the NUPI database in 1989 | NUPI (1999) |
| FEMEXP | Life expectancy in years: female 1995 | CSPP (1999) |
| GRPCAP | Regional GDP per capita in 1995 | CSPP (1999) |
| MALEXP | Life expectancy in years: male 1995 | CSPP (1999) |

| Abbreviation | Description | Sources |
|---|---|---|
| RUSSIAN | Percentage of population counted as Russian-speaking in 1989 | NUPI (1999) |
| YAB93 | Vote for the Yabloko bloc at the Duma elections in 1993: percentages | NUPI (1999) |
| YAB95 | Vote for the Yabloko bloc at the Duma elections in 1995: percentages | NUPI (1999) |

**Spain**

| Abbreviation | Description | Sources |
|---|---|---|
| INSTAUTO | Institutional autonomy; dummy variable where 1 = more of institutional autonomy and 0 = less of institutional autonomy | Based on Heywood (1995) |
| NATUN78 | National unity orientation in Spain 1978 | Wagtskjold (1978) |
| PSOE79 | Vote for the socialist party at the parliamentary election in 1979: percentages | Penniman and Mujal-Léon (1985) |
| PSOE96 | Vote for the socialist party at the parliamentary election in 1996: percentages | Congreso de los Diputados (1999) |
| REG79 | Vote for the regionalist parties at the parliamentary election in 1979: percentages | Penniman and Mujal-Léon (1985) |
| REG96 | Vote for the regionalist parties at the parliamentary election in 1996: percentages | Congreso de los Diputados (1999) |
| REGINC95 | Regional income per capita for the Spanish provinces 1995 | Institutio Nacional de Estadistica (1998) |
| REGION76 | Regionalist orientation in Spain 1976; data only for regions | Blanco *et al.* (1977) |
| REGION95 | Regionalist orientation in Spain 1995; data only for regions | Reif and Marlier (1995) |
| RELPRAT75 | Religious practice estimated for the mid-1970s | Almerich *et al.* (1975) |

**Switzerland**

| Abbreviation | Description | Sources |
|---|---|---|
| CATHOL80 | Percentage of population adhering to the Catholic creed in 1980 | Bundesamt für Statistik (1985) |

| Abbreviation | Description | Sources |
|---|---|---|
| CVP79 | Vote for the Christian Democratic Party at parliamentary elections in 1979 | Bundesamt für Statistik (1980) |
| CVP95 | Vote for the Christian Democratic Party at parliamentary elections in 1995 | Bundesamt für Statistik (1998) |
| ELF90 | Ethnic fragmentation index based on divisions into German-speakers, French-speakers, Italian-speakers, Räto-romanish-speakers and other languages in 1990 | Bundesamt für Statistik (1998) |
| FRE90 | Percentage of population speaking French in 1990 | Bundesamt für Statistik (1998) |
| GER90 | Percentage of population speaking German in 1990 | Bundesamt für Statistik (1998) |
| ITA90 | Percentage of population speaking Italian in 1990 | Bundesamt für Statistik (1998) |
| NOCONF80 | Percentage of population with no confession in 1980 | Bundesamt für Statistik (1985) |
| OTH90 | Percentage of population speaking other languages in 1990 | Bundesamt für Statistik (1998) |
| SPS79 | Vote for the Social Democratic Party at parliamentary elections in 1979 | Bundesamt für Statistik (1980) |
| SPS95 | Vote for the Social Democratic Party at parliamentary elections in 1995 | Bundesamt für Statistik (1998) |
| VOLKS90 | Regional income per capita in 1990 | Bundesamt für Statistik (1998) |
| **USA** | | |
| BLACK94 | Percentage of black population 1994 | US Department of Commerce (1997) |
| CATHOL90 | Percentages of population members of the Roman Catholic Church around 1990 | ARDA (1999) |
| DEM72 | Democrat vote in the 1972 presidential election: percentages | Austin (1986) |
| DEM96 | Democrat vote in the 1996 presidential election: percentages | US Department of Commerce (1997) |

| Abbreviation | Description | Sources |
|---|---|---|
| ELF94 | Ethnic fragmentation index based on divisions into white, Hispanic, black, American Indian, Asian 1994 | US Department of Commerce (1997) |
| GSPC94 | Gross state product per capita in current dollars 1994 | US Department of Commerce (1997) |
| HISP94 | Percentage of Hispanic population 1994 | US Department of Commerce (1997) |
| RELFRAG90 | Religious fragmentation index based on division into Catholics, non-Catholics and non-Christians around 1990 | ARDA (1999) |
| REP72 | Republican vote in the 1972 presidential election: percentages | Austin (1986) |
| REP96 | Republican vote in the 1996 presidential election: percentages | US Department of Commerce (1997) |
| UNEM96 | Total unemployment as percentage of civilian labour force in 1996 | US Department of Commerce (1997) |
| WHITE94 | Percentage of white population 1994 | US Department of Commerce (1997) |

# Appendix C:
# Micro Data Set: Variable List

| Short Abbreviation | Description | Variables in Inglehart *et al.* (2000) |
|---|---|---|
| ACHIEVE | Achievement orientation; constructed so that high scores (1) stand for achievement orientation and low scores (0) for the opposite | (V20 + V16) – (V24 + V22) |
| AGE | Age-groups; recoded so that higher scores (1) stand for the age-group 65+ and the lowest score (0) for the age-group 18–24 | AGEGROUP |
| DENOM | Denominational adherence | |
| CATHOL | Adherence to a Roman Catholic creed; a dummy variable where 1 = Catholic and 0 = non-Catholic: Belgium, Spain, USA, Switzerland | V179 |
| HINDU | Adherence to Hindu creed; a dummy variable where 1 = Hindu and 0 = non-Hindu: India | V179 |
| ORTHOD | Adherence to Russian Orthodox creed; a dummy variable where 1 = Orthodox and 0 = non-Orthodox: Russia | V179 |
| EDUCAT | Educational level; recoded so that the higher the score (1) the higher the educational level and the lower the score (0) the lower the educational level; Belgium, Spain, USA, Russia | V218 |

| Short Abbreviation | Description | Variables in Inglehart *et al.* (2000) |
|---|---|---|
| EDUCAT | Educational level; recoded so that the higher the score (1) the higher the educational level and the lower the score (0) the lower the educational level; Switzerland, India | V217 |
| ETHNIC | Ethnic identification | |
| FLEMISH | Living in a Flemish region; a dummy variable where 1 = Flemish and 0 = non-Flemish: Belgium | V234 |
| GERMAN | Using the German language; a dummy variable where 1 = German-speaking and 0 = non-German-speaking: Switzerland | V209 |
| HINDI | Using the Hindi language; a dummy variable where 1 = Hindi-speaking and 0 = non-Hindi-speaking: India | V209 |
| RUSSIAN | Using the Russian language; a dummy variable where 1 = Russian-speaking and 0 = non-Russian-speaking: Russia | V209 |
| SPANISH | Using the Spanish language; a dummy variable where 1 = Spanish-speaking and 0 = non-Spanish-speaking: Spain | V209 |
| WHITE | Belonging to the white ethnic group; a dummy variable where 1 = white and 0 = non-white | V233 |
| GENDER | Gender as a dummy variable; recoded so that 1 = female and 0 = male | V214 |
| INCOME | Income level; recoded so the higher the score (1) the higher the income and the lower the score (0) the lower the income | V227 |
| INDIV | Individualism index; constructed so that high scores (1) stands for individualism and low scores (0) for non-individualism | $(V127 - (V128 + V129))$ |

| Short Abbreviation | Description | Variables in Inglehart *et al.* (2000) |
|---|---|---|
| JOINBOY | Joining boycotts as political action; recoded to high scores (1) for joining boycotts and low scores (0) for never joining | V119 |
| LEFTRIG | Left–right self-placement where high scores stand for the right and low scores for the left; recoded to 0.1 to 1 | V123 |
| LIFESAT | Life satisfaction where high scores stand for satisfied and low scores for dissatisfied; recoded to 0.1 to 1 | V65 |
| NATPRIDE | National pride; recoded so that high scores (1) stand for very proud and low scores (0) for not at all proud | V205 |
| POLINTR | Political interest; recoded to high scores (1) for political interest | V117 |
| POSTMAT | Postmaterialism index based on four items; recoded so that 1 = postmaterialist orientation and 0 = materialist orientation | V1000mpm |
| RELSERV | Participation at religious services or church attendance; recoded so that a high score (1) stand for attendance more than once a week and a low score (0) for never attending | V181 |
| TRUST | Interpersonal trust as a dummy variable; recoded so that 1 = trust other people and 0 = one cannot be too careful | V27 |
| VOLORG | Membership of voluntary organizations; recoded to a dummy variable where 1 = membership and 0 = non-membership | V128 + V130 + V131 + V132 + V133 + V134 + V135 |

# References

Abramson, P.R. and R. Inglehart (1995), *Value Change in Global Perspective*, Ann Arbor, MI: University of Michigan Press.

Achen, C.A. (1982), *Interpreting and Using Regression*, (QASS, 29) Beverly Hills, CA: Sage.

Allardt, E. (1980), 'Prerequisites and Consequences of Ethnic Mobilization in Modern Society', *Scandinavian Political Studies*, 3, 1–20.

Almerich, P. *et al.* (1975), *Cambio social y religion en España*, Barcelona: Editorial Fontanella.

Almond, G.A. and S. Verba (1965), *The Civic Culture: Political Attitudes and Democracy in Five Nations*, Boston, MA: Little, Brown and Company.

Almond, G.A. and S. Verba (eds) (1989), *The Civic Culture Revisited*, Beverly Hills, CA: Sage.

Anderson, B. (1983), *Imagined Communities: Reflections on the Origin and Spread of Nationalism*, London: Verso.

Annett, A. (2000), 'Social Fractionalization, Political Instability, and the Size of Government', IMF Working Paper, 00/82, Washington, DC: IMF.

Anton, R. (2001), *Understanding Fundamentalism*, New York: Alta Mira.

ARDA (American Religion Data Archive) (1999), *Churches and Church Membership in the United States, 1990 (States)* by Church Growth Research Center, Kansas City, MO [investigators]; available at: http://www.arda.tm/aggregate.html/.

Austin, E.W. (1986), *Political Facts of the United States since 1789*, New York: Columbia University Press.

Avineri, S. and A. de-Shalit (1992), *Communitarianism and Individualism*, Oxford: Oxford University Press.

Ayubi, N. (1991), *Political Islam: Religion and Politics in the Arab World*, London: Routledge.

Back, L. and Solomos, J. (2000), *Theories of race and racism: a reader*, London: Routledge.

Balassa, B. (1991), *Economic Policies in the Pacific Area: Developing Countries*, London: Macmillan.

Banfield, E.C. (1958), *The Moral Basis of Backward Society*, Glencoe, IL: Free Press.

Barnes, S.H., Kaase, M. et al. (1979), *Political Action: Mass Participation in Five Western Democracies*, Beverly Hills, CA: Sage.

Barrett, David B. *et al.* (2001), *World Christian Encyclopedia: A comparative survey of churches and religions in the modern world*. 2nd edn, Oxford: Oxford University Press.

Barrett, D.B. (ed.) (1982), *World Christian Encyclopaedia: A Comparative Study of Churches and Religions in the Modern World, AD 1900–2000*, Nairobi: Oxford University Press.

Barrett, D.B. (1991), 'World religion statistics', in Encyclopaedia Britannica, *Britannica Book of the Year*, Chicago, IL: Encyclopaedia Britannica.

Barrett, D.B. (1995), 'World religion statistics', in Encyclopaedia Britannica, *Britannica Book of the Year*, Chicago, IL: Encyclopaedia Britannica.

Barrett, D.B. (1999), 'World religion statistics', in Encyclopaedia Britannica, *Britannica Book of the Year*, Chicago, IL: Encyclopaedia Britannica.

Barry, B. (2002), *Culture and Equality: An Egalitarian Critique of Multiculturalism*, Cambridge, MA: Harvard University Press.

Barth, F. (ed.) (1969), *Ethnic Groups and Boundaries: The Social Organization of Cultural Difference*, Oslo: Universitetsforlaget.

Benhabib, S. (2002), *The Claims of Culture*, Princeton: Princeton University Press.

Berelson, B. *et al.* (1954), *Voting*, Chicago, IL: University of Chicago Press.

Beyer, P. (1994), *Religion and Globalization*, London: Sage.

Black, C. (1966), *The Dynamics of Modernization*, New York, NY: Harper and Row.

Blanco, J.J. *et al.* (1977), *La conscienca regional en España*, Madrid: Centro de investigaciones sociologicas.

Blaug, M. (1992), *The Methodology of Economics*, Cambridge: Cambridge University Press.

Bollen, K. and P. Paxton (2000), 'Subjective Measures of Democracy', *Comparative Political Studies*, 33, 58–86.

Braillard, P. (2000), *Switzerland and the Crisis of Dormant Assets and Nazi Gold*, London: Kegan Paul.

Brass, P.R. (1996), *The Politics of India Since Independence*, Cambridge: Cambridge University Press.

Brecht, A. (1967), *Political Theory*, Princeton, NJ: Princeton University Press.

Brinkmann, C. (1930), 'Civilization', in E.R.A. Seligman and A. Johnson (eds), *Encyclopaedia of the Social Sciences*, Vol. 3, London: Macmillan, 525–29.

Broek, J.O.M. and J.W. Webb (1968), *A Geography of Mankind*, New York, NY: McGraw-Hill.

Bundesamt für Statistik (1980), *Statistisches Jahrbuch der Schweiz 1980*, Basel: Birkhäuser Verlag.

Bundesamt für Statistik (1985), *Statistisches Jahrbuch der Schweiz 1985*, Basel: Birkhäuser Verlag.

Bundesamt für Statistik (1998), *Statistisches Jahrbuch der Schweiz 1998*, Zürich: Verlag Neue Zürcher Zeitung.

Campbell, A. *et al.* (1954), *The Voter Decides: A Study of the Voter's Perceptions, Attitudes, and Behaviors ... Based on a Survey of the 1952 Election*, Evanston, IL: Row, Peterson and Co.

Campbell, A. *et al.* (1960), *The American Voter*, New York, NY: John Wiley.

Cantril, H. (ed.) (1951), *Public Opinion 1935–1946*, Princeton, NJ: Princeton University Press.

Cantril, H. (1958), *The politics of Despair*, New York, NY: Basic Books.

Castles, I. (1998), 'The Mismeasure of Nations: A Review Essay on the Human Development Report 1998', *Population and Development Review*, 24, 831–45.

Cavalli-Sforza, L.L. *et al.* (1994), *The History and Geography of Human Genes*, Princeton, NJ: Princeton University Press.

Census of India (1999), available at: http://www.censusindia.net/.

Chaudhuri, P. (1989), *The Economic Theory of Growth*, London: Harvester Wheatsheaf.

Choi, K. (1983), 'A Statistical Test of Olson's Model', in D.C. Mueller (ed.), *The political economy of growth*, New Haven, CT: Yale University Press, 57–78.

CIA (1999), *The World Factbook 1999* available at: http://www.odci.gov/cia/publications/factbook/.

CIA (2000) The World Factbook 2000, available at: http://www.odci.gov/cia/publications/factbook/

Coleman, J.C. (1990), *Foundations of Social Theory*, Cambridge, MA: Harvard University Press.

Collier, D. and R. Adcock (1999), 'Democracy and Dichotomies: A Pragmatic Approach to Choices about Concepts', *Annual Review of Political Science*, 2, 537–65.

Congreso de los Diputados (1999), *Resumen de los resultados de las elecciones al Congreso de los Diputados* available at: http://www.congreso.es/elecciones/home.html/.

Converse, P. (1964), 'The Nature of Belief Systems in Mass Public', in D.E. Apter (ed.), *Ideology and Discontent*, New York, NY: Free Press, 206–61.

Crick, B. (1995), *Race: The History of an Idea in the West*, (Woodrow Wilson Centre Press), Baltimore: Johns Hopkins University Press.

CRISP (1974), 'L'évolution du "monde catholique" depuis 1968: Le devenir de la pratique religieuse', *Courrier Hebdomadaire du CRISP*, no. 664, 6 December.

Crystal, D. (1997a), *The Cambridge Encyclopedia of Language*, 2nd edn, Cambridge: Cambridge University Press.

Crystal, D. (1997b), *English as a global Language*, Cambridge: Cambridge University Press.

CSPP (1999), *Russian Regional Database* available at: http://www.cspp/strath.ac.uk/.

Dalton, R.J. (1996), *Citizen Politics: Public Opinion and Political Parties in Advanced Industrial Democracies*, Chatham, NJ: Chatham House.

Dalton, R.J. (2000), 'Citizen Attitudes and Political Behavior', *Comparative Political Studies*, 33, 912–40.

Das Gupta, J. (1989), 'India: Democratic Becoming and Combined Development', in L. Diamond *et al.* (eds), *Democracy in Developing Countries. Volume 3: Asia*, Boulder, CO: Lynne Reiner, 53–104.

Davis, D.W. and C. Davenport (1999), 'Assessing the Validity of the Postmaterialist Index', *American Political Science Review*, 93, 649–64.

de Blij, H.J. (1993), *Human Geography: Culture, Society, and Space*, 4th edn, New York, NY: John Wiley.

de Blij, H.J. (1996), *Human Geography: Culture, Society, and Space*, 5th edn, New York, NY: John Wiley.

Deininger, K. and L. Squire (1997), *The Deininger-Squire Data Set* available at: http://www.worldbank.org/research/growth/dddeisqu.htm/.

Delgado, R. and Stefancic, J. (eds) (2000), *Critical Race Theory: The Cutting Edge*, Philadelphia: Temple University Press.

Delwit, P. and J.-M. De Waele (eds) (1997), *Les partis politiques en Belgique*, 2nd edn, Bruxelles: Editions de l'Université de Bruxelles.

Delwit, P. *et al.* (eds) (1999), *Gouverner la Belgique: Clivages et compromis dans une société complexe*, Paris: PUF.

Derbyshire, J.D. and I. Derbyshire (1996), *Political Systems of the World*. Oxford: Helicon.

Deutsch, K.W. (1966), *Nationalism and Social Communication: An Inquiry into the Foundations of Nationality*, 2nd edn, Cambridge, MA: The MIT Press.

Diamond, J. (1998), *Guns, Germs and Steel*, New York: Vintage.

*Dictionnaire de la Théologie Chrétienne* (1998), Paris: Encyclopaedia Universalis and Albin Michel.

*Dictionnaire de l'Islam* (1997), Paris: Encyclopaedia Universalis and Albin Michel.

*Dictionnaire du Bouddhisme* (1999), Paris: Encyclopaedia Universalis and Albin Michel.

*Dictionnaire du Judaisme* (1998), Paris: Encyclopaedia Universalis and Albin Michel.

Diener, E. et al. (1995), 'Factors Predicting the Subjective Well-being of Nations', *Journal of Personality and Social Psychology*, 69, 851–64.

DiPalma, G. (1970), *Apathy and Participation: Mass Politics in Western Societies*, New York: Free Press.

Dollar, D. and A. Kraay (2000), 'Growth is Good for the Poor' Working Paper, Washington, DC: The World Bank.

Douglas, M. and A. Wildavsky (1983), *Risk and Culture*, Berkeley, CA: University of California Press.

Dumont, F. (1996), *Genèse de la société québécoise*, Québec: Boréal.

Easterlin, R.A. (1974), 'Does Economic Growth Improve the Human Lot? Some Empirical Evidence', in P.A. David and M.W. Reder (eds), *Nations and Households in Economic Growth: Essays in Honor of Moses Abromowitz*, New York, NY: Academic Press, 89–125.

Easterlin, R.A. (1998), *Growth Triumphant: The Twenty-first Century in Historical Perspective*, Ann Arbor, MI: University of Michigan Press.

Easterly, W. and R. Levine (1997), 'Africa's Growth Tragedy: Politics and Ethnic Divisions', *Quarterly Journal of Economics*, 112, 1203–50.

Eckstein, H. (1966), *Division and Cohesion in Democracy: A Study of Norway*, Princeton, NJ: Princeton University Press.

Elazar, D.J. (1966), *American Federalism: A View from the States*, 1986. New York: Crowell.

Elazar, D.J. (1986), *Cities of the Prairie Revisited: The Closing of the Metropolitan Frontier*, Lincoln: University of Nebraska Press.

Election Commission of India (1999) available at: http://www.eci.gov.in/.

Ellis, R.J. and M. Thompson (eds) (1997), *Culture Matters: Essays in Honor of Aaron Wildavsky*, Boulder, CO: Westview Press.

Encyclopaedia Britannica (annually), *Britannica World Data*, Chicago: Encyclopaedia Britannica.

Eriksen, T.H. (1993), *Ethnicity and Nationalism*, London: Pluto Books.

Esposito, J.L. and J.O. Voll (1996), *Islam and Democracy*, New York, NY: Oxford University Press.

Esaiasson, P. and S. Holmberg (1996), *Representation from Above: Members of Parliament and Representative Democracy in Sweden*, Aldershot: Dartmouth.

Etzioni, A. (1988), *The Moral Dimension*, New York: Free Press.

Fanon, F. (1961), *Les damnés de la terre*, Paris: Maspero.

Flora, P. and S. Kuhnle (eds) (1999), *State Formation, Nation-building, and Mass Politics in Europe. The Theory of Stein Rokkan: Based on his Collected Works*. Oxford: Oxford University Press.

Franke, R.H. et al. (1991), 'Cultural Roots of Economic Performance: A Research Note', *Strategic Management Journal*, 12, 165–73.

Freedom House (1999), *Freedom in the World: The Annual Survey of Political Rights and Civil Liberties, 1998–1999*, New Brunswick, NJ: Transaction.

Freedom House (2000), *Annual Survey Of Freedom House Country Scores 1972–73 to 1999–00* available at: http://www.freedomhouse.org/ratings/.

Fromm, E. (1984), *The Working Class in Weimar Germany: A Psychological and Sociological Study*, Leamington Spa: Berg.

Fukuyama, F. (1989), 'The End of History?', *The National Interest*, (16), 3–18.

Fukuyama, F. (1995a), *Trust: The Social Virtues and the Creation of Prosperity*, New York: The Free Press.

Fukuyama, F. (1995b), 'Confucianism and Democracy', *Journal of Democracy*, 6,(2), 20–33.

Gallup, J.L. *et al.* (1999), 'Geography and Economic Development', CID Working Paper 1, Cambridge, MA: Center for International Development, Harvard University.

Gastil, R.D. (1986), *Freedom in the World: Political Rights and Civil Liberties 1985–1986*, Westport, CT: Greenwood Press.

Gastil, R.D. (1987), *Freedom in the World: Political Rights and Civil Liberties 1986–1987*, Westport, CT: Greenwood Press.

Geertz, C. (1973), *The Interpretation of Cultures: Selected Essays*, New York, NY: Basic Books, New edition 2000.

Geertz, C. (1996), *After the Fact*, Cambridge, MA: Harvard University Press.

Geertz, C. (2000), *The Interpretation of Cultures*, New York: Basic Books.

Geertz, C. (2001), *Available Light*, Princeton, NJ: Princeton University Press.

Gellner, E. (1983a), *Nations and Nationalism*, Oxford: Blackwell.

Gellner, E. (1983b), *Muslim Society*, Cambridge: Cambridge University Press.

Gibbins, J.R. and B. Reimer (1999), *The Politics of Postmodernity: An Introduction to Contemporary Politics and Culture*, Thousand Oaks, CA: Sage.

Gibson, N. (2003), *Franz Fanon: The Post Colonial Imagination* (Key Contemporary Thinkers Series), Cambridge: Polity Press.

Gilpin, R. (2000), *The Challenge of Global Capitalism*, Princeton, NJ: Princeton University Press.

Glasenapp, H. von (1957), *Die nichtchristlichen Religionen*, Frankfurt am Main: Fischer Bücherei.

Glasenapp, H. von (1963), *Die fünf Weltreligionen*, Düsseldorf: Eugen Dietrichs Verlag.

Glazer, N. and D.P Moynihan (1975), *Ethnicity: Theory and Experience*, Cambridge, MA: Harvard University Press.

Gobineau, A. de (1999), *The Inequality of Human Races*, London: Howard Fertig.

Goldberg, E. (1996), 'Thinking About How Democracy Works', *Politics & Society*, 24, 7–18.

Graham, A. (1998), *The Sociology of the Family*, Oxford: Blackwell.

Granato, J. *et al.* (1996), 'The Effect of Cultural Values on Economic Development: Theory, Hypotheses, and Some Empirical Tests', *American Journal of Political Science*, 40, 607–31.

Gray, P.H. (1996), 'Culture and Economic Performance: Policy as an Intervening Variable', *Journal of Comparative Economics*, 23, 278–91.

Grimes, B.F. (ed.) (1999), *Ethnologue: Languages of the world*, 13th edn available at: http://sil.org.ethnologue/.

Gurr, T.R. (1990), *Polity II: Political Structures and Regime Change, 1800–1986*, Boulder, CO: Center for Comparative Politics [computer file].

Gurr, T.R. and B. Harff (1994), *Ethnic Conflict in World Politics*, Boulder, CO: Westview Press.

Halliday, F. and Ozkirimli, U. (2002), *Theories of Nationalism: A Critical Introduction*, Basingstoke: Palgrave Macmillan.

Hamilton, M.B. (1995), *The Sociology of Religion*, London: Routledge.

Harris, M. (1968), 'Race', in. D.L. Sills (ed.), *International Encyclopedia of the Social Sciences*, Vol. 13, New York, NY: Macmillan, 263–69.

Harrison, L.E. and S.P. Huntington (eds) (2000), *Culture Matters: How Values Shape Human Progress*, New York: Basic Books.

Harvey, D. (1989), *The Condition of Postmodernity*, Oxford: Blackwells.

Haynes, J. (1998), *Religion in Global Politics*, London: Longmann.

Held, D. *et al.* (1999), *Global Transformations: Politics, Economics and Culture*, Cambridge: Polity.

Hellevik, O. (1993), 'Postmaterialism as a Dimension of Cultural Change', *International Journal of Public Opinion Research*, 5, 211–33.

Henderson, D. (2000), 'False Perspective: The UNDP View of the World', *World Economics*, 1(1), 1–19.

Hermet, G. (2000), *Culture et développement*, Paris: Presses de Science.

Herrnstein, R.J. and Murray, C. (1996), *Bell Curve: Intelligence and Class Studies in American Life*, New York: Simon and Schuster.

Heywood, P. (1995), *The Government and Politics of Spain*, Basingstoke: Macmillan.

Hinich, M. and M.C. Munger (1997), *Analytical Politics*, Cambridge: Cambridge University Press.

Hirst, P. and G. Thompson (1996), *Globalization in Question: The International Economy and the Possibility of Governance*, Cambridge: Polity.

Hofstede, G. (1994), *Cultures and Organizations: Software of the Mind: Intercultural Cooperation and its Importance for Survival*, London: HarperCollins.

Horowitz, D.L. (1985), *Ethnic Groups in Conflict*, Berkeley, CA: University of California Press.

Horowitz, D.L. (2001), *The Deadly Ethnic Riot*, Berkeley: University of California Press.

Hourani, A. (1991), *A History of the Arab People*, Cambridge, MA: Harvard University Press.

Huntington, S.P. (1991), *The Third Wave: Democratization in the Late Twentieth Century*, Norman, OK: University of Oklahoma Press.

Huntington, S.P. (1996), *The Clash of Civilizations and the Remaking of World Order*, New York, NY: Simon and Schuster.

Huntington, S.P. (2004), *Who Are We? America's Great Debate*, New York: Free Press.

Hutchinson, J. and A.D. Smith (eds) (1994), *Nationalism*, Oxford: Oxford University Press.

Inglehart, R. (1977), *The Silent Revolution: Changing Values and Political Styles among Western Publics*, Princeton, NJ: Princeton University Press.

Inglehart, R. (1990), *Culture Shift in Advanced Industrial Society*, Princeton, NJ: Princeton University Press.

Inglehart, R. (1997), *Modernization and Postmodernization: Cultural, Economic and Industrial Change in 43 Societies*, Princeton, NJ: Princeton University Press.

Inglehart, R. and P. Norris (2003a), *Rising tide: gender equality and cultural change around the world*. New York: Cambridge University Press.

Inglehart, R. and P. Norris (2003b), 'The true clash of civlizations', *Foreign policy*, March/April: 67–74.

Inglehart, R. and P.R. Abramson (1999), 'Measuring Postmaterialism', *American Political Science Review*, 93, 665–77.

Inglehart, R. and W.E. Baker (2000), 'Modernization, Cultural Change, and the Persistence of Traditional Values', *American Sociological Review*, 65, 19–51.

Inglehart, R. *et al.* (2000), *World Values Surveys and European Values Surveys, 1981–1984, 1990–1993, and 1995–1997* [computer file], ICPSR version, Ann Arbor, MI: Institute for Social research [producer]; Ann Arbor, MI: Inter-University Consortium for Political and Social Research [distributor].

Inglehart, R. *et al.* (2004) European Values Study Group and World Values Survey Association. EUROPEAN AND WORLD VALUES SURVEYS INTEGRATED DATA FILE, 1999–2002, RELEASE I [Computer file]. 2nd ICPSR version. Cologne, Germany: Zentralarchiv fur Empirische Sozialforschung (ZA)/Tilburg, Netherlands: Tilburg University/Amsterdam, Netherlands: Netherlands Institute for Scientific Information Services (NIWI)/Madrid, Spain: Analisis Sociologicos Economicos y Politicos (ASEP) and JD Systems (JDS)/Ann Arbor, MI: Inter-university Consortium for Political and Social Research [producers], 2004. Cologne, Germany: Zentralarchiv fur Empirische Sozialforschung (ZA)/Madrid, Spain: Analisis Sociologicos Economicos y Politicos (ASEP) and JD Systems (JDS)/Ann Arbor, MI: Inter-university Consortium for Political and Social Research [distributors], 2004.

Institut National de Statistique (1954), *Recensement général de la population 1947: Repartition au point de vue des langues parlées*, Bruxelles: Institut National de Statistique.

Institut National de Statistique (1984), *Annuaire de statistiques régionales 1984*, Bruxelles: Institut National de Statistique.

Institut National de Statistique (1994), *Annuaire de statistiques régionales 1994*, Bruxelles: Institut National de Statistique.

Institut National de Statistique (1997), *Annuaire de statistiques régionales 1997*, Bruxelles: Institut National de Statistique.

Instituto Nacional de Estadistica (1998), *Anuario estadístico 1997*, Madrid: Instituto Nacional de Estadistica.

International Monetary Fund (IMF) (1994), *Government Finance Statistics Yearbook*, Washington, DC: IMF.

Inter-Parliamentary Union (IPU) (1995), *Women in Parliaments 1945–1995: A World Statistical Survey*, Geneva: IPU.

Jackman, R.W. and R.A. Miller (1996), 'A Renaissance of Political Culture?', *American Journal of Political Science*, 40, 632–59.

Jahoda, M. *et al.* (1975), *Die Arbeitslosen von Marienthal: Ein soziographischer Versuch*, Frankfurt am Main: Suhrkamp.

Jalali, R. and S.M. Lipset (1993), 'Racial and Ethnic Conflicts: A Global Perspective', *Political Science Quarterly*, 107, 585–606.

Jameson, F. (1991), *Postmodernism*, London: Verso Books.

Kaase, M. and K. Newton (1995), *Beliefs in Government*, Oxford: Oxford University Press.

Katzner, K. (1994), *The Languages of the World*, 3rd rev. edn, London: Routledge.

Kedourie, G. (1994), *Nationalism*, Oxford: Blackwell.

Kelly, P. (ed.) (2002), *Multiculturalism Reconsidered*, Cambridge: Polity.

Kelsen, H. (1961), *General Theory of Law and State*, New York: Russell and Russell.

Khilnani, S. (1997), *The Idea of India*, London: Hamish Hamilton.

Klingemann, H.-D. and D. Fuchs (eds) (1995), *Citizens and the State*, Oxford: Oxford University Press.

Klöti, U. *et al.* (1999), *Handbuch der Schweizer Politik*, Zürich: Neue Züricher Zeitung Verlag.

Knutsen, O. (1995), 'Party Choice', in J.W. Van Deth and E. Scarborough (eds), *The Impact of Values*, Oxford: Oxford University Press, 461–91.

Knutsen, O. (2000), 'Social Structure and Party Choice in Eight West European Countries, 1970–97: A Comparative Longitudinal Study of the Impact of Religious Denomination, Church Religiosity and Education', Oslo: Department of Political Science, University of Oslo.

Knutsen, O. and E. Scarborough (1995), 'Cleavage Politics', in: J.W. van Deth and E. Scarborough (eds), *The Impact of Values*, Oxford: Oxford University Press, 492–52.

Kohli, A. (1990), *Democracy and Discontent: India's Growing Crisis of Governability*, Cambridge: Cambridge University Press.

Kottak, C. P. (2000), *Anthropology: The Exploration of Human Diversity*, Boston: McGraw-Hill.

Kroeber, A.L. and C. Kluckhohn (1963), *Culture: A Critical Review of Concepts and Definitions*, New York: Vintage Books.

Krugman, P. (1994), 'The Myth of Asia's Miracle', *Foreign Affairs*, 73(6), 62–78.

Krulic, B. (1999), *La Nation. Une idée moderne*, Paris: Ellipses.

Kuper, A. (1996), *Anthropology and Anthropologists*, London: Routledge.

Kuper, A. (2000), *Culture: the Anthropologists' Account*, Cambridge, MA: Harvard University Press.

Kuznets, S. (1966), *Modern Economic Growth*, New Haven, CT: Yale University Press.

Kymlicka, W. (ed.) (1995), *The Rights of Minority Cultures*, Oxford: Oxford University Press.

Kymlicka, W. (2001), *Politics in the Vernacular: Nationalism, Multi-culturalism and Citizenship*, Oxford: Oxford University Press.

Kymlicka, W. and N. Wayne (eds) (2000), *Citizenship in Divided Societies*, Oxford: Oxford University Press.

Landes, D.S. (1998a), *The Wealth and Poverty of Nations: Why Some are so Rich and Some so Poor*, New York: Norton.

Landes, D.S. (1998b), 'Culture Counts: Interview with David S. Landes', *Challenge*, 41(4), 14–30.

Lane, R.E. (2000), *The Loss of Happiness in Market Democracies*, New Haven, CT: Yale University Press.

Lazarsfeld, P. *et al.* (1968), *The People's Choice: How the Voter Makes up his Mind in a Presidential Campaign*, New York: Columbia University Press.

Lechner, F.J. and J. Boli (eds) (2000), *The Globalization Reader*, Oxford: Blackwell.

Lenski, G. (1965), *The Religious Factor*, London: Greenwood Press

Leton, A. and A. Miroir (1999), *Les conflits communautaires en Belgique*, Paris: PUF.

Levy, M. (1952), *The Structure of Society*, Princeton, NJ: Princeton University Press.

Lijphart, A. (1977), *Democracy in Plural Societies: A Comparative Exploration*, New Haven, CT: Yale University Press.

Lijphart, A. (1999), *Patterns of Democracy: Government Forms and Performance in Thirty-six Countries*, New Haven, CT: Yale University Press.

Lin, N. (2001), *Social Capital*, Cambridge: Cambridge University Press.

Lipset, S.M and G.S. Lenz (2000), 'Corruption, Culture and Market', in L.E Harrison and S.P. Huntington (eds), *Culture Matters: How Values Shape Human Progress*, New York: Basic Books, 112–24.

Loury, G.C. (1987), 'Why should we care about group inequality?', *Social Philosophy and Policy*, 5, 249–71.

Loury, G.C. (1995), *One by One from the Inside Out: Essays and Reviews on Race and Responsibility in America*, New York: Free Press.

Luttbeg, N.R. (1999), *Comparing the States and Communities: Politics, Government and Policy in the United States*, Dubuque, IA: Eddie Bowers.

Maddison, A. (1995), *Monitoring the World Economy 1820–1992*, Paris: OECD.

Maget, M. (1968), 'Problèmes d'ethnographie européenne', in Poirier, J. (ed.), *Ethnologie générale*, Paris: Gallimard.

Malinowski, B. (1969), *A Scientific Theory of Culture and Other Essays*, Oxford: Oxford University Press (1st edn 1944).

Manza, J. and C. Brooks (1998), 'The Gender Gap in US Presidential Elections: When? Why? Implications?', *American Journal of Sociology*, 103, 1235–66.

Masters, W.A. and M.S. McMillan (2000), 'Climate and Scale in Economic Growth', CID Working Paper 48, Cambridge, MA: Center for International Development, Harvard University.

Mauro, P. (1995), 'Corruption and Growth', *Quarterly Journal of Economics*, 110, 681–712.

Meinecke, F. (1962), *Weltbüngertum and Nationalstaat*, München: Oldenbourg.

Miller, D. (1995), *On Nationality*, Oxford: Oxford University Press.

Miller, D. (2000), *Citizenship and National Identity*, Cambridge: Polity Press.

Miller, W. E. and J.M. Shanks (1996), *The New American Voter*, Cambridge, MA: Harvard University Press.

Milton-Edwards, B. (2004), *Islam and Politics in the Contemporary World*, Cambridge: Polity.

Montero, J.R. (1998), 'Stabilising the Democratic Order: Electoral Behaviour in Spain', *West European Politics*, 21(4), 53–79.

Mortimer, E. and Fine, R. (1999), *People, Nation and State: The Meaning of Ethnicity and Nationalism*, London: IB Tauris.

Mulhall, S. and A. Swift (1996), *Liberals and Communitarians*, Oxford: Blackwell.

Muños-Perez, F. and M. Tribalat (1984), 'Mariages d'étrangers et marriages mixtes en France: Evolution depuis la première guerre', *Population*, 39, 427–62.

Myrdal, G. (1967), *Value in Social Theory: A Selection of Essays on Methodology*, London: Routledge and Kegan Paul.

Newton, K. (1999), 'Social and political trust in established democracies', in P. Norris (ed.), *Critical Citizens. Global Support for Democratic Government*, Oxford: Oxford University Press, 169–87.

Newton, K. and P. Norris (2000), 'Confidence in Public Institutions: Faith, Culture, or Performance?', in S.J. Pharr and R.D. Putnam (eds), *Disaffected Democracies: What's Troubling the Trilateral Countries?*, Princeton, NJ: Princeton University Press, 52–73.

Nieuwbeerta, P. and N.D. de Graf (1999), 'Traditional Class Voting in Twenty Postwar Societies', in G. Evans (ed.), *The End of Class Politics? Class Voting in Comparative Context*, Oxford: Oxford University Press, 23–56.

Nock, S.L. (1996), *The Sociology of the Family*, Englewood Cliffs, NJ: Prentice-Hall.

Nordlinger, E.A. (1972), *Conflict Regulation in Divided Societies*, Cambridge, MA: Center for International Affairs, Harvard University.

Norris, P. (ed.) (1999), *Critical Citizens: Global Support for Democratic Government*, Oxford: Oxford University Press.

Norris, P. and Inglehart, R. (2004), *Sacred and Secular: Religion and Politics Worldwide*, Cambridge: Cambridge University Press.

North, D. (1990), *Institutions, Institutional Change and Economic Performance*, Cambridge: Cambridge University Press.

NUPI (1999), *Centre for Russian Studies Database* available at: http://www.nupi.no/russland/russland.htm/.

Nygren, A. (1982), *Agape and Eros*, Chicago, IL: University of Chicago Press.

Ogden, S. (1999), *China*, New York: McGraw Hill.

Olson, M. (1965), *The Logic of Collective Action*, Cambridge, MA: Harvard University Press.

Olson, M. (1982), *The Rise and Decline of Nations: Economic Growth, Stagflation and Social Rigidities*, New Haven, CT: Yale University Press.

Ordeshook, P. (1992), *A Political Theory Primer*, London: Routledge.

Parker, P. (1997a), *Religious Cultures of the World*, Westport, CT: Greenwood Press.

Parker, P. (1997b), *Linguistic Cultures of the World*, Westport, CT: Greenwood Press.

Parker, P. (1997c), *Ethnic Cultures of the World*, Westport, CT: Greenwood Press.

Parker, P. (1997d), *National Cultures of the World*, Westport, CT: Greenwood Press.

Parsons, T. (1967), *Politics and Social Structure*, New York: The Free Press.

Parsons, T., Shils, E. and Smelser, N. (eds) (2001), *Towards a General Theory of Action*, New York: Transaction Books.

Penniman, H.L. and E.M. Mujal-León (eds) (1985), *Spain at the Polls 1977, 1979, and 1982*, Durham, NC: Duke University Press.

Pettigrew, T.F. (1968 ), 'Race Relations: Social-psychological Aspects', in D.L. Sills (ed.), *International Encyclopedia of the Social Sciences*, Vol. 13, New York: Macmillan, pp. 277–82.

Pettit, P. (1999), *Republicanism*, Oxford: Oxford University Press.

Peuch, H.-Ch. (ed.) (1970a), *Histoire des religions*: I, Paris: Gallimard.

Peuch, H.-Ch. (ed.) (1970b), *Histoire des religions*: I, Paris: Gallimard.

Peuch, H.-Ch. (ed.) (1972a), *Histoire des religions*: II, Paris: Gallimard.

Peuch, H.-Ch. (ed.) (1972b), *Histoire des religions*: II, Paris: Gallimard.

Peuch, H.-Ch. (ed.) (1976a), *Histoire des religions*: III, Paris: Gallimard.

Peuch, H.-Ch. (ed.) (1976b), *Histoire des religions*: III, Paris: Gallimard.

Pharr, S.J. and R.D. Putnam (eds) (2000), *Disaffected Democracies: What's Troubling the Trilateral Countries?*, Princeton, NJ: Princeton University Press.

Putnam, R.D. (1993), *Making Democracy Work: Civic Traditions in Modern Italy*, Princeton, NJ: Princeton University Press.

Putnam, R.D. (2000), *Bowling Alone: The Collapse and Revival of American Community*, New York: Simon and Schuster.

Pye, L.W. (1968), 'Political Culture', in D.L. Sills, (ed.), *International Encyclopedia of the Social Sciences*, Vol. 12, New York: Macmillan, 218–24.

Pye, L.W. (1988), *The Mandarin and the Cadre: China's Political Cultures*, Ann Arbor, MI: University of Michigan Press.

Rayside, D. (1998), *On The Fringe. Gays and Lesbians in Politics*, Ithaca: Cornell University Press.

Reif, K. and E. Marlier (1995), *Eurobarometer 43.1 bis: Regional Development, Consumer and Environmental Issues* [computer file], Cologne: Zentralarchiv für empirische Sozialforschung [producer]; Göteborg: SSD [distributor].

Renan, E. (1994), 'Qu'est-ce qu'une nation?', in J, Hutchinson and A.D. Smith (eds), *Nationalism*, Oxford: Oxford University Press.

Renner, K. (1998), *La Nation, mythe et reálité*, Nancy: Presses Universitaires de Nancy.

Reynolds, A. and B. Reilly *et al.* (1997), *The International IDEA Handbook of Electoral System Design*, Stockholm: IDEA.

Rickert, H. (1921), *Die Grenzen der naturwissenschftlichen Begriffsbildung*, Tübingen: JC Mohr.

Rokkan, S. *et al.* (1970), *Citizens, Elections, Parties: Approaches to the Comparative Study of the Process of Development*, Oslo: Universitetsforlaget.

Rose, R. (ed.) (1974), *Electoral Behavior: A Comparative Handbook*, New York: Free Press.

Rostow, W.W. (1960), *The Stages of Economic Growth: a Non-communist Manifesto*, Cambridge: Cambridge University Press.

Ruhlen, M. (1987), *A Guide to the World's Languages*, London: Edward Arnold.

Said, E.W. (1994), *Culture and imperialism*, London: Vintage.

Said, E.W. (1995), *Orientalism*, Harmondsworth: Penguin.

Sakwa, R. (1996), *Russian Politics and Society*, 2nd edn, London: Routlege.

Sanders, D. and M. Brynin (1998), 'Ordinarly Least Squares and Logistic Regression Analysis', in E. Scarborough and E. Tanenbaum (eds), *Research Strategies in the Social Sciences. A Guide to New Approaches*, Oxford: Oxford University Press, 29–52.

Sartori, G. (ed.) (1984), *Social Science Concepts*, Beverly Hills, CA: Sage.

Scarborough, E. (1995), 'Materialist–Postmaterialist Value Orientations', in J.W. van Deth, and E. Scarborough (eds), *The Impact of Values*, Oxford: Oxford University Press, 123–59.

Scheuch, E. (1990), 'The Development of Comparative Research: Towards Causal Explanation', in E. Øyen, (ed.), *Comparative Methodology: Theory and Practice in International Social Research*, London: Sage, 19–37.

Scott, M.F. (1989), *A New View of Economic Growth*, Oxford: Clarendon Press.

Sen, A. (1999), *Development as Freedom*, Oxford: Oxford University Press.

Shepsle, K.A. and M.S. Boncheck (1997), *Analyzing Politics: Rationality, Behavior and Institutions*, New York: Norton.

Shively, W.P. (1998), *The Craft of Political Research*. 4th edn, Upper Saddle River, NJ: Prentice Hall.

Sieyès, E.J. (1985), *Ecrits politiques*, Pars: Editions des Archives Contemporaines.

Singh, V.B. and S. Bose (1984), *Elections in India: Data Handbook on Lok Sabha Elections 1952–80*, New Dehli: Sage.

Smith, A.D. (1991), *National Identity*, Harmondsworth: Penguin.

Smith, A.D. (1998), *Nationalism and Modernism*, London: Routledge.

Smith, A.D. (2004), *The Antiquity of Nations*, Cambridge, Polity.

Solomos, J. and L. Back (1996), *Racism and Society*, Basingstoke: Macmillan.

Solow, R.M. (2000), *Growth Theory: An Exposition*, Oxford: Oxford University Press.

Sorokin, P. A. (1957), *Social and Cultural Dynamics: A Study of Change in Major Systems of Art, Truth, Ethics, Laws and Social Relationships*, Boston: Porter Sargent.

Sorokin, P. A. (1966), *Sociological Theories of Today*, New York: Harper and Row.

Sowell, T. (1995), *Race and Culture: A World View*, New York: Basic Books.

Spengler, O. (1926–28), *The Decline of the West*, New York: Knopf.

Stevens, J.B. (1993), *The Economics of Collective Choice*, Boulder, CO: Westview Press.

Stoetzel, J. (1983), *Les valeurs du temps présent: Une enquête*, Paris: PUF.

Summers, R. and A. Heston (1994), *Penn World Tables, Mark 5.6* available at: http://pwt.econ.upenn.edu/.

Tanzi, V. (1998), 'Corruption Around the World: Causes, Consequences, Scope, and Cure', *IMF Staff Papers*, 45, 559–94.

Taylor, C.L. (1992), *Sources of the Self*, Cambridge: Cambridge University Press.

Thompson, M., Ellis, R and A. Wildavsky (1990), *Cultural Theory*, Boulder, CO: Westview Press.

Thompson, M., Grendstad, G. and P. Selle (eds) (1999), *Cultural Theory as Political Science*, London: Routledge.

Tilly, C. (ed.) (1975), *The Formation of National States in Western Europe*, Princeton, NJ: Princeton University Press.

Tingsten, H. (1937), *Political Behaviour: Studies in Election Statistics*, London: P.S. King and Son.

Tocqueville, A. de (1990), *Democracy in America I and II*, New York: Vintage.

Todd, E. (1983), *La troisième planète: Structures familiales et systèmes idéologiques*, Paris: Seuil.

Todd, E. (1984), *L'enfance du monde: Structures familiales et développement*, Paris: Seuil.

Toynbee, A. (1987), *A study of History: Abridgement of Volumes I–VI*, New York: Oxford University Press.

Transparency International (1999), 'Corruption Perception Index' available at: http://www.transparency.org/documents/cpi/index.html; see also: http://www.gwdg.de/~uwvw/.

Triandis, H.C. (1995), *Individualism and Collectivism*, Boulder, CO: Westview Press.

Tsebelis, G. (1990), *Nested Games: Rational Choice in Comparative Politics*, Berkeley, CA: University of California Press.

Tönnies, F. (1965), *Community and Society*, New York: Harper Torchbooks (1st edn 1887).

UNDP (1990–) *Human Development Report 1990*, New York, NY: Oxford University Press.

UNDP (1994), *Human Development Report 1994*, New York, NY: Oxford University Press.

UNDP (1995), *Human Development Report 1995*, New York, NY: Oxford University Press.

UNDP (1999), *Human Development Report 1999*, New York, NY: Oxford University Press.

UNDP (2000a), *Human Development Report 2000*, New York, NY: Oxford University Press.

UNDP (2000b), Human Development Report Office: 'Response to Mr. Castles' Room Document on Human Development Report 1999' available at http://www.undp.org/hdro/fulltext.htm/.

US Department of Commerce (1997), *Statistical abstract of the United States 1997*, Washington, DC: The Agency.

van Deth, J.W. (1995a), 'Introduction: The Impact of Values', in J.W. van Deth and E. Scarborough (eds), *The Impact of Values*, Oxford: Oxford University Press, 1–18.

van Deth, J.W. (1995b), 'A Macro Setting for Micro Politics', in J.W. van Deth, and E. Scarborough (eds), *The Impact of Values*, Oxford: Oxford University Press, 48–75.

van Deth, J.W. and E. Scarborough (1995a), 'The Concept of Values', in J.W. van Deth and E. Scarborough (eds), *The Impact of Values*, Oxford: Oxford University Press, 21–47.

van Deth, J.W. and E. Scarborough (eds) (1995b), *The Impact of Values*, Oxford: Oxford University Press.

van Gunsteren, H.R. (1998), *A Theory of Citizenship*, Boulder, CO: Westview Press.

Vanhanen, T. (1999), 'Domestic Ethnic Conflict and Ethnic Nepotism: A Comparative Analysis', *Journal of Peace Research*, 36, 55–73.

Verba, S. *et al.* (1978), *Participation and Political Equality: A Seven-nation Comparison*, Cambridge: Cambridge University Press.

Wagtskjold, J.F. (1978), 'Spain: Economic, Social and Political Data for Spanish Provinces and Regions 1975–1976 [data set], Bergen: NSD, University of Bergen.

Weber, M. (1904), 'Die Protestantische Ethik und der Geist des Kapitalismus', *Archiv für Sozialwissenschaft und Sozialpolitik*, XX and XXI.

Weber, M. (1920, 1963–72), *Gesammelte Aufsätze zur Religionssoziologie* I–III, Tübingen: Mohr.

Weber, M. (1964), *The Religion of China*, New York: The Free Press.

Weber, M. (1967), *Ancient Judaism*, New York: The Free Press.

Weber, M. (1978), *Economy and Society* I and II, Berkeley, CA: University of California Press (First published 1970).

Weber, M. (1982), *Methodology of the Social Sciences*, New York: Macmillan.

Weber, M. (1993), *The Sociology of Religion*, London: Beacon Press.

Weber, M. (1996), *The Religion of India*, New York: The Free Press.

Weber, M. (2001), *The Protestant Ethic and the Spirit of Capitalism*, London: Routledge.

White, S. *et al.* (1997), *How Russia Votes*, Chatham, NJ: Chatham House Publishers.

Wildavsky, A. (1973), 'If Planning is Everything, Then Maybe it is Nothing', *Policy Sciences*, 4, 127–53

Wildavsky, A. (1987), 'Choosing Preferences by Constructing Institutions: A Cultural Theory of Preference Formation', *American Political Science Review*, 81, 3–21.

Wildavsky, A. (1991), *The Rise of Radical Egalitarianism*, Washington, DC: American University Press.

Wildavsky, A. (1995), *Is It Really True? A Citizen's Guide to Environmental Health and Safety Issues*, Cambridge, MA: Harvard University Press.

Wildavsky, A. and R.E. Ellis (1989), *Dilemmas of Presidential Leadership*, New Brunswick, NJ: Transaction Books.

Willis, P. (2000), *The Ethnographic Imagination*, Cambridge: Polity Press.

Wilson, E.O. (1999), *Consilience: The Unity of Knowledge*, New York: Vintage.

World Bank (1975), *World Bank Atlas, 1975*, Washington, DC: The World Bank.

World Bank (1987), *World Bank Atlas, 1987*, Washington, DC: The World Bank.

World Bank (1996), *World Bank Atlas, 1996*, Washington, DC: The World Bank.

World Bank (1999), *World Bank Atlas, 1999*, Washington, DC: The World Bank.

World Bank (2000), *World Bank Atlas, 2000*, Washington, DC: The World Bank.

Zubaida, S. (1993), *Islam, the People and the State*, London: Tauris.

# Index

Abramson, P.R. 245, 246
achievement orientation 263, 264, 265,
    267, 270, 272, 273, 276, 277, 285,
    286
    and micro-level outcomes 309
affluence 6, 10, 26, 39, 42
    and colonial legacy 211, 214
    distribution of 44
    and gender development 282
    and gender equality 294–5
    and individualism 282, 284
    and postmaterialism 268, 280, 282,
    287
    and poverty 44
    and religion 170–1, 176–7
    and trust 269, 282
Africa 267–70
African civilization 144
Alaouites 153
Ali (son-in-law of the Prophet) 153
Allardt, E. 116
Almond, G.A., *The Civic Culture* 32,
    59, 250–1, 253, 265
analysis, framework 2, 7, 36
Anderson, B. 73, 77
Anglo-Saxon legacy 202–3
Annett, A. 116
anthropology
    and culture 20
    *see also* cultural anthropology
Apartheid 11, 216
Arndt, E.M. 87
asceticism 158, 166
Asia 267–9
associations 15, 33, 34, 76, 77, 241, 305
    cultural 239
    neighbourhood 240
    voluntary 11, 250
atheism 146, 149, 159, 160, 161, 162
attitudes, values as 241–2, 255

Augustine, St 152
autonomy 29, 30, 85, 155, 203, 318
    institutional 123
    orientation index 299
Ayubi, N. 152

'backward society' attitude 27
Banfield, E.C. 27, 238
Banzhaf's power index 34
Barnes, S.H. 59
Barrett, D.B. 103, 104, 106, 107, 108,
    145, 160, 161, 163
Barry, B. 317, 320–3
    *Culture and Equality* 320
Barth, F. 76
Bayes' theory 34
Becker, G. 34
behaviour, values as 239–41
Belgium
    empire 204
    ethnicity 126–7
    party support 55–6, 186–7, 308
    religion 186–7
Benhabib, S. 317
    *The Claims of Culture* 320
Berbers 77, 81
Berelson, B. 58
BJP 56, 128, 129, 134, 188, 189
Bodhisattvas 151
Bollen, K. 174
boycotts, joining 63, 64, 65, 130, 132,
    134, 191, 192, 193, 286, 287
Brahmanism 148, 149
Braillard, P. 90–1
Brass, P.R. 56
Brecht, A. 142
Brinkmann, C. 141
Britain, colonial legacies 11, 207, 211
British Empire 200, 205–6, 207
Broek, J.O.M. 144, 145, 229

Brooks, 249
Buddhism 25, 46, 48, 140, 150, 151,
    156
  and economic growth 177, 310
Buddhism-Confucianism 144, 160
Buddhist world 146

Calvinism 157
Campbell, A. 58
Cantril, H. 59
capitalism 45, 113, 166
  and Protestantism 10, 139, 140, 156,
    157, 158, 164, 167, 168, 179
Catholic countries 159, 170, 173, 174,
    189, 219
Chinese civilization 144
Christian Orthodox 144
Christian world 25, 146
Christianity 25, 46, 48, 152
citizenship 1, 78
civic
  community 239, 241, 242–3
  culture 32, 59, 60, 250, 251, 253, 255
civil society 33, 238, 239, 241, 242,
    250, 316
civilization 4, 15, 26, 27
  African 144
  as culture 25, 141–2
  definitions 142
  Inuit 81, 144
  Latin American 144
  meaning 19
  Russian 144
civilizations 141–6
  Broek on 145
  classification 26, 143–5
  cycle theory 141
  and historical legacies 26
  Huntington on 141, 145
  religions as 146–7
  religious 25–6
  Toynbee on 143, 145
  *see also* 'clash of civilizations'
'clash of civilizations' 1, 6, 15, 141
clientelism 27, 239
climate, and economic development 45
Coleman, J.C. 33, 240
colonial experience 203, 208, 209, 212,
    310

colonial legacies 203–12
  and affluence 211, 214
  Britain 11, 207, 211
  and corruption 214
  and economic development 209–11,
    216
  France 205, 207, 209, 210
  and human development 214
  and outcomes 206–9
  significance 212–16
  Spain 209, 211
  Third World 210–11, 217
colonial rule 162, 200, 203, 206, 207,
    209, 210, 212, 213, 214, 216, 310
colonialism 25, 111, 116, 161
  characteristics 203
  consequences 209–12
  as culture 1
communalism 7, 29, 305
communism 15, 31, 160, 221, 223, 227,
    231
communitarianism 3, 61, 315, 316, 317,
    322
communities 1, 3, 4, 6, 7, 15, 26, 36, 76,
    77
  ethnic 79, 82, 95, 101, 102, 143
  imagined 73, 83, 95, 314
  linguistic 102
Confucianism 25, 27, 139, 140, 142,
    144, 146, 150–1, 156–7, 158, 310
Congress Party 56, 128, 188
consociationalism 43, 180, 181, 318
Converse, P. 239, 244, 246
Coptes 77
corruption 33, 42, 48, 176, 179, 202,
    263, 269, 277, 312
  and colonial legacies 214
  and religion 173–5
Crystal, D. 103, 104, 105, 106
cultural analysis 1, 2, 7–9, 10, 12, 29,
    35, 36, 37, 39, 41, 108, 113, 199,
    219, 238, 239, 252, 254, 255, 257,
    258, 259, 260, 263, 289
cultural anthropology 33–4
cultural approach 2–3, 11, 37, 41–2, 305
cultural cleavage, sex as 290–2
cultural effects 1, 2, 3, 5, 6, 8, 11, 16,
    42, 57, 115, 226, 231, 243, 255,
    275, 306, 312

cultural equation 60–1
cultural factors
  and gender equality 296
  impact 309–12
cultural identity 3–4, 18, 36
  as ethnicity 78
  and groups 4–5, 15
cultural outcomes 5–6, 8–9, 305–23
  key variables 9–10
  longitudinal perspective 200
  macro levels 39, 40–1, 42–8, 307
  micro levels 39, 60–6, 308–9
  regional levels 39, 51–7, 308
cultural preferences 40, 41, 42
cultural research 20, 311
cultural studies 10, 11–12
cultural thesis (CT) 8, 306, 312
culture 3–5
  ambiguity of 24–7
  and anthropology 20
  civilization as 25, 141–2
  colonialism as 1
  concept 17–18, 18–20, 35
  connotations 21–4
  definitions 17
  denotation 25
  and economic development 44–5
  ethnicity as 73
  and fundamentalism 315–16
  and globalization 8
  kinds 6
  meaning 3
  role 39
  significance 312–13
  theories 27–31
  typology 28–31
  *see also* political culture; subcultures

Dalton, R.J. 132, 149
Darwin, C. 92
Das Gupta, J. 56
data sets
  macro-level 327–34
  micro-level 57–60, 341–3
Davenport, C. 245
Davis, D.W. 245
de Blij, H.J. 107, 204
de Graaf, N.D. 249
De Waele, J.-M. 55

Delgado, R. 114
  *Critical Race Theory* 94
Delwit, P. 55
democracy
  consociational 318
  and family structures 227–8, 230
  index 42
  measurement 42–3
  and religion 173–5
Derbyshire, I. 204
Derbyshire, J.D. 204
Deutsch, K.W. 73
development, and religion 139
developmental outcomes 94, 167, 176,
    213, 214, 216
  and postmaterialism 279, 280
Diamond, J. 45
diasporas 78–9
Diener, E. 265
*Diesseits* 158
  vs *Jenseits* 157
DiPalma, G. 132
Dollar, D. 44
Douglas, M. 29, 252, 263, 264
Dubois, W.E.B. 93

Easterlin, R.A. 44
Easterly, W. 117
Eckstein, H. 227
economic development
  and climate 45
  and colonial legacies 209–11, 216
  and culture 44–5
  geographical factors 49
  historical factors 49
  and human development 45–6
  and quality of life 46
  and religion 158, 167–8, 170, 173,
    174, 176, 179
economic growth
  and Buddhism 177
  and religion 170–2
egalitarianism 1, 4, 29, 30, 47
Elazar, D.J. 28
Ellis, R. 2, 254
equality 46–7
  multiculturalism, conflict 315, 321
equator, distance from 49, 50
Eriksen, T.H. 75

Esaiasson, P. 132
Eskimos *see* Inuit civilization
Esposito, J.L. 174
essentialist approach 147, 152
ethnic cleavages 96, 98, 99, 115–17
    and human development 117
ethnic fragmentation 10, 96, 115
    USA 120
ethnic groups 76–9, 96, 114–15
    characteristics 77
    definition 76, 82–3
    as imagined communities 77
    lateral 78, 79–80
    and nations 82–3
    vertical 78, 80
ethnic identity 73
ethnic mobilization 79, 80
ethnicity 2, 4, 8, 10, 95–8, 128, 133–4
    Belgium 126–7
    as cultural identity 78
    as culture 73
    and globalization 6
    India 127–8, 129
    and interest in politics 132, 133
    and language 95, 98–9, 101, 101–2,
        109, 111–14
    and left-right placement 132
    and life satisfaction 131
    models 97
    and national pride 130
    outcomes 101–34, 310
    Russia 120–3
    Spain 123–5
    Switzerland 125–6
    USA 119–20, 121
    and voluntary organisations 132, 133
ethnicity theory 40, 97–8, 116
ethnie 35, 96, 97, 98, 155, 313, 314,
    316, 318
ethnogenesis 79–80
Etzioni, A. 2, 34
Eurobarometer surveys 60, 244, 245, 258
European Values Study (EVS) 59–60
extra-worldly 147, 156, 157
    *see also* inner-worldly

family cultures 220–3
    classification 224–6
    outcomes 227–30

family structures 219–31
    and democracy 227–8, 230
    and political systems 227–30
    typologies 220–3, 224–6
    variations 223–4
family values 197, 223, 224, 227, 228,
    229, 231, 312
Fanon, F. 91, 95, 216
fatalism 29, 30, 238, 252
Fichte, J.G. 87
Flora, P. 116
France, colonial legacies 205, 207, 209,
    210
Franke, R.H. 44
Freedom House 42, 43
French Empire 203, 210
Fromm, E. 58
Fukuyama, F. 1, 33, 45, 48, 251, 255,
    263, 264, 282
fundamentalism, and culture 315–16

game theory 34
Geertz, C. 1, 2, 17, 20, 35
    works
        *Available Light* 34
        *The Interpretation of Cultures* 34
        *Works and Lives* 33–4
Gellner, E. 84, 152
gender development 173, 263, 290, 312
    and affluence 282
    and gender empowerment 293–5
    and religion 177
    and trust 282
Gender Development Index (GDI) 47,
    172, 173, 290
gender empowerment
    and gender development 293–5
    and Islam 298
Gender Empowerment Measure (GEM)
    47, 172, 173, 290
gender equality 42, 47–8, 109, 181, 276,
    279, 289, 290
    and affluence 294–5
    and cultural factors 296
    and human development 47
    and Protestantism 297
gender orientations, and value
    orientations 298–9
geographical location 49

German Empire 204
Gini coefficient 47
Glasenapp, H. 151
Glazer, N. 119
globalization 6–7, 89, 305–6
    and culture 8
    and groups 102
    and religion 6
    and universal values 3, 6
Gobineau, J.A., *The Inequality of Human Races* 92
Goldberg, E. 243
Graham, A. 220
Granato, J. 42
Gray, P.H. 44
Greek Orthodox 25, 27, 31, 146, 160, 162, 173
Grimes, B.F. 103, 104, 125
groups
    and cultural identity 4–5, 15
    culture-based/interest-based 15
    and globalization 102
    language 107–9
    *see also* primordial groups
Gurr, T.R. 116

Hamilton, M.B. 43, 45, 148
Harff, B. 116
Harris, M. 92
Harrison, L.E. 42, 43
Harvey, D. 261
Haynes, J. 140
Herder, J.G. von 84, 86, 88
    *Outline of a Philosophy* 87
hermeneutics 12, 20, 152, 313
Hermet, G. 42
Hernstein, R.J., *The Bell Curve* 94
heterogeneity
    cultural 7, 51, 313, 320
    ethnic 54, 102, 119
    religious 141, 158, 179, 180, 181
Heywood, P. 53, 123
hierarchy 27, 28, 29, 30, 31, 252
Hindu civilization 144
Hindu nationalism 79, 81, 162
Hinduism 2, 25, 46, 48, 149–50, 151
Hinduist/Buddhist world 25
Hinich, M. 2, 258
Hofstede, G. 265

Holmberg, S. 132
Holocaust victims, and Switzerland 90–1
homogeneity 115, 119, 122, 128
    cultural 7
homosexuality 292
    attitudes to 300, 301, 302
Horowitz, D.L. 41, 43, 95–6, 116, 117
Hourani, A. 101
human development 6, 94, 113, 114, 181, 214, 282
    and colonial legacy 214
    and economic development 45–6
    and ethnic cleavages 117
    and gender equality 47
    and postmaterialism 279
    variation 177
Human Development Index (HDI) 6, 45, 46, 172
    and attitudes to homosexuality 302
human rights 5, 10, 140, 173, 176, 231, 251, 279, 307, 310
Humboldt, A. 87
Huntington, S. 1, 11, 15, 26, 41, 42, 43, 144, 145, 229
    *The Clash of Civilisations* 141
    *Who are We?* 314
Hutchinson, J. 73

Iberian legacy 200–2, 209, 210, 211, 216
ideology, nationalism as 85
IFOP 59
income, and religion 169–70
income distribution 6, 42, 47
    and colonial legacy 214
    measurement 172
    and religion 173, 176, 177
India
    ethnicity 127–8, 129
    party support 56, 187–8, 308
    religion 187–8, 189
individual values 11, 39, 57
individualism 11, 28, 29, 30, 43, 263, 264, 265, 266, 282
    and affluence 282, 284
Inglehart, R. 1, 11, 41, 42, 57, 59, 62, 129, 243, 244, 245, 246, 247, 248, 253, 254, 263, 264, 265, 268, 274, 280, 282, 290, 291, 303, 304

inner-worldly 147, 156, 157, 165, 166
  *see also* extra-worldly
institutional analysis 37
institutions 7, 17, 23, 24, 40, 49
  economic 33, 201, 202
  educational 241
  family 221, 227, 229
  governmental 142
  historical 37
  market 171
  political 31, 32, 33, 239, 242, 275,
    317
interpretive approach 1, 12, 20, 57,
  259
Inuit civilization 81, 144
irrationality, vs rationality 157, 158
Islam 2, 11, 25, 46, 48, 152–5
  caliphate 153–4
  essentialist perspective 152–4
  and gender empowerment 298
  relativist perspective 154
  Shia 146, 153, 158
  sources 153
  Sunni 146, 152, 153, 158
Islamic fundamentalism 152, 154, 162,
  314
Isma'ilis 153
Italy
  political variations 239
  trust in 242–3

Jackman, R.W. 42, 282
Jahoda, M. 58
Jainism 142
Jalali, R. 116
Jameson, F. 261
Japanese Empire 209
*Jenseits* 158
  vs *Diesseits* 157
Judaism 2, 139, 142, 146, 147, 151,
  151–2, 158, 162, 167, 235
justice 46, 48, 90, 91, 277, 316, 322

Kaase, M. 59
  *Beliefs in Government* 11
Katzner, K. 103
Kedourie, G. 84
Kelly, P., *Multiculturalism
  Reconsidered* 323

Khilnani, S. 56
Klemm, G.E., *Allgemeine
  Kulturgeschichte der Meenschheit*
  19
Klöti, U. 54
Kluckhohn, C. 19, 20, 24
Knutsen, O. 249
Kohli, A. 56
Kohn, H. 85
Koran 152
Kottak, C.P. 20, 24–5, 144
Kraay, A. 44
Kroeber, A.L. 19, 20, 24
Krugman, P. 171
Kuhnle, S. 115
*Kultur* 18, 19
*Kulturwissenschaft* 20
Kuper, A. 144
Kurds 81
Kuznets curve 46, 47
Kymlicka, W. 1, 11, 317–18

Landes, D.S. 44, 49
language
  English 105
  and ethnicity 95, 98–9, 101, 101–2,
    109, 111–14
  families 103–5, 106–14
  and modernity 111
languages, users 104
Lao-Tse 151
Latin American civilization 144
Lazarsfeld, P. 58
Le Play, Frederic 220, 224
leadership, modernized 49, 50
left-right placement 65–6
  and ethnicity 132
legacies
  historical 2, 7, 10, 11, 25, 26, 35, 36,
    87, 137, 141, 143, 199, 199–217,
    200, 205, 207, 211, 217, 238, 280,
    295, 309, 310–11
  and civilizations 26
  *see also* Anglo-Saxon legacy;
    colonial legacies; Iberian legacy
Lenski, G. 43
Lenz, G.S. 48
Leton, A. 126
Levine, R. 117

Levy, M. 227
libertarianism 4
life satisfaction 10, 60, 62, 66, 67, 133,
    285, 308, 309
  and ethnicity 130, 131, 134
  and religion 190, 191
  and values 285, 286, 287
Lijphart, A. 43, 181
  *Democracy in Plural Societies* 318
linguistic group 104, 108
Lipset, S.M. 48, 116
longitudinal perspective 7, 37, 41
Lutheranism 162

McMillan, M.S. 49
Maget, M. 77
Malinowski, B. 17, 21, 199
Manza, J. 249
Maronites 77, 79
Masters, W.A. 49
materialism 7, 17, 246, 255, 260, 263
  postmaterialism 249
Mauro, P. 48
Meinecke, F. 87
*Mezzogiorno* 27, 33, 238, 253
Mill, J.S. 227
Miller, D. 47, 89, 90, 91
Miller, R.A. 282
Miller, W.E. 42, 119
*Millet* system 206
Milton-Edwards, B., *Islam and Politics
    in the Contemporary World*
    154–5
minorities 1
  cultural support 318–19
  and nationalism 90–1
Miroir, A. 126
modernity, and language 111
modernization theory 43
Montero, J.R. 53
moralism 28
Moynihan, D.P. 119
multiculturalism 1, 7, 75, 83
  critique 320–3
  definition 320
  equality, conflict 315, 321
  mutual respect 317–19
  nationalism, conflict 314–15
  recognition mechanisms 317–18

relevance 313–17
  restrictions on 316
  vs universalism 322–3
Munger, M.C. 2, 258
Murray, C., *The Bell Curve* 94
Muslim Brotherhood 154
Muslim world 25, 146, 170
mutual respect
  multiculturalism 317–19
  politics of 318–19
Myrdal, G. 26
mysticism 151, 156, 158, 166

N-person game theory 34
Nash's equilibrium 34
nation 15, 24, 25, 26, 26–7, 73
  concept 15, 84
  definition 314
  and ethnic groups 82–3
  meaning 81
  without states 81, 88–9
nation-building 39, 79, 80–2
nation-state 43, 45, 73, 75, 79, 80, 82,
    83, 84, 85, 87
national identity 5, 6, 26, 75, 83, 84
  and nationalism 85, 89
national pride 60, 129, 130, 131, 132,
    133, 134, 310
  and ethnicity 130
nationalism 1, 2, 48
  civic 85, 87
  concept 84–5
  definition 85
  examples 86, 90
  French model 86, 88–9
  genealogical 85, 87
  German model 86, 87–8
  as ideology 85
  and minorities 90–1
  multiculturalism, conflict 314–15
  and national identity 85, 89
  and nationality 83–9
  theories 87
  typology 85–6
nationality 4
  and nationalism 83–9
New Cultural Theory (NCT) 29–31,
    36–7, 238, 255
  typology 29, 252

*Culture and Politics*

'new politics' 258
Newton, K. 11, 33, 43, 60, 241, 242,
    251–2
    *Beliefs in Government* 11
Nieuwbeerta, P. 249
Nock, S.L. 220
Nordlinger, E. 181
Norris, P. 33, 49, 290, 291
North, D. 26, 41, 43, 49, 200–3
Nygren, A. 152

occidental civilization 103, 144
OECD 50, 63, 64, 65, 66, 67, 68, 130,
    189, 190, 214, 248, 266, 267, 268,
    269
Ogden, S. 27–8
old culture theory 11, 252, 313
Olson, M. 44, 49
Ordeshook, P. 2, 258
orientalism 2
Orthodox world 170
Ottoman Empire 203, 206
Ottoman legacy 204
outputs
    political 1, 5, 90, 245, 249, 263
    and values 274, 311

Palestinians 81
Parker, P. 103, 104
Parsons, T. 227
party support 10, 11, 51–7
    Belgium 55–6, 186–7, 308
    India 56, 187–8, 308
    and postmaterialism 249–50
    and religious structure 182–9
    Spain 53–4, 183–4, 185, 308
    Switzerland 54–5, 184–6, 308
    USA 51–2, 183, 184, 308
path-dependency 200
Paxton, P. 174
Pettigrew, T. 93
Pettit, P. 48
Peuch, H-Ch. 137, 148, 152
Pietism 162
policy-making 3, 5, 61, 255, 263, 276,
    278, 280, 318, 319, 322
political culture 17, 31–3
    definition 31
    typology 32

political systems, and family structures
    227–30
politics
    activity 63–4
    interest in 61–3
        and ethnicity 132, 133
        and religion 190
    of mutual respect 318–19
    of recognition 1
    *see also* left-right placement
postmaterialism 1, 11, 31, 61, 263, 264,
    268–9
    and affluence 268, 280, 282, 287
    and developmental outcomes 279,
        280
    and human development 279
    macro-level outcomes 278–85
    and party support 249–50
    theory 239, 244–50, 263
    values 245–6, 249–50, 276, 279–80
poverty, and affluence 44
preferences 37, 40, 41, 42, 49, 275–6
primordial groups 95, 254
prophets 148
*Proporz* 181, 315
Protestantism 2, 43
    and capitalism 10, 139, 140, 156,
        157, 158, 164, 167, 168, 179
    and gender equality 297
Puritanism 156–7
Putnam, R.D. 1, 11, 33, 43, 238,
    239–40, 241, 242, 243, 251, 253,
    254, 263, 264, 274
Pye, L.W. 17, 27, 31

quality of life, and economic
    development 46
Quebec 5, 319

race 73, 91–5
    meaning 94
rational choice approach 2, 34, 36, 37,
    40, 42, 305
rationality 14, 34, 157, 165
    economic 155
    and religion 170
    social 97
    vs irrationality 157, 158
Rawls, J. 322

regional-level
  data set 335–9
  impact
    culture 307
    ethnicity 126–7, 128, 134
    religion 183–9
relativist approach 147
religion 8
  and affluence 170, 170–1, 176, 176–7
  Belgium 186–7
  and corruption 173–5
  and democracy 173–5
  and development 139
  and economic development 158,
    167–8, 170, 173, 174, 176, 179
  and economic growth 170–2
  essentialist approach 147
  and gender development 177
  and globalization 6
  and income 169–70
  India 187–8, 189
  information sources 138
  and joining boycotts 192
  outcomes 167–93, 310
    correlations 175
    regression analysis 178, 193
  and rationality 170
  relativist approach 147
  and social development 172–3
  Spain 183–4, 185
  Switzerland 184–6
  USA 183, 184
  and voluntary organization
    membership 190–1
  *see also* sociology of religion
religions
  adherents 161, 163
  as civilizations 146–7
  classifications 146–7, 147–55
  countries 160
  mapping 159–63
  Weber's typology 157–8
religious fragmentation 5–6, 25, 43, 141
  outcomes 179–82
religious fundamentalism 2
religious heterogeneity 140–1
religious services, attendance 189–90
religious structure, and party support
  182–9

Renan, E. 88–9, 91
Renner, K. 76
Rickert, H., *Kulturwissenschaft und
  Naturwissenschaft* 20
rights 1
  *see also* human rights
Rokkan, S. 43, 98, 116
Roman Catholicism 25, 31, 158, 160,
  161, 174, 176, 266
  *see also* Catholic countries
Rose, R. 249
Rostow, W.W. 45
Ruhlen, M. 103
Russia
  ethnicity 120–3
  party support 52
Russian civilization 144
Russian Empire 206
Rwanda 116, 217

Said, E. 1, 2, 11
Sakwa, R. 52
Samis 81
Sartori, G. 18
Scarborough, E. 239, 244, 245, 250,
  259
Schelling, F.W.J. 87
sects 4, 15, 40, 141, 148, 149, 157, 317
secularization 140, 141, 159, 160, 162,
  181, 189
Sen, A. 46
sex, as cultural cleavage 290–2
Shari'a 153
Shia 146, 153, 158
Shintoism 25, 146, 150
Sieyès, E.J. 88
Sikhs 81
Smith, A.D. 1, 77, 79, 80, 88, 91, 98
  *The Antiquity of Nations* 96–7, 98
social capital 240–1, 251
  meaning 240
social development
  indicators 172
  and religion 172–3
social structure 7, 40, 49, 56, 240, 249,
  307, 312, 320, 321, 323
society
  divided 57, 140, 182, 184
  dual 27–8

sociology of religion 40, 45, 148
Sombart, W. 158
Sorokin, P.A. 142–3
Sowell, T. 114
Spain
    colonial legacies 209, 211
    ethnicity 123–5
    party support 53–4, 183–4, 185, 308
    religion 183–4, 185
Spanish Empire 200, 201, 209
Spencer, H. 92
state
    definition 81
    and nation 81, 88–9
Stefancic, J., *Critical Race Theory* 94
subcultures 24–5
Sunni 146, 152, 153, 158
survey approach 57, 58
Switzerland
    ethnicity 125–6
    and Holocaust victims 90–1
    party support 54–5, 184–6, 308
    religion 184–6

Tamils 81
Tanzi, V. 48
Taoism 151, 158, 310
Taylor, C. 1, 320
    *The Sources of the Self* 317
Third World 41, 47, 209
    colonial legacies 210–11, 217
Thompson, M. 2, 27, 28, 29, 30, 238,
    252, 254
Tibetans 81
Tingsten, H. 58
Tocqueville, A. de 33, 241, 250, 251
    *Democracy in America* 119
Todd, E. 41, 219, 220–3, 224–6, 227,
    228–9, 230–1
Tönnies, F. 15
Toynbee, A. 144, 145, 229
    on civilizations 143
traditionalism 28
triadic society 28
Triandis, H.C. 265
Trobriand Islands 199
trust 11, 241–2, 263, 264, 269, 282, 283
    and affluence 269, 280, 282
    and gender development 282

    interpersonal 242, 243, 264, 269,
        282, 283, 285
    in Italy 242–3
    political 33
    social 33
trust society 1
trust theory 239–40, 250–2
Tylor, E.B., *Primitive Culture* 18–19

UNDP 45
universal values 5, 10, 40, 237–55, 262,
    265–70
    and globalization 3, 6
    theories 237, 264
universalism, vs multiculturalism 322–3
USA
    ethnic fragmentation 120
    ethnicity 119–20, 121
    party support 51–2, 183, 308
    religion 183, 184

value orientations 257–87
    central 263–5
    and gender orientations 298–9
    inquiry 258–60
    relevance 260–3
values
    as attitudes 241–2, 255
    as behaviour 239–41
    changes 302
    impacts 276–7
    individual 11
    macro level correlation 272
    macro level outcomes 278–85
    meaning 259
    micro level correlation 271
    micro level outcomes 285–6
    orientations 237–43
    outcomes 252–4, 311–12
    and outputs 274, 311
    postmaterialism 245–6, 249–50, 276,
        279–80
    postmaterialist 245–6, 249–50
    significance 273–7
    survey approach 58–60
    and voluntary organisations 286
    *see also* European Values Study;
        universal values; World Values
        Survey

van Deth, J.W. 239, 259, 260, 261
van Gunsteren, H.R. 11
Vanhanen, T. 116
Verba, S., *The Civic Culture* 32, 59, 250–1, 253, 265
*Verstehen* 20, 158, 313
virtuosi 148, 150, 158
*Volk* 78
*Volksgeist* 85, 87, 97
Voll, J.O. 174
Voltaire, *Essai sur les Moeurs et l'Esprit des Nations* 19
voluntary organisations 11, 63
    and ethnicity 132, 133
    membership 64
    and religion 190–1
    and values 286

Wagon, 'Little Wagon, Big Wagon' 150
WAPOR 59
Webb, J.W. 144

Weber, A. 141
Weber, M. 20, 73, 83, 98, 138, 307
    theory of religion 8, 10, 45, 139–40, 148, 155–9, 164–5, 167–8, 310
    works
        *Economy and Society* 82, 139
        *The Protestant Ethic and the Spirit of Capitalism* 146
        *The Religion of China* 165
        *The Religion of India* 165–6
White, S. 52
Wildavsky, A. 1, 2, 11, 21, 29, 31, 36, 47, 252, 263, 264, 265, 274, 313
Wilson, E.O. 12
World Bank 47
World Values Survey (WVS) 11, 57, 60, 61–6, 189, 244, 258, 264
    countries 68–9

Zoroastrianism 147, 151
Zubaida, S. 152